Getting to Zero

GETTING TO ZERO

THE PATH TO NUCLEAR DISARMAMENT

Edited by

Catherine McArdle Kelleher and Judith Reppy

Stanford Security Studies

An Imprint of Stanford University Press

Stanford, California 2011

Stanford University Press
Stanford, California

Printed in the United States of America

Library of Congress Cataloging-in-Publication Data

Getting to zero : the path to nuclear disarmament / edited by Catherine McArdle Kelleher and Judith Reppy.
p. cm.
Includes bibliographical references and index.
ISBN 978-0-8047-7394-2 (cloth : alk. paper) —
ISBN 978-0-8047-7702-5 (pbk.)
1. Nuclear disarmament. 2. Nuclear weapons—Government policy. I. Kelleher, Catherine McArdle, editor of compilation. II. Reppy, Judith (Judith Voris), editor of compilation.

JZ5675.G49 2011
327.1'747—dc22 2010043065

Typeset at Stanford University Press in 10/14 Minion

CONTENTS

WHAT NEXT?

FIGURES AND TABLES

FIGURES

TABLES

ACKNOWLEDGMENTS

Books, like families, require myriad sources for success: strong personal relationships, supportive environments, funding, and considerable luck. We have been fortunate in all these domains and wish to extend our thanks to those individuals and institutions whose contributions and confidence in the enterprise have helped us bring this volume to fruition.

The book represents the last step in a fascinating decade-long research project launched under two titles, the Dialogue of Americans, Russians, and Europeans (DARE) and its predecessor, Germans, Americans, and Russians in Dialogue (GARD), both made possible by generous grants from the Carnegie Corporation. Deana Arsenian, now Carnegie vice president, provided intellectual and financial support from the very first days at Aspen Berlin. We were also aided by funding for this volume from the Watson Institute of International Studies at Brown, the home of DARE since 2002, and its Project on Nuclear Dilemmas of the 21st Century. Cornell University's Peace Studies Program under the leadership of Jonathan Kirshner and Elaine Scott generously allowed Sandra Kisner to serve as copy-editor extraordinaire. We could not have finished the project without her help.

Our abiding thanks for the book itself go to our contributors, who were not only excellent partners but also patient and responsive collaborators throughout all the problems of editing and writing on two continents. Particular gratitude goes to David Holloway, who got us started and was there for the finish as well. Our deep appreciation, too, to those who provided all manner of help in the production process: Simon Moore and Philip Maxon in College Park, and Scott Warren in Providence. Sheila Fournier, Ellen White, and Christine Kilgus were the outstanding Brown masters in financial management and meeting organization.

We have also been fortunate in the people and locations who allowed us to test and improve our thoughts along the way. Carlo Schaerf and ISODARCO provided a stage for the first public presentations of our arguments in January 2009 at the ISODARCO Winter Course in Andalo, Italy. We are grateful to the Italian funders that made that possible: the physics departments of the Universities of Rome Tor Vergata and of Trento; The Fondazione Opera Campana dei Caduti of Rovereto and in particular its *Reggente*, Prof. Sen. Alberto Robol; the Giunta della Provincia Autonoma di Trento and the presidencies of the Trentino Alto Adige regional council and of the Trentino provincial council. Physicians for Social Responsibility through Jill Marie Lewis supported our authors' meeting in May 2009 in Washington, DC.

The Center for International and Security Studies at Maryland (CISSM) provided Catherine much needed stimulation, space, and services. Catherine wishes also to give particular thanks to Thomas Biersteker, Barbara Stallings, and Michael Kennedy, all Watson Institute directors, for their personal support of DARE activities, and to John Birkelund, long-time chairman of the Watson Board for his critical interest.

Catherine McArdle Kelleher, College Park, Maryland
Judith Reppy, Ithaca, New York

ABBREVIATIONS

ABM	Anti-Ballistic Missile (Treaty)
AMS	(Chinese) Academy of Military Sciences
ASMP	*à Air-Sol Moyenne Portée* (medium-range air-to-surface missile)
ASOC	Air Sovereignty Operation Centers
AWE	[UK] Atomic Weapons Establishment
BMD	ballistic missile defense
CAEP	Chinese Academy of Engineering Physics
CAI	Cooperative Airspace Initiative
CD	(Geneva) Conference on Disarmament
CDU	Christian-Democratic Union (Germany)
CEA	*Commissariat à l'Energie Atomique* (French Atomic Energy Commission)
CEP	circular error probable
CFE	Conventional Forces in Europe
CFSP	Common Foreign and Security Policy
CIRUS	Canada-India-Reactor-United States
CISAC	Committee on International Security and Arms Control
CNS	[Russian] Concept of National Security
CSGAC	Chinese Scientists Group for Arms Control
CSU	Christian Social Union (Germany)
CTBT	Comprehensive (Nuclear) Test Ban Treaty
DE	damage expectancy
DOD	[U.S.] Department of Defense
DOE	[U.S.] Department of Energy

EADS	European Aeronautic Defense and Space Co.
ENDC	Eighteen Nation Disarmament Committee
EPR	European Pressurised Reactor
ESDP	European security and defense policy
FDP	Free Democratic Party (Germany)
FMCI	Fissile Material Control Initiative
FMCT	Fissile Material Cut-Off Treaty
GCD	general and complete disarmament
GIRM	Graphite Isotope Ratio Method
HEU	highly-enriched uranium
HLW	high-level radioactive waste
IAEA	International Atomic Energy Agency
ICAN	International Campaign to Abolish Nuclear Weapons
ICBM	Intercontinental Ballistic Missile
INF	Intermediate Range Nuclear Forces (Treaty)
IPFM	International Panel on Fissile Materials
IISS	International Institute for Strategic Studies
JSTPS	Joint Strategic Targeting Planning Staff
LANL	Los Alamos National Laboratory
LEU	low-enriched uranium
LLNL	Lawrence Livermore National Laboratory
LOW	launch-on-warning
LUA	launch-under-attack
MAD	mutually-assured destruction
MinAtom	Ministry for Atomic Energy
MIRV	multiple independently-targeted re-entry vehicle
MoD	Ministry of Defence
MUF	material unaccounted for
NIE	National Intelligence Estimate
NNSA	National Nuclear Security Administration
NPR	Nuclear Posture Review
NPT	Non-Proliferation Treaty
NRC	National Research Council
NSG	Nuclear Suppliers Group
NWFZ	nuclear weapon free zones
NWS	nuclear weapons states
OECD	Organization for Economic Co-operation and Development

PALEN	Préparation à la limitation des essais nucléaires (Preparation for the limitation of nuclear testing)
PNI	Presidential Nuclear Initiative
PrepCom	NPT Preparatory Committee
PTBT	Partial Test Ban Treaty
R&D	research and development
RevCon	Review Conference
RNEP	Robust Nuclear Earth Penetrator
RRW	Reliable Replacement Warhead
S&T	science and technology
SAC	Strategic Air Command
SALT	Strategic Arms Limitations Talks
SBIRS	Space-Based Infrared System
SDI	Strategic Defense Initiative
SED	Strategic and Economic Dialogue
SIOP	Single Integrated Operational Plan
SLBMs	Submarine Launched Ballistic Missiles
SM-3	Standard Missile-3
SNEP	Subterranean Nuclear Explosion Project
SORT	(Strategic Offensive Reductions Treaty)
SPD	Social Democratic Party (Germany)
SSBNs	nuclear ballistic missile submarines
SSP	Stockpile Stewardship Program
START	Strategic Arms Reduction Treaty
THAAD	Terminal High Altitude Area Defense
TNA	*tête nucléaire aéroportée* [airborne nuclear warhead]
TNO	*tête nucléaire océanique* [oceanic nuclear warhead]
TNW	tactical nuclear weapons
WMD	weapons of mass destruction

FOREWORD BY WILLIAM J. PERRY

In April 2009, in the beautiful Old World capital of Prague, President Obama delivered an eloquent speech in which he made a simple but dramatic declaration: "I state clearly and with conviction America's commitment to seek the peace and security of the world without nuclear weapons."

He repeated that commitment in a speech to the UN General Assembly in September, and then introduced a resolution to the Security Council calling for steps that move toward a world without nuclear weapons. The president invited the "Gang of Four"—George Shultz, Henry Kissinger, Sam Nunn, and myself—to be part of his delegation that day, and graciously credited our two op-eds as having had an important influence on his position. Of course a world without nuclear weapons is still a distant goal, but the president's two speeches have launched us on a journey toward that goal.

Why did the four of us take such a dramatic position on nuclear weapons? What has developed since our first op-ed was published? And what is the path forward?

On the first question, I will not presume to speak for my three colleagues, but I will give you an account of how my own thinking was shaped. I have come to believe that the gravest security danger the world faces today is the detonation of a nuclear bomb in Washington or Moscow or Mumbai, and that this danger is increasing every year. But I must also acknowledge that my views on the danger of nuclear weapons have been shaped by my experiences during the Cold War. I will describe one of those experiences to you.

One night when I was the Under Secretary of Defense for Research and Engineering, I was aroused by a phone call at 3:00 a.m. As I sleepily picked up the phone I heard a voice identifying himself as the watch officer at NORAD. The general got right to the point, telling me that his computers were indicating 200 intercontinental ballistic missiles on the way from the Soviet Union to the United States.

I woke up immediately. The computer alert was, of course, a false alarm. The general was calling me in the hopes that I could help him determine what had gone wrong so that he had some answers when he briefed the president the next morning. That call is engraved in my memory, but it is only one of three false alarms that I know have occurred in the United States, and I don't know how many more might have occurred in the Soviet Union.

I describe this experience to make the point that the risks of a nuclear catastrophe have never been theoretical to me—I experienced those dangers at first hand.

Ironically, during the same period that I experienced the false warning of an attack by Soviet nuclear weapons, I was responsible for the development of America's nuclear weapons: the B-2 bomber, the MX missile, the Trident submarine, the Trident missile, the air-launched cruise missile (ALCM), and the Tomahawk. I saw all too clearly the risks in building such deadly weapon systems, but I believed that it was necessary to take those risks given the very real threats we faced.

However, after the Cold War ended, I believed that it was no longer necessary to take those terrible risks, and I believed that we should begin to dismantle the deadly nuclear legacy of the Cold War. My first opportunity to act on that belief came in 1994, when I was asked by President Clinton to be his secretary of defense. As secretary, my first priority was working to reduce the dangers of the Cold War nuclear arsenal.

Our greatest immediate danger was that the nuclear weapons in Ukraine, Kazakhstan, and Belarus would fall into the hands of terrorists. When the Soviet Union collapsed, these new republics had inherited the nuclear weapons on their soil. Ukraine, for example, had more nuclear weapons than the United Kingdom, France, and China combined. And the country was going through great social, economic, and political turbulence. Through adroit diplomacy we were able to get these new republics to agree to give up their nuclear weapons. Then, using the Nunn-Lugar program, we assisted them in the dismantlement process.

I personally supervised the dismantlement process in Ukraine, visiting the largest and most modern intercontinental ballistic missile (ICBM) site, at Pervomaysk, four times. During my time in office I oversaw the dismantlement of about 8,000 nuclear weapons in the United States and the former Soviet Union, and helped three nations go non-nuclear: Ukraine, Kazakhstan, and Belarus. That was the first time since the dawn of the nuclear age that nuclear proliferation had been reversed.

Also in my last year in office, with the help of the national lab directors, I steered the Comprehensive Test Ban Treaty (CTBT) through the Pentagon so that President Clinton could sign it. At the time, I believed that we were well on our way to mitigating the deadly nuclear legacy of the Cold War.

Since then the effort has stalled, even reversed. The U.S. Senate rejected the ratification of CTBT. Russia and China are building a new generation of nuclear weapons. North Korea already has a small nuclear arsenal, and Iran is following in their footsteps. If we cannot contain those two latter nations, it is very likely that there will be widespread proliferation in the Middle East, and possibly in Northeast Asia as well. Additionally, Pakistan is a growing danger. The government in Pakistan is being challenged by Al Qaeda and Taliban militias in an increasingly violent insurgency. And, to add to the danger, the Pakistani government has released A. Q. Kahn.

It is not an exaggeration to say that these dangerous actions have put the world at a tipping point of proliferation. If Iran and North Korea cannot be stopped from building nuclear arsenals, I believe that we will cross that tipping point, with consequences that will be dangerous beyond most people's imagination.

I have gone through this background so that you can understand my state of mind in October 2006, when George Shultz decided to hold a workshop at Stanford on the twentieth anniversary of the Reykjavik Summit meeting between presidents Reagan and Gorbachev. Reagan was considered to be a hawkish president, but his views on nuclear weapons were far from hawkish, as expressed in his statement: "A nuclear war cannot be won and must never be fought." To the surprise of many of his own supporters, he really believed what he said. And at the Reykjavik Summit he seriously explored with Gorbachev the idea of moving toward the elimination of nuclear weapons and ballistic missiles, the key weapons of the Cold War.

The two presidents actually came close to an agreement but in the end backed away. Those of you who remember that summit meeting will also remember that most political and academic specialists were incredulous that the two presidents would even discuss such a rash idea. But twenty years later, at the Stanford workshop, we concluded that we ought to revive the idea that Reagan and Gorbachev discussed at that summit, moving toward a world without nuclear weapons.

We believed that some really dramatic action was needed to stop this terrible drift to a nuclear catastrophe, and our two op-eds, in January of 2007 and January of 2008, prescribed such dramatic actions. We did not expect much more from our first op-ed than the usual responsive articles from academics in this field, so the actual reaction caught us by surprise.

We were swamped with news articles and letters from colleagues, mostly of the view that the world was overdue for a serious reevaluation of nuclear arsenals and postures. Buoyed by this response, we scheduled meetings with senior government officials and former officials in the United States, Russia, China, India, Japan, the United Kingdom, Italy, and Norway.

In parallel with our actions, groups of former officials in other countries also began working to move toward a world without nuclear weapons. Other groups of four were established in Germany and the United Kingdom. Bruce Blair and Barry Blechman formed a group called "Global Zero." But such unofficial activities can only go so far—the actions that make a real difference must be taken by governments.

The first indication that our op-eds were taken seriously by governments came in late 2008 with a speech by Margaret Beckett, who was the United Kingdom's foreign minister. During the presidential campaign in 2008 both candidates, Senator McCain and Senator Obama, expressed qualified support. So we ended 2008 with more response and more support than we had truly expected, but, in fact, no real governmental action.

Then in 2009, some truly unprecedented actions were taken by governments. Just ten weeks after he was inaugurated, President Obama made his famous speech in Prague, from which I quoted at the beginning of this foreword. At their April 2009 bilateral in London, President Obama and President Medvedev jointly declared their support for a world without nuclear weapons. That was followed by their summit meeting in Moscow, at which both presidents made a commitment to move forward to a new arms reduction treaty by the end of the year, and President Obama said that he would work for a Fissile Material Cut-Off Treaty (FMCT) and the ratification of CTBT. At that time, several prominent Americans across the political spectrum stepped forward to call for a world without nuclear weapons, including General Colin Powell and Governor Arnold Schwarzenegger.

And governments all over the world weighed in. British prime minister Gordon Brown officially endorsed moving to a world without nuclear weapons, and the United Kingdom is taking the lead in research on the supportive verification technology. Norway, Italy, and Finland each have sponsored conferences on nuclear disarmament and are funding non-proliferation projects. Japan and Australia formed an International Commission on Nuclear Non-Proliferation and Disarmament, of which I was the American commissioner. In December of 2009, the commission held its fourth and final meeting in Hiroshima.

The commissioners agreed on recommendations that spell out a three-phase plan of action. The first phase deals with the near-term actions on START, CTBT, and FMCT, as well as curtailing the nuclear programs of Iran and North Korea. The commissioners call for that phase to be completed by 2012.

The second phase is no less daunting. It calls for the United States and Russia to dismantle their 22,000 nuclear weapons at a rate of 1,500 per year until they are down to a level of 500 each, while other nations hold or decrease their arsenals. The commission called this new level the "minimization point." This second phase will necessarily entail a high level of verification of the weapons dismantlement and the associated fissile material. Remember that to date we have never verified the removal of warheads, only delivery vehicles. The commissioners estimate that the nuclear powers could reach this "minimization point" by 2025. At that point the world would take a deep breath and see if the geopolitical conditions at the time permit moving to zero.

The third and final phase, which entails moving to zero, would require a different geopolitical environment than now exists. It is possible, of course, that the process of dismantlement and verification in the second phase would itself promote the trust and confidence that would help build such an environment.

So this past year we have seen unprecedented actions and planning that none of us could have predicted at the beginning of the year. It truly has been an *Annus Mirabilis*, a "Year of Miracles."

That term has been used to describe two different miraculous years in science: 1666, when Newton published his landmark papers on the theory of gravitation and optics; and 1905, when Einstein published three landmark papers, including his famous paper on the theory of relativity. In my lifetime, I can remember Vaclav Havel calling 1989 an *Annus Mirabilis* as all of the Eastern European nations gained their independence, nearly bloodlessly. And of course that year culminated with the fall of the Berlin Wall.

I do not mean to suggest that the developments of this year are equal in significance to those remarkable events, but considering my expectations going into 2009, I must say that I consider the developments of that year as nothing short of miraculous.

Which brings me to my last question and to this book. What remains to be done is much, much more difficult than what has been done. In the next two years, for example, the United States and Russia need to ratify the New START. The United States needs to ratify the CTBT. The international community needs to negotiate a new FMCT. The international community needs to find a way to stop nuclear weapons programs in North Korea and Iran. And the nuclear powers need to start making significant annual reductions in their nuclear weapons arsenals, to be sustained for more than a decade.

These are daunting challenges. None of them will be achieved with business as usual; indeed, their achievement will call for brilliant diplomacy sustained over many years.

Getting to Nuclear Zero examines some of the key issues that will need to be addressed. More important, authors from different countries explore these issues from an international perspective. It is clear that international cooperation is required to be successful in realizing the vision that so many now embrace. This book greatly contributes to the international discussion of the steps required and the obstacles to overcome if we are to make progress on the path to a world free of nuclear weapons.

Palo Alto, California, Spring 2010

Getting to Zero

Introduction

Catherine McArdle Kelleher

If one decided to get rid of all nuclear weapons in the world, the first question would be how to go about it. But a second, equally important but less frequently asked question, would be: what else would you then have to do to ensure the safety and security of citizens and the peace and stability of the global community? Ridding the world of nuclear weapons is desirable only if a safer world is actually brought into being. How can we do that?

In this project we took as given that complete nuclear disarmament will happen and focused our attention on what that will imply. We agreed to take as our guiding principle that any proposals for policy should advance the cause of going to zero. Thus, the chapters in the book do not debate whether going to zero is feasible or a good idea. Instead, they address in some detail what nuclear zero will mean for existing institutions, issues, and practices. What has to change for nuclear states to embrace nuclear disarmament as a pressing goal, not a far-distant vision to be disregarded in making policy today? How can countries chafing against, or even outside, the nonproliferation regime be persuaded to abandon their nuclear ambitions? The chapters seek to offer the beginnings of a roadmap to a world in which nuclear weapons will no longer be the currency of power, but instead a historical memory.

This book emerged from a series of conversations and exchanges that took place under the aegis of a generous Carnegie Corporation grant for "Dialogue among Americans, Russians, and Europeans," or DARE. A group of experts and policy-makers from all three geographic areas were recruited to meet periodically over the past decade to assess issues of transformational significance and to explore the potential for trilateral cooperation. Of particular importance for nuclear zero issues was a small DARE seminar held in Milan in January 2009, with contributions from that meeting then reflected in lectures during the 2009 ISODARCO Winter School at Andalo, Italy.

These discussions were initially stimulated by the remarkable January 2007 *Wall Street Journal* article by George Shultz, William Perry, Henry Kissinger, and Sam Nunn. In marking the anniversary of the 1986 Reykjavik Summit between Ronald Reagan and Mikhail Gorbachev, the group stressed the real disarmament opportunity that had been lost in Iceland, called for a world free of nuclear weapons, and outlined a series of practical steps toward reaching that goal. Soon known as the "Gang of Four," or "The Four Horsemen," the group has since issued reports, held major conferences, and engaged in a global campaign to emphasize the challenges of eliminating nuclear weapons and the need to move toward that difficult goal. Their initiative galvanized a new discussion of nuclear disarmament and the alternate paths to its achievement in many circles. They led then-senators Barack Obama, Hilary Clinton, and John McCain to endorse the cause during the 2008 U.S. presidential primary campaign. President Obama carried the movement forward when he declared in a stirring speech given in Prague on April 5, 2009, that the United States was committed to seek the peace and security of a world without nuclear weapons.

In practical terms, the first steps by President Obama have been more expectable than revolutionary, but they do emphasize renewed American leadership. Working primarily with its leading European allies, the United States has undertaken a diplomatic "reset" with Russia, and altered the national ballistic missile defense system to relocate installations in Eastern Europe. All of these steps have helped alleviate some tensions with Russia, the country that must be the foremost partner of the United States in arms control talks. Work on formal Strategic Arms Reduction Talks (Start III) increased in intensity and led to a new agreement. The president's second year also saw an April Washington summit on securing all fissile materials, followed in May 2010 by the periodic global nuclear review and renewal of the now-extended Nuclear Non-Proliferation Treaty (NPT) regime. There was even an intensive campaign toward Senate approval for the Comprehensive Test Ban Treaty (CTBT), unratified for more than a decade, a treaty that, if observed, will significantly hinder both horizontal and vertical proliferation. Obama was awarded (some argued prematurely) the 2009 Nobel Peace Prize: his comments and intentions on nuclear disarmament were among the reasons cited by the panel for giving the award to the president so early in his first term.

All of this is promising news after more than a decade in which the issues posed by nuclear weapons were largely eclipsed by concerns over ethnic wars and the threat of terrorism. There is no doubt about serious renewed interest among surprising numbers of foreign policy elites toward the goal of nuclear disarmament. There is, for the first time in decades, a limited bandwagon effect among elites and mass publics. The general public, at least as probed in opinion polls, is more interested in the issue and more willing to support nuclear elimination or limitation. A number of European governments and governmental officials, past and present, including those of Britain, France, Germany, Italy, and Norway, have added to the momentum. They have either endorsed the Obama initiatives or gone beyond them to offer specific plans for further cuts in nuclear weapons, improvements in verification technology, and safeguards for nuclear fuel stockpiles.[1]

There is, of course, pervasive skepticism as well. Some of it is from predictable sources: from policy "realists," from self-styled conservatives, and from those who believe the nuclear revolution has unalterably changed the core formulas of state power and the relationship of the weak to the strong. Others question the possibility of technological constraint: can we really restore the genie to its bottle, given the global spread of civil nuclear technologies, the near instantaneous distribution of technical literature, and a global commerce system poised to deliver any and all necessary components through a myriad of legal and illegal channels? Still others note with disdain the absent national voices: what beyond the usual lofty rhetoric of "perpetual peace through nuclear abolition" has been heard on nuclear zero from the Russians, the Chinese, or the Indians, not to mention the Pakistanis and the Israelis? What of the restless threshold states, Iran and North Korea? Policy-makers striving for nuclear zero must also still those voices cautioning against excessive cost or insurmountable risk. Even those who do accept the goal of zero must appreciate the significant costs and risks that must be managed.

Moreover, President Obama's strong words from Prague have fallen on a largely unprepared audience, both in the United States and around the world. Despite a long history of individual and group activism in behalf of nuclear disarmament, such issues have not been high on the public agenda in recent years. The causes are many. Most obvious are the preferences of the George W. Bush administration and perhaps at the end, that of Bill Clinton.[2] These were political choices to marginalize nuclear disarmament by administrations that, ironically, actually oversaw major reductions in many categories of nuclear launchers and warheads (by more than half in some instances), as well as the destruction, under the Cooperative Threat Reduction regime and other frameworks, of many of the components of the former Soviet nuclear establishment.

Perhaps more important, the George W. Bush team also came to see the end of the Cold War as a closing of the nuclear chapter in terms of great power conflict. His critics, but also some of his supporters, began to define nuclear limitation as the key to stopping further nuclear proliferation, including to terrorist or other nonstate organizations. With Russia and the United States now strategic partners, the Bush administration considered arms control an outdated concept. Complex treaties and negotiated agreements took too long to complete, or could always be circumvented by cheaters or, in the struggle to ratify, generated increased hostility and perceptions of confrontation and adversarial bargaining. So a minimalist SORT (Strategic Offensive Reductions Treaty) signed in 2002 was sufficient.

For the move to nuclear zero ultimately to succeed, the discussion of the issues at stake must be expanded to engage a broader cross-section of citizens, scholars, and policy-makers in countries around the world. The task is particularly hard given the present circumstances—the international financial crisis with the attendant fears of economic collapse, unemployment, and social pain; the reform of markets and health care; the winding down of the war in Iraq in circumstances of fragile peace; the ramping up of counterinsurgency by the United States and its allies in Afghanistan; and the challenge of global climate change—all occupy presidential time and attention. The cost for a U.S. president to focus on this issue, early in his first term in office, has been high, and likely to be higher in both financial and electoral terms.

This book takes on the nuclear zero objectives, those hard, long-range yet serious policy questions, and tries to delineate and test practical steps for the nuclear nations to take. Few of the contributors suggest such a process will be easy or swift, gauging the process in decades rather than years. Nuclear weapons, in the sixty-five years since their invention, have come to take up a preeminent position in the strategies and militaries of the countries that own them. Because of that, eradicating them will be more complex than scrapping any other marginally effectual weapons systems—land mines, for example, or chemical and biological weapons. Nuclear weapons defined the superpower relationship for the larger part of the twentieth century. At times populations in both Russia and the United States registered majorities for prohibition, or at least nonuse.

Depending on whom you ask—even in the expert community—their presence brought stability or terror, or perhaps both, to the Cold War. As the ultimate weapon, destructive potency was their biggest advantage, but also their biggest hindrance. The political and ethical barriers to their use (known as the nuclear taboo) and the catastrophe of nuclear retaliation (under Mutually Assured Destruction [MAD], or almost any other formula of deterrence) kept their use constrained throughout the Cold War and especially at its end. Nuclear weapons became as much symbols as weapons, markers of prestige. They purportedly showed that a country had wealth, technical expertise, and a right to have a say in world events.

Among the many challenges we face in ridding the world of these weapons is the need to find a new way of thinking for the international community to conceive of them—not in terms of pride, but of abhorrence. Richard Rhodes has suggested an analogy to a disease that, like smallpox, polio, and other identified public health scourges, is to be controlled and eventually eradicated.[3] Rhodes reminds us that public health came to be an expected function of government only in the last 150 years. Now it is a field in which international cooperation is expected and ultimately enforced, where monitoring and mitigating action are now routine, even among individuals and states with few other relations or much mutual admiration.

Others, including the late Randy Forsberg, and Matthew Evangelista in his chapter in this book, have suggested that a better comparison (or at least a history from which to learn lessons) would be the eradication of slavery in the West. The abolition of slavery involved the forgoing of direct economic profit on investment in the name of both moral principle and political-social risk. It had sudden spurts of activity and state enthusiasm, but the slow, deliberate momentum was largely carried forward under British political leadership at a time of its global dominance. Of great interest is the substantial role civil society groups played in changing public opinion in Britain and throughout the world, and the passion and persistence with which they waged their campaigns. We have largely forgotten the various strategies a series of British governments employed, using both hard and soft power, making promises of gain and punishment to states and individuals—methods available for nuclear disarmament advocates today.

Neither analogy captures the risks involved in a non-nuclear world in which a rogue or pariah state might indeed try to be king. Nevertheless, they are suggestive of how a change of thinking about possible outcomes, rather than a blanket rejection of all potential alternative futures, can move policy discussion and action forward. Few outside of the committed bureaucracies believe the NPT regime in its present form, or the nuclear status quo that has endured since the end of the Cold War, will or can continue unchanged and unchallenged. The question is rather what direction of change to choose and pursue. Through the DARE initiative, we invited leading scholars and practitioners to offer their thoughts in the framework of the zero movement. The result is this book.

The first section of the book focuses on the history of the nuclear zero movement, documenting the successes and failures of six decades of nuclear weapons. David Holloway describes the Gang of Four's vision of a world without nuclear weapons, reviewing its architects and the various historical attempts to bring it about. Randy Rydell looks at the history of prohibition discussions at the international level and the role played by or proposed for the international community, and especially the United Nations, in achieving progress on getting to zero. Götz Neuneck strikes an optimistic note with a description of the growing activity in Europe in support of nuclear zero.

Each nuclear weapon state faces different domestic politics, different international commitments, and different foreign policy challenges. Each has established different rules and different principles for its nuclear programs and deployment strategies. Untangling this web of sometimes-contradictory policies will be necessary as diplomats seek to get the verifiable reductions needed to maintain confidence and retain domestic support. Only then will they be able not only to demonstrate their fidelity to the NPT obligations they assumed many decades ago but also to meet the critical test: to bolster the morale and the resolve of the adherent states that remain in compliance, regardless of the behavior of the rogue states.

The second section of the book looks at the past decisions and future perspectives of the major nuclear states in an effort to address this issue. Lynn Eden looks at targeting, lethality, and strategy as critical drivers in the United States. Alexei Arbatov examines Russian views on deterrence. Ian Anthony explains the debate in the United Kingdom with large decisions imminent; Venance Journé investigates France's unique passion for all things nuclear, and how that will impact the disarmament debate; and Jeffrey Lewis spotlights China as it adapts its nuclear policy for the modern age.

In the third section, we turn to regional powers and their policies and prospects for nuclear zero. Nadia Alexandrova-Arbatova describes the international relations dynamics in a postnuclear world, with Europe as her case study; Avner

Cohen wonders what will become of Israel's policy of opacity in a disarming world or in a Middle East that includes a nuclear Iran; Jill Marie Lewis, with Lacie A. N. Olson, describes the evolving Iranian situation and the potential to affect Iran's decisions on nuclear weapons through a broader engagement across other policy areas. Completing the section, Waheguru Pal Sidhu looks at a country that was once at the forefront of the nuclear zero movement but was then tempted by the power of atomic weapons, and asks what the prospects are for India to relinquish its nuclear arms.

After this look at separate countries, the fourth part of the book goes on to consider some of the issues that confront them all. It is on these issues that the combined efforts and experience of the international community will be most applicable. Joint solutions will be needed and shared understandings developed to ensure forward momentum. In contrast to past efforts, short-term expediency or offsetting conditions in getting an agreement or achieving the broadest and lowest level of compliance should not be allowed to trump the long-term goal. James Acton assesses verification solutions; Judith Reppy looks at the institutional future for weapons laboratories in a postnuclear world; Marco de Andreis and Simon Moore connect the worlds of nuclear weapons and civilian nuclear power, and ask whether nuclear energy can ever cease to be a proliferation hazard; Matthew Evangelista discusses military strategy in a world beyond nuclear deterrence, a discussion that Dennis Gormley adds to with his study of how to understand and mitigate the conventional strategic imbalance that will become more prominent as we move even the first steps to nuclear zero. Finally, in the last section, David Holloway and Peter Dombrowski offer their expectations and suggestions for practical steps toward the future.

To conclude, emerging generations of security analysts, as well as many in the attentive publics, have come to see nuclear issues as settled or stabilized, or on the way to being "solved." Present levels of nuclear armament are viewed as "acceptable" and the risk of accident, miscalculation, or unauthorized use is "manageable." In this frame, however, the policy dialogue on nuclear zero is significantly impoverished. The "unknowing" of the previous history of efforts to constrain or eliminate nuclear weapons is especially apparent among younger generations, including present public officials as well as students. Most are hard pressed to remember the ins and outs of critical arms control deals that form the backbone of the present stability. There is a fundamental unfamiliarity with the issues raised by prospects of nuclear disarmament and with the many previous efforts to develop or at least catalog constructive approaches.

Moreover, it is still the early days in the implementation of Obama's commitment to this issue area. The hope for a major change is still strong in many of the interested constituencies, but the length of the national and international road to implementation is still hard to assess. Throughout the administrations of George W. Bush and Bill Clinton, the United States failed to engage in a rigorous dialogue on these complex issues at home or abroad. It did not, as it had in the past, reach out to scholars and policy-makers in Europe and Russia to explore cooperative solutions, or push for education and dialogue, with emerging states that have developed, for example, an interest in civil nuclear power. Leadership of the international nuclear discussion, despite the challenges of Iran or North Korea, the successes of South Africa or Libya, or even of Bush's effective Proliferation Security Initiative, often went elsewhere—or evaporated altogether.

With this volume, we hope to raise the questions and propose some of the answers that will be needed in the years ahead as this debate advances. We believe these essays can provide some signposts to point policy-makers in the right direction, and to bring attentive publics to a new appreciation of both the opportunities and the challenges involved in adopting this ambitious policy goal. More than anything, we hope that the volume will help the global community in taking the beginning steps to zero.

NOTES

1. Vassailos Savvadis and Jessica Seiler, "Nuclear Disarmament Proposals from 1995 to 2009: A Comparative Chart" (3 December 2009), at http://cns.miis.edu/stories/091203_disarmament_proposals.htm.

2. See Dennis Gormley, Catherine Kelleher, and Scott Warren, "Missile Defense Systems: Global and Regional Implications," Geneva Center for Security Policy (2009), at http://www.gcsp.ch/e/publications/geneva_papers/geneva_paper_5.pdf.

3. Richard Rhodes, "Reducing the Nuclear Threat: The Argument for Public Safety," *Bulletin of the Atomic Scientists* (Web Edition), 14 December 2009, at http://www.thebulletin.org/web-edition/op-eds/reducing-the-nuclear-threat-the-argument-public-safety.

HOW WE GOT TO WHERE WE ARE

1 The Vision of a World Free of Nuclear Weapons

David Holloway

INTRODUCTION

The Reykjavik Summit meeting between General Secretary Mikhail Gorbachev and President Ronald Reagan, which took place in October 1986, was a very dramatic occasion. Deep reductions in strategic nuclear forces were discussed, and agreements seemed very close at hand. An additional session was arranged to try to resolve differences over SDI (the Strategic Defense Initiative). In the end no agreements were reached. At the time Reykjavik seemed to many to be a terrible failure, but historians now regard it as one of the most important of the Cold War summit meetings.

The possibility of getting rid of nuclear weapons altogether came up at the Reykjavik meeting, but it was not the central issue. Neither side formally proposed the elimination of nuclear weapons, though Gorbachev had made such a proposal in January 1986. The issue arose at Reykjavik in the heat of a discussion about the shape of START (the Strategic Arms Reduction Treaty) and the elimination of strategic weapons. Reagan and Gorbachev found themselves at cross purposes. The United States proposed that each side reduce its strategic offensive arms by 50 percent in the first five years of an agreement; during the following five years "the remaining fifty percent of the two sides' offensive ballistic missiles shall be reduced." Gorbachev wanted to know what would happen to the bombers in the second five years. What ensued seems from the transcript to have been an increasingly testy exchange, in which Reagan said, in apparent irritation: "It would be fine with [me] if we eliminated all nuclear weapons." Gorbachev responded: "We can do that. We can eliminate them." Secretary of State George Shultz added, "Let's do it." Reagan then went on to say that if they could agree to eliminate all nuclear weapons, [Reagan] thought they could turn it over to their Geneva people with that understanding, for them to draft up that agreement, and Gorbachev could come to the U.S. and sign it."[1] Gorbachev agreed and then went on to talk about the treaty on strategic arms reductions.

Not everyone was happy that the issue of eliminating nuclear weapons had been raised at Reykjavik. There was a great deal of criticism in the United States and from NATO allies. According to Shultz, Secretary of Defense Casper Weinberger, National Security Advisor John Poindexter, and many in the State Department regarded Reykjavik "as a blunder of the greatest magnitude."[2] Admiral William Crowe, chairman of the Joint Chiefs of Staff, told Reagan that the chiefs were alarmed by the idea of giving up ballistic missiles.[3] Margaret Thatcher, who believed that nuclear weapons were absolutely essential for British security and for NATO, soon flew to Washington to make her displeasure clear to President Reagan.[4] "Any leader who indulges in the Soviets' disingenuous fantasies of a nuclear-free world courts unimaginable perils," former president Richard Nixon and Henry Kissinger wrote six months later.[5]

The brief discussion at Reykjavik of the elimination of nuclear weapons elicited another, more propitious, response. In October 2006, the Hoover Institution at Stanford University held a conference to mark the twentieth anniversary of the Reykjavik meeting. (Hoover is a conservative research institute often associated with the Republican Party.) The primary organizers were George Shultz, Reagan's secretary of state, and Sidney Drell, a Stanford physicist with a long involvement in national security issues and arms control. The aim of the conference was to rekindle the Reagan-Gorbachev vision of a world free of nuclear weapons. The participants were overwhelmingly American, and many of those present had taken part in the Reykjavik meeting.[6]

The atmosphere at the conference was gloomy about the nuclear state of the world; the first North Korean nuclear test had taken place some days earlier. The Bush administration's efforts to stop nuclear proliferation were not working. The nonproliferation regime appeared to be failing, and there was a sense that something radical needed to be done, that the status quo was drifting to a bad outcome.[7] The most important result of the conference was an article in the *Wall Street Journal* in January 2007 calling for a world free of nuclear weapons. George Shultz and former Secretary of Defense William Perry, who had both attended the conference, were joined by former Secretary of State Henry Kissinger and former Senator Sam Nunn in signing the article. This was a bipartisan group—or "nonpartisan," as Shultz likes to call it—with two Republicans and two Democrats.[8] The article was the product of serious discussion among the four principals, with Sidney Drell playing an important role. Shultz and his colleagues paid careful attention to the wording of the article. Before the end of the month Mikhail Gorbachev supported the call for urgent action in an article of his own in the *Wall Street Journal*.[9]

The article by Shultz et al. (sometimes referred to as the "Gang of Four," the "Four Horsemen of the Apocalypse," or the "Quartet") elicited enormous interest, in the United States and beyond. Its authors were surprised and gratified. To judge by the letters received and by newspaper editorials published around the world, the response was overwhelmingly favorable. It was clear that they had tapped into a deep-seated anxiety about the way in which the nuclear order was developing. They called for a number of steps to lay the groundwork for a world free of nuclear weapons: further reductions in nuclear forces; the de-alerting of U.S. and Russian strategic nuclear forces; the elimination of short-range nuclear weapons designed to be forward deployed; ratification of the Comprehensive Test Ban Treaty; and so on.

These proposals were not new. What was new was that it was these men, with vast experience in the making of U.S. national security policy, that were advocating them; as Gorbachev put it in his article, they were not men known for utopian thinking. Yet by itself that is not enough to explain the response to the *Wall Street Journal* article, for eminent men make many appeals to little effect, and many others have called for getting rid of nuclear weapons without attracting public attention. It was some combination of the men and the moment that produced the powerful response. In October 2007 a second conference was held at the Hoover Institution to discuss the various steps that might be undertaken to move toward a world without nuclear weapons.[10] All four horsemen took part in that conference; they wrote a second article, which appeared in the *Wall Street Journal* in January of 2008.[11]

About two-thirds of the former American secretaries of state, secretaries of defense, and national security advisors have given general support to the appeal of Shultz and his colleagues.[12] So too did Barack Obama when he was still a candidate for the presidency. In an interview in September 2008 (that is, before the election), he said:

> As president, I will set a new direction in nuclear weapons policy and show the world that America believes in its existing commitment under the Nuclear Nonproliferation Treaty to work to ultimately eliminate all nuclear weapons. I fully support reaffirming this goal, as called for by George Shultz, Henry Kissinger,

William Perry, and Sam Nunn, as well as the specific steps they propose to move us in that direction.[13]

Apart from Iran's nuclear ambitions, nuclear weapons were not an issue in the 2008 presidential election; they did not become the focus of differences between the candidates. Senator John McCain, the Republican candidate, also endorsed the goal of a world free of nuclear weapons.[14]

Foreign governments have taken the Hoover Initiative seriously. The British foreign secretary, Margaret Beckett, expressed her support in June 2007, and in February 2008 the Norwegian government organized a conference to explore how the vision of a world without nuclear weapons could be turned into reality. Four senior German statesmen published an article in the *Frankfurter Allgemeine Zeitung*, in response to, and in general support of, the Hoover Initiative.[15] Similar groups in Britain and Italy have published articles in the press offering their support.[16] In a speech to the Conference on Disarmament in August 2009, the Chinese foreign minister, Yang Jiechi, noted that "the complete prohibition and thorough destruction of nuclear weapons and a nuclear-weapon-free world have become widely embraced goals, and various initiatives on nuclear disarmament have been proposed."[17] He welcomed these developments.

In a speech in Prague on April 5, 2009, President Obama reiterated his commitment to the vision of a world free of nuclear weapons: "I state clearly and with conviction America's commitment to seek the peace and security of a world without nuclear weapons."[18] He laid out a list of practical measures that his administration would pursue to move in that direction. On September 24, 2009, he chaired a UN Security Council summit (the first time a U.S. president had done so) on nuclear nonproliferation and nuclear disarmament, and he invited the four "horsemen" to be present. The Security Council unanimously adopted a resolution (Resolution 1887) enshrining a shared commitment to the goal of a world without nuclear weapons and setting out a framework for action.[19] On October 9, 2009, Obama was awarded the Nobel Peace Prize for his "extraordinary efforts to strengthen international diplomacy and cooperation between peoples." The Nobel Committee "attached special importance to Obama's vision of and work for a world without nuclear weapons."[20]

Nuclear disarmament has now moved into the mainstream of American—and international—politics, becoming the focus of intense debate and discussion. Before looking in a later chapter at some of the steps that have been taken to turn the vision of a world free of nuclear weapons into reality, it will be useful to consider, if only briefly, past efforts at nuclear disarmament. This is not the first time that there has been a call for the abolition of nuclear weapons. After World War II negotiations were held under the auspices of the United Nations to eliminate the bomb. The Russell-Einstein Manifesto of 1955—which provided the basis for the Pugwash Meetings—also urged that nuclear weapons be eliminated.[21] So too did the Nuclear Non-Proliferation Treaty of 1968. After the end of the Cold War there were several commissions and reports calling for the elimination of nuclear weapons.[22] Here I shall discuss briefly two of these efforts: the negotiations on the international control of atomic energy in the late 1940s and the Reykjavik Summit meeting of October 1986. The former provides a template against which later disarmament proposals have frequently been measured; the latter provides a prologue of sorts to the current effort to move toward a world free of nuclear weapons.[23]

THE INTERNATIONAL CONTROL OF NUCLEAR WEAPONS

Many of the scientists involved in the Manhattan Project believed that the world, as it was then organized, could not cope with the atomic bomb. They had just lived through the most destructive war in history, and memories of the carnage of World War I were still strong. How could an international system in which large-scale wars appeared to be a natural and recurrent phenomenon cope with a weapon as destructive as the atomic bomb? Robert Oppenheimer put the point succinctly in October 1945 when he said: "[T]he peoples of this world must unite or they will perish."[24]

Already during World War II the great physicist Niels Bohr, who learned of the Manhattan Project when he escaped from Denmark in September 1943, had advocated international cooperation in dealing with nuclear weapons after the war. Bohr feared that political differences would lead to a breakdown in the wartime alliance and to an arms race between the Soviet Union and the Western powers. He did not believe that this was inevitable, because he saw the bomb as an opportunity as well as a danger. The very magnitude of the threat it posed to the human race would make it necessary for states to cooperate, and that might provide the basis for a new approach to international relations. Bohr won support from senior officials in Washington and London for his idea that the way to avoid an arms race was to bring atomic energy under international control, but he did not succeed in convincing either Roosevelt or Churchill of the need for an initial approach to Stalin on that score.[25]

The idea of international control nevertheless remained on the political agenda. In November 1945, Truman, along with the British and Canadian prime ministers, called for a UN commission to study how atomic weapons might be eliminated and atomic energy applied to peaceful uses. The Soviet government agreed to this proposal. The UN Atomic Energy Commission was established in January 1946 to make recommendations in four areas: (a) the exchange of basic scientific information; (b) the control of atomic energy to ensure its use for peaceful purposes; (c) the elimination of atomic weapons; and (d) safeguards against the "hazards of violations and evasion."[26]

Two months later, in March 1946, the U.S. State Department published *A Report on the International Control of Atomic Energy*, which outlined a plan to achieve the two goals of *preventing* the use of atomic energy for destructive purposes and *promoting* its use for the benefit of society. It became known as the Acheson-Lilienthal Report (after Dean Acheson, then undersecretary of state, and David Lilienthal, chairman of the Tennessee Valley Authority (TVA) and soon to be the first chairman of the Atomic Energy Commission), but Robert Oppenheimer was the key influence on the report.[27]

The Acheson-Lilienthal report proposed that all dangerous activities be placed under an international Atomic Development Authority, while safe activities such as research and the peaceful uses of atomic energy were to be left under the control of individual states. The report defined as "dangerous" any activity that offered a solution to one of the three major problems of making atomic weapons: (a) the supply of raw materials; (b) the production of plutonium and uranium-235; and (c) the use of these materials to make atomic weapons. The Atomic Development Authority would control world supplies of uranium and thorium, construct and operate plutonium production reactors and uranium isotope separation plants, and license the construction and operation of power reactors and other activities in individual countries.[28]

This report provided the basis for the U.S. proposal presented to the UN Atomic Energy Commission in June 1946 by Bernard Baruch. Five days later, Andrei Gromyko, Soviet ambassador to the United Nations, presented the Soviet plan calling for an international convention banning the production, stockpiling, and use of atomic weapons, and for the destruction of all existing bombs within three months. The two proposals were based on very different premises. The Baruch Plan, like the Acheson-Lilienthal Report, proposed a powerful international agency. Baruch did make important modifications to the report's recommendations, insisting that the permanent members of the Security Council forgo the right of veto in this area and stressing that states must be punished for violations. The Soviet proposal echoed the 1925 Geneva Protocol banning chemical weapons, though it went further in prohibiting production and stockpiling as well as use. Like the protocol it lacked provisions for international control, and relied on individual governments for enforcement, though Stalin soon modified the proposal to include full international control.[29]

The two proposals can be characterized as follows, with the American position stated first: (a) international organization vs. national governments; (b) no veto vs. veto; (c) international control vs. national control; and (d) international enforcement vs. national enforcement. In December 1946, at the urging of the United States, the UN Atomic Energy Commission approved the Baruch Plan, with ten countries voting for it and the Soviet Union and Poland abstaining. The Soviet veto ensured that the Security Council would not endorse the commission's report.

Discussions continued in the commission, but the prospects for an agreement dimmed as U.S.-Soviet relations deteriorated. The Soviet Union made a new proposal in June 1947. This still called for a convention banning atomic weapons, but it now put forward the idea of an international control commission with the right to inspect "all facilities engaged in mining of atomic raw materials and in production of atomic materials and atomic energy." These facilities would remain in national hands, but they would be subject to inspection. This proposal fell far short of the international control envisaged by the Baruch Plan. It received only desultory consideration in the UN commission and was formally rejected in 1948.[30] The effort to bring atomic energy under international control, in which many hopes and much effort had been invested, came to nothing.

THE REASONS FOR FAILURE

The failure of international control has been blamed on many factors, among them Soviet intransigence and Baruch's modifications to the Acheson-Lilienthal Report, but there is a more basic explanation. Neither Truman nor Stalin saw the bomb solely or even primarily as a common danger to be addressed by cooperative action; in other words, they did not see the bomb as Niels Bohr thought they should. For Truman the bomb was a powerful instrument of diplomatic pressure at a time when the United States and the Soviet Union were competing in shaping the postwar world. For Stalin the bomb was an instrument of diplomatic pressure that Truman would use to try to intimidate and demoralize the Soviet Union and therefore something the Soviet Union should counterbalance by acquiring a bomb of its own as quickly as possible.

Truman was at best ambivalent on international control. He ignored Secretary of War Henry Stimson's warning that only a direct approach would be taken seriously by Stalin, adopting instead Secretary of State James Byrnes's proposal that negotiations take place under the auspices of the United Nations. There is no evidence to suggest that Stalin, for his part, wanted international control of atomic energy or that he believed the United States was seriously interested in it. The United States and Britain had tried to keep their atomic work secret from the Soviet Union when the three countries were allies in the war against Germany: why expect cooperation now, when they were rivals in shaping the postwar world? The Baruch Plan did not allay these suspicions, since it would have required the Soviet Union to renounce the atomic bomb, and to accept a powerful international agency, before the United States yielded control over its own atomic bombs and facilities.[31]

In the event, each country placed more reliance on its own capacity to defend its interests than on an international regime about which both had doubts. With the failure of international control, deterrence moved to the fore as the basis on which nuclear relationships came to be managed. Indeed the first formulations of nuclear deterrence in the United States were advanced in opposition to those who claimed that disaster would follow if international control of atomic energy were not established. The goal of eliminating nuclear weapons, though often invoked, was widely seen to be unrealistic as long as the Cold War continued. The goal of disarmament came to be replaced by that of arms control, which focused more on stabilizing the deterrent balance than on eliminating nuclear weapons altogether.[32]

ARE THERE LESSONS TO BE LEARNED FROM THIS EXPERIENCE?

Just as in 1945–46, we are once again at a point where the international system seems to many people to be unable to cope with the danger of nuclear weapons. The period of optimism that followed the end of the Cold War has been replaced by the more pessimistic assessment that our current nuclear order is, if not quite broken, under immense strain. New nuclear threats—especially from new nuclear powers and nonstate actors—have assumed a dominant role in American thinking about nuclear weapons, and those threats do not appear to be quite as amenable to deterrence as the Cold War threats were judged to be. One reads and hears today many nostalgic references to the Baruch Plan: if only it had been adopted and were now in place!

The nuclear order today is, of course, very different from what it was in 1945–

46. In spite of the differences, there are two broad lessons to be drawn from the failure of the Baruch Plan. First, the political context is crucial in thinking about nuclear disarmament. Agreement on international control would have had to be based on a common understanding of how the postwar world could, and should, develop, but no such common understanding existed. The crux of the Cold War was indeed the competition between rival visions of how the world should be organized. Bohr believed that the bomb was a common threat to which cooperation would be the appropriate response, but that is not how either Truman or Stalin viewed the bomb. Oppenheimer came to understand the importance of the political context: "[He] feels that the weakness of the Acheson-Lilienthal Report is that it did not sufficient[ly] define the state of the world necessary for any effective plan of control," a colleague recorded early in 1948.[33] The same point is made in a report prepared by a panel of consultants chaired by Oppenheimer in 1953: "[No] regulation of armaments, however limited, has ever proved feasible except as part of some genuine political settlement."[34]

This point is certainly relevant for any attempt to push forward with nuclear disarmament. Some degree of common understanding is needed—in the first instance among the nuclear powers—about the way in which the world is going to develop, if there is to be progress to a world without nuclear weapons. Nuclear disarmament is a profoundly political undertaking, and difficult to pursue if we do not have a conception of the world—and of how it might develop—that we can all live with. During the Cold War that was impossible, but the strategic context has become much more fluid since the end of the Cold War, and that gives the political context a new salience. The relatively stable structure of the international system during the Cold War made it possible to focus on the more technical aspects of arms control, but the political context has assumed a new importance as we try to think through the problems of disarmament in the current international system.

A second and related point is that it is essential that the nuclear powers—and other major powers too (Germany and Japan in particular)—have a sense that any program of nuclear disarmament is *their* program. Though it would hardly have made a difference to the final outcome, Bohr was surely right to suggest to Churchill and Roosevelt that they make a preliminary approach to Stalin to discuss what might be feasible. Stimson gave similar advice in September 1945 when he urged Truman to make a direct approach to Stalin, on the grounds that if other, smaller powers were involved, Stalin would not take the idea of international control seriously. That might have been a more productive approach than an ambitious plan presented on a take-it-or-leave-it basis. Seen from that angle, the Acheson-Lilienthal Report, for all its brilliance, was a classic example of a technocratic, rather than a political, approach to dealing with international politics.

By way of contrast, Shultz and his colleagues underlined that they were putting forward their ideas not as a blueprint but as a means of initiating discussions with other countries, and the Obama administration, while it has focused on specific steps in the short term, has taken a similarly open-ended approach to the goal of nuclear disarmament. This point is especially important because one major line of criticism of the vision of a world free of nuclear weapons is that if the vision were realized it would merely make the world safe for American conventional military power; in other words, the idea of getting rid of nuclear weapons is no more than the pursuit of national interest under the guise of a noble vision. It is precisely because such suspicions exist that it is important to engage other countries in dialogue about the conditions that would make it possible to rid the world of nuclear weapons. The goal will not be attainable unless all states see it as being in their interest.

THE REYKJAVIK MEETING

In the early 1990s George Shultz asked Mikhail Gorbachev what he thought was the most important turning point in bringing the Cold War to an end. Gorbachev answered: the Reykjavik Summit in October 1986, because that was where he and Ronald Reagan had discussed a whole range of issues in depth, thus providing the basis for future progress. Figure 1.1 suggests that Reykjavik was indeed a turning point in the U.S.-Soviet nuclear arms race. The year 1986 appears to have been the year in which the number of nuclear weapons in the world peaked, and the overwhelming majority (about 95 percent) belonged to the United States and the Soviet Union. (Figure 1.1 is based on estimates of nuclear stockpiles, and these may be inaccurate, since most governments do not publish precise data about their total inventory of nuclear warheads.)

Gorbachev and Reagan had met in Geneva in November 1985, and that meeting had brought some easing in the relationship between the United States and the Soviet Union after several very difficult and dangerous years. The two men agreed that "a nuclear war cannot be won and must never be fought," and they planned to hold two summit meetings, one in Washington and one in Moscow.[35] The meeting at Reykjavik was unscheduled, and the idea of it came

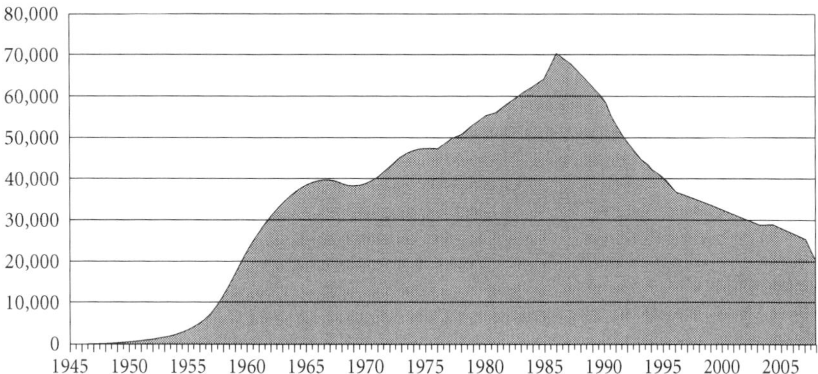

Figure 1.1. Global Nuclear Stockpiles 1945–2008. ©2008 Hans M. Kristensen and Robert S. Norris, Federation of American Scientists and Natural Resources Defense Council.

to Gorbachev in August 1986, when he was on vacation in the Crimea. He was frustrated by the slow progress of the arms control negotiations in Geneva and wanted to breathe new life into the process of arms reduction. Reagan agreed to Gorbachev's proposal for a presummit meeting in Reykjavik in October.[36]

Gorbachev instructed his foreign policy advisor Anatolii Cherniaev to ask the Foreign Ministry to work out the specifics for the meeting with Reagan. Cherniaev was very disappointed with the result; the important thing, he told the Foreign Ministry, was "big politics," not the details of negotiation.[37] Gorbachev and Cherniaev pushed for a set of daring proposals that would sweep Reagan off his feet. A few days before Gorbachev left for Reykjavik, the Politburo met to discuss draft directives that had been prepared by the General Staff and the Foreign Ministry. Gorbachev was not satisfied with the directives; he was prepared to make concessions in order to elicit concessions from the American side. According to Cherniaev, Gorbachev summed up the Politburo meeting as follows:

> Our main goal now is to prevent another new stage in the arms race from taking place. If we do not do that, the danger for us will grow. By not retreating on some specific, even very important questions, from what we have stood firm on for a long time, we will lose the main thing. We will be drawn into an arms race that is beyond our strength. We will lose, because now for us that race is already at the limit of our possibilities.[38]

Gorbachev set off for Reykjavik with a set of proposals that included a 50 percent reduction in strategic nuclear forces and the elimination of medium- and intermediate- range missiles in Europe. This marked a significant shift in the Soviet position. In return Gorbachev expected limitations on the Strategic Defense Initiative, the program of research on missile defense that Reagan had launched with his so-called Star Wars speech on March 23, 1983.

The delegations accompanying Reagan and Gorbachev engaged in hard negotiation during the two days in Iceland and made great progress toward agreements on both strategic and intermediate-range forces, but SDI proved to be a stumbling block. Reagan would not accept the restrictions that Gorbachev wanted to impose on the program, while Gorbachev would not conclude agreements on offensive systems unless the United States accepted limits on SDI. Nevertheless, the negotiations at Reykjavik were not wasted. They laid the basis for the INF (Intermediate Range Nuclear Forces) Treaty signed in Washington in December 1987 and START I (the Strategic Arms Reduction Treaty) signed in July 1991.

Does Reykjavik have lessons for nuclear disarmament today? It is quite a different case from the early negotiations to bring atomic energy under international control. Notwithstanding the brief but important exchange between Reagan and Gorbachev on getting rid of nuclear weapons, the main focus of the meeting was the reduction, not the elimination, of nuclear weapons. Although no agreements were reached at Reykjavik, the meeting was by no means wholly a failure, when broadly considered. Figure 1.1 suggests that it started a process of nuclear arms reductions that has continued to this day.

Like the negotiations on international control, Reykjavik points to the importance of the political context. The meeting was, as Gorbachev noted, a major turning point in bringing the Cold War to an end. The agreements almost reached at Reykjavik were a portent of the changing political relationship between the United States and the Soviet Union. It was the changing political relationship that made possible the reductions in nuclear forces that began in the late 1980s, but progress in arms control contributed in turn to the reduction of tension. To say that the political context must be right is not to say that no steps should be taken toward disarmament until the context is right. Steps toward disarmament can contribute to the creation of the right political context.

THE HOOVER INITIATIVE

The Hoover Initiative did not create a new agenda. Many individuals and groups have worked over the years to advocate nuclear disarmament, and many of the steps proposed by the initiative are already enshrined in international agreements or have been the subject of international negotiations. What the Hoover Initiative has done is to move nuclear disarmament into the mainstream of American and international politics. Other groups—the Nuclear Threat Initiative and Global Zero, for example—have taken up the goal of ridding the world of nuclear weapons. Most important, President Obama has espoused the goal of a world free of nuclear weapons and has taken a number of steps to move in that direction. Among these steps are: a commitment to reduce the role of nuclear weapons in U.S. national security strategy; negotiations with Russia on the reduction of strategic nuclear forces; preparations to send the Comprehensive Test Ban Treaty to the Senate for ratification (the United States signed the treaty in 1996, but the Senate refused to ratify it in 1999); and a global summit on the security of nuclear materials. I discuss these steps in more detail in Chapter 18.

The renewed interest in nuclear disarmament springs from a belief that the nuclear nonproliferation regime needs to be strengthened in order to respond to nuclear threats from irresponsible "rogue" states and terrorist groups. Shultz and his colleagues judge deterrence to be an ineffective strategy for dealing with these new nuclear threats. To that extent the Hoover Initiative accepts a key premise of the Bush Doctrine, as set out in the National Security Strategy of September 2002, which argued that deterrence was not an effective way of dealing with the new threats.[39] The Hoover Initiative does not, however, accept the Bush Doctrine's corollary—namely, that the United States should be willing to act preemptively (that is, to use preventive force) to deal with "emergent" and not just "imminent" threats. More precisely, the initiative gives preventive force a low priority among the available options for dealing with potential nuclear threats; it does not elevate it to the status of a national strategy, though it certainly does not rule it out completely. The initiative can be read as a rejection of the Bush doctrine, insofar as it implies that preventive force ("preemption" in the Bush Doctrine's terms) is not a satisfactory instrument on which to place primary reliance in dealing with new nuclear threats. This conclusion is reinforced by the war in Iraq—not because it turned out that Iraq had no nuclear weapons, but because preventive war proved to be a much more difficult undertaking than the Bush administration had understood.

It is a crucial premise of the Hoover Initiative that a nuclear order based on discrimination—with some countries possessing nuclear weapons and others denied the right to have them—will not work over the long term. It is not only that there will be additional states wanting to acquire nuclear weapons of their own. The nuclear regime will not be legitimate in the eyes even of those states that do not wish to have nuclear weapons. They may be less willing, therefore, to sustain and enforce a discriminatory nuclear regime than a regime in which nuclear weapons are prohibited altogether. Obama has stressed this point. "Rules must be binding," he said in Prague. "Violations must be punished. Words must mean something. The world must stand together to prevent the spread of these weapons." In his remarks to the UN Security Council on September 24, 2009, he said: "The Security Council has both the authority and responsibility to determine and respond as necessary when violations of [the Nuclear Non-Proliferation Treaty] threaten international peace and security.... And we must demonstrate that international law is not an empty promise, and that treaties will be enforced."[40]

CONCLUSION

President Obama has adopted the elimination of nuclear weapons as a goal for his administration. Previous attempts at nuclear disarmament point to the importance of the political context and of political consultation in taking steps to rid the world of nuclear weapons. The Hoover Initiative and, more important, the policies advanced by Obama have opened up political space for renewed efforts to deal with the nuclear danger.

NOTES

1. "Memorandum of Conversations," in *Implications of the Reykjavik Summit on Its Twentieth Anniversary: Conference Report*, ed. George P. Shultz and Sidney D. Drell (Stanford: Hoover Institution Press, 2007), pp. 210–11.

2. George P. Shultz, *Turmoil and Triumph: My Years as Secretary of State* (New York: Scribner's, 1993), p. 778.

3. Ibid., p. 776.

4. Margaret Thatcher, *The Downing Street Years* (New York: Harper Collins, 1993), pp. 471–73.

5. Richard M. Nixon and Henry A. Kissinger, "An Arms Agreement—on Two Conditions," *The Washington Post*, April 26, 1987.

6. The proceedings were published in Shultz and Drell, *Implications of the Reykjavik Summit.*

7. I base these comments on my own participation in the meeting.

8. George P. Shultz, William J. Perry, Henry A. Kissinger, and Sam Nunn, "A World Free of Nuclear Weapons," *Wall Street Journal*, January 4, 2007.

9. Mikhail Gorbachev, "The Nuclear Threat," *Wall Street Journal*, January 31, 2007.

10. George P. Shultz, Steven P. Andreasen, Sidney D. Drell, James E. Goodby, eds., *Reykjavik Revisited: Steps Toward a World Free of Nuclear Weapons* (Stanford: Hoover Institution Press, 2008).

11. George P. Shultz, William J. Perry, Henry A. Kissinger, and Sam Nunn, "Toward a Nuclear-Free World," *Wall Street Journal*, January 15, 2008.

12. Ibid.

13. "*Arms Control Today* 2008 Presidential Q&A," *Arms Control Today*, December 2008. Accessed at http://www.armscontrol.org/system/files/Obama_Q-A_Final_Dec10_2008.pdf.

14. John McCain's speech at the University of Denver on May 27, 2008. Accessed at http://www.clw.org/elections/2008/presidential/mccain_speech_nuclear_weapons/.

15. Margaret Beckett, "A World Free of Nuclear Weapons?" Remarks delivered to the Carnegie International Nonproliferation Conference, June 25, 2007. Accessed at http://www.carnegieendowment.org/events/?fa=eventDetail&id=1004&prog=zru. On the Norwegian conference, see: http://www.7ni.mfa.no/norway/opact/International+Conference+on+Nuclear+Disarmament.htm. Helmut Schmidt, Richard von Weizsäcker, Egon Bahr, and Hans-Dietrich Genscher, "Fár eine atomfreie Welt," *Frankfurter Allgemeine Zeitung*, January 9, 2009.

16. Douglas Hurd, Malcolm Rifkind, David Owen, and George Robertson, "Start Worrying and Learn to Ditch the Bomb," *The Times*, June 30, 2008; Massimo D'Alema, Gianfranco Fini, Giorgio La Malfa, Arturo Parisi, and Francesco Calogero, "Per un mondo senza armi nucleari," *Corriere della Sera*, July 24, 2008.

17. Address by H. E. Yang Jiechi, minister of foreign affairs of the People's Republic of China, at the Conference on Disarmament, Geneva, August 12, 2009.

18. Remarks by President Barack Obama in Prague, April 5, 2009. Accessed at http://www.whitehouse.gov/the_press_office/Remarks-By-President-Barack-Obama-In-Prague-As-Delivered/.

19. Obama's remarks at the Security Council Summit can be accessed at http://www.whitehouse.gov/the_press_office/Remarks-By-The-President-At-the-UN-Security-Council-Summit-On-Nuclear-Non-Proliferation-And-Nuclear-Disarmament/. The text of the resolution can be found at http://www.iaea.org/NewsCenter/News/PDF/N0952374.pdf.

20. The citation can be found at http://www.iaea.org/NewsCenter/News/PDF/N0952374.pdf.

21. The text of the manifesto can be found at http://www.pugwash.org/about/manifesto.htm.

22. See, for example, the 1996 Report of the Canberra Commission on the Elimination of Nuclear Weapons, at http://www.dfat.gov.au/cc/index.html.

23. On the history of disarmament movements, see Lawrence S. Wittner, *The Struggle against the Bomb*, 3 vols. (Stanford: Stanford University Press, 1993, 1997, 2003).

24. Robert Oppenheimer, speech at Los Alamos, October 16, 1945, in Oppenheimer, *Letters and Recollections*, ed. Alice Kimball Smith and Charles Weiner (Stanford: Stanford University Press, 1995 [1980]), pp. 310–11.

25. This story is well told by Margaret Gowing, *Britain and Atomic Energy* (London: Macmillan, 1964).

26. Richard G. Hewlett and Oscar E. Anderson, Jr., *A History of the United States Atomic Energy Commission . Volume 1: The New World, 1939/1946* (University Park: Pennsylvania State University Press, 1962), pp. 461–69, 531–33.

27. "A Report on the International Control of Atomic Energy," Prepared for the Secretary of State's Committee on Atomic Energy (U. S. Government Printing Office, Washington, DC, March 16, 1946).

28. Ibid., pp. 34–36, 39–44.

29. R. M. Timerbaev, *Rossiia i iadernoe nerasprostranenie* (Moscow: Nauka, 1999), pp. 44–51.

30. Bertrand Goldschmidt, *The Atomic Complex: A Worldwide Political History of Nuclear Energy* (La Grange Park, IL: American Nuclear Society, 1982), pp. 77–81.

31. For a shrewd discussion of the American policy on international control, see McGeorge Bundy, *Danger and Survival: Choices about the Bomb in the First Fifty Years* (New York: Random House, 1988). See also Campbell Craig and Sergey Radchenko, *The Atomic Bomb and the Origins of the Cold War* (New Haven: Yale University Press, 2008).

32. Two classic texts on arms control are Thomas C. Schelling and Morton H. Halperin, *Strategy and Arms Control* (New York: Twentieth Century Fund, 1961); and Donald G. Brennan, ed., *Arms Control, Disarmament, and National Security* (New York: G. Braziller, 1961).

33. Frederick Osborn, diary entry for February 18, 1948. Quoted in Michael D. Gordin, *Red Cloud at Dawn: Truman, Stalin, and the End of the Atomic Monopoly* (New York: Farrar, Straus and Giroux, 2009), p. 58.

34. "Armaments and American Policy," Report by the Panel of Consultants of the Department of State to the Secretary of State, January 1953, *FRUS, 1952–1954, National Security Affairs volume II, part 2* (Washington, DC: U.S. Government Printing Office, 1984), p. 1075.

35. Jack Matlock, *Reagan and Gorbachev: How the Cold War Ended* (New York: Random House, 2004), pp. 149–73. The quotation is on p. 165.

36. A. S. Cherniaev, *Shest' let s Gorbachevym* (Moscow: Kul'tura, 1993), pp. 105–17.

37. Ibid., p. 107.

38. Ibid., pp. 112–13. These notes correspond to the minutes of the Politburo meeting given in *V Politburo TsK KPSS… Po zapisiam Anatoliia Cherniaeva, Vadima Medvedeva, Georgiia Shakhnazarova (1985–1991)* (Moscow: Al'pina, 2006), pp. 85–87. The minutes of the Politburo meeting in English can be found, along with other relevant documents, in *The Reykjavik File* at the National Security Archive at http://www.gwu.edu/~nsarchiv/NSAEBB/NSAEBB203/index.htm.

39. *The National Security Strategy of the United States of America, September 2002* (Washington, DC: The White House, 2002). Accessed at http://georgewbush-whitehouse.archives.gov/nsc/nss/2002/nss.pdf.

40. "Remarks by the President at the United Nations Security Council Summit on Nuclear Non-proliferation and Nuclear Disarmament" (The White House: Office of the Press Secretary, September 24, 2009). Accessed at http://www.whitehouse.gov/the_press_office/Remarks-By-The-President-At-the-UN-Security-Council-Summit-On-Nuclear-Non-Proliferation-And-Nuclear-Disarmament/.

2 Advocacy for Nuclear Disarmament: A Global Revival?

Randy Rydell

Ever since nuclear weapons were first used at the end of World War II, there have been proposals to eliminate them. The world today is largely united on the merits of this goal but remains deeply divided over how to achieve it. Some commentators call for mass popular movements. Some urge the states with the largest nuclear arsenals to lead the way. Some have sought to redefine what "zero" means, saying that "virtual" arsenals or nondeployed weapons are an acceptable goal. Some insist on absolute preconditions. Some address disarmament as merely a "vision" or "ultimate goal." A few seem to believe that achieving this goal will require nothing less than world government.

Now that "global nuclear disarmament" is finally receiving the attention it deserves, this is a good time to examine some of the recent proposals for achieving it, their antecedents, and some of the challenges that such efforts will need to address if they are to prove successful.

THE REDISCOVERY OF NUCLEAR DISARMAMENT

If Rip van Winkle had awoken on January 4, 2007, and read his *Wall Street Journal*, he could well have concluded that former U.S. secretaries of state George Shultz and Henry Kissinger, former secretary of defense William Perry, and former senator Sam Nunn (D-Ga.) had just invented a wonderful new idea: the vision of a world free of nuclear weapons.[1]

He would not have known that "disarmament" appeared twice in the UN Charter, which was adopted before the first nuclear test, and that the General Assembly had identified the goal of eliminating all nuclear weapons and other "weapons adaptable to mass destruction" in its first resolution, adopted in London on January 24, 1946. This was the same year that the U.S. government produced the Acheson-Lilienthal report and Baruch Plan, and the Soviet Union offered what came to be called the Gromyko Plan, all ostensibly aimed at achieving a nuclear weapon–free world.

He would not have known about the near miss in May 1955, when the nuclear powers came very close to agreement on a plan for nuclear disarmament in Geneva. Nor could he have known that the General Assembly put "general and complete disarmament [GCD] under effective international control"—aiming at the *elimination* of weapons of mass destruction and the *limitation* of conventional arms—on its agenda in 1959, where it has been ever since. He would not have known that President John Kennedy introduced his own detailed GCD proposal in the General Assembly on September 25, 1961, or that the United States and Soviet Union released that month the McCloy-Zorin statement of "agreed principles" for achieving GCD, a concept that would later be incorporated in a dozen multilateral treaties.

He would not have known about the conclusion of the Nuclear Non-Proliferation Treaty (NPT) in 1968, which addressed both nuclear disarmament and GCD. A decade later, the General Assembly would convene its first special session on disarmament and agree that although GCD was the world community's "ultimate objective," nuclear disarmament would be its top priority. He would not have known about the Reykjavik summit in 1986, when U.S. president Ronald Reagan and Soviet leader Mikhail Gorbachev discussed the elimination of nuclear weapons and long-range ballistic missiles.

He would also not have been aware of the five treaties creating regional nuclear weapon–free zones that also address GCD, nor the hundreds of resolutions that the General Assembly had adopted over six decades for global nuclear disarmament. He would not have heard of the 1996 advisory opinion by the International Court of Justice, which held that the NPT parties had a duty not just to negotiate to achieve this goal but also to bring such negotiations to a conclusion.

Although these combined activities have not yet produced a nuclear weapon–free world, they did play a key role in shaping a global political environment that has been conducive to stockpile reductions over the last twenty years, to the gradual delegitimization of such weapons (still a work in progress), and to the generation of practical proposals for achieving nuclear disarmament.

As a result, it is less common today to see nuclear disarmament summarily dismissed as utopian, impractical, or as Margaret Thatcher once said, "pie in the sky."[2]

A CASCADE OF DISARMAMENT PROPOSALS

Nobody disputes that the January 2007 op-ed in the *Wall Street Journal* stimulated public interest in disarmament as a serious response to nuclear weapons threats. Since its publication there have been a cascade of disarmament proposals. The world today is arguably closer to a "tipping point" for new progress in nuclear disarmament than it is to a global nuclear weapon free-for-all, as some have feared (Table 2.1).[3]

These nuclear disarmament initiatives have come from many diverse sources. The approach of having former officials or statesmen publish op-eds on this issue has now been replicated in Australia, Belgium, Canada, France, Germany, Italy, The Netherlands, Norway, Poland, Sweden, and the United Kingdom.[4] More will likely follow. Newspapers around the world have published countless editorials in support of this goal. It was endorsed by both leading candidates in the 2008 U.S. presidential campaign, as well as by senior officials in virtually all other states that possess such weapons.

Several nuclear weapon states have taken some steps in the right direction, if not always officially linking this progress to their legal commitments under Article VI of the NPT. The French government has announced a significant cut in its arsenal, after having already shut down its nuclear test site along with its plants to produce fissile material for weapons. The British government has proposed a conference of experts from the nuclear weapon states to examine the challenge of verifying nuclear disarmament.

For their part, the United States and Russian Federation—which have more than 95 percent of the world's nuclear weapons—concluded a new bilateral treaty on April 8, 2010, to replace the expired START treaty.[5] The new treaty sets a ceiling for each side of 1,550 deployed strategic offensive nuclear warheads and limits their respective number of deployed delivery vehicles for such warheads at 700. The treaty fulfills joint commitments made by presidents Obama and Medvedev in 2009; in his April 5, 2009, speech in Prague, President Obama also stated a U.S. commitment "to seek the peace and security of a world without nuclear weapons," adding that this would entail the pursuit of further reductions beyond the START follow-on treaty.[6]

These are just some of the efforts that are under way by states with nuclear weapons, efforts that by no means will alone produce global nuclear disarmament but that may help in achieving further reductions.

Other initiatives have come from diverse coalitions of states, consisting of what are often called the "middle-power states." The New Agenda Coali-

TABLE 2.1

Getting to Zero: Some Recent Initiatives

In the last few years a number of private groups and governments have offered proposals for moving toward nuclear disarmament. Some of the most prominent are listed below.

Private Sector	
Abolishing Nuclear Weapons [Perkovich/ Acton, International Institute for Strategic Studies, Adelphi Paper 396] (2008)	<http://www.carnegieendowment.org/ files/abolishing_nuclear_weapons_ debate.pdf>
Abolition 2000 (1995)	http://www.abolition2000.org/
Appeal for U.S. Leadership for a Nuclear Weapons-Free World (2009)	http://www.wagingpeace.org/
Article VI Forum [Middle Powers Initiative]	http://www.middlepowers.org/
Global Zero (2008)	http://www.globalzero.org/
Hoover Plan [Shultz, Perry, Kissinger, Nunn]	http://www.hoover.org/publications/ digest/6731276.html
ICAN (International Campaign to Abolish Nuclear Weapons) (2007)	http://www.ippnw.org/Programs/ ICAN/index.html
International Luxembourg Forum on Preventing Nuclear Catastrophe (2007)	http://luxembourgforum.org/eng/ events/aboutforum/
NGO Response to Blix Commission (2006)	http://wmdreport.org/
Weapons of Mass Destruction Commission (Blix Commission) (2006)	http://www.wmdcommission.org/
Public Sector	
European Union disarmament initiative [Sarkozy letter to Ban Ki-moon] (2008)	http://www.franceonu.org/ spip.php?article3533
Five-point proposal by Secretary-General Ban Ki-moon (2008)	http://www.un.org/News/Press/ docs/2008/sgsm11881.doc.htm
Follow-up to the advisory opinion of the International Court of Justice [Malaysia, UNGA Res 63/49] (2008)	http://disarmament.un.org/ vote.nsf/
International Commission on Nuclear Non-Proliferation and Disarmament [Australia and Japan] (2008)	http://www.icnnd.org/
Norwegian initiative (2005)	http://www.norway.org.au/policy/ organizations/norwegianinitiative.htm
NPT's "13 steps" adopted at 2000 NPT Review Conference (2000)	http://www.reachingcriticalwill.org/ legal/npt/13point.html
Nuclear disarmament (Myanmar for majority of Nonaligned Movement, UNGA Res 63/46), 2008	http://disarmament.un.org/vote.nsf/
Renewed determination towards the total elimination of nuclear weapons (Japan, UNGA Res 63/73), 2008	http://disarmament.un.org/vote.nsf/
Towards a nuclear-weapon-free world (South Africa, for New Agenda Coalition, UNGA Res 63/58), 2008	http://disarmament.un.org/vote.nsf/
British Foreign and Commonwealth Office, "Lifting the Nuclear Shadow," (2008)	http://www.fco.gov.uk/en/fco-in-action/counter-terrorism/ weapons/nuclear-weapons/nuclear-paper/

tion (Brazil, Egypt, Ireland, Mexico, New Zealand, Sweden, and South Africa) continues to advance its joint proposals for progress in nuclear disarmament, notably by means of annual resolutions in the General Assembly. The states behind the Norwegian initiative (Australia, Chile, Indonesia, Norway, Romania, South Africa, and the United Kingdom) have been advancing their own set of disarmament and nonproliferation proposals since 2005, focusing mainly on measures to strengthen the NPT.

Several international coalitions of nongovernmental actors have also emerged in recent years to champion this cause, including long-standing efforts by Pugwash Conferences, which won the Nobel Peace Prize for its work on nuclear weapons in 1995.[7] Other groups offering steps for disarmament include the Global Zero initiative, the International Luxembourg Forum on Preventing Nuclear Catastrophe, Mayors for Peace, and the Middle Powers Initiative and its Article VI Forum (organized by the Global Security Institute), as well as other coalitions focused more on building support at the grass-roots level, such as ICAN (the International Campaign to Abolish Nuclear Weapons), Abolition 2000, the Nuclear Age Peace Foundation, and others too numerous to list here.

Various international commissions have also focused on the disarmament challenge, building on the earlier work by the Palme and Canberra commissions (1982 and 1996, respectively). In 2006 the international Weapons of Mass Destruction Commission chaired by Hans Blix issued a report with thirty recommendations dealing just with nuclear weapons.[8] Two years later, Australia and Japan jointly launched the International Commission on Nuclear Non-Proliferation and Disarmament in a common effort to reinvigorate global efforts in these fields; its final report, issued in late 2009, produced seventy-six recommendations.[9] Also noteworthy are the annual reports issued by the International Panel on Fissile Materials, an independent group of arms control and nonproliferation experts that since 2006 has been studying specific technical measures to control and dispose of weapon-usable nuclear materials.[10]

In 2008 the European Union sent a proposal to the UN secretary-general, outlining an eight-point initiative to address several nuclear weapon challenges, including disarmament. In December 2008, Javier Solana, the EU high representative for common foreign and security policy, addressed the EU disarmament and nonproliferation proposals at a conference held at the European Parliament.[11]

Nuclear disarmament is what Dag Hammarskjöld used to call a "hardy perennial" at the United Nations, which has served as a global forum for cultivating this perennial for over six decades. On October 24, 2008, Secretary-General Ban Ki-moon delivered a major address devoted just to nuclear disarmament, the first such address by a UN secretary-general exclusively on this subject in many years. In December 2009, he issued his Action Plan for nuclear disarmament and nonproliferation, identifying several ways to implement his 2008 proposal.[12] He has also raised this issue repeatedly in his official remarks at many multilateral gatherings, inside and outside the United Nations, and he even launched a multimedia Twitter, Facebook, and MySpace campaign called "WMD-WeMustDisarm" leading up to the International Day of Peace, September 21, 2009.[13] On September 24, 2009, the UN Security Council held its first high-level summit to address nuclear disarmament and nonproliferation, which resulted in the adoption of Resolution 1887, though it dealt primarily with nonproliferation issues.

Meanwhile, efforts are continuing in the General Assembly to advance specific nuclear disarmament proposals, although they seldom receive the credit they deserve for their persistence and level of detail. These include specific resolutions on nuclear disarmament offered by Japan, Myanmar (on behalf of a majority of the Non-Aligned Movement), the New Agenda Coalition, and Malaysia (on a nuclear weapons convention).[14] These resolutions are debated and adopted year after year by overwhelming majorities.

Nuclear disarmament has also been a specific focus of meetings that take place in NPT arenas, as registered, for example, in the thirteen "practical steps for the systematic and progressive efforts" to implement Article VI of the treaty, agreed at the 2000 NPT Review Conference. The 1995 NPT Review and Extension Conference politically tied the indefinite extension of the treaty to a package deal of commitments that included a "programme of action" relating to Article VI of the treaty and the Middle East Resolution, which called for efforts to establish a nuclear weapon–free zone in the region. Each of the 2007, 2008, and 2009 annual sessions of the Preparatory Commission for the 2010 NPT Review Conference also addressed nuclear disarmament issues in some depth, and each of these sessions also allowed for some participation by groups from civil society (including presentations, attendance at plenary meetings, and the distribution of publications).

In addition, nuclear disarmament has been the focus of several recent books that have helped to clarify the historical context, prescribe specific steps, and stimulate a dialogue between advocates and critics of disarmament.[15] The entire Fall 2009 and Winter 2010 issues of *Daedalus*, the journal of the American Academy of Arts and Sciences, were dedicated to the subject "On the Global Nuclear Future."

ASSESSING THE ROAD MAPS TO ZERO

Several points emerge from this brief survey of only a few of the many nuclear disarmament proposals that have emerged in recent years. First, these proposals come from a wide variety of sources, including very different types of countries—such as nuclear weapon states and coalitions of industrialized and developing states—as well as regional organizations and a growing number of diverse nongovernmental organizations. The champions of nuclear disarmament are not only non–nuclear weapon states and peace groups; literally all states profess to support this goal, as do growing numbers of current and former leaders of government and former military experts. The constituency of nuclear disarmament has significantly expanded in recent years to include the world's religions, women's groups, environmentalists, scientists, scholars, lawyers, human rights advocates, mayors, and legislators.

Second, although anti–nuclear weapon movements have historically placed a very heavy emphasis—best documented by Lawrence Wittner[16]—on the threats posed by such weapons and fears of their possible use, recent proposals are stressing such themes as the positive security benefits that would result for all countries from the elimination of such weapons. Meanwhile, more commentators are also stressing the military disutility[17] or irrelevance of nuclear weapons in addressing security concerns in the twenty-first century, including terrorism, proliferation, the prevention of armed conflict within and between states, as well as many other emerging issues relating to cybersecurity, space weapons, and the development and transfers of conventional weaponry. Although appeals to fear and basic morality persist in many of these initiatives, there is also more of an emphasis on hope and the prospects for a safer world without nuclear weapons.

Third, there is much cross-fertilization among these various proposals. Many of their "steps toward zero" have long appeared in General Assembly resolutions. The four most fundamental criteria for assessing future nuclear disarmament initiatives—that is, that they should be verifiable, transparent, irreversible, and legally binding—have appeared for many years in these resolutions and in consensus documents agreed upon at meetings of representatives from the NPT states parties. Many of these criteria were addressed by groups of governmental experts in reports requested by the General Assembly decades ago.

This process of cross-fertilization goes far beyond these basic principles and encompasses some very specific proposals. These most commonly include deep cuts in the largest nuclear arsenals, held by the Russian Federation and the United States; reductions in nuclear weapon delivery systems; the destruction of nondeployed weapons; the safeguarding of fissile material recovered from such weapons; the entry into force of the Comprehensive Nuclear Test Ban Treaty and the start of negotiations on a multilateral fissile material treaty; disarmament actions by other states with nuclear weapons; the no-first-use doctrine; the withdrawal of nonstrategic nuclear weapons deployed outside national territories; de-alerting; security assurances for non–nuclear weapon states; adherence by the nuclear weapon states to the protocols of nuclear-weapon-free-zone treaties; parallel efforts to eliminate other types of weapons of mass destruction while limiting conventional arms; and numerous other confidence-building measures to facilitate the process of nuclear disarmament.

Fourth, a great weakness in these proposals—virtually all of them—is that they go only so far in specifying what specific actors must do in specific circumstances; in short, the proposals tend, with only rare exceptions, to avoid issues relating to the political tactics of implementation. For example, such proposals seldom, if ever, get into the weeds of the domestic politics of states to identify what new laws and regulations must be created to give greater weight to international commitments, or how specific governmental institutions need to be adapted to meet this challenge. Some proposals recognize the need to integrate international disarmament commitments into the domestic policies, laws, regulations, and bureaucracies of states, but they are typically silent on precisely how this is to be achieved. International commissions understandably have been reluctant to prescribe such reforms in specific states. More surprising is the reluctance of nongovernmental proposals to address these challenges. In short, the proposals are much stronger on what needs to be done than on how to do it.

Fifth, future proposals for global nuclear disarmament must do a better job of responding to criticisms that have been raised about the wisdom of pursuing zero.[18] Critics say that the goal is utopian or impractical; that it is dangerous, encouraging states once covered by foreign nuclear umbrellas to seek their own nuclear deterrents; that it is irrelevant, because a given set of "bad countries" will inevitably seek nuclear weapons regardless of what the rest of the world does; that it is unenforceable (what would the world community really do if, in a nuclear weapon–free world, a state cheated and developed its own clandestine nuclear arsenal?); that it would open the door to large-scale conventional war; that it is unverifiable; and that it fails to understand that nuclear weapons are dangerous only when they are in the "wrong hands." Also, most commonly, it must respond to the dictum that such weapons "cannot be dis-invented."

All of these arguments have sound rebuttals. Former military leaders and nuclear weapon policy-makers have potentially much to contribute in clarifying the positive security benefits from disarmament and, above all, in exposing the many frailties of its alternatives.

Sixth, many of these zero initiatives suffer from zero follow-up. Meetings are held, various pieces of paper are issued, and that is that. The act of making such proposals has become an end in itself in some ways. Given that many of the proposals are quite similar, disarmament proponents might well examine more closely what has happened to past proposals, why they have not been implemented, or how they could be advanced through additional actions by governments and international organizations. This suggests the great importance of regular assessments of the consistency of empirical facts with agreed normative goals.

To promote accountability and compliance with past policy commitments, various public arenas already play important roles, and could well become even more relevant in the years to come as the nuclear arsenals continue to decline. With respect to nuclear disarmament, these especially include the various sessions of the NPT preparatory committees and once-every-five-years review conferences, which together comprise the NPT review process.[19]

One of the key decisions leading to the indefinite extension of the NPT in 1995 provided that the treaty review process "should look forward as well as back."[20] This is how accountability occurs in a multilateral treaty setting: behavior is assessed against agreed normative standards, which in the case of the NPT are found in the text of the treaty itself and in interpretative statements adopted by consensus at the review conferences. Another such multilateral arena is in the work of the UN General Assembly and its First Committee, which annually considers about fifty resolutions, including many that deal with specific measures to promote global nuclear disarmament. Complementary follow-up efforts and assessments can also occur within the governmental processes of individual states, through the oversight, speech, and debate functions of the legislatures; especially useful are assessments intended to ensure that a state's laws, policies, and practices are in line with its international commitments.

Though the various arenas may differ, the essential process of accountability is largely the same, consisting of three fundamental components: commitment, behavior, and assessment. Much of the case for the eventual negotiation of a multilateral nuclear weapon convention follows very similar logic: an agreed disarmament norm is needed—in this case, agreement on the norm of zero. The norm has behavioral consequences. This behavior is authoritatively assessed through a procedure widely accepted as legitimate. And judgments are reached on the achievement of the intended purpose.

The process of accountability is very important both in confirming progress and in exposing departures from the agreed norm, especially since some of these departures—while originally intended to apply to single states—could well evolve into new multilateral norms. A good example is the often-proposed doctrine that would treat nuclear weapons as legitimate to possess for the "sole purpose" of deterring nuclear attacks.[21] It remains to be seen whether current calls for such a doctrine would serve as a stepping stone toward—or away from—zero. One need only consider a world in which more and more states were acquiring their own nuclear weapons for this sole purpose, while current possessors defer disarmament indefinitely. A review and accountability process is therefore indispensable in identifying and preventing the evolution of new multilateral norms that are contrary to the goal of disarmament.

The seventh and final point about these proposals is their common tendency to ignore issues relating to the UN disarmament machinery (including the Conference on Disarmament), reforms that are needed, and its past contributions and successes in advancing disarmament. The United Nations serves as an indispensable arena for deliberating disarmament norms, for converting such norms into multilateral treaty obligations, for promoting their universality and legitimacy, and, of course, for establishing accountability.

A GLOBAL REVIVAL—BUT OF WHAT?

This survey should leave little doubt that there has been a significant revival of worldwide interest in the goal of eliminating nuclear weapons worldwide. This revival is not limited to initiatives launched by individuals or groups in civil society; it is also manifested in efforts by states and coalitions of states.

Yet throughout the history of global nuclear disarmament efforts, the various "partial measures" that have been pursued have tended over time to become ends in themselves, as disarmament has typically been approached as a distant aspiration or "vision" rather than as a serious focus of public policy.

More than thirty years ago, Swedish disarmament diplomat Alva Myrdal wrote of the "game of disarmament,"[22] and there are indications that this game is still being played. With disarmament relegated to the status of a dream, concrete policy actions have tended to bear a closer resemblance to arms control than to disarmament. Thus the original twin goals agreed in the early years of the United Nations—namely, the *elimination* of all weapons of mass destruction and the *regulation* of conventional arms—have become switched, and much of the global effort now appears to be centered on regulating nuclear weapons.

Evidence for this is seen in the efforts by the nuclear weapon states to reduce the number of deployed strategic nuclear weapons and their delivery systems, to halt the global proliferation of such weapons, to strengthen controls and physical security over fissile materials, to tighten up export controls, and other such measures, while at the same time affirming the continued indispensability of such weapons for purposes of deterrence.

So the revival of nuclear disarmament as a goal does not necessarily translate into the revival of governmental efforts to achieve it. Such efforts would logically include the establishment of disarmament agencies in the nuclear weapon states, the adoption of domestic legislation and regulations specifically addressing disarmament, the development of national plans with timetables and benchmarks for achieving disarmament goals, the appearance of disarmament as line-items in national budgets, and the termination of research and development of modifications to existing weapons or efforts to "modernize" facilities constituting the nuclear weapon complex. The doctrine of nuclear deterrence has been modified here and there, but it remains viewed as an indispensable basis for security in about ten states directly, and tens more indirectly under the nuclear umbrella. There are no disarmament "complexes" or disarmament "stewardship programs."

Yet virtually all of the various nuclear disarmament initiatives currently on the table have some potential to contribute in bridging this gap between future ends and current means. Different initiatives are obviously targeted at different constituencies. Policy-makers and experts in regional and international organizations will find much that is useful in the reports of the International Commission on Nuclear Non-Proliferation and Disarmament, and the International Panel on Fissile Materials. Meanwhile, the Global Zero Campaign, the International Campaign Against Nuclear Weapons (ICAN), Abolition 2000, the Women's International League of Peace and Freedom, and countless other civil society groups aim at wider audiences. Religious groups that will surely continue to promote disarmament include Pax Christi, the Quakers, Soka Gakkai International, and the World Council of Churches, to name only a few.

The transition from affirming the goal of disarmament to achieving it will occur only if there is sufficient political will, which is most likely to be found in the union of a compelling idea with diverse political actors willing to advance it.

LOOKING AHEAD

Future efforts to rid the world of nuclear weapons—to achieve zero—will therefore succeed or fail depending on the outcome of two parallel trends. The first is the achievement of an international consensus on certain substantive issues relating to nuclear weapons per se—namely, their irrelevance as military instruments, the security hazards posed by their very existence, their cost, the human and environmental consequences of their production and use, and their widespread identification as an anathema rather than as a source of prestige or status. The second is a multidimensional political process to build and sustain such a consensus, a process involving, in various ways, the participation of individual citizens, nongovernmental groups, political parties, mayors, national legislators, and regional and international organizations. Navigating to zero, in short, requires both an anchor (a stable goal) and a sail (some dynamic means of propulsion).

Zero will not be achieved strictly by the action of elites nor by an exclusive reliance on many other worthy but insufficient measures, including those relating to nonproliferation, safeguards, physical security controls over nuclear materials, and other such activities. Together, these are better viewed as complementary means to advance disarmament. The great advantage of the zero-norm is that it offers a universal, nondiscriminatory standard, which makes it far more likely to obtain the international cooperation and consent needed to achieve full compliance and sustainability.

Yet many still believe that nuclear weapons will be around forever—that they have "kept the peace"; that they represent the triumph of national genius over the forces of nature; and that they offer the ultimate protection against fearsome threats emanating from a violent and unpredictable world that exists in an enduring, immutable condition of anarchy. Pax atomica, they say, is here to stay.

Perhaps George S. Patton had the best response. He wrote in a 1933 paper on military tactics:

> When Samson took the fresh jawbone of an ass and slew a thousand men therewith he probably started such a vogue for the weapon . . . that for years no prudent donkey dared to bray. . . . History is replete with countless other instances of military implements each in its day heralded as the last word—the key to victory—yet each in its turn subsiding to its useful but inconspicuous niche. Today machines hold the place formerly occupied by the jawbone, the elephant, armor, the long bow, gun powder, and latterly, the submarine. They too shall pass.[23]

NOTES

This chapter is based on an article that originally appeared in the April 2009 issue of *Arms Control Today*, and is published here with the permission of the Arms Control Association.

1. International readers might not know that Rip van Winkle is a fictional character who appeared in a short story by Washington Irving about a lazy farmer in New York who sleeps for twenty years through the U.S. Revolutionary War. In the present article, he sleeps even longer. George P. Shultz, William J. Perry, Henry A. Kissinger, and Sam Nunn, "A World Free of Nuclear Weapons," *Wall Street Journal*, 4 January 2007, p. A15. The same authors later published "Toward a Nuclear-Free World," *Wall Street Journal*, 15 January 2008, p. A13; and "How to Protect Our Nuclear Deterrent," *Wall Street Journal*, 19 January 2010, p. A17.

2. Margaret Thatcher, interview cited in Geoffrey Smith, "Thatcher to Reagan: Put Some Hindsight in Summit Vision," *Los Angeles Times*, 14 November 1986.

3. For a contrary view, see William J. Perry and James R. Schlesinger et al., "America's Strategic Posture: The Final Report of the Congressional Commission on the Strategic Posture of the United States" (Washington, DC: United States Institute of Peace, 2009), which made twelve references to the impending nuclear "tipping point." See also "The Nuclear Tipping Point," a documentary film released in January 2010 by the Nuclear Security Project, in coordination with the Nuclear Threat Initiative and the Hoover Institution on War, Revolution and Peace, and the press release describing the film at http://www.nti.org/c_press/press_release_NTP_012710.pdf.

4. For links to each of these statements, see http://www.pugwash.org/reports/nw/nuclear-weapons-free-statements/NWFW_statements.htm.

5. "Treaty between the United States of America and the Russian Federation on Measures for the Further Reduction and Limitation of Strategic Offensive Arms," at http://www.state.gov/documents/organization/140035.pdf.

6. Texts of the Prague speech of 5 April, the Joint Statement of 1 April, and the Joint Understanding of 6 July are available at www.whitehouse.gov.

7. The Pugwash Council identified eleven steps for nuclear disarmament in its statement issued after the 57th Pugwash Conference in 2007. See www.pugwash.org/reports/pac/57/statement.htm.

8. Weapons of Mass Destruction Commission, *Weapons of Terror: Freeing the World of Nuclear, Biological and Chemical Weapons* (Stockholm: Weapons of Mass Destruction Commission, 1 June 2006), at www.wmdcommission.org/files/Weapons_of_Terror.pdf.

9. Gareth Evans and Yoriko Kawaguchi (co-chairs), *Eliminating Nuclear Threats: A Practical Agenda for Global Policymakers* (Canberra and Tokyo: International Commission on Nuclear Non-proliferation and Disarmament, November 2009).

10. International Panel on Fissile Materials, "Global Fissile Material Report 2009: A Path to Nuclear Disarmament" (Princeton: International Panel on Fissile Materials, 2009).

11. Javier Solana, "European Proposals for Strengthening Disarmament and the Non-Proliferation Regime," Address, European Parliament, Brussels, 9 December 2008, at www.eu-un.europa.eu/articles/en/article_8354_en.htm.

12. Secretary-General Ban Ki-moon, "Secretary-General, at Breakfast Meeting, Spells Out Steps to 'Move Ball Forward' on Nuclear Disarmament, Non-Proliferation Ahead of Review Conference," Press Release SG/SM/12661, 8 December 2009, at http://www.un.org/News/Press/docs/2009/sgsm12661.doc.htm.

13. "Secretary-General Launches Multiplatform Campaign to Promote Nuclear Disarmament and Non-proliferation," UN Press Release DC/3179, 13 June 2009, at http://www.un.org/News/Press/docs/2009/dc3179.doc.htm.

14. On 18 January 2007, and on the request of Malaysia and Costa Rica, Secretary-General Ban Ki-moon circulated their draft Model Nuclear Weapons Convention to member states as an official UN document, A/62/650.

15. Examples include Bruce Larkin, *Designing Denuclearization* (New Brunswick: Transaction Publishers, 2008); George Perkovich and James M. Acton, *Abolishing Nuclear Weapons: A Debate* (Washington, DC: Carnegie Endowment, 2009); and Barry M. Blechman and Alexander K. Bollfrass (eds.), *Elements of a Nuclear Disarmament Treaty* (Washington, DC: Stimson Center, 2010).

16. Lawrence Wittner, *The Struggle against the Bomb* (Stanford: Stanford University Press, 1995, 1997, 2003).

17. See Ward Wilson, "The Winning Weapon? Rethinking Nuclear Weapons in Light of Hiroshima," *International Security* 31, no. 4 (Spring 2004): 162–79; and Wilson, "The Myth of Nuclear Deterrence," *Nonproliferation Review* 15, no. 3 (November 2008): 421–39.

18. There are notable exceptions. See John Holdren, "Getting to Zero: Is Pursuing a Nuclear-Weapon-Free World Too Difficult? Too Dangerous? Too Distracting?" Discussion Paper 98-24 (Cambridge, MA: Belfer Center for Science and International Affairs, April 1998), at http://belfercenter.ksg.harvard.edu/publication/2919/getting_to_zero.html.

19. For a further discussion of the NPT review process and accountability, see Jayantha Dhanapala with Randy Rydell, *Multilateral Diplomacy and the NPT: An Insider's*

Account, UNIDIR/2005/3 (Geneva: UN Institute for Disarmament Research, 2005), pp. 115–42.

20. "Decision 1: Strengthening the Review Process for the Treaty," NPT/CONF.1995/32 (Part 1), Annex, para. 7, at www.un.org/disarmament/WMD/Nuclear/1995-NPT/pdf/NPT_CONF199532.pdf.

21. Several publications support this "sole purpose" doctrine, including William J. Perry and Brent Scowcroft (Chairs), *U.S. Nuclear Weapons Policy*, Independent Task Force Report No. 62 (New York: Council on Foreign Relations, 2009); and Federation of American Scientists, Natural Resources Defense Council, Union of Concerned Sciences, *Toward True Security: Ten Steps the Next President Should Take to Transform U.S. Nuclear Weapons Policy* (Washington, DC: Union of Concerned Scientists, 2001, 2008) at http://docs.nrdc.org/nuclear/files/nuc_08021201A.pdf.

22. Alva Myrdal, *The Game of Disarmament* (New York: Pantheon Books, 1976).

23. "Notable & Quotable," *Wall Street Journal*, 14 November 1995, p. A14.

3 Is a World without Nuclear Weapons Attainable? Comparative Perspectives on Goals and Prospects

Götz Neuneck

INTRODUCTION

After years in the doldrums, there is once more wind in the sails of nuclear arms control. U.S. president Obama, in his Prague speech of April 5, 2009, declared—to considerable global astonishment—that America was committed "to seek the peace and security of a world without nuclear weapons." He laid particular emphasis on the great moral responsibility of the United States: "[As] a nuclear power, as the only nuclear power to have used a nuclear weapon, the United States has a moral responsibility to act. We cannot succeed in this endeavor alone, but we can lead it, we can start it." Important aims and proposals of the arms control community, which in recent decades have been worked on by nongovernmental organizations, think tanks, and commissions (Palme 1982, Canberra 1996, Blix Commission 2006, Evans and Kawaguchi 2009)[1], are once again an integral part of world politics. During the eight years of the George W. Bush administration the arms control and disarmament process that was launched after the Cold War ended was systematically enfeebled and reversed. A UN commission warned in 2004 that "[we] are approaching a point at which the erosion of the non-proliferation regime could become irreversible and result in a cascade of proliferation."[2]

Now pledges have been made. It remains to be seen, however, whether they can be converted into concrete steps toward a world that is more secure, more just, and more peaceful. If this opportunity for an "everything-must-go" clear-out of nuclear doctrines and arsenals is botched, further progress in disarmament is highly unlikely.

The proximate triggers for the renewed interest were the two op-eds written by former U.S. secretaries of state George Shultz and Henry Kissinger, former defense secretary William J. Perry, and former senator Sam Nunn.[3] At the beginning of 2007 and again in January 2008, these men, who had done so much to shape U.S. foreign and security policy, garnered worldwide attention with their nonpartisan call for a world without nuclear weapons and the concrete steps they proposed. The American quartet was supported and bolstered by the declarations of high-ranking politicians from Great Britain, Italy, Germany, Norway, The Netherlands, Poland, France, and Belgium.[4] Some governments—one might mention the interventions by British prime minister Gordon Brown and German foreign minister Frank-Walter Steinmeier—welcomed the proposals. A parallel "Global Zero" initiative was launched in Paris in December 2008, within a framework in which more than a hundred prominent figures—including former statesmen such as Jimmy Carter and Mikhail Gorbachev—from the political, economic, military, and civil spheres will work on a step-by-step policy plan for the complete elimination of nuclear weapons by 2030.

In the meantime, the debate on whether and to what extent a nuclear weapons–free world is desirable, feasible, or realistic is proceeding all over the world in newspapers, blogs, and conferences. The Four Horsemen, as they came to be called, have compared the aim of a nuclear weapons–free world to a mountain peak that is shrouded in clouds but has to be reached. There are many ways to the summit, and the precise route has not yet been established. Needless to say, there will be bumpy stretches, precarious abysses, and insurmountable slopes along the way, but strength and will must be brought to bear in order to reach the goal.

Nuclear weapons are unusable but deployable tools of war; they destroy cities and countries and are the only weapon that could obliterate modern civilization in short order. The Evans-Kawaguchi Commission put it bluntly: "Nuclear Weapons are the most inhumane weapons ever conceived, inherently indiscriminate in those they kill and maim, and with an impact deadly for decades."[5] In his Prague speech, President Obama warned against raising our hopes too high, however: "I'm not naive. This goal will not be reached quickly—perhaps not in my lifetime. It will take patience and persistence." In this chapter, current proposals will be presented in the first section, the opportunities and obstacles bound up with them cited in the second section, and further routes suggested in the third section.

RESUSCITATION OF THE GOAL OF A NUCLEAR WEAPONS–FREE WORLD

The American Narrative

The first article by the American "Gang of Four"—George Shultz (secretary of state under Ronald Reagan 1982–89), Henry Kissinger (secretary of state under Richard Nixon 1973–77), William J. Perry (secretary of defense under Bill Clinton 1994–97), and Sam Nunn (U.S. senator, 1972–97)—appeared on January 4, 2007, in the *Wall Street Journal* as a so-called "op-ed" under the title "A World Free of Nuclear Weapons."[6] It explicitly took up President Reagan's dream of the elimination of all nuclear weapons. The former president had regarded nuclear weapons as "totally irrational, totally inhumane, good for nothing but killing, possibly destructive of life on earth and civilization." Mikhail Gorbachev and Ronald Reagan had almost reached agreement on the total abolition of all superpower nuclear weapons at the Reykjavik Summit in 1986, but Reagan was unwilling to give up the Strategic Defense Initiative (SDI) program and his advisers persuaded him against it. The vision of a nuclear weapon–free world is once more in play because the world is now confronted by a "new and dangerous nuclear era." The article continues: "Apart from the terrorist threat, unless urgent new actions are taken, the U.S. soon will be compelled to enter a new nuclear era that will be more precarious, psychologically disorienting, and economically even more costly than was Cold War deterrence."

In advocating this approach, the authors call into question any resort to old deterrence strategies: "It is far from certain that we can successfully replicate the old Soviet-American 'mutually assured destruction' with an increasing number of potential nuclear enemies world-wide without dramatically increasing the risk that nuclear weapons will be used."[7] The risk that nuclear weapons might fall into the hands of terrorists is increasing, as are the ambitions of a whole new set of countries to acquire nuclear weapons of their own. North Korea and Iran are the most notorious examples. The op-ed called upon the United States—in other words, the Bush administration—to assume a leadership role and to take concrete steps, including the substantial reduction of nuclear arsenals, the withdrawal of nuclear weapons already deployed, and the ratification of the Comprehensive Test Ban Treaty (CTBT).

Former Soviet president Gorbachev had his say a few days later, also in the *Wall Street Journal*.[8] In his article, he regretted the downgrading of global arms control treaties, drew attention to the still enormous nuclear weapons stocks of the superpowers, and declared that the current situation was due to a failure of political leadership in the wake of the end of the East-West conflict: "This glaring failure has allowed nuclear weapons and their proliferation to pose a continuing, growing threat to mankind."

The second contribution by the "Gang of Four"—"Toward a Nuclear-Free World," January 15, 2008—was far more comprehensive and specific.[9] It drew on a conference at Stanford University in October 2007, in which other secretaries of state and experts from former administrations participated. Comprehensive proposals for a "dramatic reduction of nuclear dangers" take up almost two-thirds of the op-ed and specify, among other things, the strengthening of the Non-Proliferation Treaty (NPT) and improving security standards for the storage of nuclear weapons and nuclear materials. A new demand is to begin negotiations with Russia on a cooperative solution to missile defense. Another important proposal is to scrap the operational and strategic planning of massive nuclear strikes as redolent of approaches based on "mutually assured destruction" (MAD), because the United States and Russia are allies in the war on terrorism. Also remarkable is the backing of several other former U.S. secretaries of state and defense ministers, including Madeleine Albright, James Baker, Zbigniew Brzezinski, Warren Christopher, and Colin Powell. The two op-eds not only exerted considerable influence on presidential candidates Barack Obama and John McCain but also triggered various new disarmament proposals by international organizations and institutions.

During the presidential campaign Democratic nominee Obama stated: "And I will make the goal of eliminating nuclear weapons worldwide a central element of U.S. nuclear policy,"[10] whereas Republican candidate John McCain focused more on nuclear security and nonproliferation issues.[11] The role of nuclear disarmament was not central in the public phase of the campaign, but the nuclear crises of North Korea and Iran certainly emphasized the need for new policies.

Responses: Start Worrying

Responses by the different European quartets were meant to support the U.S. discussion on nuclear zero. After the experiences of the Cold War, which involved the massive deployment of nuclear weapons for military use, the European public is overwhelmingly in favor of further nuclear reductions. A poll from 2007 showed that Germany and Italy are more oriented toward nuclear disarmament than the two European nuclear weapon states, Britain and

France.[12] In a letter at the end of 2008 to UN Secretary-General Ban Ki-moon on behalf of the European Union, the French president stated:

> Europe, two of whose members have nuclear weapons, is particularly concerned. Europe has already done much for disarmament. Keenly aware of the fact that its own security encourages the pursuit of global disarmament efforts, Europe is prepared to do more. Our ambition extends to every aspect of disarmament, for we are convinced of the need to strive for general disarmament.[13]

Reaction from other former politicians came on June 30, 2008, in Great Britain. Under the title "Start Worrying and Learn to Ditch the Bomb," three former British foreign ministers—Douglas Hurd, Malcolm Rifkind, and David Owen—and former NATO general secretary George Robertson identified themselves with the U.S. articles.[14] The United States and Russia, which have the largest nuclear arsenals, should begin the disarmament process, but "[if] we are able to enter into a period of significant multilateral disarmament Britain, along with France and other existing nuclear powers, will need to consider what further contribution it might be able to make to help to achieve the common objective." Their aims are similar to those of the U.S. politicians, calling, above all, for the renunciation of new nuclear weapons production developments, as discussed in the United States.

One month later, on July 24, 2008, an article appeared in the *Corriere della Sera* written by former Italian foreign ministers Massimo D'Alema and Gianfranco Fini, together with leading Italian political intellectuals Giorgia La Malfa, head of the Republican Party and a former member of the European Parliament as well as of the Italian Parliament; Arturo Parisi; and physicist Francesco Calogero, former secretary general of Pugwash.[15] The authors called for the swift entry into force of the CTBT and the commencement of negotiations on a Fissile Material Cut-off Treaty (FMCT) at the Geneva Conference on Disarmament. The United States and Russia would have to improve relations, and "Italy and Europe can and must play their role to foster initiatives and agreements which may help to create the conditions conducive to the goal of eliminating nuclear weaponry." The remarks are of a very general nature, however: an explicit reference to the withdrawal of tactical nuclear weapons from Europe or Italy is missing.

On January 9, 2009, in the *Frankfurter Allgemeine Zeitung*, another cross-party quartet of famous former politicians spoke out. Former chancellor Helmut Schmidt of the Social Democratic Party (SPD), former president of

Germany Richard von Weizsäcker of the Christian-Democratic Union (CDU), retired minister of state Egon Bahr (SPD), and former foreign minister Hans-Dietrich Genscher of the Free Democratic Party (FDP), under the title "Toward a Nuclear-Free World: A German View for an Atomic Weapons-Free World," nailed their colors to the mast of a nuclear weapons–free world and called for drastic reductions in nuclear arsenals.[16] They wrote: "All short-range nuclear weapons must be destroyed," and called explicitly for "all remaining [U.S.] nuclear warheads [to] be withdrawn from German territory," as well as a renunciation of the "first-use" option by NATO and Russia: "Relics from the age of confrontation are no longer adequate for our new century. Partnership fits in badly with the still-active NATO and Russian doctrine of nuclear first use, even if neither side is being attacked with such arms. A general non-first-use treaty between the nuclear weapon states would be an urgently-needed step." The then-active American plan for basing missile defense facilities in Poland and the Czech Republic was regarded as a "return to the era of confrontation."

Only the German op-ed covered the need to address conventional disarmament as well. It pointed to the failure to adapt the Treaty on Conventional Armed Forces in Europe (CFE) to reflect the implications of NATO enlargement: an Adapted Treaty on Conventional Armed Forces in Europe (ACFE), which is seen as a central component of European security, has so far not been ratified by the NATO countries, and Russia has "suspended" the CFE. Many proposals have been presented, but a solution to this problem is unfortunately still not in sight.[17] The German op-ed was also the only one to mention Russian president Medvedev's proposal to establish a comprehensive security system in Europe. The politicians emphasized that German reunification was achieved through détente and cooperation between the former opposing blocs, which made possible "historic progress in disarmament and arms control for the whole of Europe."

All parties in the German Parliament except the Conservative CDU/CSU now call for the withdrawal of tactical nuclear weapons from German soil.[18] The Green Party has long stood for the removal of NATO nuclear weapons from Germany and a world free of nuclear weapons, combined with the phasing-out of nuclear energy. The relatively new Left Party argues not only for the withdrawal of tactical nuclear weapons but also for abandonment of NATO by Germany.

Moreover, in October 2009 the newly formed Conservative-Liberal government in Germany released its "coalition treaty," which said that it "will advocate within NATO and toward our U.S. allies a withdrawal of remaining nuclear weapons from Germany."[19] The new German foreign minister, Guido Westerwelle, began a round of visits to discuss with likeminded states the withdrawal of U.S. nuclear tactical weapons (TNW).[20] At the Munich Security Conference in 2010 Westerwelle not only explained the influence of the American and German op-eds on the current German policy but he also said: "The last remaining nuclear weapons in Germany are a relic of the Cold War. They no longer serve a military purpose. That is why, through talks with our partners and allies, we, the German Government, are working to create the conditions for their removal."[21] This seems to be the first time that a German government has not only declared itself to be working actively for a nuclear weapon–free world but has advocated removing nuclear weapons from German territory without mentioning the Russian tactical nuclear weapons. This could trigger a decisive debate on the future of NATO's nuclear weapons, within the discussion of the new NATO Strategic Concept or outside of it.

Op-eds were also published by former statesmen from many other countries. A paper dated April 6, 2009, by former Polish president Aleksander Kwaśniewski, former prime minister Tadeusz Mazowiecki, and former Polish president Lech Wałęsa, called for "urgent steps towards nuclear disarmament" and that the United States and Russia "will begin the process of freeing the world from the nuclear menace."[22] A Norwegian call dated June 4, 2009, came from six former politicians in Norway: four former prime ministers—Odvar Nordli, Gro Harlem Brundtland, Kåre Willoch, and Kjell Magne Bondevik—and former foreign minister Thorvald Stoltenberg, all from the Norwegian Labour Party; and also from Kjell Magne Bondevik of the Conservative Party.[23] They stressed the need to combine vision and action, quoting from the U.S. "Four Horsemen" article from 2007: "Without the bold vision, the actions will not be perceived as fair or urgent. Without the actions, the vision will not be perceived as realistic or possible." The relatively brief declaration asserted that not only nuclear weapons but also production facilities for weapons-grade nuclear materials must be eliminated. New negotiations on reducing nuclear arsenals between the United States and Russia are supported and the inclusion of tactical nuclear weapons called for. Existing arms control agreements, such as the INF Treaty, the CFE Treaty, and the NPT, must be maintained and strengthened. Missile defense, in contrast, would only trigger further rearmament.

The next quartet was French: former prime ministers Alain Juppé (Conservative Party), Michel Rocard together with former defense minister Alain Richard, both from the Socialist Party, and retired general Bernard Norlain released an op-ed on October 14, 2009, with the title "For Global Nuclear Disarmament, the Only Means to Prevent Anarchic Proliferation."[24] The current nonproliferation crisis on North Korea and Iran is seen as very dangerous for the NPT regime: "There is a risk that this phenomenon will snowball, with a mutually reinforcing circle of institutional instability and an increasing number of protagonists. International security is thus at risk." As obstacles for further reductions, the authors identify "the vested interests in the political and military establishments of the US and Russia, the mistrust of change amongst the Russian and Chinese leaders," and regional conflicts between India and Pakistan. The authors then see "a special role" for France as a "dynamic and creative actor" in the debate. They call for "appropriate consequences" for "disarmament and its resolution, when the time comes, for France's own nuclear capabilities." The call remains vague, but clearly shows that a debate in French democratic institutions is not yet underway, but must be held. President Nicolas Sarkozy in his speech on board the nuclear submarine *Le Terrible* in Cherbourg on March 21, 2008, promised more transparency, a no-target policy of France, and a reduction by one-third of its nuclear weapons.[25]

An op-ed by foreign ministers of Sweden Carl Bildt and of Poland Radek Sikorski on February 2, 2010, dealt explicitly with the remaining tactical nuclear weapons in Europe. They called on the American and Russian leadership "to commit themselves to early measures to greatly reduce so-called tactical nuclear weapons in Europe."[26] They also asked Russia (which holds, in their opinion, 2,000 warheads in the western part of its country) to withdraw its tactical weapons, for example, from the Kaliningrad region or the Kola peninsula, and they continue: "The time has come to cover sub-strategic nuclear weapons with an arms control regime, which would look like the one that was established long ago for strategic arms."

A Belgian quartet, formed by former NATO secretary general Willy Claes, former prime ministers Guy Verhofstadt and Jean-Luc Dehaene, and former minister of foreign affairs Louis Michel, issued a statement on February 19, 2010.[27] They strongly supported the other op-eds and Obama's commitment to move toward the goal of abolishing all nuclear weapons. They clearly stated that "[it] is impossible to continue to deny nuclear weapons to other states as long as we ourselves have them" and requested "a drastic reduction of all deployed and non-deployed tactical and strategic nuclear weapons." They called on their government "to take active steps within NATO for the rapid removal of these nuclear weapons, as the German government has done" and added that the "withdrawal should not be linked to the missile defense debate."

This statement alludes to the fact that after the new Obama plan for deploying missile defense in Europe was released, the argument shifted to emphasize that U.S. land- or sea-based medium-range interceptors could/should be hosted in Poland, Romania, and Bulgaria. These countries are also looking for the deployment of U.S. forces to strengthen their national security needs in the neighborhood of their big neighbor Russia. Interestingly, the Belgian prime minister, Yves Leterme, underlined in a press release on the same day that his government supports the overall nuclear weapons–free vision. He also noted that Belgium would work with a number of other NATO members to take the nuclear disarmament and nonproliferation agenda forward during the review of the Alliance's Strategic Concept.[28]

These various declarations, including a statement by four Canadian statesmen on March 26, 2010,[29] have given rise to global political as well as expert debates, debates that should have been held by decision-makers and policy planners in the 1990s after the end of the Cold War but are now unavoidable due to the undermining of the arms control architecture and the incipient dangers of proliferation. Most of the proposals are on the pragmatic side and call for the revival of arms control dialogue.[30] A nuclear weapons–free world is regarded as desirable, but only as a distant goal on the horizon. The path now taken is crucial, since it determines the ultimate goal of a world free of all nuclear weapons. The precise conditions of a nuclear weapons–free world require further discussion. Nevertheless, it is remarkable that former nuclear pragmatists, such as Henry Kissinger and William J. Perry, regard a nuclear weapons–free world as desirable and feasible, and the strategy of deterrence as inadequate and outdated. This has kindled renewed interest among the public, politicians, and government officials, which is long overdue, given the growing nuclear threat.

A number of governments, nongovernmental organizations, and political parties responded positively to the former politicians' interventions. The Obama administration will be measured by the extent to which it is able to implement its proposals. Other nuclear weapons states have begun to come about to take up the course that has been laid. The French government, for example, has promised a further reduction of its nuclear arsenal, and it has already closed its nuclear test site along with its plants to produce fissile material for weapons.[31]

British activity has been notable. British prime minister Gordon Brown, in a speech delivered in New Delhi in January 2008, emphasized the need "to accelerate disarmament amongst possessor states, to prevent proliferation to new states, and to ultimately achieve a world that is free from nuclear weapons."[32] Three former high-ranking generals from the UK stressed in a supporting statement in January 2009 that "nuclear weapons have shown themselves to be completely useless as a deterrent to the threats and scale we currently, or are likely to face—particularly international terrorism." They argued that the UK "deterrent has become virtually irrelevant except in the context of domestic policy."[33] The British government has proposed a conference of experts from the nuclear weapons states to examine the challenge of verifying nuclear disarmament. As early as 2007, British foreign minister Margaret Beckett suggested that Great Britain might serve as a "disarmament laboratory." Defense Minister Des Browne stated on March 4, 2008, before the Geneva Conference on Disarmament, that "the UK [will become] a role model and testing ground for measures that we and others can take on key aspects of disarmament."[34] At the Special UN Security Council Meeting "Nuclear Non-proliferation and Nuclear Disarmament" on September 24, 2009, in New York, Prime Minister Gordon Brown said, "Nuclear-weapon States must pursue active disarmament with a credible road map that will command confidence of all non-nuclear-weapon States," and he stressed what is mostly missing: a credible time scheme for "active and irreversible disarmament."[35]

Other calls have been more conditional. Indian prime minister Manmohan Singh declared, at the opening of the conference "Towards a World Free of Nuclear Weapons" in New Delhi in June 2008, that "India is fully committed to nuclear disarmament that is global, universal and non-discriminatory in nature."[36] A former coordinator of the Indian Pokhran nuclear test in 1998, however, has said that due to national security concerns, India must conduct further tests and therefore cannot sign the CTBT—obviously a maneuver to derail further arms control steps in the region.[37] Russian prime minister Vladimir Putin remarked, at a meeting with German foreign minister Frank-Walter Steinmeier in June 2009, that the Kremlin would consider giving up its nuclear arsenal if other countries did the same.[38] But a crucial act of commitment by these countries would bring the debate decisively forward. UN secretary general Ban Ki-moon, in a speech given on October 24, 2008—the first speech addressing nuclear disarmament by a UN secretary general for a long time—presented a Five-Point Plan, which, among other things, called for heightened research and development efforts by governments in relation to verification, as well as greater transparency, provisions of international law, security measures, and the prospect of commencing negotiations on a nuclear weapons convention.[39]

Various international coalitions of nongovernmental organizations have, for decades, proposed concrete steps toward a nuclear weapon–free world. The Pugwash Conferences on Science and World Affairs, awarded the Nobel Peace Prize in 1995, issued an Eleven-Point Program on their 50th Anniversary in 2007.[40] These steps range from implementing de-alerting and a no-first-use policy, removing nuclear weapons from forward-basing, and accelerating the dismantlement of nuclear warheads, to drastic reduction of nuclear forces and making a "nuclear weapon convention" a reality. The Middle-Power Initiative and its Article VI Forum, as well as other groups, such as the International Campaign to Abolish Nuclear Weapons, the International Physicians for the Prevention of Nuclear War, Mayors for Peace, Abolition 2000, and International Engineers and Scientists against Proliferation, have developed extensive proposals and materials at the level of civil society. Center stage in this context stands the establishment of a nuclear weapons convention that, similar to the conventions banning biological and chemical weapons, would globally ban the production, testing, possession, and deployment of nuclear weapons, covering all states.

Naturally, criticism, skepticism, and disapproval of the various op-eds have not been lacking. Democrat defense experts Harold Brown and John Deutch, both former Defense Department luminaries, wrote that "the goal, even the aspirational goal, of eliminating all nuclear weapons is counterproductive."[41] U.S. senator Jon Kyl, a Republican, said that "the national security of the USA—and that of all our friends and allies—will not permit a nuclear weapons–free world in the foreseeable future."[42]

These assertions broach some of the fundamental arguments of opponents of global nuclear zero, arguments heard mainly in the NWS themselves. They include keeping nuclear weapons in readiness in order to protect friendly nations ("extended deterrence"), and the ambiguity of nuclear weapons as a last resort against all possible threats, including from states and groups that do not possess nuclear weapons themselves. In many non–nuclear weapons states, the nuclear zero initiatives are regarded with some skepticism and, to some extent, as propaganda or mere rhetoric.

We may, nevertheless, assume that the goal of bringing into being a nuclear weapon–free world is generally regarded as desirable. The exact route and prevailing constraints for a nuclear weapon–free world have, however, barely been outlined so far. Only the first phase—namely, the clearing out of horrendous nuclear arsenals and deployment doctrines—could be embarked upon at present. Additionally, a working and verifiable FMCT regime can lay the foundations for effective identification, notification, and control of fissile materials, and an implemented CTBT would not only prohibit nuclear testing by new states but also constrain vertical proliferation. The hope remains that an enhanced debate will bring humanity closer to the ultimate goal.

OPPORTUNITIES AND OBSTACLES IN TODAY'S NUCLEAR WORLD

More than twenty years after the end of the East-West conflict there are still around 23,000 nuclear weapons in the arsenals of the nuclear weapons states, more than 90 percent of them held in the United States and Russia alone. Around 9,000 are operational, and several thousand American and Russian warheads are on high alert. Furthermore, the number of so-called tactical nuclear weapons on both sides is not precisely known. Some former high-ranking generals are arguing that a new policy of forward-based nuclear weapons is required, which also has to include nuclear sharing arrangements.[43] NATO continues to support the deployment of around 150 to 240 American warheads in Europe, while Russia justifies its estimated 2,000 or so tactical warheads—albeit in storage facilities on its own territory—on the basis of NATO's conventional superiority.[44] The nuclear doctrines of both sides are based on first-use of nuclear weapons in a political environment in which the deployment of such weapons for military purposes is now inconceivable. The appallingly large arsenals of the two nuclear powers are the result of the Cold War's first- and second-strike scenarios. A study by the CISAC Committee of the U.S. National Academy of Sciences in 1997 proposed a "core deterrence" capacity of a few hundred nuclear warheads.[45]

Modernization Efforts of the Two Superpowers

Both major nuclear powers are continuing to think about modernizing their nuclear arms, and Russia has also gone on a higher state of alert. For example, in 2008 patrol flights by Russian nuclear bombers were resumed, and in August 2009 two modern Russian nuclear submarines were sighted off the East Coast of the United States, after a fifteen-year absence. In the United States, the conversion—proposed during the George W. Bush administration—of strategic missiles, such as the seaborne Trident, into launchers bearing precision-guided munitions has been put on hold. With such a "Prompt Global Strike" program it might be possible to destroy at extreme ranges targets, including Russian missile silos, with pinpoint accuracy—with either conventional or nuclear weapons, at least in the perception of the Russian military.[46] Russia and China are increasingly concerned about these developments, alongside the extensive U.S. use of space for reconnaissance and early warning purposes, because in a crisis they would create many uncertainties and problems of perception for other countries.

While the United States already has a modernized arsenal at its disposal on land and sea, as well as in the air, the Russian armed forces are working on new strategic carrier delivery systems, such as the intercontinental Topol-M missile, the destabilizing R-27 missile with multiple warheads, and the submarine-launched Bulava missile. The existing Russian missile arsenal is aging, so despite the planned modernization, Russia's strategic arsenal will continue to shrink over the next few years.

From the Russian standpoint, the strategic stability of nuclear arsenals has at times been called into question by a number of developments in the United States. The multitiered global missile defense program announced by former president George W. Bush can, from the viewpoint of Russian planners, undermine the Russian arsenal's second-strike capability over the long term. The strategic "balance of terror" between the United States and Russia rests on the mutual capability for a nuclear second strike. It is emphatically not based on a mutual capability for defense against a nuclear strike. Russian planners must assume, based on the limited functionality of the planned defense system, that the missile defense system in the United States, as well as the one that is now planned for Europe, will be spread widely and that the interceptor missiles will be continually updated. Other missile defense programs are under discussion: for example, a defense system in space. Two antisatellite tests by China (2007) and the United States (2008), in which missiles destroyed their own satellites, show that in a crisis military conflict in space is now possible.[47]

Experience shows that armament programs costing billions tend to expand over time, both quantitatively and qualitatively. Over the longer term, this casts the credibility of the currently shrinking Russian missile arsenal into doubt. Some U.S. experts have drawn attention to the fact that U.S. nuclear forces, due to their technological superiority, could wipe out the opposing arsenal in a first strike and establish a state of "nuclear primacy."[48] Even though this sounds sensational, the possibility may constrain other nuclear weapon states from reducing their own arsenals.[49] In this way, fears concerning the feasibility or possibility of nuclear war re-enter the strategic planning of smaller nuclear weapon countries.

"Minor" Nuclear Powers and Declared Nuclear Weapons States

Great Britain, France, and the People's Republic of China have much smaller strategic arsenals than the United States and Russia. France has 300 strategic warheads, and in March 2008, President Sarkozy announced that this number was to be reduced even further. Great Britain has 160 operational strategic warheads and China has around 180 nuclear warheads. The two Western European nuclear powers each have four nuclear submarines with seaborne missiles and maintain one submarine always at sea. France also has airborne standoff weapons. At the UN Security Council meeting on September 24, 2009, Prime Minister Brown stated that the UK government aimed "that, when the next class of nuclear submarines enters service in the mid-2020s, our fleet should be reduced from four boats to three."[50]

China's nuclear modernization program can be described as modest. The development of a U.S. seaborne missile defense in the Pacific, however, poses a problem for Chinese planners. China has around 20 ICBMs capable of reaching the United States. The United States would like to deploy around 150 seaborne defense missiles on Aegis class ships within five years. The development of the system's interception capabilities against long-range missiles is very likely and could undermine the Chinese second strike potential.

Then there are the three nuclear states that have not yet signed the NPT. So far, the international community has not been able to integrate these "nuclear outsiders" into a limitation regime or to extract a disarmament roadmap from them. India and Pakistan—both emerging nuclear states—have been engaged in a nuclear armament and missile race for years. They seem to be tied to each other and perhaps also include China in this analytic circle. But further progress in nuclear disarmament would increase the pressure on India and Pakistan to stop their nuclear race. According to Western estimates, the two states each have sixty warheads, are testing longer range missiles, and are building up their navies. In August 2009, India unveiled its first nuclear submarine and plans to build others. Pakistan regards the strategic balance as having been massively disturbed and has been increasing its defense budget for years. Both countries are developing cruise missiles that can be fitted with nuclear warheads and are interested in purchasing conventional, diesel-powered submarines from France and Germany. Since, according to some scientific experts, India's nuclear tests were not entirely successful, a number of voices in India are advising against signing the CTBT so that further tests can be conducted.[51]

In early 2009 India and the United States finalized an agreement on civilian nuclear uses, which had been initiated four years earlier during the Bush administration. The boost given to India as a nuclear power by the U.S.-India deal is putting a strain on the calls for "universal proliferation norms."[52] After controversial debates, the Nuclear Suppliers Group (NSG) approved an exception for India from the group's trade restrictions on September 6, 2008.[53] In the end, only smaller countries criticized the trade of nuclear technologies to India and argued for reimposing sanctions if India resumed nuclear testing, but they could not withstand the political pressure from the Bush government.

There is a real danger that a distinction between "good" and "bad" nuclear powers will become established. The West has willingly acquiesced in Israel's "opaque" nuclear arsenal without a serious attempt at an arms control solution.[54] Israel as a small country would be confronted with a monstrous existential threat if some of its Arab neighbors were to go nuclear. Therefore in the longer run, a regional zone free from nuclear weapons (NWFZ) must be in the interest of Israel.

Other nondeclared nuclear states pose different problems, especially North Korea, which has withdrawn from the NPT and is subject to UN sanctions. In 2006 and 2009 it conducted underground nuclear tests, and it maintains an aggressive missile program. It is responsible, according to A. Q. Khan, the "father of the Pakistani nuclear program," for the spread of missile and nuclear production technology, in particular to Libya, Iran, and Syria. The Khan Laboratories are accused of having established a network of intermediaries to transfer equipment and blueprints for producing weapon-grade nuclear material.[55] Recently, North Korea announced that it is in the final stages of a uranium enrichment program. The six-party talks between North Korea, the United States, China, Japan, Russia, and South Korea have largely been put on ice.

As Jill Marie Lewis and Avner Cohen discuss in their chapters, the disagreement about the Iranian nuclear program has so far not been resolved, despite the Obama administration's declared willingness to engage in dialogue. Uranium enrichment is continuing, UN sanctions seem to have had no effect, and the calls for a military solution are getting louder. A military solution to the conflict could destabilize the Middle East just as much as the unrestrained proliferation of nuclear technology in the region. Political solutions, backed by technical models for the disputed fuel production, are still possible, however, if there were the political will to bridge a thirty-year standstill between the United States and the Islamic Republic of Iran.

Weapons-Grade Fissile Material and the Future of Nuclear Energy

Focusing on the reduction of strategic weapons tends to overshadow the problem of the security of the production, storage, and disposal of weapons-grade materials. These fissile materials—such as enriched uranium or plutonium—can be found in both the military and civil spheres of various states that engage in civil nuclear power generation. With regard to large-scale, partly unsecured stocks of fissile material, the question of how to secure the storage and production sites recurs constantly. Stocks of highly enriched uranium worldwide amount to around 1,670 tonnes and those of separated weapons-grade plutonium to 500 tonnes[56] Half of the latter derives from the civil sphere, and the stock is growing at an alarming rate. Eight kilograms of plutonium are enough to build a nuclear bomb.

Former IAEA director-general El Baradei talks of thirty "virtual nuclear weapons states," those states that have the knowledge and the means to enrich uranium or reprocess plutonium. These include not only the nuclear powers but also non–nuclear weapons states such as Brazil, Egypt, Turkey, and South Africa. The anticipated "renaissance of nuclear energy" will serve only to intensify the proliferation problem, especially because the non–nuclear weapons states—including, of course, Iran—are entitled to engage in civil nuclear energy generation. The International Atomic Energy Agency has come out in favor of 1,400 new nuclear reactors by 2050. It cannot be merely by chance that, besides Iran, thirteen other countries throughout the Middle Eastern states have declared a revived interest in civil nuclear power fuel cycle generation.[57]

Quite apart from the security of fissile materials, an end to the production of weapons-grade materials within the framework of an FMCT is a central aim of arms control efforts. An FMCT is called for in virtually all the op-eds. The established nuclear weapons states have ceased the production of fissile material for bomb production, since for the time being they have enough. De facto nuclear weapons states Israel and, especially, India and Pakistan, on the other hand, continue to produce fissile material for bomb production. Issues of definition, notification, and verification, as well as the inclusion of the civil nuclear fuel cycle, are important in this regard. The Geneva Conference on Disarmament (CD) has had a program of work in this area since May 2008, and in May 2009 it agreed that existing stocks must be included and inspected. Despite the tabling of specific proposals in May 2009, however, concrete work on the FMCT has not yet begun. Progress has been stymied by Pakistan, which argues that its security interests have not been respected. Looking toward India's continuing fissile material production, which is bolstered by the U.S.-India deal, it called for a "holistic and non-selective approach." There is some hope this stalemate can be overcome, but the key issue remains: how to integrate nuclear outsiders such as India and Pakistan in the arms control regime.

START: Resetting Bilateral Strategic Disarmament

The bilateral START I treaty of 1991 between the United States and Russia included an expiration date of December 5, 2009, when it was to be replaced by a successor agreement. A framework agreement was reached at the summit between presidents Medvedev and Obama in July 2009, according to which there would be a reduction to 1,500 to 1,675 warheads and 500 to 1,100 strategic launch systems, numbers that largely correspond to Russia's programmed reduction targets. The final agreement, signed in April 2010, limits both sides to 1,550 deployed warheads and 700 deployed strategic vehicles. Given the unresolved disagreement about strategic missile defense, NATO's conventional superiority, and the superior military technology capability of the United States, Russia, for the time being, is showing little interest in further rounds of cuts.

In Prague, President Obama declared: "To put an end to Cold War thinking, we will reduce the role of nuclear weapons in our national security strategy." The new administration must now make good on this promise. There are a number of proposals on the table.[58]

The End of Vertical Proliferation: CTBT

All of the op-eds we have mentioned are at one in calling for the rapid coming entry into force of the CTBT. U.S. President Obama has described the ratification of the Comprehensive Test Ban Treaty by the U.S. Congress as an important goal of his foreign and arms control policy. The Treaty, already ratified by 149 states, can come into force only if nine hold-out states—the United States, China, India, Pakistan, Iran, Israel, Egypt, Indonesia, and North Korea—also ratify it. The United States has the key role here. In the U.S. Senate, the majority of 67 Senators required for ratification is not ensured. Recently, the Perry/Schlesinger Commission gave an account of the lack of unanimity in the Congress and the arguments of both advocates and opponents.[59] There is a danger that ratification will be submerged in a confused tangle of technical and political counterarguments. The Reliable Replacement Warhead (RRW) program, which was rejected by Congress in 2008, and barred in the 2010 Nuclear Posture Review, still garners support in some circles. However, the development of new nuclear warheads would be a fatal signal to the world: the United States could be reproached with seeking to keep on modernizing its arsenal indefinitely and making new technical developments for new nuclear weapon options more attractive to other countries.

NPT Review Conference 2010

The conclusion of a START successor treaty, the prospects of further deep cuts in the nuclear arsenals of the two major nuclear powers, and the initiation of CTBT ratification will surely be magnified by the successful results from the NPT Review Conference in May 2010. After the failure to implement the 13-Point Program set forth in 2000, and the lack of progress in 2005, failure in 2010 could not have escaped being seen by most analysts as a fatal blow for the NPT. Multilateral consensus, cooperation, and agreement are reinforced because the Conference in hindsight can be claimed as at least a partial success. For the longer term, however, the future of the nuclear world order is still up for debate. In George Perkovich's words, "A nuclear order based on a double standard—a handful of states determined to keep nuclear weapons and also trying to prevent 185 from getting them—is inherently unstable."[60]

The aims of the Obama administration are ambitious. They include the START successor agreement, negotiation of a FMCT, and the ratification of the CTBT, as well as other treaties by Congress. On 22 October 2009, Secretary of State Hillary Rodham Clinton called for a strengthened IAEA regime with better resources and verification methods, the establishment of a new international framework for nuclear civil energy cooperation, and more efficient measures to prevent nuclear terrorism.[61] She welcomed prompt negotiation of a FMCT and a quick entry into force of the CTBT.

The extent to which the Obama administration succeeds will depend on its ability to bring around the nuclear bureaucracy and create some measure of bipartisan support in Congress for a reduction in the role of nuclear weapons in the twenty-first century. The enormous cost of maintaining nuclear weapons, the threat of nuclear terrorism, and the fact that nuclear weapons are the only tools of war that, over the long term, can pose an annihilating danger to the United States should go a long way toward fostering the view that current arsenals must be drastically reduced and the international nonproliferation regime strengthened.

THE NEXT STEPS: WHAT OTHER WAYS ARE POSSIBLE TOWARD A NUCLEAR WEAPON-FREE WORLD?

If the two major nuclear powers were each to achieve a target figure of 500 to 1,000 warheads, the three other established nuclear powers could be brought on board to make further reductions and disarm proportionately. Multilateral negotiations—which also settle such important issues as procedures for disposing of warheads, improved safeguards, and the inspection of treaty implementation—should be included. Finally, a third step would involve striving toward and working out an agreement among all nuclear weapons states aiming at nuclear zero—in other words, the complete renunciation of the production, possession, and deployment of nuclear weapons. The smaller arsenals become, the more urgently will important questions arise, questions that have to be worked out on the basis of international cooperation. Have all warheads really been eliminated? Has weapons-grade material been disposed of irreversibly? Is it certain that no state is conducting a secret production program? Can it be ascertained with sufficient surety that civil nuclear sites are not being used for weapons programs? Will it be possible for states to break ranks and engage in nuclear re-armament? What role will missile defense play in a nuclear zero world?

Certainly, many of these questions will be difficult to answer. However, the op-eds of the various four (or more) horsemen and President Obama's Prague speech constitute a challenge to surmount the attitudes, instruments, and doctrines of the Cold War once and for all, and to proscribe the use of nuclear weapons. The United States, as still the strongest military power on earth, has taken the lead in setting out toward a nuclear weapons–free world. This cannot be done without the cooperation of friendly states, organizations, and experts, not to mention patience, time, and scientific and security-policy expertise. The overwhelming European public, while not yet captured by the debate, does not see a special role for nuclear weapons in Europe and largely wants to remove these weapons of mass destruction from their soil. Certainly, there is still a split between the remaining European nuclear weapon states, France and to a lesser extent Great Britain, as well as East-European countries which still see a threat from Russia. Were nuclear disarmament, including significant reduction or abolition of tactical nuclear weapons, to proceed, the voice for maintaining this capability would be marginalized.

A global effort is needed to overcome the hurdles, but if a beginning is now made in all earnestness, it can help to ensure that nuclear weapons will never be used again. In the twenty-first century new challenges, threats and problems for mankind are emerging where nuclear weapons do not play any role except to put states and people in gravest danger.

NOTES

This is an updated and extended version of the article by Götz Neuneck, "Globalizing Nuclear Zero: Is a World without Nuclear Weapons Really Attainable?" in *Internationale Politik und Gesellschaft*, 4/2009, pp.46–64, at http://library.fes.de/pdf-files/ipg/ipg-2009-4/4-09_neuneck_us.pdf. This chapter profited greatly from the research done by Lynne Welton for her master's thesis, "The Vision of a World Free of Nuclear Weapons: A Comparative Analysis of the Op-Eds of Elder Statesmen and Defense Experts" (University of Hamburg, 2009), published as Working Paper No. 14, IFSH/IFAR, February 2010.

1. The Independent Commission on Disarmament and Security (Palme Commission), *Common Security: A Blueprint for Survival* (New York: Simon & Schuster, 1982); Canberra Commission on the Elimination of Nuclear Weapons, *Report of the Canberra Commission on the Elimination of Nuclear Weapons* (Canberra, Australia: Dept. of Foreign Affairs and Trade, 1996); Weapons of Mass Destruction Commission (Blix Commission), *Weapons of Terror: Freeing the World of Nuclear, Biological and Chemical Arms* (Stockholm: WMD Commission, 2006); Gareth Evans and Yoriko Kawaguchi (Co-Chairs), "Eliminating Nuclear Threats: A Practical Agenda for Global Policymakers," Report of the International Commission on Nuclear Non-proliferation and Disarmament, Canberra 2009, at http://www.icnnd.org/reference/reports/ent/pdf/ICNND_Report-EliminatingNuclearThreats.pdf.

2. United Nations, "A More Secure World," New York, 2005.

3. George P. Shultz, William J. Perry, Henry A. Kissinger, and Sam Nunn, "A World Free of Nuclear Weapons," *Wall Street Journal*, 4 January 2007, p. A15, and "Toward a Nuclear-Free World," *Wall Street Journal*, 15 January 2008, p. A13.

4. See the comprehensive collection of opinion pieces for a nuclear weapons–free world at Pugwash Online at http://www.pugwash.org/reports/nw/nuclear-weapons-free-statements/NWFW_statements.htm.

5. Evans and Kawaguchi, "Eliminating Nuclear Threats.

6. Shultz et al., "A World Free of Nuclear Weapons."

7. Ibid.

8. Mikhail Gorbachev, "The Nuclear Threat," *Wall Street Journal*, 31 January 2007, at http://www.wagingpeace.org/articles/2007/01/31_gorbachev_nuclearthreat.htm.

9. Shultz et al., "Toward a Nuclear-Free World."

10. "2008 Presidential Q&A," *Arms Control Today*, 24 September 2008.

11. See "McCain Remarks on Nuclear Security," *Washington Post*, 24 May 2008.

12. "Global Public Opinion on Nuclear Weapons," September 2007. Commissioned by The Simons Foundation and conducted in the US, Britain, France, Germany, Italy and Israel in July and August 2007 by the polling firm, Angus Reid Strategies. Available at http://thesimonsfoundation.ca/nuclear-disarmament/global-public-opinion-on-nuclear-weapons-2/.

13. Letter of French president Nicolas Sarkozy to Secretary-General Ban Ki-moon, made public on 8 December 2008, at http://www.carnegieendowment.org/files/Sarkozy_UN_letter_20081208.pdf.

14. Pugwash Online: http://www.pugwash.org/reports/nw/nuclear-weapons-free-statements/NWFW_statements.htm.

15. Ibid.

16. Ibid.

17. Wolfgang Zellner, Hans-Joachim Schmidt, and Götz Neuneck (eds.), *Die Zukunft der Konventionellen Rüstungskontrolle in Europa/The Future of Conventional Arms Control in Europe* (Baden-Baden: Nomos, 2009).

18. Resolution 17/1159 of the German Parliament "Der Bundestag" from March 24, 2010.

19. The CDU/CSU-FDP Coalition Treaty can be found in German at http://www.cdu.de/doc/pdfc/091024-koalitionsvertrag-cducsu-fdp.pdf.

20. See Martin Butcher, "The German Coalition and NATO Nuclear Policy Debate," *NATO Monitor Issue Brief*, 8 January 2010; for the domestic discussions in Germany, see Oliver Meier, "German Nuclear Stance Stirs Debate," *Arms Control Today*, December 2009, at http://www.armscontrol.org/print/3984.

21. Federal Minister of Foreign Affairs Guido Westerwelle, speech at the 46th Munich Security Conference, 6 February 2010, at http://www.securityconference.de/Westerwelle-Guido.451.0.html?&L=1.

22. Pugwash Online: http://www.pugwash.org/reports/nw/nuclear-weapons-free-statements/NWFW_statements.htm.

23. Ibid.

24. Ibid.

25. Speech by Nicolas Sarkozy, president of the French Republic, "Presentation of *Le Terrible* in Cherbourg," 21 March 2008, at http://www.acronym.org.uk/docs/0803/doc09.htm; see also the chapter by Venance Journé in this volume.

26. Carl Bildt and Radek Sikorski, "Next, the Tactical Nukes," op-ed, *New York Times*, 2 February 2010, at http://www.nytimes.com/2010/02/02/opinion/02iht-edbildt.html.

27. Pugwash Online: http://www.pugwash.org/reports/nw/nuclear-weapons-free-statements/NWFW_statements.htm.

28. "Communiqué de presse: un monde sans armes nucléaires est également l'objectif du gouvernement Leterme," 19 February 2010. An unofficial translation is

available at http://www.premier.fgov.be/fr/nieuws/communiqu%C3%A9-de-presse-un-monde-sans-armes-nucl%C3%A9aires-est-%C3%A9galement-l%E2%80%99objectif-du-gouvernement-.

29. Pugwash Online: http:// www.pugwash.org/reports/nw/nuclear-weapons-free-statements/NWFW_statements.ht.

30. The Russian statement of October 14, 2010 is exceptional in its emphasis on the need for a "deep reorganization of the entire international system" as a necessary condition for nuclear disarmament. See Yevgeny Primakov, Igor Ivanov, Yevgeny Velikov, and Mikhail Moiseev, "Moving from Nuclear Deterrence to Mutual Security," at http://www.pugwash.org/reports/nw/nuclear-weapons-free-statements/NWFW_statements_Russia.htm.

31. See the chapter by Venance Journé in this volume.

32. Gordon Brown, speech at the Chamber of Commerce in New Delhi, 21 January 2008, at http://www.number10.gov.uk/Page14323; Cabinet Office, "The Road to 2010: Addressing the Nuclear Question in the Twenty First Century," London, July 2009, at http://www.cabinetoffice.gov.uk/media/224864/roadto2010.pdf.

33. Field Marshal Lord Bramall, General Lord Ramsbotham, and General Sir Hugh Beach, "UK Does Not Need a Nuclear Deterrent," *The Times*, 16 January 2009, at http://www.timesonline.co.uk/tol/comment/letters/article5525682.ece.

34. Des Browne, "Laying the Foundations for Multilateral Disarmament," speech before the UN Conference on Disarmament, Geneva, 5 February 2008, at http://www.mod.uk/defenceinternet/aboutdefence/people/speeches/sofs/20080205layingthefoundationsformultilateraldisarmament.htm.

35. Gordon Brown, speech at the 6191st meeting of the UN Security Council on 24 September 2009 (S/PV.6191) in New York, at http://daccessdds.un.org/doc/UNDOC/PRO/N09/523/14/PDF/N0952314.pdf?OpenElement.

36. Manmohan Singh, "Inauguration of the International Conference 'Towards a World Free of Nuclear Weapons,'" New Delhi, 9 June 2008, at http://pibhyd.ap.nic.in/er0906080 4.pdf.

37. "No CTBT, India Needs More Nuclear Tests: Pokharan II Coordinator," *Times of India*, 27 August 2009, at http://timesofindia.indiatimes.com/india/No-CTBT-India-needs-more-nuclear-tests-Pokhran-II-coordinator-/articleshow/4940502.cms.

38. "Putin Could Imagine a Russia with No Nuclear Weapons," *Deutsche Welle*, 10 June 2009, at http://www.dw-world.de/dw/article/0,,4315776,00.html.

39. Ban Ki-moon, "Five Steps to a Nuclear-Free World," *The Guardian*, 23 November 2008, at http://www.guardian.co.uk/commentisfree/2008/nov/23/nuclear-disarmament-united-nations.

40. Pugwash Conferences on Science and World Affairs, "Pugwash Conferences on Science and World Affairs and the Middle Powers Initiative: Revitalizing Nuclear Disarmament," Policy Recommendations of the Pugwash 50th Anniversary Workshop,

Pugwash, Nova Scotia, 5–7 July 2007, at http://www.pugwash.org/reports/nw/pugwash-mpi/Pugwash-MPI-Communique.htm.

41. Harold Brown and John Deutch, "The Nuclear Disarmament Fantasy," *Wall Street Journal*, 19 November 2007.

42. Quoted in George Perkovich, "Rebuttal to Senator Kyl," 3 July 2008, at http://www.carnegieendowment.org/publications/index.cfm?fa=view&id=20275. See also Kyl's op-ed, "Why We Need to Test Nuclear Weapons," *Wall Street Journal*, 21 October 2009.

43. Hugh Beach, "The End of Nuclear Sharing? US Nuclear Weapons in Europe," *RUSI Journal* 154, no. 6 (December 2009): 48–53.

44. Hans C. Kristensen, "U.S. Nuclear Weapons in Europe: A Review of Post-Cold War Policy, Force Levels, and War Planning," *Natural Resources Defense Council*, 2005, at http://www.nrdc.org/nuclear/euro/contents.asp.

45. Committee on International Security and Arms Control, National Academy of Sciences, *The Future of U.S. Nuclear Weapons Policy* (Washington, DC: National Academy Press, 1997).

46. Elaine M. Grossman, "U.S. Military Eyes Fielding 'Prompt Global Strike' Weapon by 2015," Global Security Newswire, Wednesday, 1 July 2009, at http://www.globalsecuritynewswire.org/gsn/nw_20090701_5635.php.

47. On this subject, see Subrata Ghoshroy and Götz Neuneck (eds.), *South Asia at a Crossroads: Conflict or Cooperation in the Age of Nuclear Weapons, Missile Defense, and Space Rivalries* (Baden-Baden: Nomos, 2010).

48. Keir A. Lieber and Daryl G. Press, "The Rise of U.S. Nuclear Primacy," *Foreign Affairs* (March/April 2006), at http://www.foreignaffairs.com/articles/61508/keir-a-lieber-and-daryl-g-press/the-rise-of-us-nuclear-primacy.

49. In the United States also, they are viewed as sensationalists. See Keir A. Lieber and Daryl G. Press, "The Nukes We Need," *Foreign Affairs* 88, no. 6 (November/December 2009): 31–51.

50. Gordon Brown, speech at the 6191st meeting of the UN Security Council.

51. "No CTBT, India Needs More Nuclear Tests."

52. Oliver Meier, "The US-India Nuclear Deal: The End of Universal Non-Proliferation Efforts?" *Internationale Politik und Gesellschaft* (April 2006): 28–43, at http://www.fes.de/ipg/inhalt_d/pdf/Meier_GB.pdf.

53. Nuclear trade restrictions had been initially imposed in response to India's first nuclear test in 1974 and reaffirmed after the Indian 1998 tests. The NSG now has forty-six members; see http://www.nuclearsuppliersgroup.org.

54. See the chapter by Avner Cohen in this volume.

55. See William J. Broad, David E. Sanger, and Raymond Bonner, "A Tale of Nuclear Proliferation: How Pakistani Built His Network," *New York Times*, 12 February 2004, A1. See also William Langewiesche, *The Atomic Bazaar* (London: Penguin Books, 2007).

56. International Panel on Fissile Materials (IPFM), "A Fissile Material (Cut-Off)

Treaty: A Treaty Banning the Production of Fissile Materials for Nuclear Weapons or Other Nuclear Explosive Devices with Article-by-Article Explanation," 16 March 2009, at http://www.fissilematerials.org/ipfm/site_down/fmct-ipfm_mar2009draft.pdf.

57. In 2008 the International Institute for Strategic Studies (IISS) Strategic Dossier listed Algeria, Egypt, Jordan, Kuwait, Bahrain, Qatar, Libya, Morocco, Saudi Arabia, Syria, Turkey, the United Arab Emirates, and Yemen. See International Institute for Strategic Studies, *Nuclear Programmes in the Middle East: In the Shadow of Iran*, IISS Strategic Dossier (London: ISSS, May 2008).

58. Hans M. Kristensen, Robert S. Norris, and Ivan Oelrich, *From Counterforce to Minimal Deterrence: A New Nuclear Policy on the Path toward Eliminating Nuclear Weapons*, Occasional Paper No. 7 (Washington, DC: Federation of American Scientists, 2009), at http://www.fas.org/pubs/_docs/OccasionalPaper7.pdf.

59. William J. Perry, James R. Schlesinger, et al., *America's Strategic Posture. Final Report of the Congressional Commission on the Strategic Posture of the United States* (Washington, DC: United States Institute of Peace, 2009), at http://www.usip.org/strategic_posture/final.html.

60. George Perkovich, *Abolishing Nuclear Weapons: Why the United States Should Lead* (Washington, DC: Carnegie Endowment for International Peace, 2008).

61. Remarks by Secretary of State Hillary Rodham Clinton at the United States Institute of Peace, 21 October 2009, at http://www.state.gov/secretary/rm/2009a/10/130806.htm.

PAST DECISIONS, FUTURE PERSPECTIVES

4 The U.S. Nuclear Arsenal and Zero: Sizing and Planning for Use—Past, Present, and Future

Lynn Eden

As we consider significantly reducing the U.S. nuclear arsenal—through unilateral actions and in conjunction with others—it is important to consider the historical contours of the U.S. nuclear arsenal. What drove the spectacular U.S. arms buildup during the Cold War? How should we understand the post–Cold War reductions? And what are the barriers to reductions to much lower numbers?

The key to understanding is the internal and largely hidden logic of U.S. plans to use nuclear weapons should deterrence fail. U.S. nuclear war planning is not a barrier to cutting to an arsenal of 1,500 or somewhat fewer strategic nuclear weapons, but the deep logic that guides planning for use is likely, *if not contravened*, to prove a barrier to a significantly smaller arsenal, on the order of 100 to 500 nuclear weapons, on the way to zero.

First, I sketch out the contours of the U.S. strategic nuclear arsenal from its inception to the present. Over time, the U.S. arsenal grew remarkably more lethal—that is, more able to destroy specific "hard targets" such as missile silos and command bunkers. Most notable is the exponential increase in lethality from 1980 to 1990, and the peak reached in 2002—more than a decade *after* the collapse of the Soviet Union.

Second, I explain the underlying logic and process of planning for nuclear war. Nuclear war plans are contingency plans that shape the options available in the event deterrence fails. The planning process drives weapons numbers and is an arena in which battles over numbers are fought. The basic idea is to be able to limit damage from an enemy's attack through an ability to *destroy* enemy forces, command structure, and communications prior to their launch; *disrupt* an attack early in the launch process; or *stop* an enemy's ability to continue to fight. All have been part of U.S. nuclear war planning, but the first two have been the most important. Their logic is incorporated in and inseparable from detailed organizational routines for targeting nuclear weapons—including designating targets, rating target "hardness," and evaluating the overall effectiveness of the U.S. attack. These routines, and the logic they embody, have been surprisingly persistent. Unless changed, they are likely to prove an insuperable barrier to achieving deep nuclear arms reductions and, ultimately, getting to zero.

Third, I examine the role of this targeting logic in the post–Cold War era. How did the United States arrive at approximately 2,200 strategic weapons on alert in 2010? What role is targeting logic likely to play at 1,000 weapons, or 500 weapons? And what will allow for a drop to a force that is an order of magnitude smaller? As we will see, reaching a nuclear stockpile of a few hundred, or a few tens of weapons, on the way to zero will require radical changes in the basic assumptions of U.S. nuclear war planning.

THE U.S. NUCLEAR ARSENAL

In the Real World

The scale of destruction that nuclear weapons cause is important to understand but difficult to grasp. The atomic bombs detonated at Hiroshima and Nagasaki in August 1945 are frequently referred to as "small," the equivalent of the explosive power of 15,000 and 21,000 tons of dynamite, respectively. But these are "small" only in comparison to the destructive potential of the post–World War II nuclear weapons arsenals, including today's.

McGeorge Bundy, national security advisor to presidents John F. Kennedy and Lyndon Johnson, provides a sense of scale: "In the real world of real political leaders . . . a decision that would bring even one hydrogen bomb on one city of one's own country would be recognized in advance as a catastrophic blunder; ten bombs on ten cities would be a disaster beyond history; and a hundred bombs on a hundred cities are unthinkable." Wise words, but according to historian David A. Rosenberg, the U.S. Air Force had identified a hundred city centers for atomic attack by the fall of 1947, and by the fall of 1949, the U.S. atomic war plan "called for attacks on 104 urban targets with 220 atomic bombs, plus a re-attack reserve of 72 weapons."[1] Today's arsenal is capable of inflicting far greater damage.

Overall Contours

From the end of World War II to the late 1980s, both the United States and Soviet Union/Russia steeply increased the total numbers of warheads in their bomber, ICBM, and SLBM forces, ultimately reaching levels of 11,500 to 14,000 strategic nuclear weapons each (and, counting nonstrategic weapons, 30,000 to 40,000 weapons each).[2] In the post–Cold War period, both countries greatly decreased those forces. Historically, the overall arsenals have grown and shrunk roughly in tandem. The United States has had a preponderance of its warheads in the strategic bomber force and the SLBM force; the Soviet Union/Russia has had a preponderance of warheads in its ICBM force. In this chapter we will look at the U.S. side.

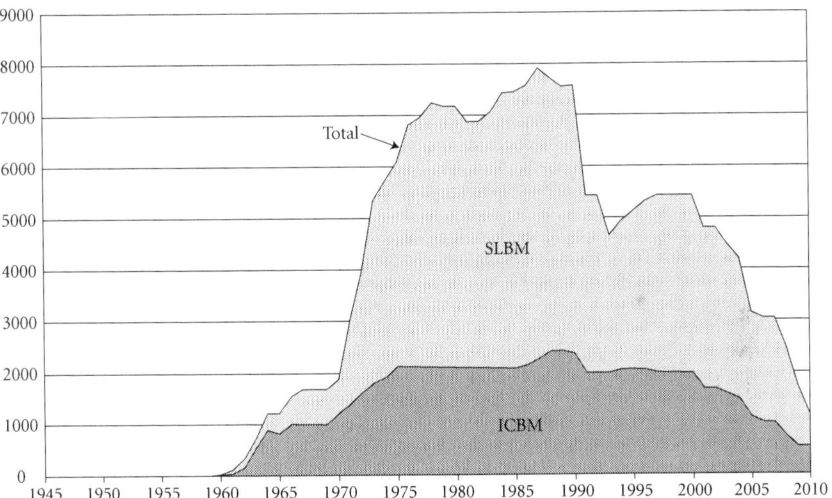

Figure 4.1. U.S. ICBM and SLBM warheads, 1945–2010. Sources: Archive of Nuclear Data from Natural Resources Defense Council's Nuclear Program, http://www.nrdc.org/nuclear/nudb/dafig4.asp, and dafig6.asp; and Robert S. Norris and William M. Arkin, "Nuclear Notebook: U.S. Nuclear Forces, 2000," *Bulletin of the Atomic Scientists* (May/June 2000): 69–71, and succeeding "nuclear notebooks," *Bulletin*, 2001–10.

Lethality

The picture is very different when we use a broad measure that compares ICBM and SLBM destructive capabilities over time (see Figure 4.2). Specifically, *lethality*, K, is a comparative measure of "hard-target kill capability": the greater

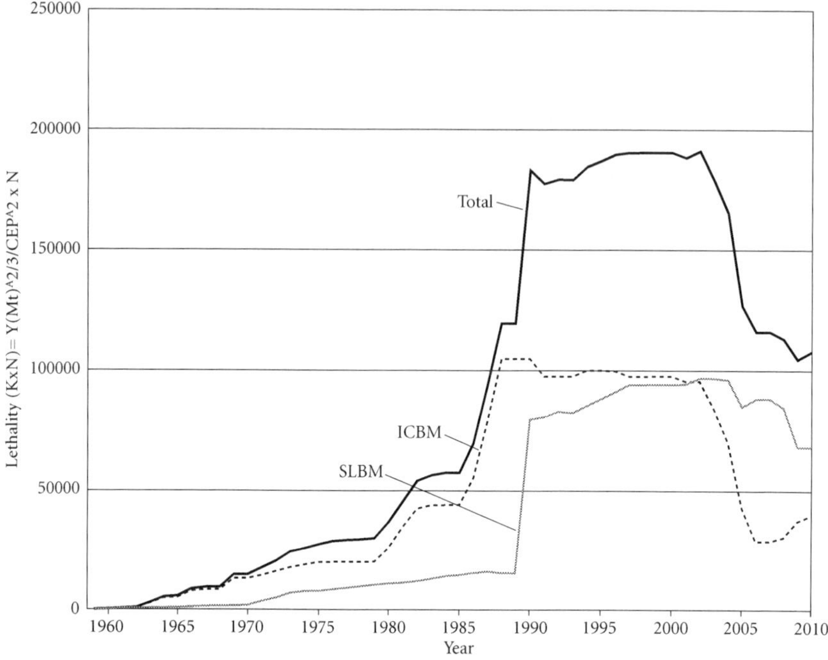

Figure 4.2. Comparative and total lethality of U.S. ICBMs and SLBMs, 1959–2010. Sources: http://www.nrdc.org/nuclear/nudb/dafig3.asp#fiftynine, datab5.asp; datab7.asp; Robert S. Norris and William M. Arkin, "Nuclear Notebook: U.S. Nuclear Forces, 2000," *Bulletin of the Atomic Scientists* (May/June 2000): 69–71; and succeeding "nuclear notebooks," *Bulletin*, 2001–10.

the lethality, the greater the ability of a weapon, or a class of weapons, to destroy hard targets such as missile silos, hardened communication sites, and command bunkers. Comparing different values of K shows the relative ability of nuclear weapons of varying yields and accuracy to destroy enemy hard targets.[3] Lethality is not a measure of the full destructive potential of nuclear weapons. It does not measure the fire damage caused by nuclear weapons on targets or on human beings, nor the radiological effects, nor potential effects on climate.[4] It is, however, a concept highly consonant with the deep logic of nuclear war planning.

The measure for lethality does not depend on knowing the capability to destroy *specific* hard targets, nor does it require specification of all the structures being targeted at a particular time or over time.[5] Instead, by taking into account yield and accuracy, lethality gives us a simple way to compare weapons systems. The most important component of lethality is accuracy: making a warhead twice as accurate has the same effect as increasing the yield—that is, the explosive power—eight times.

Lethality can be measured per warhead or in aggregate. To get a feel for lethality, let us compare the first U.S. ICBM warhead deployed, the W-49 Atlas, in 1959, to the lethality of the Trident D-5 W88 warhead, first deployed in 1990 and currently deployed. The Atlas warhead had an explosive power (yield) of 1.44 megatons and an accuracy, measured as circular error probable (CEP) of 1.8 nautical miles (n.m.), or approximately 11,000 feet. CEP is the radius of a circle within which half the warheads aimed at a target are expected to fall. Thus a CEP of 1.8 nautical miles means that half the warheads are expected to fall within that distance, and the other half beyond. The Trident warhead has a yield of 0.475 megaton and a CEP of 0.06 nautical mile, or an accuracy of a little over the length of a football field. The lethality per re-entry vehicle (K) was 0.4 for the Atlas; for the Trident it is 169. In other words, with approximately one-third the yield and thirty times the accuracy, a single Trident D-5 W-88 warhead is approximately 425 times as lethal as was the Atlas.

Lethality gives us a very different sense of destructive capability than simpler measures that focus on numbers of warheads. If we look just at numbers (Figure 4.1), we see a precipitous drop in warhead numbers in 1991 and then a more sustained drop beginning in 2001, until, by 2009, the total number of strategic missile warheads is the same as in 1969. Focusing on lethality (Figure 4.2) shows us that just as the Cold War began to thaw, the lethality of the U.S. missile force *increased* exponentially. This was because of the deployment of the Minuteman III W-78 in 1980 (accurate to 0.12 nautical mile), the highly accurate MX warhead in 1986 (accuracy 0.06 n.m.), and the equally accurate Trident D-5 W-88 in 1990. At the same time, the Poseidon C-3 (accuracy 0.25 n.m.) was retired in 1990, and, beginning in 1991, the Trident D-5 W-76 (0.12 n.m.) began to replace the older Trident C-4 (accuracy 0.25 n.m.). Indeed, the lethality of the U.S. missile force increased more than three times from 1985 to 1990 and actually increased slightly more until it peaked in 2002, more than a dozen years after the collapse of the Soviet Union. In 2009, lethality was almost half its peak level. Although in 2010, the U.S. had about the same number of deployed warheads as it did in 1969, the lethality of the force was more than seven times greater.

THE LOGIC OF NUCLEAR WAR PLANNING

The damage-limiting logic of nuclear war planning and the organizational routines based on that logic have been, and remain, deeply ingrained in decisions about the numbers and capabilities of the U.S. nuclear arsenal.

To get a sense of proportion, let us turn to late 1960, when the U.S. government first integrated a series of regional nuclear war plans into one plan called the Single Integrated Operational Plan, or SIOP. The first SIOP was designated by the fiscal year for which it was operative: SIOP-62. Not surprisingly, the planning took place at the headquarters of the Strategic Air Command (SAC) in Omaha, Nebraska. The commander of SAC also directed the multiservice staff in charge of the SIOP, the Joint Strategic Targeting Planning Staff (JSTPS).

At this time, America's overwhelming destructive power lay in its bomber force of more than 3,000 nuclear weapons. The ICBM and SLBM force of 137 warheads—30 Atlas D and 27 Atlas E warheads with individual yields of 1.4 and 3.75 megatons, respectively, and 80 Polaris warheads of 600 kilotons each—was a huge force by historical standards, and small only in comparison to the bomber force.

According to journalist Fred Kaplan, the nuclear war plan "SIOP-62 ... called for sending in the full arsenal of the Strategic Air Command—2,258 missiles and bombers carrying a total of 3,423 nuclear weapons—against 1,077 'military and urban-industrial targets' throughout the 'Sino-Soviet Bloc.'"[6] More than 800 of these targets were military. Of the military targets, about 200 were nuclear forces: 140 bomber bases, approximately 30 submarine bases, and 10 to 25 Soviet ICBMS.[7] Of the total targets, about 200 were urban-industrial targets—that is, industrial targets largely located in populated areas.

In an internal government memo, economist Carl Kaysen described the consequences of executing SIOP-62. At the time, he was trying to craft a much smaller first-use nuclear option for President Kennedy for possible use during the Berlin crisis. According to Kaysen, if all U.S. strategic nuclear forces were executed as planned in SIOP-62, they would be expected to kill 54 percent of the population of the Soviet Union, "including 71% of the urban population, and . . . to destroy . . . 82% of the buildings, as measured by floor space." Further, Kaysen continued, "there is reason to believe that these figures are underestimated; the casualties, for example, include only those of the first 72 hours."[8]

Built into the targeting plan above was a set of algorithms—abstract to handle and catastrophic to realize—based on determination of the following:

- What counts as a target and how many are there?
- How "hard" or resistant are those targets to damage?
- Given a planned attack, what damage is to be expected against enemy assets?

These three questions involved a great deal of investigative and analytical work, but also embodied highly subjective collective judgments colored by intense interservice, industrial, and political rivalries. The eventual answers had broad implications for the numbers, characteristics, and types of weapons systems procured. Moreover, once judgments were embedded in routines, they became difficult to undo, either because they had resulted from hard political negotiations or because people came to take them for granted.

The U.S. nuclear war plan, the SIOP, was a "capabilities plan" that allocated existing weapons to specific targets.[9] The allocation process was complicated. But decisions about targeting also resulted from "pull" and "push" dynamics that both led to and justified arguments for more nuclear weapons. Anticipation of more and "harder" targets provided a "pull" to procure more weapons that could destroy those targets. The arrival of new nuclear weapons in the arsenal provided a "push" to find and justify targets at which to aim those warheads.

What Counts as a Target and How Many Are There?

U.S. nuclear war planning—the planning process in which specific weapons are allocated to be delivered and to destroy specific targets—comes directly out of the experience of World War II strategic bombing. Despite the fact that large areas would inevitably be destroyed by strategic nuclear weapons, planners treat these weapons as though they destroy specific targets. Wider "collateral" damage does not "count" as an organizational goal and therefore is not "credited"—in fact, it is generally invisible—in war plans. Individual targets are classified into types—for example, strategic nuclear forces, other military targets, or urban-industrial targets.

In addition, all targets are characterized in terms of their geographic coordinates, function, and structural type. This mapping and categorizing is a huge analytical enterprise that I have elsewhere termed a vast "census of . . . destruction." Like all censuses, the results reflected purpose and invented categories. In this case, war planners enumerated the specific structures and equipment slated for destruction, determined the aim points for U.S. weapons, and worked out the complicated logistics of routing weapons and timing possible attacks.[10]

The activity was explained to the public in terms of deterrence, but it seems better to think of the detailed and highly secret process as one of contingency planning should deterrence fail. (According to an official history, in the early 1970s, the targeting staff considered recommending the "inclusion of 'deterrence' as a major objective of the SIOP" but decided against it "since the SIOP was a capabilities plan rather than an objectives plan." Objectives were listed in the war plan, but these were objectives once war began.)[11]

Finally, the armed services—especially the Air Force—used current and especially projected targets to argue for future weapon requirements in a process that David Rosenberg dubbed "bootstrapping." According to Rosenberg, in January 1952, Air Force chief of staff General Hoyt Vandenberg told President Dwight Eisenhower, "Even allowing for incomplete intelligence . . . there appeared to be 'perhaps *five or six thousand* Soviet targets which would have to be destroyed in the event of war' [emphasis added]." Rosenberg continued, "This would require a major expansion in weapons production. . . . Air Force–generated target lists were used to justify weapons production, which in turn justified increased appropriations to provide matching delivery capability. . . . As intelligence improved, Air Force target lists steadily outpaced accelerating stockpile growth."[12]

The targets that drove most of the Air Force's weapons requirements and soaked up the vast majority of its warheads were Soviet strategic nuclear forces. Hence, the Air Force's preferred strategy was "counterforce": U.S. nuclear forces to counter, or attack, Soviet forces to "limit damage" to the United States.

The more that Soviet forces increased or were projected to, the more the target lists expanded, which then "pulled" weapons requirements up to be able to meet damage goals against those targets. The Air Force had organizational interests in maintaining a strong defense industrial base, but this does not mean war planners did not genuinely believe the scope of the threat.

The logic of "bootstrapping" continued throughout the Cold War—and after. A year and a half after the 1985 Reykjavik meeting between President Ronald Reagan and Soviet premier Mikhail Gorbachev that had led to a warming in relations, and more than a year after Gorbachev had made a serious and detailed nuclear arms reduction proposal, an Air Force general assigned to the joint strategic target planning staff explained, "The U.S. is in a weapon-poor target-rich environment. The Soviets are in the opposite situation. We find ourselves in a deficit position." A decade later, after the Soviet Union had dissolved, the United States was still described as being in a "target-rich environment."[13]

For the Navy, for much of the Cold War, the process worked somewhat differently. Here the dominant mission was not to limit damage in the event of war but to penetrate Soviet missile defenses—a mission dictated in part by the challenges of launching missiles from submarines at sea, which resulted in much lower accuracies than Air Force land-based missiles. MIRV technology provided a path to more warheads per launcher for both the Air Force and the Navy. While the Air Force chose relatively few high-yield warheads (until the deployment of the MX in 1986, with ten warheads per missile), the Navy chose more numerous lower-yield—and, largely by necessity, less accurate—weapons. When the Poseidon C-3 missiles carrying ten warheads began to replace Polaris missiles carrying one or three warheads, a "push" dynamic began, requiring the target planning staff to find more targets. An official history of the targeting staff cites "spectacular growth" in SIOP warheads from mid-1971 to mid-1972. The same history notes: "The introduction of Multiple Independently Targeted Reentry Vehicles (MIRVs) in the inventory has resulted in an increase in the number of weapons *as well as an increase in the number of [Designated Ground Zeros] required to efficiently utilize these new weapons.*"[14] In plain English: more targets were put into the war plan so that weapons could be aimed at them. Greater growth lay ahead: from 1971 to 1978, ICBM warheads increased from 1,444 to 2,144. Primarily because of increases in Poseidon C-3 warheads, SLBM warheads increased from 1,664 to 5,120.

At the same time, 1971–72, John S. Foster, the Pentagon's director of defense research and engineering, led a closely held targeting review panel that worked to rationalize the targeting of this "profusion of warheads in excess of those needed to fulfill the major attack options against Soviet strategic [nuclear] forces and key economic facilities." The review, and subsequent targeting, placed much greater emphasis on "other military targets" and "economic recovery targets," both, not coincidentally, amenable to destruction by Poseidon warheads.[15]

Analytically more interesting were economic recovery targets. Formally, the government's new goal was to be able to "retard significantly the ability of the USSR to recover from a nuclear exchange and regain the status of a 20th century military and industrial power more quickly than the United States."[16] Destroying an enemy's industrial base had always been part of the U.S. nuclear war plan. However, ensuring that the enemy's economy will recover more slowly than your own required many more warheads. According to a Foster panel participant, the question was, "Could you *really* keep a country from recovering economically? The answer is no, you can't do it with one strike. Everybody agreed to that. . . . We found out . . . that there is something worse than nuclear war. It's two nuclear wars in succession . . . two to six weeks apart."[17]

Then, unexpectedly, the push dynamic—the necessity to target the vast number of warheads coming into the arsenal—turned back into a pull dynamic. When the government asked academics to develop economic recovery models, they found that the Soviet economy could recover surprisingly quickly to prewar levels. RAND analysts Michael Kennedy and Kevin Lewis explained,

"The U.S. force committed to the attack in such models often runs to several thousand warheads," yet "typical results suggest full recovery to prewar GNP within about five years." Varying assumptions still led to "perhaps fifteen years" at the outside to make a full recovery.[18] According to political scientist Scott Sagan, one implication was that "*significantly larger numbers of weapons were required* to achieve the counter-recovery objective," and he suggests that by the late 1970s more than half of the targets were urban-industrial.[19]

In President Jimmy Carter's administration, reviews of targeting policy began to shift emphasis away from economic recovery and toward greater damage to Soviet military targets. Most important was the 1978 Nuclear Policy Targeting Review led by government analyst Leon Sloss. In political scientist Janne Nolan's words, "Instead of cutting weapons to fit the shrinking target list, the study 'kept the same number of weapons and allocated more to each target,' according to one analyst. It justified this by raising the damage criteria, a more exacting standard imposed to determine what was needed to destroy the targets." According to Sagan, Reagan administration policy was consistent with policy under the Carter administration: a decreased emphasis on economic targets, an increased emphasis on counterforce targeting, and also an increased emphasis on "holding the Soviet leadership directly at risk."[20]

Consistent with these doctrinal shifts, both the Carter and Reagan administrations accelerated counterforce programs such as the MX and the Trident D-5 programs,[21] which would not, however, be deployed until 1986 and 1990, respectively. The MX had a yield of 300 kilotons and an exceptional accuracy of 0.06 nautical mile, or 365 feet. With the deployment of the Trident D-5 W-88 warhead with a yield of 475 kilotons and accuracy equal to that of the MX, for the first time the Navy had a weapon with a hard-target kill capability as good as or better than the Air Force's. Not coincidentally, with the anticipated D-5 deployment, and the very significant political problems encountered by the Air Force, as one after another survivable basing mode for the MX was eliminated, the Navy began to exhibit a willingness to take on the Air Force directly in making claims for survivable counterforce capability.[22]

Harder Targets and Damage Criteria

Over time, U.S. intelligence also discerned that the Soviets were "hardening" their weapons and command structures. This sounds like a claim about modifying the structures, as in digging deeper underground bunkers or using more reinforced concrete. Indeed, it can mean this.

But in the engineering community, hardness also identifies a point of failure. An engineer might say a building is resistant to, or can withstand, a magnitude 8 earthquake but not an 8.2 quake. The choice of the point of failure is crucial. For engineers and architects, it determines the design, construction, and cost of putting up structures. For nuclear targeteers, it works in reverse: it allows them to decide what is required to *cause* "moderate" damage (often referred to as turning the structure into "gravel"), or "severe" damage ("dust"). The greater the required damage, the "harder" the structure. Targeting a building for severe damage boosts its hardness rating, while targeting it for moderate damage would result in a lower hardness rating.[23] In other words, damage criteria result from goals, not from inherent characteristics of structures and are written into the vocabulary of physical vulnerability. The implications are important: saying the Soviet or Russian target base got harder could mean a difference in construction, or it could mean a U.S. decision that "severe," not "moderate," damage was now required, or both.

Target hardness has great implications for weapons procurement: the "harder" the targets, the stronger the claims for more accurate weapons, and sometimes for higher-yield weapons. That logic operated in the early 1970s, when the Strategic Air Command said it required a new more accurate and higher yield ICBM, the MX, because the Soviet target base had hardened. According to Air Force general Russell Dougherty, who became the commander-in-chief of SAC in 1974, and, as commander, was also the director of JSTPS, "In the early '70s . . . we needed the accuracy. . . . That was one of the big drivers for the MX [because the Soviet target base] had changed character, it had hardened."[24]

Damage Expectancy

Both targets and damage criteria were, and are, incorporated into an algorithm that calculates, for every weapon type matched to relevant targets, the expected effectiveness of attack.[25] The overall calculation is termed expected damage, or damage expectancy, abbreviated DE; it is a compound probability composed of four other probabilities:

- that a weapon or class of weapons survives before being launched (prelaunch survivability, or PLS);
- that a weapon does not fail for mechanical or other internal reasons (probability weapon is reliable, or PRE);
- that a weapon penetrates enemy air or other defenses (probability of penetration, or PTP);

- that a weapon destroys the target, determined by a combination of accuracy, weapon yield, height of burst, and target hardness (probability of "kill," or PK).

Stated otherwise:

DE = PLS x PRE x PTP x PK

If an insufficient number of weapons is available to "cover" the chosen targets or if the targets are deemed too hard for those weapons to destroy, then the probability of kill will be considered unacceptably low—leading to calls for more and "higher-quality" weapons.

Every aspect of damage expectancy is subject to the politics and negotiation of interservice rivalry and weapons procurement. For example, retired Navy vice admiral Gerald E. Miller, who was detailed to the joint planning staff as the Navy representative when the first SIOP was being developed in late summer 1960, describes how the staff established a policy committee to interpret the brief political guidance it had received and to iron out many other issues. The committee, with voting representatives from each of the four services plus other experts, met almost every day to work through problems.[26]

According to Admiral Miller:

> When we came to Polaris, eight had been fired [obviously in tests]. *Four* got to the target.... So the weapons system reliability [PRE] is only going to be 50%. Well, Jesus, if ... you're down here to 50%, what kind of a weapon system is that?! And we haven't even talked about the probability of the weapon not doing the damage because its accuracy's not very good. So you're talking about a useless weapon system if its reliability isn't very good. So a big battle goes on in the conference room ... for a couple, three days. And finally [the head of SAC and the director of JSTPS] General Power himself came down and sat at the head of the table and said, "All right, I'll resolve this. Let it be."[27]

Prelaunch survivability (PLS), or what is called "planning factor," is also a highly negotiated number. Indeed, in the original negotiations over Polaris missiles, General Power had argued that the PLS for Polaris was *not* 1, but less. However, the policy committee determined—not surprisingly, given that submarines could not be detected—that the correct value was 1.[28]

Conversely, the Strategic Air Command has historically argued for a very high PLS for the ICBM force, somewhere between 0.98 and 1.00.[29] To get a prelaunch survivability number that high does not require going first, but requires a *launch* either on warning or very early in the course of a nuclear attack on the United States. This contradicts more common notions of survivability, such as being able to "ride out an attack," as submarines can do for long periods of time. To the Air Force, PLS is composed of two probabilities: the probability of survival (PS), which extends to the moment before the impact of incoming warheads, and the probability of launch (PL). The Air Force believes that "the probability of survival for each silo has been unity . . . but erodes very quickly following a [nuclear] attack on the force. . . . Before impact of . . . weapons, the PS is unity and the PL governs the PLS value."[30] It seems a tortured use of ordinary language to think of *pre*-launch survivability as *including* the probability of launch. But for the Air Force, "survive" is a transitive verb: a commander can "survive" his forces by launching them.[31]

Thus the logic of nuclear war planning sets the terms by which military personnel understand threat and by which goals and requirements shape the development of weapons systems. At the same time, the war planning process sets the terms of competition for political, military, and industrial rivalry. Planners justify weapons in terms of the compound algorithm of damage expectancy. The most important damage goals are "severe damage" to "hard targets," including hardened communication and command sites and, especially, nuclear forces.

NUCLEAR DOCTRINE IN THE POST–COLD WAR ERA

In 2000, defense analyst Bruce Blair wrote an op-ed explaining why top American military officers insisted that current nuclear policy prevented them from shrinking the arsenal to fewer than 2,000 to 2,500 strategic nuclear weapons: "The reason for [the military's] position is a matter of simple arithmetic, buried in the nation's strategic war plan and ultimately linked to presidential guidance." Blair's "simple arithmetic" derives from the numbers and types of nuclear targets in the war plan and the level of expected damage, as discussed above. Not counting hundreds of targets in China and elsewhere, Blair said:

> [T]here are about 2,260 so-called vital Russian targets on the list today, only 1,100 of them actual nuclear arms sites within Russia. [In addition,] we have nuclear weapons aimed at 500 "conventional" targets—the buildings and bases of a hollow Russian army on the verge of disintegration; 160 leadership targets, like government offices and military command centers, in a country practically devoid of leadership; and 500 mostly crumbling factories that produced almost no armaments last year.[32]

The Bush administration had a somewhat different set of targets, but the target categories were fundamentally the same as those in 2000 and earlier, including "critical war-making and war-supporting assets such as WMD forces [read: nuclear forces] and supporting facilities, command and control facilities, and the military and political leadership."[33]

When President Barack Obama took office in 2009, the United States had approximately 2,200 strategic nuclear weapons on alert—about the same number it had in 2000. In the first year, the new administration eliminated a few hundred of those weapons. More important, in early April 2010, the administration completed two major documents on nuclear forces and doctrine. President Obama and Russian president Medvedev signed a new arms control agreement, the New START treaty. The U.S. and Russian strategic nuclear arsenals will each be reduced to 1,550 warheads. A decade after Blair's op-ed, the U.S. military has agreed to "cover" somewhat fewer targets, and therefore requires fewer weapons.

Even more revealing, the Obama administration completed a far-reaching Nuclear Posture Review (NPR), requiring myriad negotiations among the military, the departments of defense, state, energy, and the White House. A crucial issue was the purpose of nuclear weapons: in particular, should the NPR say that the *sole* purpose of nuclear weapons is to deter? Had it said so, achieving much smaller numbers of nuclear weapons would have been on the table. Instead, and no doubt in deference to military preferences, the NPR says, "The *fundamental* role of U.S. nuclear weapons . . . is to deter attack on the United States, our allies, and partners." In other words, besides deterrence, U.S. nuclear weapons have another role: actual use if deemed necessary. Relatedly, a declaration of no first use was removed from an early draft of the document, again indicating that in some situations the United States reserves the right to use nuclear weapons. Given possible use, what determines force size? The NPR is clear: "Russia's nuclear force will remain a significant factor in determining how much and how fast we are prepared to reduce U.S. forces." The deep logic of U.S. nuclear war planning has not changed. The United States targets Russian nuclear forces; until the Russians eliminate those targets, the U.S. military will resist much deeper reductions in U.S. forces. Had the Nuclear Posture Review explicitly directed the military to cut the nation's deployed nuclear weapons arsenal to, say, 500 warheads, it would have forced the military to revise its definition of target coverage and damage criteria.[34]

GETTING TO VERY LOW NUMBERS—AND TO ZERO

Since the end of the Cold War—and especially since the post-2007 movement to create a nuclear-free world, and as seen in the Nuclear Posture Review—the military's logic has diverged sharply from civilian analysts' assumptions about the use of nuclear force.[35] The latter views as neither legitimate nor credible the possibility of launching hundreds or more nuclear weapons, possibly first, for military purposes against an adversary's nuclear forces or closely related command and communication nodes.

Instead, in a post–Cold War twist on what earlier had been termed "punitive retaliation," "minimum deterrence," or "existential deterrence," various analysts have called for a commitment to no first use. They generally argue that the only purpose of nuclear weapons is to deter and, if necessary, to respond to the use of nuclear weapons by other countries. In either case, damage should be as "small" as possible.[36] In the words of an influential study by the National Academy of Sciences' Committee on International Security and Arms Control, "The United States should adopt a strategy . . . that would be based neither on predetermined prompt attacks on counterforce targets nor on automatic destruction of cities. . . . If they were ever to be used, [nuclear weapons] would be employed against targets . . . in the smallest possible numbers. . . . The operational posture of the much smaller forces must be designed for deliberate response rather than reaction in a matter of minutes."[37] How small is "much smaller forces"? Some analysts focus on initial reductions to 1,000 nuclear weapons; others foresee a "minimization point" of 500 weapons by 2025; others a total in the "low hundreds."[38]

Getting from 500 or somewhat fewer deployed weapons to elimination will be much more difficult. Some advocate a thorough reassessment of possibilities at 500. Others claim that to get to zero it is necessary "to create cooperative geopolitical conditions, regionally and globally, making the prospect of major war or aggression so remote that nuclear weapons are seen as having no remaining deterrent utility."[39] Still others argue that very low numbers of weapons, and zero, would create strong incentives to rearm, and those who retained only a few weapons, or who quickly built back up to a few weapons, would have large advantages over those who did not "break out." The anxiety over the actions of others could, or would, increase the risk of war.[40] By some accounts, stability and deterrence near or at a zero level require the ability to reconstitute nuclear arsenals. In particular, the United States must have a virtual or latent capacity to build nuclear weapons: a "responsive nuclear infrastructure" composed of excellent facilities, skilled weapons designers who can assess and solve potential problems, and a strong scientifically based experimental program to retain and hone skills.[41] This may not sound like nuclear abolition, but for some, an agile, "capability-based deterrent" is precisely the requirement for achieving and maintaining a world free of nuclear weapons.[42]

Clearly, the problems of achieving stability at very low numbers, and zero, are formidable. Nonetheless, we must first get from here to there. To reach 500 weapons or fewer will require nothing less than the upending of the fundamental assumptions of U.S. nuclear war planning: a counterforce strategy that threatens an adversary's or adversaries' strategic nuclear forces, leadership, and communications.

Only a few analysts have discussed what targeting options at very low numbers should, or could, look like. A force of a few hundred strategic nuclear warheads, the National Academy committee says,

> implies a drastic change in strategic target planning. A force of a few hundred can no longer hold at risk a wide spectrum of the assets of a large opponent, including its leadership, key bases, communication nodes, troop concentrations, and the variety of counterforce targets now included in the target lists. The reduced number of weapons would be sufficient to fulfill the core function [of deterrence], however, through its potential to destroy essential elements of the society or economy of any possible attacker.[43]

Despite the acknowledgment that much lower numbers will require drastic changes in targeting procedures, the National Academy study does not spell out which "essential elements of society" should be targeted.

Political scientist Charles Glaser is braver in his specificity, arguing that limited nuclear options can range from "pure demonstration attacks, which inflict no damage but communicate U.S. willingness to escalate further" to "more damaging countervalue attacks . . . made against isolated industrial facilities, a small town, or even a small city. Without minimizing the horror of attacks against people, we should acknowledge that there is a vast difference between these attacks and a full-scale attack against major Russian population centers."[44]

Only a single detailed study, *From Counterforce to Minimal Deterrence: A New Nuclear Policy on the Path toward Eliminating Nuclear Weapons* (2009), has analyzed the consequences of a U.S. nuclear attack on a "small" set of targets.

Analysts from the Federation of American Scientists and the Natural Resources Defense Council devised a target set that is a "tightly constrained subset set of countervalue targets," which they term "infrastructure targeting," of twelve large industrial targets in Russia: three oil refinery targets; three iron and steel works; two aluminum plants; one nickel plant; and three thermal electric power plants. They ran a number of possible attacks on these plants, some of which are isolated from population centers. The results were, as we would expect, devastating. "With weapons equivalent to the . . . most common U.S. warhead [the 100 kiloton W-76], over a million people would be killed or injured by an attack of just one dozen warheads. This suggests to us that the current U.S. arsenal is vastly more powerful than needed."[45]

We are faced, then, with deep contradiction. On the one hand, a number of civilian analysts call for a no-first-use, limited retaliation policy with an arsenal ranging from a few hundred to 1,000 nuclear weapons. But these analysts offer no argument about how and with what *political* effect one nuclear weapon or tens of nuclear weapons could be used in war—other than some implicit notion of shock or inflicted punishment leading to the enemy's capitulation. They do predict very large numbers of casualties, making it difficult to see how the benefits of such use could outweigh the moral recoil and loss of international standing that would result. But perhaps the implicit idea is more radical: the U.S. government may threaten to use nuclear weapons but, in fact, cannot use them at all, or can use them only after being attacked to then wreak vengeance—thus deterring a direct attack.[46] This does not seem unreasonable. But it runs counter to military logic, identity, and entrenched organizational algorithms.

On the other hand, the U.S. military personnel involved in nuclear targeting operate with deeply ingrained understandings and organizational routines that led to exceedingly large numbers of nuclear weapons during the Cold War and to very high levels of lethality afterward. Weapons numbers have since come down, but they appear to be "sticky" at about 1,500 deployed strategic warheads. If the military were amenable to eliminating another 1,000 weapons, the National Academy committee is persuasive in arguing that a force of a few hundred weapons will have to be organized around very different principles.

What will it take to get there? Certainly it will require a more far-reaching internal agreement than we can see in the Obama administration's 2010 Nuclear Posture Review. Such an agreement will cut against deeply ingrained military understandings, and against some vested interests as well. Politically, such an agreement cannot be imposed, and but will require strong allies within the military who are willing to accept and implement it. Whether such allies already exist is unclear. The best chance for success rests in finding or creating military leaders who are willing to rethink the basis of U.S. nuclear war planning, and who are able to persuade their colleagues about the advantages of doing so.

NOTES

1. McGeorge Bundy, "To Cap the Volcano," *Foreign Affairs* 48, no. 1 (October 1969): 10; David Alan Rosenberg, "The Origins of Overkill: Nuclear Weapons and American Strategy, 1945–1960," *International Security* 7, no. 4 (Spring 1983): 15, 17.

2. Committee on International Security and Arms Control, National Academy of Sciences, *The Future of U.S. Nuclear Weapons Policy* (Washington, DC: National Academy Press, 1997), p. 16.

3. I have used Bruce G. Blair's formula in *Strategic Command and Control: Redefining the Nuclear Threat* (Washington, DC: Brookings Institution, 1985), Table A-3, "Lethality of U.S. and Soviet Strategic Missile Forces, 1975 and 1978," p. 310. K is lethality per re-entry vehicle: (K) = Yield of warhead (in megatons)$^{2/3}$/accuracy of re-entry vehicle (circular error probable, or CEP^2). Intuitively, K, lethality, is a ratio, an area divided by an area, normalized to megatons. I am grateful to Theodore A. Postol for explaining this to me in an intuitive way. I thank Michael Chaitkin, Jane Esberg, Michael Kent, and Carmella Southward for excellent assistance in collecting, analyzing, and presenting the data in Figures 4.1 and 4.2.

4. See Lynn Eden, *Whole World on Fire: Organizations, Knowledge, and Nuclear Weapons Devastation* (Ithaca, NY: Cornell University Press, 2004); Alan Robock and Owen Brian Toon, "Local Nuclear War, Global Suffering," *Scientific American* 302, no. 1 (January 2010): 74–81.

5. To measure the ability to destroy specific targets, one uses *single-shot kill probabilities*; see Matthew G. McKinzie et al., *The U.S. Nuclear War Plan: A Time for Change* (Washington, DC: Natural Resources Defense Council, June 2001), pp. 42–45.

6. Fred Kaplan, "JFK's First-Strike Plan," *Atlantic* (October 2001), n.p.

7. Scott D. Sagan, "SIOP-62: The Nuclear War Plan Briefing to President Kennedy," *International Security* 12, no. 1 (Summer 1987): 26–28.

8. Carl Kaysen to General Maxwell Taylor, Military Representative to the President, "Strategic Air Planning and Berlin," 5 September 1961, Top Secret, excised copy, with cover memoranda to Joint Chiefs of Staff Chairman Lyman Lemnitzer, released to National Security Archive, pp. 2–3. Source: U.S. National Archives, Record Group 218, Records of the Joint Chiefs of Staff, Records of Maxwell Taylor, in "First Strike Options and the Berlin Crisis," September 1961, William Burr, ed., National Security Archive Electronic

Briefing Book No. 56 (25 September 2001), at http://www.gwu.edu/~nsarchiv/NSAEBB/NSAEBB56/.

9. See Rosenberg, "Origins of Overkill," p. 7; Headquarters, Strategic Air Command, History and Research Division, "History of the Joint Strategic Target Planning Staff: Preparation of SIOP-63 [effective 1 July 1962]," January 1964, Top Secret, excised copy, p. 14, in "New Evidence on the Origins of Overkill," in *The Nuclear Vault*, William Burr, ed., National Security Archive Electronic Briefing Book No. 236 (1 October 2009), at http://www.gwu.edu/~nsarchiv/nukevault/ebb236/index.htm.

10. Eden, *Whole World on Fire:* "census of . . . destruction," p. 107; "enumerated specific structures . . . routing and timing," pp. 32–24, 97, 108.

11. M. E. Hayes, Strategic Air Command Historical Staff, "History of the Strategic Target Planning Staff, SIOP-4 H/I, July 1970–June 1971," 6 January 1972, pp. 2, 3, at DoD FOIA online Reading Room, at http://www.dod.gov/pubs/foi/reading_room/467.pdf.

12. Rosenberg, "Origins of Overkill," p. 22 (emphasis added).

13. Not for attribution comment, Bellevue, Nebraska, 21 May 1987; Hans Kristensen, "Targets of Opportunity," *Bulletin of Atomic Scientists* (September/October 1997): 27.

14. Walton S. Moody, Strategic Air Command Historical Staff, "History of the Joint Strategic Target Planning Staff, SIOP-4 J/K, July 1971–June 1972," n.d., p. 21; Appendix "F," p. 69 (emphasis added), at DoD FOIA online Reading Room, at http://www.dod.gov/pubs/foi/reading_room/468.pdf.

15. Terry Terriff, *The Nixon Administration and the Making of U.S. Nuclear Strategy* (Ithaca, NY: Cornell University Press, 1995), pp. 133–34.

16. Janne E. Nolan, *Guardians of the Arsenal: The Politics of Nuclear Strategy* (New York: Basic Books, 1989), pp. 110–11, quoting from *Annual Defense Department Report for Fiscal 1978* (Washington, DC: GPO, 1977), p. 68.

17. Unattributed interview with Lynn Eden, Arlington, Virginia, 3 November 1987.

18. When academics were asked: Nolan, *Guardians of the Arsenal*, pp. 110–11; Michael Kennedy and Kevin N. Lewis, "On Keeping Them Down; or, Why Do Recovery Models Recover So Fast?" in *Strategic Nuclear Targeting*, Desmond Ball and Jeffrey Richelson, eds. (Ithaca, NY: Cornell University Press, 1986), pp. 195–96.

19. Scott D. Sagan, *Moving Targets: Nuclear Strategy and National Security* (Princeton: Princeton University Press, 1989), pp. 46–47 (emphasis added).

20. Nolan, *Guardians of the Arsenal*, pp. 134–35; Sagan, *Moving Targets*, pp. 50–53, quotation at p. 51.

21. Sagan, *Moving Targets*, p. 52.

22. Graham Spinardi, *From Polaris to Trident: The Development of US Fleet Ballistic Missile Technology* (Cambridge: Cambridge University Press, 1994), pp. 150–51.

23. On damage criteria, see Eden, *Whole World on Fire*, pp. 32–34; 288–89.

24. General Russell Dougherty (USAF, ret.), interview with Lynn Eden, McLean, Virginia, 30 October 1987.

25. See the excellent discussion of the algorithms of targeting in Theodore A. Postol, "Targeting," in *Managing Nuclear Operations*, John D. Steinbruner, Ashton B. Carter, and Charles A. Zracket, eds. (Washington, DC: Brookings Institution, 1987), pp. 379–80.

26. Vice Admiral Gerald E. Miller (USN, ret.), interview with Lynn Eden, Arlington, Virginia, 10 July 1989.

27. Ibid.

28. Ibid.

29. The argument for a very high PLS was made in what the Air Force called its "Minimum Risk Briefing," a briefing on what forces were required in order to "minimize risk" to the United States. Theodore A. Postol, conversations with Lynn Eden, Stanford, California, 8 February 1988, and 16 June 2009.

30. George J. Seiler, *Strategic Nuclear Force Requirements and Issues* (Air Power Research Institute, Maxwell Air Force Base, Alabama: Air University Press, 1983), pp. 60–61.

31. Air Force general, conversation with Lynn Eden, Bellevue, Nebraska, 20 May 1987. "Time dependent variable": Seiler, *Strategic Nuclear Force Requirements*, p. 60.

32. Bruce G. Blair, "Trapped in the Nuclear Math," op-ed, *New York Times*, 12 June 2000; see also Hans M. Kristensen, "Obama and the Nuclear War Plan," Federation of American Scientists Issue Brief, 25 February 2010.

33. "Critical war-making": Hans M. Kristensen, Robert S. Norris, and Ivan Oelrich, *From Counterforce to Minimal Deterrence: A New Nuclear Policy on the Path toward Eliminating Nuclear Weapons*, Federation of American Scientists and the Natural Resources Defense Council, Occasional Paper No. 7, April 2009, p. 9, also p. 22.

34. U.S. Department of Defense, *Nuclear Posture Review Report* (April, 2010), pp. 15, 30. Compare Gary Schaub, Jr. and James Forsyth, Jr., "An Arsenal We Can All Live With," *New York Times*, May 23, 2010.

35. See the "Gang of Four": George P. Shultz, William J. Perry, Henry A. Kissinger, and Sam Nunn, "A World Free of Nuclear Weapons," *Wall Street Journal*, 4 January 2007; Shultz et al., "Toward a Nuclear-Free World," *Wall Street Journal*, 15 January 2008.

36. "Punitive retaliation": Charles Glaser, *Analyzing Strategic Nuclear Policy* (Princeton: Princeton University Press, 1990), pp. 52–54; "minimum deterrence": Robert Jervis, *Psychology and Deterrence* (Baltimore, MD: Johns Hopkins University Press, 1985), p. 146; "existential deterrence": McGeorge Bundy, "The Bishops and the Bomb," review of *The Challenge of Peace: God's Promise and Our Response*, pastoral letter of the U.S. Bishops on War and Peace, *New York Review of Books* 30, no. 10 (16 June 1983): 4.

37. Committee on International Security and Arms Control, *Future of U.S. Nuclear Weapons Policy*, pp. 6–8.

38. On 1,000 weapons, see David Holloway, "Further Reductions in Nuclear Weapons," in *Reykjavik Revisited: Steps toward a World Free of Nuclear Weapons*, George P. Shultz, Steven P. Andreasson, Sidney D. Drell, and James E. Goodby, eds. (Stanford:

Hoover Institution Press, 2008), pp. 1–45; on 500 weapons, see Report of the International Commission on Nuclear Non-Proliferation and Disarmament, Gareth Evans and Yoriko Kawaguchi, cochairs, *Eliminating Nuclear Threats: A Practical Agenda for Global Policymakers* (15 December 2009); on 1,000 and then reductions to "roughly 300 nuclear weapons—of which at least 100 were secure, survivable, and deliverable," see Committee on International Security and Arms Control, *Future of U.S. Nuclear Weapons Policy*, pp. 76–78, quotation here on p. 80.

39. Thorough reassessment at 500: unattributed statement, Stanford University, 2 November 2009; creating "cooperative geopolitical conditions": International Commission on Nuclear Non-Proliferation and Disarmament, *Eliminating Nuclear Threats*, p. 205.

40. Thomas C. Schelling, "The Role of Deterrence in Total Disarmament," *Foreign Affairs* 40, no. 3 (April 1962): 392–406; Schelling, "A World without Nuclear Weapons?" *Daedalus* 138, no. 4 (Fall 2009): 124–29; Charles L. Glaser, "The Flawed Case for Nuclear Disarmament," *Survival* 40, no. 1 (Spring 1998): 112–28.

41. An early argument to this effect is Jonathan Schell, *The Fate of the Earth*, first published in 1982 and now available in Schell's *The Fate of the Earth and The Abolition* (Stanford: Stanford University Press, 2000).

42. Joseph C. Martz, "The United States' Nuclear Weapons Stockpile and Complex: Past, Present and Future," talk at Center for International Security and Cooperation, Stanford University, 10 November 2009.

43. Committee on International Security and Arms Control, *Future of U.S. Nuclear Weapons Policy*, p. 80.

44. Charles L. Glaser, "Nuclear Policy without an Adversary: U.S. Planning for the Post-Soviet Era," *International Security* 16, no. 4 (Spring, 1992): 52.

45. Kristensen et al., *From Counterforce to Minimal Deterrence*, pp. 31, 34, 41.

46. This assumes that an attack can be attributed; one cannot retaliate if one does not know whom to address.

5 Nuclear Deterrence, Disarmament, and Nonproliferation

Alexei G. Arbatov

Since the end of the Cold War, nuclear deterrence between Russia and the United States has receded into the background in terms of day-to-day foreign policy and official public relations.[1] Although both countries retain thousands of nuclear warheads, they have ceased to be global rivals, and the chances of a deliberate war between them have fallen close to zero. There are serious differences on some issues, such as Yugoslavia (1999), Iraq (2003), Russian domestic politics and their effect on elections in Ukraine (2004), the eastward expansion of the North Atlantic Treaty Organization (1999, 2003, and 2007), the war in Georgia (2008), a growing U.S. presence in several of the former Soviet republics, and the planned deployment of U.S. ballistic missile defense (BMD) sites in Europe.

Nonetheless, Moscow and Washington are no longer the leaders of two coalitions of states and political-ideological movements that had made bipolarity and severe rivalry the global norm in international relations for almost five decades. Their relations—despite continuous ups and downs, friction, disagreements, and mutual recrimination—include numerous and important areas of cooperation.

This cooperation has embraced various economic and political spheres: peacekeeping operations, resolution of regional conflicts, nonproliferation of weapons of mass destruction (WMD), the struggle against terrorism, joint ground and naval exercises, programs to secure and eliminate stockpiles of nuclear and chemical weapons, safe disposal of nuclear materials and decommissioned nuclear submarines, salvage operations at sea, and joint human space systems.

The legacy of the Cold War—mutual nuclear deterrence—is becoming less and less relevant as an instrument for dealing with post–Cold War international realities, threats, and risks. Eventually either nuclear deterrence will be abandoned, or the deterrence will lead to the collapse of international security through nuclear proliferation and actual use of nuclear weapons, either in combat, through an accident, or as a terrorist act.

POST–COLD WAR PARADOXES

Since the early 1990s, the United States and Russia (and in a more limited way, Britain and France unilaterally) have halved their deployed strategic nuclear forces in terms of nuclear reentry vehicles (warheads) under the 1991 Strategic Arms Reduction Treaty (START I), and are expected to reduce them by another 60 percent by 2012 under the 2002 Strategic Offensive Reduction Treaty (SORT) and a new START agreement. Combined with cuts in both sides' tactical nuclear arms, the reductions will apparently amount to more than 80 percent over the twenty-year period since the middle 1980s.

But there is the other side of the coin. The decade and a half that has elapsed since the end of the Cold War has demonstrated at least three great paradoxes in regard to nuclear weapons.

The first is that mutual nuclear deterrence between the United States and the Soviet Union (and now Russia) has quietly outlived the two states' global rivalry and confrontation, with which it was closely associated from 1945 to 1991, and which continued in its self-perpetuating momentum even after the collapse of one of the main subjects of deterrence—the Soviet superpower. These inexorable dynamics of mutual nuclear deterrence have acquired a growing and negative "feedback effect" on political relations between former opponents, sustaining a muted, though multifarious, fear: of the supposed evil intentions of the "strategic partner"; of inadvertent or accidental nuclear attack; of possible loss of control over nuclear weapons leading to their acquisition by rebel groups or terrorists; of the one's plans to gain control over the other's nuclear weapons or to deliver a disarming strike against nuclear sites—all this in the absence of any real political basis for suspecting such horrific scenarios or actions.

The second paradox is that, with the removal of the fear of escalation of any nuclear weapon use to a global catastrophe, the United States, Russia, and some other nuclear weapon states have become much more casual about contemplating initiation of the actual combat use of nuclear weapons in service to specific military missions. Thus, the end of the Cold War has actually lowered, not raised, the nuclear threshold, to say nothing of not bringing an end to nuclear warfare planning altogether.

During the George W. Bush administraton, Washington emphasized the right to launch preemptive selective nuclear strikes, thereby promoting a doctrine of actual nuclear warfare rather than of traditional nuclear deterrence. This example is being followed by Russia, although with some reservations and a variety of controversial official declarations. After a rather weak resistance, Moscow resigned itself to the Bush administration's lack of interest in arms control treaties. Instead, despite scarce funding, Russia unwisely is attempting to carry out a "balanced modernization" of all three legs of its nuclear triad (that is, air-, land-, and sea-based systems); shrinking from discussing tactical nuclear weapons; and seeking to make up for its setbacks through the export of civilian nuclear technologies and materials, as well as massive arms sales abroad.

As early as 1993, democratic Russia officially repudiated the no-first-use commitment made by the totalitarian Soviet Union in 1982. During 2000 and 2001 Moscow reconfirmed that position, and it now says that nuclear weapons play a leading role in ensuring Russian national security. Moscow even acknowledges the possibility of "a selective and limited combat use" of strategic nuclear weapons in order to "de-escalate the aggression."[2] This implies accomplishing specific tasks involved in conducting and terminating nuclear warfare, rather than merely deterring aggression through the capacity to inflict "devastating retaliation," as previously claimed by Soviet official military doctrine.

Not surprisingly, Great Britain, France, and China are not going to undertake any limitations of their nuclear forces through arms control treaties, alleging that they lag far behind the two major nuclear powers. Indeed, all three are implementing planned long-term modernizations and, in some weapon systems, a buildup of nuclear arsenals. Besides, Britain and France are elaborating limited nuclear strike options of their own.

Now, as never before, nuclear deterrence looks like the factor most likely to remain a permanent part of international relations, at least until a more devastating or efficient weapon is invented. Moreover, this posture is taken not because of the colossal technical or political difficulties of achieving "general and complete nuclear disarmament," but because of the presumably considerable "inherent advantages" of nuclear weapons as a means of sustaining national security and "civilizing" international relations.

Obviously, the Big Five (the United States, Russia, Great Britain, France, and

China) openly or tacitly treat nuclear deterrence as an indispensable and legitimate instrument of their security and military policies, even as they claim that other countries have no right to acquire nuclear weapons.

SMOOTH THEORY AND HARSH REALITY OF NUCLEAR DETERRENCE

It will never be proved with finality whether nuclear weapons and nuclear deterrence saved the world from a third world war during the Cold War decades. Fortunately history does not have a subjunctive mood. Certainly the USSR and the United States conducted their foreign policy and military actions abroad with much greater caution than otherwise might be the case, and avoided direct armed conflict.

There was only one example when the great powers came to the brink of war and after some maneuvering stepped back out of the horror of possible nuclear conflagration. This was the Cuban missile crisis of October 1962. However, the irony of that case was that the crisis was provoked by the very nuclear deterrence that is now portrayed by many as an insurance against nuclear war. Moscow had decided to secretly deploy medium range missiles in Cuba to catch up with the U.S. crash missile buildup of 1961–64, which was provoked by Nikita Khrushchev's bluff of Soviet missile superiority after the triumph of Sputnik in 1957. Hence, the "remedy" (nuclear deterrence) barely saved the world from the catastrophe provoked by the application of that very "remedy" (arms race within the context of nuclear deterrence).

Be that as it may, the realities of nuclear deterrence are much more frightening and controversial than it seems in peacetime, when nuclear deterrence is no more than a theoretical notion buried in the deep background of day-to-day international affairs. If a new crisis happens, which cannot be excluded and which may be much more difficult to resolve in multipolar and uncontrolled international affairs, deterrence may once again move to the foreground of practical politics and fail, with catastrophic consequences. A miniature reminder of such a possibility occurred during the August 2008 conflict in the Caucasus.

It is commonly assumed that the sense of nuclear deterrence is making nuclear weapons not tools for conducting war, but a political instrument, which guarantees that nuclear weapons will not be used in practice—neither within the context of a premeditated attack nor as a result of the escalation of a nonnuclear conflict between nuclear nations. Now, in the sixth decade of the nuclear era, this circumstance is seen as being perfectly natural. Some even talk about the "civilizing" effect of nuclear weapons on politicians and the military and on international politics. However, the reality of nuclear deterrence is much more controversial, because there is no clear watershed between nuclear deterrence and nuclear war-fighting.

Even the most destructive strategic nuclear forces carry out their political mission of deterrence specifically through their ability to carry out assigned combat missions—that is, destroy certain targets—and nothing else. These missions are embodied in operational plans, target lists, and flight programs loaded into ballistic and cruise missiles' onboard computers. These operational plans provide for the use of weapons with varying degrees of expected effectiveness in a first strike, a launch-on-warning (LOW) strike, a launch-under-attack (LUA) strike, or delayed retaliatory second strike. These options envision massive salvos, limited groupings, or even single missile nuclear strikes at various combinations of states and targets.

The "gray area" of no clear distinction between the concepts of deterring and waging nuclear war relates even more to operational-tactical and tactical nuclear systems (TNW) than is the case with strategic forces. Since TNW are viewed as means to promote success in a theater or at the battlefield level more rapidly or to offset an enemy's superiority in conventional forces, it is nearly impossible to draw a distinction between deterrence and war-fighting.

Moreover, the division of nuclear weapons into strategic and tactical categories is also quite conditional. For the USSR/Russia, American forward-based systems in Europe have always been equated to strategic weapons, since from their forward bases they can reach deep into the territory of the USSR/Russia. For Eastern Europe and Russian neighbors in Asia, in turn, Russia's tactical nuclear weapons are also seen as equivalent to strategic weapons, both in operational range and destructive consequences of their use.

Still more dangerous is the so-called hair-trigger nuclear posture, associated with weapons that must be launched quickly upon receiving information about an opponent's attack in order to avoid destruction on the ground. Altogether there are now probably about 2,000 nuclear warheads on hair-trigger alert in line with LOW/LUA concepts and operational plans: most of the U.S. and Russian ICBMs, and the Russian SLBMs on submarines at bases.

With ICBM flight time being about 30 minutes and SLBM about 15 to 20 minutes, these concepts provide political leaders with a decision-making time of only 4 to 8 minutes (subtracting the time of missile attack detection and confirmation, and the time for the response launch sequence and fly-away). And this time would be available only if the leaders are safe and ready, and everything works perfectly according to planned procedures. Besides, the leaders will have to operate under enormous stress, receiving controversial intelligence information and the on-duty officers' interpretation of data from early warning systems. On top of all this, there is no difference between the upgrading of the alert status of strategic forces for the first (preemptive) or the second (retaliatory) strike. Operations officers would most probably interpret the actions of the other side in the most conservative way, and they would hardly have either the time or authority to educate political leaders on the details and possible misperceptions of strategic forces' crisis activities.

No doubt, maintaining several thousand nuclear warheads on hair-trigger alert is the ultimate absurdity of nuclear deterrence twenty years after the end of the Cold War, when political, economic, and security relations, at least among the P5 (the five permanent members of the UN Security Council), render deliberate nuclear attack virtually unthinkable. Moreover, it was and remains extremely dangerous. During the Cold War years there were dozens of false alarms on both sides, and the fact that nuclear war did not erupt out of a technical malfunction or a decision-maker's miscalculation should be to an important degree attributed to sheer luck.

Nowadays a number of new dangers are contributing to such a catastrophic possibility. Proliferation of nuclear weapons and ballistic missiles to an expanding number of states with inadequate negative control makes unauthorized or deliberate provocative launch of a missile much more probable and threatening as a trigger of massive nuclear exchange. Of special concern is the proliferation of long-range cruise missiles and sea-based ballistic and cruise missiles, which are capable of delivering an anonymous strike. Some new nuclear states are politically unstable, and a launch of nuclear weapons may happen there as a result of civil war, putsch, or a contest among rival groups or between political and civilian leaders for control over nuclear weapons. As a result of nuclear proliferation there is a growing danger of terrorists getting access to nuclear materials or weapons. A terrorist nuclear explosion in one or several capitals might provoke a spontaneous nuclear exchange by great powers' forces on hair-trigger alert.

DISINTEGRATION OF ARMS CONTROL

The third paradox is that with the end of the Cold War, the focus has been on doing away with nuclear arms limitations and reductions, transparency, and confidence building, rather than doing away with nuclear deterrence and eventually the nuclear weapons themselves. The victims of this process (primarily at the initiative of U.S. policy makers of 2001–8) already include the ABM treaty, START II, and the START III Framework Treaty, an Agreement on delineation between strategic and tactical BMD systems of 1997, as well as the entry into force of the Comprehensive Test Ban Treaty (CTBT), and negotiations on the Fissile Material Cut-off Treaty (FMCT). Emulating U.S. policy, Russia suspended its adherence to the Treaty on Conventional Force Reduction in Europe (CFE) in 2007 and threatened to withdraw from the Intermediate Nuclear Forces and Short Range Nuclear Forces Elimination Treaty of 1987, if the U.S. plan of deploying ballistic missile defense sites in Europe were to be implemented. Potentially, even the Nuclear Non-Proliferation Treaty (NPT) might fall apart—at least that is how it looked from the results of a disastrous NPT Review Conference of May 2005. The whole structure of nuclear arms control is collapsing, with most dire predictable consequences from the growth of new threats and risks.

The new beginning of a nuclear free world, started by the article of four respected American former state figures and later supported by the new U.S. administration of Barack Obama, has been a promising change, but it is yet to be substantiated by practical policy.

HOW RELEVANT IS NUCLEAR DETERRENCE?

Of the main reasons why nuclear deterrence should be superseded by some type of constructive strategic relationship between the United States and Russia, and eventually among all nuclear weapon states, the first is nuclear deterrence's irrelevance to the real threats and challenges of the post–Cold War era.

Deterrence remains effective against the least probable or nonexistent threats: nuclear or massive conventional attacks by great powers (and their alliances) against each other. But it does not work against the new real and present dangers, such as nuclear proliferation, international terrorism, ethnic and religious conflicts, drug and arms trafficking, transborder crime, and illegal migration, to say nothing of climate warming and world economic crisis. It has been a highly debatable point—whether nuclear disarmament could prevent nuclear proliferation in the past or might do it in the future. It is certain, however, that nuclear deterrence cannot stop proliferation, and it is quite probable that deterrence encourages further expansion of the "nuclear club."

The second reason for replacing deterrence with a new strategic relationship is that the relations involved in mutual nuclear deterrence place tangible limitations on the ability of great powers to cooperate genuinely in dealing with new threats and challenges. The degree of cooperation during Cold War times, when most arms control treaties, including the Nuclear Non-Proliferation Treaty, were concluded, is not enough for the new era. Such endeavors—cooperation between the leading states' secret services and special forces, joint counterproliferation policies (for example, Russian participation in the Proliferation Security Initiative, and the envisioned actual U.S.-Russian combat operations against terrorists and rogue and failed states), officially initiated joint early missile launch warning and BMD systems—virtually imply a common security alliance of a new type. Much stricter nuclear and missile export control regimes, greater emphasis on securing and accounting for nuclear warheads and nuclear materials (which implies broad transparency and access to each other's secret sites), verifiable cessation of production of weapons-grade nuclear materials throughout the world, common policy on internationalization of nuclear fuel cycle facilities, and ambitious Global Partnership projects—all these require a greater magnitude of trust and cooperation among partner states.

But all of these are impossible to imagine while the United States and Russia still aim thousands of nuclear warheads at each other, keep missiles on hair-trigger alert, and modernize nuclear forces to preserve devastating retaliatory capabilities against each other. Besides, as was mentioned above, the momentum of nuclear deterrence, in combination with new threats and missions and technological developments, may destabilize strategic relations among the great powers, further undercutting their ability to think and act together.

The current crisis over the Iranian nuclear program, despite the apparent similarity of the U.S. and Russian positions, provides a good illustration of this point. Neither the United States nor Russia wants Iran to have uranium enrichment or plutonium reprocessing capabilities, to say nothing of Teheran's potential acquisition of nuclear weapons. However, action in the form of United Nations Security Council sanctions against Iran, or a UN authorization of the use of military force, is where U.S.-Russian unanimity stops. For the United States, the prospect of eventually being targeted by Iranian nuclear missiles is totally unbearable and warrants all means of prevention. For all conservative Russians, the dire political, economic, and security implications of supporting (even if passively) UN sanctions or U.S. military action against Iran—Russia's long-standing partner—may be seen as too high a price to pay. After all, as hard-liners would point out, Russia is already targeted by thousands of U.S. nuclear weapons, as well as by the nuclear weapons of American allies and partners (Britain, France, Israel, and Pakistan). A nuclear-armed Iran would not add much to this picture, and it probably would target its missiles elsewhere anyway.

The prospect of Iranian nuclear materials or weapons being leaked to Islamic terrorist organizations is much more frightening. However, Russian hawks would claim that this is a hypothetical scenario, while actual transactions of that kind might have been already attempted or done through A. Q. Khan's black market connections with the Taliban, al Qaeda, and Iran—without ensuing aggressive U.S. attempts to investigate and prosecute the case. Apparently this benign position was motivated by Washington's desire not to destabilize its partner regime in Pakistan, which is important for other American interests. As for Russia, the majority of its political-strategic elite would not support sacrificing cooperation with its partner regime in Iran, which is likewise important for many Russian interests, in favor of cooperation with the United States, particularly in view of the state of U.S.-Russian strategic relations.

The third reason for initiating a new strategic relationship in place of mutual nuclear deterrence is the problem of resource allocation. In annual defense budgets the allocations for nuclear weapons are relatively small (10–15 percent).[3] But the costs of the whole 20- to 30-year service life cycle of strategic systems (R&D, procurement, deployment, maintenance, and eventual dismantling and utilization) are staggering. Sustaining nuclear deterrence at current levels, or even at reduced levels (such as the 1,550 deployed warheads called for under the New START treaty), is an expensive luxury, given that the two biggest powers assign the bulk of these forces the mission of destroying each other, as well as serving "as a hedge against future uncertainty." This aimless "hedge" may be relatively inexpensive for the United States, which has the largest overall defense budget in the world (about as big as the sum of all military spending by the other major powers), and which fully modernized its strategic nuclear force during the 1980s and 1990s, investing in "strategic capital" that will last for decades into the future. Still, even for the United States it would be easy to find a much better allocation for these resources, whether within its defense budget or outside it, in particular in times of harsh economic crisis.

The burden of maintaining robust nuclear deterrence is much heavier for Russia, which is now implementing a "balanced modernization" of all elements of its strategic triad and planning to keep up with the New START treaty ceilings. Faced with a severe deficiency of appropriations for an expensive military reform, as well as modernization and restructuring of its conventional forces,

Russia nonetheless has to spend huge sums on nuclear weapons. The budget share for nuclear deterrence is relatively still bigger for France, Britain, and China.

By maintaining mutual nuclear deterrence, the great powers are wasting resources that otherwise could be applied to more appropriate military and security tasks and missions. Moreover, significant scientific and technical intellectual resources are tied up by nuclear deterrence. Powerful state, business, research, and political organizations are locked into sustaining nuclear confrontation in economic, technical, and mental respects, instead of addressing the more realistic and urgent needs of national and international security.

TRANSFORMING NUCLEAR DETERRENCE

There are three principal routes for doing away with mutual nuclear deterrence, at least as a principal operational mode of U.S.-Russian military relationship.

The first of the three avenues toward the end of nuclear deterrence is to further reduce and "de-alert" Russian and American strategic nuclear forces. The second is to develop and deploy a joint ballistic missile early warning system and a missile proliferation monitoring system. The third is to develop and deploy joint BMD systems. Initially, the second and third avenues might be limited to nuclear and missile proliferation threats, but eventually—in parallel with transformation of the nuclear forces of both sides—they could embrace a growing part of the strategic assets of the two powers and their allies, and thus would transform their present mutual nuclear deterrence into a qualitatively new type of strategic relationship.

This new relationship could be called "strategic nuclear partnership," "cooperative nuclear weapons policies," "a common nuclear security framework," "a mutual nuclear insurance [or assurance] strategy," or any number of other names, depending on one's tastes and semantic skills. In any case, the main problem is not the term, but the substance.

The first two steps on this long way are the ratification of CTBT by the United States, China, and other nations, without which the treaty cannot enter force, and successful ratification of the New START treaty by the United States and Russia to replace START I, which expired in December 2009.

After a decade of mockery and neglect, nuclear disarmament has returned to U.S.-Russian and other nuclear powers' official documents and political commitments. This was due to the famous article by four respected Ameri-

can statesmen in favor of moving toward a nuclear-free world. The change of administration in Washington and President Barack Obama's commitment to this idea have made nuclear disarmament once again a subject of practical diplomacy.

The new U.S. president promised to achieve the ratification of CTBT. In the spring of 2010, Washington and Moscow signed the New START treaty, which envisions reductions in the number of operationally deployed strategic delivery vehicles to 700 and of warheads to 1,550 for each side. However, besides the problems of ratification which the new treaty met in the U.S. Senate, a number of issues remain disturbing for Russia, and they may reappear in the negotiations for a follow-on to New START. One is the future of the U.S. BMD deployment plan, in particular in Europe. The first stages of deployment on ships in the Mediterranean, Rumania, and Bulgaria pose no serious challenge to Russia's deterrence. However, there is no U.S. commitment to limit or coordinate with Moscow further deployments in any clear way, while Russia has to plan its strategic forces and arms control policies ten to fifteen years in advance. Other problems are the U.S. insistence on counting strategic warheads by their actual (operational) deployment, instead of maximum missile and bomber loadings, as in START I. Also, a growing concern of Moscow is the American deployment of thousands of strategic (long-range) air-launched and sea-launched cruise missiles and dozens of ballistic missiles with conventional precision-guided warheads on heavy bombers and submarines, capable of a counterforce strike at opponents' strategic forces.

In contrast to President Obama's call for a nuclear-free world, the practical policy of the United States for the first disarmament step is quite conservative, to say nothing of the open opposition of a part of the American political elite to New START. The Pentagon wishes to implement most of the New START reductions through removal of some MIRV warheads from missiles to storage, and by conversion of many strategic weapons for delivering conventional munitions. The first would leave the United States with a big reconstitution potential (the possibility of returning warheads from storage to missiles), and the second with a new conventional counterforce capability. Both are quite disturbing for Moscow.

Despite all general reservations about nuclear disarmament, Russia has been gradually becoming more receptive to the idea of further nuclear disarmament. On the other hand, Russia is reluctant to commit itself to much deeper reductions after the New START, in view of U.S./NATO advantages in BMD technol-

ogies and conventional weapon systems and forces, the potential threat from other nuclear weapon states (all eight of which have weapons that can reach Russian territory), and American space support and potential strike capabilities, as embodied in the Prompt Global Strike concept and systems.

If these obstacles are overcome, the process of nuclear disarmament will gain momentum and, eventually, involve other nuclear states and address the problems of tactical nuclear weapons, nuclear weapons in storage, fissile materials production and stocks, as well as numerous interacting military, political, and economic problems.

We may hope that, in the long run, nuclear disarmament will do away with nuclear deterrence, which would permit stopping and reversing nuclear proliferation. It goes without saying that this would be a long and difficult process. A future nuclear-free world cannot be just the present world minus nuclear weapons. It would have to be a very different world, not free only from nuclear weapons but also from weapons based on new physical principles, from large conventional wars, and from any arbitrary use of force by strong nations against weak ones. All in all it will have to be a world with a very different system of international security. But wouldn't it be better to strive for a new foundation of international security instead of the mutual capacity of states to kill in several hours dozens of millions of each other's citizens?

NOTES

1. This essay draws on earlier work done with Vladimir Dvorkin published in *Beyond Nuclear Deterrence* (Washington DC: Carnegie Endowment for International Peace, 2006).

2. *Aktualnye zadachi razvitia Vooruzhennykh Sil Rossiyskoi Federatsii* [Urgent tasks of the armed forces of the Russian Federation] (Moscow, 2003), pp. 41–42.

3. http://www.whitehouse.gov/omb/budget/fy2010/assets/summary.pdf.

6 British Thinking on Nuclear Weapons

Ian Anthony

INTRODUCTION

It is an interesting time to assess British attitudes toward nuclear weapons, since it appears that something is afoot in Westminster, at least in regard to UK positions on nuclear arms control. Senior British political figures made major speeches calling for nuclear disarmament in each of the years 2007, 2008, and 2009.

In 2007, speaking at a conference in the United States, the foreign secretary at that time, Margaret Beckett, called for a new disarmament initiative based on two separate but mutually reinforcing elements: vision (by which she meant a scenario for a world free of nuclear weapons), and action (by which she meant progressive steps to reduce warhead numbers and limit the role of nuclear weapons in security policy).[1]

Addressing the Conference on Disarmament in Geneva in February 2008, former secretary of state for defense Des Browne said that "the international community needs a transparent, sustainable and credible plan for multilateral nuclear disarmament."[2]

In March 2009 Prime Minister Gordon Brown included a call for a serious commitment to disarmament by nuclear weapon states in his speech to a conference on the international nuclear fuel cycle in London.[3] In his speech Brown promised to publish a credible road map toward disarmament by all the nuclear weapon states, through measures that will command the confidence of all the non-nuclear weapon states, in the summer of 2009. In July 2009 the UK published a document called "The Road to 2010," containing what the prime minister called "an ambitious but achievable set of reforms across the entire nuclear question" intended to "re-invigorate the bargain at the heart of the Nuclear Non-Proliferation Treaty."[4]

As recently as December 2006—six months before the speech by Margaret Beckett—the UK published the result of a major policy review focused on the future of the British nuclear capability. The main conclusion was that under present circumstances it was necessary for the UK to retain "the minimum nuclear deterrent capability necessary to provide effective deterrence." To that end, the UK has put in place the first elements of a program to sustain national nuclear forces for the indefinite future by preparing the ground for a decision to build a new class of submarines to carry nuclear-tipped ballistic missiles and by revitalizing the scientific and engineering capacities of the atomic weapon research establishment. Speaking at the 2009 summit meeting of the G8 industrialized powers, Prime Minister Brown emphasized that there was no need to adjust the current UK plans to modernize nuclear forces at present, stating that "we have to show that we can deal with this by collective action. Unilateral action by the UK would not be seen as the best way forward."[5]

In June 2009 the leader of one mainstream UK political party, the Liberal Democrats, indicated that he would not support renewing Britain's nuclear deterrent with an equivalent modernized system should his party form the next government.[6] Although it seemed extremely unlikely at the time that the Liberal Democrats would come to power, following the May 2010 election they joined in a coalition government with the Conservative Party. A strategic defense review was announced immediately, but nuclear weapons were not on the table. On publication in October 2010, *Securing Britain in an Age of Uncertainty: The Strategic and Defense Security Review*,[7] had to take into account a difficult context. The government has to examine defense policy against a background of reduced resources, extensive commitments, and a current approach that does not adequately explain how the present UK force posture and operations by UK armed forces support national security. If there is a threat to maintaining the independent UK deterrent it might come from the combination of financial pressure and what Cornish and Dorman call "campaign tribalism"—the tendency to shape medium- and long-term decisions about force posture based on the short-term needs of current operations.[8]

The UK government takes a long-term and incremental approach to nuclear disarmament, and does not see any inconsistency in making the political case for arms reductions and developing specific proposals intended to further that objective while still modernizing national nuclear forces.

It is legitimate to ask whether recent public diplomacy signals a change in approach in thinking about the role of nuclear weapons or whether it is aimed at heading off national and international criticism of what is essentially continuity in nuclear policy.

BRITISH NUCLEAR POLICY AND FORCE POSTURE

The framing of nuclear policy would logically have become more complicated with the passage of time after the end of the Cold War. Even within the framework of deterrence it would have been necessary to reconsider the threats to which a nuclear deterrent might apply and to ensure that the threat to use nuclear weapons in any identified contingency (however remote) remains credible in the mind of any potential adversary. However, from what can be seen in public documents, recent reviews have not engaged in detail with the issue of what role nuclear deterrence should play in British security and defense policy. Instead of an explicit rationale, nuclear policy has been based more on a widely held and essentially unchallenged assumption that possessing nuclear weapons must confer some benefit in an uncertain world.

The end of the Cold War could have been a watershed in British thinking about nuclear weapons because the rationale for maintaining a nuclear deterrent was exclusively put forward in terms of the threat from a nuclear-armed Soviet Union. The official report on which the 1980 decision to modernize British nuclear weapons was based used an intelligence assessment that nuclear planning need take into account only the nuclear threat posed by the Soviet Union.[9]

The decisive argument in favor of an independent nuclear capability was the need to maintain a second center of decision-making in Europe in order to create uncertainty in the mind of Soviet military planners. According to this line of thinking, any Soviet planners who doubted whether the United States would in reality use nuclear weapons in defense of European allies would have to take into account the risk that in extreme circumstances the UK could launch a nuclear strike in defense of its own vital interests.

The use of British nuclear weapons could have been either strategic or substrategic. For the British the substrategic use of nuclear weapons in the Cold War context would have been for purposes of war termination once hostilities with the Soviet Union had broken out. Nuclear weapons could have been used, as Michael Quinlan has put it, to transmit to the enemy "the political message that he had underrated NATO's resolve and that for his own survival he must back off.[10]

In a strategic sense, the function of nuclear weapons during the Cold War was war avoidance. From a British point of view, the general line of thinking was expressed by Michael Howard in a 1964 lecture when he noted that

> those Powers which possess sufficient wealth, scientific expertise and industrial capacity have developed weapons systems which poise the threat of inescapable and unacceptable destruction over the heads of their rivals even in time of deepest peace; and for nations so threatened military security can no longer be based on traditional principles of defence, mobilization and counter-attack. It can be based only on the capacity to deter one's adversary by having available the capacity to inflict on him inescapable and unacceptable damage in return.[11]

The critical parameter for "inescapable and unacceptable damage" in UK planning was to retain the technical capability to destroy completely a target in the Soviet Union of central importance to Russian decision-makers—normally believed to be Moscow.

In the early 1990s UK decision-makers were very reserved in modifying this rationale for retention of nuclear weapons, for example by ascribing them a role in deterring "new threats" of the kind suggested by the discovery of the full extent of Iraq's illegal nuclear weapon program. Speaking in 1993, Minister of Defence Malcolm Rifkind argued that, once outside the existing bilateral East-West framework, "it is difficult to be confident that an intended deterrent would work in the way intended, in the absence of an established nuclear deterrent relationship."[12]

At the same time, the Cold War ended at the point where the UK was just about to begin deployment of its new submarine-based nuclear deterrent (the Vanguard Class submarines armed with Trident D5 missiles tipped with a British-designed warhead believed to be adapted from the U.S. W76 warhead).[13] Thus, at the point where the rationale of an independent nuclear deterrent might have been questioned, the financial burden of acquisition had already been absorbed and the anticipated running costs for the Trident force were rather low (probably around $1 billion per year).

This does not mean that nuclear posture went unchanged. On the contrary, UK nuclear forces were extensively rationalized and streamlined as a result of decisions taken after the end of the Cold War. In the early 1990s the UK nuclear forces were not limited to submarine-launched nuclear-tipped missiles. At that time artillery regiments of the British Army were trained in the use of Lance missiles and nuclear-capable 155-millimeter field guns—delivery systems that would have been supplied with nuclear weapons by the U.S. Army for use on the battlefield in certain contingencies. After 1992 the UK participation in these sharing arrangements was ended in the context of the September 1991 U.S. Presidential Nuclear Initiative (PNI) under which George H. W. Bush pledged to withdraw all ground-launched short-range nuclear weapons deployed overseas and destroy them along with existing U.S. stockpiles of the same weapons.

The Bush PNI went further and promised to end the deployment of tactical nuclear weapons on surface ships, attack submarines, and land-based naval aircraft under normal circumstances. Shortly afterward the United Kingdom decided to eliminate all maritime nuclear capability other than Trident, so that the capability of Royal Navy surface ships to carry or deploy nuclear weapons (in the form of nuclear depth charges to be used against submarines) was removed. The Royal Air Force owned several hundred WE177 gravity bombs for delivery by Tornado bombers, and a decision was taken to phase out all UK air-launched nuclear weapons. In 1993 the UK cancelled plans to develop a nuclear-armed air-launched cruise missile, and the nuclear mission was finally taken away from the dual-capable Tornado bombers in 1998.

At the same time, the UK determined that there was still a need for a substrategic nuclear capability, and in future this task would necessarily be allocated to Trident—as the only British nuclear system available.[14] From the mid-1990s UK submarines were armed with a mix of some Trident missiles with multiple warheads and some with only one "live" warhead. Moreover, it was decided that those warheads to which a substrategic role was ascribed would be configured to allow for an explosive yield significantly lower than the 80 to 100 kilotons believed to be the norm for each UK Trident warhead.

The rationalization of nuclear systems led to a decrease in the number of UK nuclear warheads from roughly 450 during the 1980s to approximately 225 by 2010.[15] Taking into account U.S. nuclear weapons earmarked under sharing arrangements, UK nuclear forces are said to have been reduced by 75 percent since the end of the Cold War.

The UK decision to rationalize and reduce nuclear forces was taken in the context of a change in NATO thinking about the role assigned to nuclear weapons. The nuclear sharing arrangements involving British armed forces were obviously keyed to Alliance contingencies, while half of the roughly 100 British nuclear-capable Tornado bombers were based at RAF Bruggen in Germany.

The next chronological "decision point" for nuclear weapons policy occurred after the change of government in 1997 that brought the Labour Party into power, led by Tony Blair. While the incoming government was committed to carry out a Strategic Defence Review, the terms of reference for the 1998 review were dictated by the determination of the Labour government to implement election manifesto pledges. During the election campaign, Labour made a commitment to maintain a national nuclear deterrent in order to reduce a political vulnerability that had plagued the Labour Party in previous election campaigns. Therefore, the working groups set up to conduct the defense review limited themselves to considering how existing nuclear capabilities and support could be adjusted to meet Britain's needs in the changed strategic environment. Given the rationalization and reduction of UK nuclear forces already noted above, in 1998 there was only scope for further trimming of the Trident force. To that end it was announced that each submarine on deterrent patrol would in future carry no more than forty-eight warheads (as opposed to the capacity of ninety-six) and that no more Trident missiles would be bought beyond those already delivered or on order.[16]

The 2003 Defence White Paper (the first after the terrorist attacks of September 2001) did not contain any change to nuclear policy or force posture, but did highlight the need "to be prepared to prevent, deter, coerce, disrupt or destroy international terrorists or the regimes that harbor them and to counter terrorists' efforts to acquire chemical, biological, radiological and nuclear weapons."[17]

The Labour Party election manifesto in 2005 included a commitment to retain an independent nuclear deterrent, and on re-election the government began to consider the options for replacing the Trident system. The future of the British nuclear weapons establishment was one area of concern. Michael Clarke has noted that the workforce within the atomic weapons research establishment of the UK was shrinking and aging to the point that "as engineers retire and leave the workforce it is not clear that the essential skills will still exist after 2010 without a specific design programme on which to work."[18] One of the first decisions made by the new government in 2005 was to allocate roughly £1 billion to refurbish the atomic weapons research establishment at Aldermaston and recruit a new generation of scientists and engineers.[19]

In this political environment the decisions about when and how to modernize strategic nuclear forces have been driven primarily by technical factors. For planning purposes officials have worked on the assumption that the normal lifecycle of the strategic nuclear weapons in the British arsenal was expected to be around twenty-five to thirty years, and roughly fifteen years has been estimated as the lead-time needed to design and build the first replacement submarine. Applying these rules of thumb meant that a first replacement for the Vanguard Class submarine would be expected to enter into service around 2023 and, counting back from that date, a decision to begin the process would be needed around 2008.[20]

In 2005–6 the government established an Official Group on the Future of the Deterrent to prepare a decision on how to sustain the UK deterrent over the period 2020–50. The group considered four generic options for a replacement to the Trident system, and concluded that the most sensible would be a new generation of submarines equipped with Trident ballistic missiles. The work of this group led to a government decision, published in a white paper in December 2006, to build a new class of submarines and to participate in the U.S. life extension program for the Trident D5 missile.[21] In February 2010 the government published a discussion document laying out the elements of a future defense review. In that document "the provision of an operationally independent strategic nuclear capability, including its protection" was included as a defense planning assumption.[22]

Following the May election, the new coalition government decided to retain and renew the independent nuclear deterrent but, citing the need to obtain value for money, reduced the number of operational launch tubes planned for each submarine from twelve to eight, and the number of warheads carried by each submarine from forty-eight to forty.[23]

On November 2, 2010, the British and French governments signed a path-breaking treaty on collaboration in the technology associated with nuclear stockpile stewardship.[24] Under the terms of the treaty the UK and France would construct and operate two facilities, one in each country, by 2015. According to the Treaty, French and British scientists will cooperate, including through the exchange of relevant classified information, on the safety and security of nuclear weapons; nuclear warhead stockpile certification; and countering nuclear or radiological terrorism.[25] The program of work at the facilities will measure the performance of relevant materials at extremes of temperature and pressure, allowing the scientists to model the performance and safety of British and French nuclear weapons without carrying out nuclear explosive tests—which are illegal under the CTBT that both France and the UK have ratified.

The Treaty does not require cooperation on substantive aspects of the work program (though cooperation is not excluded), but facilitates independent work needed for national programs in a safe and security environment at the lowest cost. Under the terms of the Treaty both joint facilities must include the necessary features to guarantee the security of national information and operations. In the statement accompanying the signature of the Treaty, the UK Minister of Defence underlined that nothing in the agreement with France in any way weakened British nuclear cooperation with the United States.

BRITISH THINKING ABOUT THE ROLE OF NUCLEAR WEAPONS

The previous section has underlined that the British nuclear force structure has changed very significantly in the past twenty years. However, while the question of "what" is available in terms of nuclear forces can largely be answered using official public documents, it is more difficult to answer the questions "why" and "how" weapons might be used from the same sources. To what extent has thinking evolved about the military contingencies in which nuclear weapons might have to be used? Is there evidence of a change in the nuclear mission?

There appears to have been relatively little discussion of the nuclear dimension of strategic issues since the early 1990s. There has certainly been little emphasis on initiating a wider public debate on nuclear weapon issues other than the need to prevent further proliferation. As noted by Michael Quinlan in 2006,

> Government ministers, while giving several indications of a disposition towards continuance, have declared the government's readiness for full and open debate—by implication, in advance of a firm decision rather than, as in 1980, in examination and defence of a decision taken. It has as yet, however (at the time of writing), neither entered debate in any substantial degree nor provided much information to sustain that debate knowledgeably.[26]

In June 2008 four senior political figures published a newspaper article intended to stimulate discussion and debate in the United Kingdom around options for nuclear arms control. Subsequently the issue of nuclear arms control has been taken up by a cross-party group of sixteen senior parliamentarians.[27]

Senior politicians in the Labour Party remain committed to maintaining nuclear forces primarily on the grounds that giving up the national nuclear deterrent would give domestic political opponents an argument to be deployed in a general election. Thinking in the Conservative Party is also normally described essentially in terms of domestic politics. As one veteran commentator on military affairs put it in 2009, "The Tories are most unlikely to make waves about Trident ahead of an election, because they see no votes in it. If [then party leader] David Cameron committed himself to dumping the deterrent, he would merely provoke a gratuitous and possibly fatal party split."[28]

It is widely believed that the current nuclear force is as small as it can be without giving up the requirement that nuclear weapons will be available for use on a permanent basis. As noted above, the submarine platform and ballistic missile delivery system are widely agreed to be the best way of reducing vulnerability to a disarming strike and ensuring a relatively secure second-strike capability.[29]

As a result, decisions have been driven mainly by technical questions about replacing equipment as it becomes old and sustaining a minimum deterrent at the lowest cost. Issues related to nuclear weapons do not appear to impinge greatly, if at all, on British thinking about how military force can and should be applied after the end of the Cold War. Arguments in official documents have been put forward in general terms.

The *National Security Strategy of the United Kingdom*, published in 2008, included the judgment that

> no state currently has both the intent and the capability to pose a direct nuclear threat to the United Kingdom or its vital interests. But we cannot rule out the risk that such a threat will re-emerge over future decades. We also monitor: the possibility of nuclear weapons or material or technology (including commercial) falling into the hands of terrorists, who we know have ambitions to acquire it; and the proliferation of the technology behind ballistic missiles, which increases the chance of either new states or non-state actors being able to threaten the United Kingdom directly in the future.

Consequently, the maintenance of the UK nuclear deterrent is explained as necessary because "we cannot rule out a nuclear threat to the United Kingdom re-emerging over the next 50 years."[30] No specific rationale is put forward and no information is supplied about how nuclear weapons might be employed to enhance UK security.

During the Cold War great effort was put into minimizing any risk that the armed forces of the two adversarial blocs would confront each other or engage in military operations in close proximity to one another partly because any risk, however small, that escalation could lead to a nuclear conflagration was unacceptable. The critical threshold was between peace and war because of a lack of certainty over whether and when other thresholds (between conventional and nuclear weapon use, and between battlefield use of nuclear weapons and attacks on cities in the homeland of nuclear weapon states) would be crossed.[31] On occasions where confrontations did occur, even if by proxy, the two main adversaries went out of their way to reduce the possibility for escalation or misunderstanding by ensuring communication with each other and among their respective allies and partners.

With the end of the Cold War the very cautious approach to the use of force and high emphasis on deterrence has progressively given way to a different kind of discourse. The use of force has come to be seen as a tool to be used actively to promote beneficial outcomes (that is, beneficial to the user), rather than a last resort to be employed only in the most extreme circumstances. Beginning in 1991, with the use of a large multinational coalition to expel Iraqi forces from Kuwait under the banner of the United Nations, peace operations became both more frequent and more varied. Subsequently, the line between peace operations and other forms of use of force were blurred, first in 1999 in the Western Balkans and then in 2003 in the Persian Gulf.

Current UK military planning is predicated on being prepared for operations outside the Euro-Atlantic area, sometimes under a United Nations mandate and sometimes as part of a looser U.S.-led coalition of states. Looking out to 2030, the Joint Doctrine and Concepts Centre (JDCC) within the UK Ministry of Defence forecasts that

> international law will remain subject to interpretation, with the most powerful Western states providing the will and the means to enforce international law on behalf of the "international community." Other states, in particular the least developed and non-state actors, may refuse to comply with its strictures and may increasingly contest claims that the West equates to the "international community." International law will become increasingly permissive about when outside force can be used to intervene in a nation's domestic affairs, if there are strong humanitarian grounds for that intervention.[32]

The thinking of the JDCC was perhaps influenced by what was seen as a successful intervention in Sierra Leone in 2000 when British forces rapidly broke the resistance of the irregular forces of the Revolutionary United Front that had humiliated UN peacekeeping forces and defeated the forces of the government of Sierra Leone. British forces were then able to withdraw after an operation that lasted less than two years.

While the UK has developed a capability for operations against a range of nonstate actors, thinking is based heavily on operating alongside the United States in other contingencies. The 2003 Defence White Paper noted that

> expeditionary operations, involving intervention against state adversaries, can only plausibly be conducted if US forces are engaged, either leading a coalition or in NATO. Where the UK chooses to be engaged, we will wish to be able to influence political and military decision making throughout the crisis, including during the post-conflict period. The significant military contribution the UK is able to make to such operations means that we secure an effective place in the political and military decision-making processes. To exploit this effectively, our Armed Forces will need to be interoperable with US command and control structures, match the US operational tempo and provide those capabilities that deliver the greatest impact when operating alongside the US.[33]

To summarize, the prevailing view at the time of the last significant defense review in 2003 was that the UK armed forces would be called on fairly frequently, but that operations would involve relatively small numbers and be of fairly short duration. This has not turned out to be the case. As one recent analysis has pointed out, in contrast to expectations, large numbers of UK forces have been tied down in two locations, Iraq and Afghanistan, for an extended period. This was not the scenario envisaged, and as a result military planning has been driven by the day-to-day management of events in an "apparent vacuum at the political/strategic level."[34]

The change in thinking about the use of force should logically have had an impact on UK nuclear policy if only because of emerging evidence that a steady proliferation of materials, technologies, and equipment might increase the number of nuclear armed states in proximity to places where UK forces might reasonably expect to be deployed in the future.

Cold War planning was tailored to the need for rapid military action in the face of aggression because conflict scenarios left little time to evaluate options and reformulate strategies. Preplanning for many possible scenarios was one factor that created demand for large numbers of nuclear weapons and a diverse range of delivery means, but it also required procedures for rapid delegation of authority to use nuclear weapons to military commanders. With the end of preplanned nuclear operations, signaled in the NATO Strategic Concept adopted in 1991, Allies now emphasized the need "to modify the principle of flexible response to reflect a reduced reliance on nuclear weapons."[35]

The 1991 Strategic Concept recognized that NATO no longer faced a situation of numerical inferiority in key conventional weapon systems, as well as the dramatically improved security environment. While NATO remained committed to maintain an appropriate mix of nuclear and conventional forces based in Europe, the dissolution of the Warsaw Treaty Organization in 1991 and the beginning of the withdrawal of Soviet armed forces from Central Europe meant that the role of nuclear forces was to ensure the prevention of war. Since conventional forces could now be relied on in most contingencies, the theories of escalation that had underpinned flexible response in conditions of forward defense became redundant.

In spite of these developments, the progressive elimination of UK short-range nuclear forces did not eliminate the need for what UK officials in the past had dubbed substrategic nuclear weapons. However, while shorter-range delivery systems for nuclear weapons were seen as an important element in flexible response during the Cold War, after 1991 the task assigned to substrategic nuclear delivery systems remained keyed to the risk of a major confrontation between nuclear-armed adversaries—which in effect meant that they were a "hedge" against any dramatic deterioration of relations with Russia.

In 1993 Malcolm Rifkind, the minister for defense at that time, underscored that

> the ability to undertake a massive strike with strategic systems is not enough to ensure deterrence. An aggressor might, in certain circumstances, gamble on a lack of will ultimately to resort to such dire action. It is therefore important to the credibility of our deterrent that the United Kingdom also possesses the capability to undertake a more limited nuclear strike in order to induce a political decision to halt aggression by delivering an unmistakable message of our willingness to defend our vital interests to the utmost.[36]

In the past, the UK approach to the use of short-range nuclear weapons was limited to this support for strategic deterrence, and no other scenario appears to have been used in planning. For example, when the Royal Navy diverted ships to help recover the Falkland Islands from illegal Argentine occupation in 1982, the nuclear depth charges on board were transferred to other ships in mid-Atlantic and returned to the UK.[37]

After the end of the Cold War senior officials continued to play down the role that nuclear weapons might play in any contingency outside the Euro-Atlantic area, including in one case—Iraq in 1991—where an adversary was known to possess a stockpile of weapons of mass destruction. The fact that Iraq had large quantities of chemical weapons was known in 1991, and it was also widely suspected that Iraq had developed biological weapons, even if the full extent of the biological weapons program was not fully understood at that time. However, asked about the possibility of nuclear weapons being used in any scenario in 1991, Prime Minister John Major replied that "we [do] not envisage the use of nuclear weapons." After a short pause Major added the more categorical "we would not use them."[38]

During the period in which the UK participated in the political and strategic buildup to the invasion of Iraq in 2003—ostensibly to prevent and guard against the emergence of a new and dangerous arsenal of weapons of mass destruction in the Middle East—the role of nuclear weapons in such scenarios was periodically discussed in public.

At different times statements by the minister of defense in the United Kingdom appeared to give nuclear weapons a new core mission in strategic planning: namely, to deter or respond to attacks by a non-nuclear weapons state armed with chemical or biological weapons. This tendency appears to have been a largely subjective and psychological response after the mass impact terrorist attack on the United States in 2001, rather than the product of strategic analysis. Political leaders were suddenly forced to come to terms with the idea that a small and poor opponent might acquire capabilities against which there is no defense. In a period when the UK was contemplating the more frequent use of force, the thought that an essentially weak player might be able to paralyze stronger players by acquiring unconventional weapons, and even severely wound them by actual use, was an uncomfortable one. The combination of mass-impact terrorism and the proliferation of nuclear and biological weapons knocked political decision-makers in major powers off balance, and this began to be reflected in their public statements.

In March 2002, when the invasion of Iraq was already under active discussion in public, British Minister of Defence Geoff Hoon told a parliamentary committee that states like Iraq "can be absolutely confident that in the right conditions we would be willing to use our nuclear weapons." Two days later, appearing on a television current affairs program, Hoon told presenter Jonathan Dimbleby, "[If] there is a threat to our deployed forces, if they come under attack by weapons of mass destruction, and by that specifically chemical or biological weapons, then we would reserve the option in an appropriate case, subject to the conditions that I have referred to when I was talking to the select committee, to use nuclear weapons."[39]

The remarks made in 2002 led to public discussion about how an attack using chemical or biological weapons on British armed forces in the field far from the United Kingdom could ever meet the criteria of last resort or extreme self-defense. When later asked to clarify his comments in an official setting, and presumably having had the time for consultation with officials, Mr. Hoon qualified his remarks and used a formulation closer to the more established understanding of the role of nuclear forces. In the House of Commons Hoon said that "the use of nuclear weapons is still a deterrent of last resort. However, for that to be a deterrent, a British Government must be able to express their view that, ultimately and in conditions of extreme self-defence, nuclear weapons would have to be used."[40]

At around the same time several strategic analysts inside and outside government published papers that considered what role, if any, nuclear weapons might play in expeditionary operations. All of the papers concluded that the military rationale behind a role for nuclear weapons in such operations was unconvincing at best, while the political barriers (internal as well as international) to thinking in these terms were high.[41] In 2009 the UK confirmed that "the use of any nuclear weapon would be strategic in nature," and therefore British officials have "stopped using the terms 'sub-strategic,' 'tactical,' 'non-strategic,' or 'battlefield' nuclear weapon."[42]

Public information in official documents asserts that any decision to use British nuclear weapons could now only be taken in a matter of weeks from the time the executive received a request from an operational commander.[43] Whereas previously authorization to use a weapon could be obtained in twenty-four hours, there does not now seem to be any procedure that would allow the use of a Trident missile within that time frame. This discussion raises a number of questions over how British nuclear weapons would be employed in practice. Given what was said above about assumptions underpinning military operations, a request from a British commander in the field would presumably come in conditions where UK forces were operating alongside U.S. counterparts—since there is no circumstance where an operation of the Sierra Leone type could require a nuclear response. The request might also come in the framework of operations undertaken as part of NATO. In either case there would have to be extensive consultations about whether and when the use of a nuclear weapon might be authorized.

At an operational level, in contrast to the Cold War, there are no existing plans involving preplanned targets for nuclear weapons. To the extent that there are standard procedures for NATO consultations on the use of nuclear weapons, they seem to consist of annual desktop exercises involving all allies (the exercises are known as Able Ally and were carried out at least through 2006).[44] The United Kingdom also maintains a liaison cell within the United States Strategic Command with a direct link to the UK nuclear operations center. However, while a system for technical communication between the UK, the United States, and NATO still exists, the need for extensive political consultation over when and how nuclear weapons might be employed would presumably contribute to the period of several weeks said to be required for authorization of use.

Given the central priority accorded to operating in tandem with the United States, UK thinking must also have been influenced by the emerging approach of the Bush administration. In his speech at the National Defense University in May 2001 the president identified a need to "seek security based on more than the grim premise that we can destroy those who seek to destroy us" and called for "a new policy, a broad strategy of active nonproliferation, counterproliferation, and defenses."[45] This way of thinking was later reflected in the Nuclear Posture Review report released in January 2002, which developed the idea of a "New Triad" in which a greater role would be allocated to non-nuclear strategic capabilities "to strengthen the credibility of our offensive deterrence."[46]

The logic of the 2002 Nuclear Posture Review was that the United States could not respond in kind to an attack using chemical or biological weapons and therefore the risk of a nuclear response to a mass casualty attack was unacceptably high. The review recommended developing improved non-nuclear capabilities (including conventional weapons, but also information warfare options) to substitute for some missions for which nuclear weapons were earmarked. In common with the UK approach, the U.S. documents did not specify in any detail how nuclear weapons might be used in any given circumstances. However, the issue of whether a threat based on the first use of nuclear weapons in a limited conflict could be credible in the eyes of the target was clearly one important problem that U.S. planners were addressing. As one analyst expressed it, "[T]he NPR recognized that large-scale nuclear attacks in response to some actions taken by some adversaries are simply not credible."[47]

The U.S. approach was consistent with British preferences in that it focused on pushing the role of nuclear weapons into the background and de-emphasizing their role in security policy, while retaining a smaller but very modern nuclear arsenal. At the same time there is little in the public literature to suggest that the UK has any interest in discussing the nuclear dimension of tailored deterrence in detail, given that there is no longer a set of operational plans in place for how to use nuclear weapons, no established procedures for timely in-conflict command and control of nuclear forces, and very limited flexibility in the nuclear force structure.

Future thinking about deterrence in the UK is likely to retain the central element of a conditional response to aggression based on calculation of costs and benefits and backed by the threat of punishment. However, in addressing the cost/benefit calculations made by future adversaries, as well as the instruments available to punish aggression, nuclear weapons are unlikely to play a central role.

The UK position is therefore to emphasize that nuclear weapons have a purely political role, taking as a starting point that significant nuclear arsenals remain in the world (some of which are being modernized and expanded) and that the number of states possessing nuclear weapons and ballistic missile delivery systems for them has continued to grow incrementally. Therefore the government has reached a very broad judgment that "we cannot rule out the risk either that a major direct nuclear threat to the UK's vital interests will re-emerge or that new states will emerge that possess a more limited nuclear capability, but one that could pose a grave threat to our vital interests."[48] The Conservative-Liberal Democrat coalition government elected in 2010 has the same commitment in declaratory policy as the previous Labour government: to work to create the conditions for eventual nuclear disarmament but in the mean time to maintain a modern and effective minimum deterrent.[49]

UK PERSPECTIVES ON NUCLEAR ARMS CONTROL

As noted in the introduction, the UK has recently come out strongly in support of a revitalization of nuclear arms control. This has included strong support for efforts to resume U.S.–Russian bilateral negotiations after a roughly fifteen-year hiatus in which the only accomplishment was the 2002 Moscow Treaty, which was regarded by most analysts as an inadequate basis for transparent, verified, and irreversible arms reductions. The government has made it clear that there is no objection in principle to the UK giving up its nuclear weapons entirely under the right circumstances.[50] Moreover, while it is not an official document from the UK government, a study sponsored by the UK Foreign Office and carried out by the London-based IISS perhaps gives an indication regarding what these conditions might be.

To give up its nuclear weapons (in the framework of a binding commitment by all nuclear weapon states to do the same) the UK would require a "watertight" nonproliferation regime, a highly intrusive verification system, and a new package of political, military, and institutional arrangements that would provide adequate collective security guarantees.[51] The overall set of arrangements would have to gain the support of all states with nuclear weapons, not only the nuclear weapon states in the sense of the 1968 Treaty on the Non-Proliferation of Nuclear Weapons (NPT).

The UK has also strongly supported some of the specific incremental steps along the way to the long-term vision of a nuclear weapon–free world. The UK has strongly supported the entry into force of the 1996 Comprehensive Test Ban Treaty, and has supported the negotiation of a Fissile Material Cut-off Treaty (FMCT), but with a much more reserved position in regard to a verification protocol for the treaty. While the reservations about FMCT verification during the Bush administration partly reflected a desire not to be out of step with the United States, the UK has proposed a technical conference for representatives of weapon laboratories in the P5 countries with a view to starting the process of thinking about the verification of global nuclear disarmament. Objections to FMCT verification may not continue now that the Obama administration has come out in favor of negotiations on such measures.

The UK thinking about arms control is partly motivated by concerns about the risk that over the medium to long term the number of states with nuclear weapons will continue to grow. If the nonproliferation regime suffers a series of setbacks, then the value of the regime as a source of security becomes progressively more questionable. At some point the norms against proliferation might be reversed, with states arguing that the norm for security in a world where nuclear weapons continue to play an important role is proliferation, rather than nonproliferation. Widespread proliferation is most likely to occur in conditions where nuclear weapons come to be seen as not only acceptable but essential. The probability would increase still further if nuclear weapons were believed to have an overall positive impact on international security.

As the probability of this worst-case being realized has grown, the UK has increased its support for processes that might reduce the salience of nuclear weapons in the thinking of states. This also explains the publication of national statements and policy documents that underline the diminishing role ascribed to nuclear weapons in UK planning, the increased efforts to strengthen international regimes and processes, as well as British support for the development of new forms of international cooperation that might erect new technical, political, or legal barriers in the way of nuclear weapon development.

The UK authorities have concluded that a new commitment to multilateral arms control must be one element in a strategy to head off this potential proliferation dynamic, or at least reduce its extent. Furthermore, they have concluded that in order for the multilateral approach to deliver its full potential there must be a new commitment to rebalance the underlying bargain between nuclear weapons states and non-nuclear weapons states contained in the 1968 Treaty on the Non-Proliferation of Nuclear Weapons (NPT). In the speeches by Foreign Minister Beckett the need for a new effort to reduce nuclear weapons by the five permanent members of the UN Security Council was highlighted. In the speech by Gordon Brown great emphasis was also placed on the need to ensure that the commitment in the NPT for cooperation in the peaceful use of nuclear technology is fully respected by all parties to the treaty.

In light of the changes in UK thinking about how armed forces might be used, the interest in strengthening the nonproliferation regime also becomes both pragmatic and logical. Although senior decision-makers sometimes underline that "all options are on the table" in scenarios where nuclear weapons may be present, in fact the spread of nuclear weapons and ballistic missile delivery systems for them to more states in the region where UK military planners believe that forces are most likely to be used—the Middle East and Southwest Asia—would undoubtedly be a major complicating factor in any future military operations.

As noted above, analyses suggest that the UK national deterrent may not confer any particular advantage on the UK vis-à-vis potential adversaries in regional scenarios, and UK forces would in any case only be committed alongside the United States. However, managing the transatlantic dimensions of a confrontation with a country that has nuclear weapons and a delivery system that could target Europe but not North America would raise new issues for extended deterrence. Or perhaps more accurately it would raise the old issues of credibility and solidarity in a very new context.

CONCLUSIONS

The brief survey of British nuclear policy presented above suggests that there is currently a political space opening up in which a thorough and detailed review of the case for British nuclear weapons might be undertaken. However, there is also considerable evidence for the view that political, technical, and industrial issues create a very large inertia that would have to be overcome before the current decision to maintain a national deterrent could be reversed. While it was always true that the most probable outcome of the review of nuclear policy planned for 2010 would mirror the deliberations conducted in 2006—which were limited to discussing what type of nuclear deterrent is needed—there are a few factors that might lead to a different decision.

The first is that senior political leaders in the UK appear to have a genuinely open mind on the long-term goal of eliminating nuclear weapons, though policy is still based on a conviction that this is not a realistic objective for the short or medium term. A great deal of activity was aimed at creating the best conditions for advancing the preferred UK proposals at the 2010 conference to review the NPT. This included an effort to strengthen nonproliferation instruments that are regarded as a necessary adjunct to the anticipated expansion in the nuclear industry worldwide. Therefore, significant progress in nuclear nonproliferation and reductions in the arsenals of the largest nuclear powers would have a strong impact on UK nuclear policy.

A second factor is the pressure exerted on nuclear planning by the combination of the immediate operational needs of the armed forces and a financial situation that demands close scrutiny of all discretionary spending. If the view that nuclear forces were not central to UK security became widespread, then the large investment in new platforms and delivery systems for nuclear weapons might also come to be seen as unaffordable.

NOTES

1. Margaret Beckett, Secretary of State for Foreign and Commonwealth Affairs, "A World Free of Nuclear Weapons?" Keynote address to the Carnegie International Nonproliferation Conference, 25 June 2007, at http://www.carnegieendowment.org/events/index.cfm?fa=eventDetail&id=1004.

2. Des Browne, Secretary of State for Defence, "Laying the Foundations for Multilateral Disarmament," Conference on Disarmament, Geneva, 5 February 2008, at http://www.labour.org.uk/des_browne_conference_on_nuclear_disarmament.

3. Rt. Hon. Gordon Brown, Prime Minister of the United Kingdom of Great Britain and Northern Ireland, opening address to International Nuclear Fuel Cycle Conference, 17–18 March 2009, at http://ukinaustria.fco.gov.uk/en/uk-mission-un-in-vienna/meetings-and-conferences.

4. 16 July 2009, at http://www.cabinetoffice.gov.uk/reports/roadto2010.aspx.

5. Patrick Wintour, *The Guardian*, 9 July 2009, at http://www.guardian.co.uk/world/2009/jul/09/britain-nuclear-stockpile-summit-obama.

6. Patrick Wintour and Nicholas Watt, *The Guardian Online*, 16 June 2009, at http://www.guardian.co.uk.

7. *Securing Britain in an Age of Uncertainty: The Strategic Defence and Security Review*, Command Paper 7948 (London, October 2010).

8. These issues are explored in particular by Paul Cornish and Andrew Dorman in their articles *International Affairs* 85, no. 2 (March 2009); and "National Defence in the Age of Austerity," *International Affairs* 85, no. 4 (May 2009).

9. Peter Hennessy, *Cabinets and the Bomb*, British Academy Occasional Paper 11 (Oxford: Oxford University Press, 2007), p. 345.

10. Michael Quinlon, *Strategic Analysis* 33, no. 3 (May 2009): 345.

11. Michael Howard, "Military Power and International Order," *International Affairs* 40, no. 3 (July 1964): 399–400.

12. Malcolm Rifkind, *UK Defence Strategy: A Continuing Role for Nuclear Weapons?* Speech to the Centre for Defence Studies, London, November 16, 1993.

13. Michael Clarke, "Does My Bomb Look Big in This?" *International Affairs* 80, no. 1 (January 2004).

14. Statement to the House of Commons by Minister of Defence Malcolm Rifkind, 9 February 2003.

15. Of these warheads no more than 160 are in operational deployment with the remainder undergoing routine maintenance or held in storage. James Blitz, *Financial Times*, 27 May 2010, p. 2, at http://www.ft.com/cms/s/0/d204db92-6925-11df-aa7e-00144feab49a.html.

16. UK Ministry of Defence, "Modern Defences for the Modern World," *Strategic Defence Review* (July 1998).

17. *Delivering Security in a Changing World*, Defence White Paper presented to Parliament by the Secretary of State for Defence, Cm 6041-I, December 2003, p. 3.

18. Clarke, "Does My Bomb Look Big In This?"

19. Peter Hennessy, *Cabinets and the Bomb*, British Academy Occasional Paper 11 (Oxford: Oxford University Press, 2007), p. 331.

20. The decision to purchase Trident was taken in 1980 and the first submarine became operational around 1994.

21. UK Ministry of Defence, *The Future of the United Kingdom's Nuclear Deterrent*, 4 December 2006.

22. *Adaptability and Partnership: Issues for the Strategic Defence Review*, presented to Parliament by the Secretary of State for Defence, Cm 7794, February 2010, p. 47.

23. *Securing Britain in an Age of Uncertainty*, p. 5.

24. Secretary of State for Defence Liam Fox statement to the House of Commons on Defence Treaties (France), Hansard, 2 November, Column 780.

25. Treaty between the United Kingdom of Great Britain and Northern Ireland and

the French Republic relating to Joint Radiographic/Hydrodynamics Facilities, London, November 2, 2010.

26. Michel Quinlan, "The Future of United Kingdom Nuclear Weapons: Shaping the Debate," *International Affairs* 82, no. 4 (July 2006).

27. Douglas Hurd, Malcolm Rifkind, David Owen and George Robertson, "Start Worrying and Learn to Ditch the Bomb," *The Times*, 30 June 2008. For more information on the Top Level Group of UK Parliamentarians for Multilateral Nuclear Disarmament and Non-proliferation see http://toplevelgroup.org/.

28. Max Hastings, "If Defence Is to Be Strategic Rather than Politically Expedient, Dump Trident," *The Guardian Online*, 19 January 2009, at www.guardian.co.uk.

29. In 2009 the Institute for Public Policy Research (IPPR) convened a Commission on National Security in the 21st Century that included many eminent names from the British defense establishment. The IPPR commissioners did challenge the view that a submarine-based deterrent was the best alternative and called for a review. However, it is not clear on what grounds such a review would overturn the technical analysis made by the Ministry of Defence as recently as 2006. *Shared Responsibilities: A National Security Strategy for the United Kingdom*, final report of the IPPR Commission on National Security in the 21st Century (June 2009).

30. The Cabinet Office, *The National Security Strategy of the United Kingdom: Security in an Interdependent World* (March 2008).

31. For a British view on escalation during the Cold War see Lawrence Freedman, "Escalation and Arms Control," in *Nuclear Strategy and World Security*, ed. Joseph Rotblat and Sven Hellman (Basingstoke: Macmillan, 1985).

32. Joint Doctrine and Concepts Centre, *Strategic Trends*, Ministry of Defence (March 2003).

33. UK Ministry of Defence, *Delivering Security in a Changing World* (December 2003).

34. Paul Cornish and Andrew Dorman, "Blair's Wars and Brown's Budgets: From Strategic Defence Review to Strategic Decay in Less than a Decade," *International Affairs* 85, no. 2 (March 2009).

35. *The Alliance's New Strategic Concept*, agreed by the North Atlantic Council, Rome, 7–8 November 1991, at http://www.nato.int/docu/comm/49-95/c911107a.htm.

36. Malcolm Rifkind, speech delivered at King's College, London, 16 November 1993, quoted in Bruce D. Larkin, *Nuclear Designs: Great Britain, France and China in the Global Governance of Nuclear Arms* (New Jersey: Transaction Publishers, New Brunswick, 1996), p. 38.

37. Rob Evans and David Leigh, "Falklands Warships Carried Nuclear Weapons, MoD Admits," *The Guardian*, 6 December 2003.

38. Major quoted in Hugo Young "Hoon's Talk of Pre-emptive Strikes Could Be Catastrophic," *The Guardian*, 6 June 2002.

39. Richard Norton-Taylor, "Bush's Nuke Bandwagon," *The Guardian*, 27 March 2002. The transcript of the interview from the ITV Jonathan Dimbleby Show is available at http://cndyorks.gn.apc.org/news/articles/uknukepolicy.htm.

40. Hoon's response to a parliamentary question is reproduced in the House of Commons, Hansard Debates for 29 April 2002.

41. See, for example, Commander Robert Green, "Conventionally-Armed UK Trident?" *RUSI Journal* 147, no. 1 (February 2002); and Michael Clarke, "Does My Bomb Look Big in This?" On this particular point the conclusions reached in this period were very similar to those arrived at by analysts ten years earlier. See Nicholas K. J. Witney, *The British Nuclear Deterrent after the Cold War* (RAND Corporation, 2005).

42. UK Foreign and Commonwealth Office, *Lifting the Nuclear Shadow: Creating the Conditions for Abolishing Nuclear Weapons* (9 February 2009).

43. Ibid.

44. Patrick A. McVey, Joint Exercises and Training Division/J37, *USSTRATCOM Joint Exercise Briefing* (9 February 2005).

45. George W. Bush, Remarks at the National Defense University, 1 May 2001.

46. Elements of the Nuclear Posture Review Report submitted to Congress on 31 December 2001 at http://www.globalsecurity.org/wmd/library/policy/dod/npr.htm.

47. M. Elaine Bunn, "Can Deterrence Be Tailored?" *Strategic Forum* (January 2007).

48. UK Ministry of Defence, *The Future of the United Kingdom's Nuclear Deterrent*, 4 December 2006.

49. "Securing Britain in an Age of Uncertainty: The Strategic Defence and Security Review," Command Paper 7948, October 2010, p. 37, at http://www.direct.gov.uk/prod_consum_dg/groups/dg_digitalassets/@dg/@en/documents/digitalasset/dg_191634.pdf.

50. Sir Lawrence Freedman, "British Perspectives on Nuclear Weapons and Nuclear Disarmament," in Barry Blechman, ed., *Unblocking the Road to Zero: Perspectives of Advanced Nuclear Nations*, Stimson Center February 2009, p. 24.

51. George Perkovic and James Acton, *Abolishing Nuclear Weapons*, Adelphi Paper 396 (London: IISS, 2008).

7 France's Nuclear Stance: Independence, Unilateralism, and Adaptation

Venance Journé

OVERVIEW

Since 1945, nuclear matters have been, in a very discreet way, at the core of major French policies, foreign and domestic, in the energy, industrial, and defense sectors. France has developed an advanced nuclear arsenal, although limited quantitatively, and official support for the French nuclear program has enjoyed a remarkable continuity. All along, the most authoritative French speakers have reiterated that French nuclear weapons are not for use—"not for a military purpose during a conflict." In the years after the fall of the Berlin wall, France, like other nuclear weapon states, reassessed its nuclear policy in the new international context: the hardware and doctrine have somehow evolved, and the possibility of nuclear weapon use is now more credible. Weapons have been made more flexible to take care of a wider range of circumstances and have been adapted for use in limited missions. Moreover, the nuclear program was developed in secret until 1958, and the legacy of secrecy has become a fact of nuclear life in France.

Equally consistent has been the response of French authorities to recent calls from a number of leading figures—many of them known as hardliners on nuclear issues—for real progress toward nuclear disarmament. The French authorities' response to the push for nuclear zero is that the nuclear deterrent is the best way to respond to nuclear proliferation, and it will remain at the core of France's security for the foreseeable future. The French response can be understood in the light of its policy of independence and autonomy and its specific history.

In this chapter, I will examine the evolution of the French nuclear weapons program. I will highlight the fact that disarmament or limitation measures have been carried out in a way that does not alter the French stance of deterrence. I will also discuss the absence of debate in France on the steps to be taken toward an abolition of nuclear weapons and conclude with some proposals for specific steps toward disarmament.

THE EARLY EVOLUTION OF THE FRENCH NUCLEAR FORCE

French scientists played an important role in the early development of nuclear science, but they were not included in the Manhattan Project. Several French scientists did go to Canada, where they played a leading role in the Canadian nuclear program. On October 18, 1945, two months after the explosions at Hiroshima and Nagasaki, the French interim government presided over by General de Gaulle created by ordinance the French Atomic Energy Commission (CEA—Commissariat à l'Energie Atomique). Its mission was to implement "all measures that can be helpful to benefit the use of atomic energy in the field of Science, Industry and National Defense."[1] The CEA was directly under the highest executive authority and had an unusual level of administrative and financial autonomy.

In the early years, domestic conditions were very unfavorable for the development of a military nuclear program. The Fourth Republic was very unstable, and governments turned over frequently. Moreover, given the ongoing colonial wars in Indochina and Algeria, many decision-makers and the military did not favor embarking on a long-term program that would require considerable financial and human resources. Most political parties shared this view; the general public was against nuclear weapons; and with very few exceptions, all the scientists in CEA were strongly opposed to any military use of nuclear energy. The international context was also unfavorable: specifically, the United States was against any other national program, and two civilian nuclear agreements, the European Defense Community and Euratom, were being negotiated in Europe.

Nonetheless, the French military nuclear program started in the early 1950s. From the beginning, the French military nuclear program was shrouded in secrecy. No head of government had taken a firm decision on the issue; nevertheless, the necessary facilities were constructed. On May 20, 1955, the minister of defense, Pierre Koenig, and the minister of atomic affairs, Gaston Palewski, signed a secret memorandum of understanding explicitly giving CEA the responsibility for the development of nuclear weapons and allowing the secret transfer of funds from the Ministry of Defense to CEA. The work was always presented as "studies," and the agreements between CEA and the Ministry of Defense were secret. Only the president of the Council of Ministers and a very few others involved knew about the real state of affairs.

In November 1956, the fate of the Suez military expedition and what it revealed about the lack of French power led to a real, but still secret, political decision to pursue the development of nuclear weapons. On November 30, 1956, a new protocol was signed that defined the objectives of a national nuclear weapons program: preparatory studies for nuclear explosives, manufacture of prototypes, and tests.

June 1958 marked a turning point in the French nuclear program: after thirteen years away from the public political scene, General de Gaulle came back to lead the French Republic. De Gaulle was well informed about the nuclear work, and on July 22, 1958, he publicly gave a high priority to the nuclear bomb project. The time of clandestine operations had ended. Soon after, France became a nuclear power: the first nuclear A-bomb test was conducted in Reggane on February 13, 1960.

THE DETERRENCE OF "THE WEAK TO THE STRONG"

De Gaulle gave precedence to foreign policy over domestic affairs, and his diplomacy rested on "realpolitik." He wanted France to participate in discussions as an equal with the "great powers," and was convinced that military independence was the key to diplomatic independence. From the 1940s onward, de Gaulle was a strong proponent of an independent nuclear force. He understood that the nuclear weapon was also an equalizer, allowing a balance between powers with an unequal level of armament.

It should be underlined that an independent policy was not a given at the time. The nuclear policy of strict independence implied autonomy of effort, choice, and forces: it meant renouncement of foreign help and no sharing of resources with foreign countries because they could have different aims. Therefore: (1) France had to be free to decide when, how, and against which adversary the force would be used—the basis for the often misunderstood *tous azimuts* concept; (2) the French deterrence force had to be free from a military integrated command; and (3) France could not extend its deterrence to neighboring countries without undermining its concept of deterrence.

Beyond the policy of independence, several other reasons led de Gaulle early on to envisage French withdrawal from the NATO integrated military command: the U.S. opposition to French nuclear forces; the obvious U.S. supremacy over Europe and the risk that France might be engaged in a war against her own interests; and the concern that relying too much on the United States might lead France to reduce its own defense efforts.

In 1957, the successful launch of Sputnik and the possibility that Soviet ballistic missiles could reach U.S. territory made it obvious that no U.S. president would risk a nuclear attack on U.S. soil to defend Europe. In 1962 McNamara's flexible response doctrine cleared the way for de Gaulle to reject NATO's responsibility to defend France and, in 1966, to withdraw the French forces from the NATO military integrated command.

The French deterrence force was initially meant to secure French vital interests—insuring the integrity of the national territory and the existence of the nation—against possible threats arising from a more powerful country. The original French nuclear policy was therefore strictly defensive, in order to prevent war. It was a deterrence "of the weak to the strong," the strong being the USSR during the Cold War.

With limited means, the purpose was to have weapons in sufficient number so that enough would survive a first strike, and be able to inflict unacceptable damages out of proportion to the stakes in the conflict if vital interests were endangered. France has always maintained ambiguity in defining her vital interests, considering that it enhances deterrence because a possible adversary would have difficulty in assessing its margin for action.

Deterrence was the nonevent: instead of comparing forces, the point was to compare the damage inflicted. During the Cold War, the French deterrence posture was an anticity strategy, aimed at convincing the enemy (the USSR) that attacking France would not be worth the gain. It was a straight and simple deterrence policy, but paradoxically, if it had ever been executed, France would have been wiped out.

Who is to decide? The Fifth Republic gives increased executive power to the president, who is "the person with the final word on our deterrent and the only one with the power to decide."[2] As President Mitterrand has explained: "As a matter of fact, conditions in which France could have to reply to an aggression or a threat of aggression could leave only a few minutes. It is for this reason that, in principle, the head of the State decides, and decides alone."[3]

A FORCED MARCH: THE CONSTRUCTION OF THE DETERRENCE FORCE

By the 1960s, the colonial wars were over, and it was possible to allocate substantial funds and manpower to the nuclear program. Although the French nuclear force was mainly intended for its political value, nevertheless it had to be militarily credible, with an advanced arsenal. Although not matching the numbers deployed by the superpowers, France developed a nuclear strategic triad, with surface, air, and submarine components, and including both strategic and tactical weapons.

The initial phases of the French nuclear force development met with three types of challenges: timing, finance, and technology.

Rapid development had the highest priority in order to close the technological gap with the other nuclear powers and to make the French nuclear force irreversible. The latter was necessary because of domestic opposition (socialists, communists, and Europeanists) and international opposition (mainly the United States), as well as pressure from disarmament initiatives (Partial Test Ban Treaty negotiations and the start of the discussions for the Nuclear Non-Proliferation Treaty [NPT]).

Technological developments proceeded in three main areas:[4]

1. Making the force as invulnerable as possible. To insure the survivability of the second-strike launchers, the nuclear submarines were built early; construction of the *Redoutable* started in 1963.

2. Increasing the yield. Deterrence of "the weak to the strong" required the ability to inflict the maximum damage possible, and it led to the development of very powerful weapons of several megatons. After a troubled process, the first H-bomb was successfully tested in 1968.[5] The high-yield warheads were placed on surface-to-surface ballistic missiles situated on the Plateau d'Albion in the south of France.

3. Expanding the penetration power. In reaction to the U.S.-Soviet arms race, France developed a series of smaller weapons and of missiles with increasing range. In the late 1970s MIRV technology was mastered.

After the end of the Cold War, in the early 1990s, the authorities in CEA anticipated that the Comprehensive Test Ban Treaty (CTBT) being discussed at the time would prevent any more testing in the future. In order to ensure the maintenance of the weapons, or even to build new weapons in a nuclear test prohibition regime, France launched a simulation program.

Low Yield Weapons and ultime avertissement

The original deterrence policy was strictly defensive, excluding military use on the battlefield, and thereby giving nuclear weapons solely a political role. With French withdrawal from NATO military integrated command, however, the French authorities knew that their forces stationed in Germany would be deprived of NATO's tactical nuclear weapons. De Gaulle decided in 1966 to build tactical weapons. Once France had developed a triad with strategic and tactical weapons, and given that it was not possible to exclude a foreign invasion of French territory, it was tempting to conceive of a possible use for nuclear weapons. This was true, in particular, for the short-range, low-yield weapons for use on the battlefield outside of French territory. Weapons of a yield of 30 to 40 kilotons were developed and installed on the Pluton (deployed from 1974), followed by the Hadès ground-ground missiles, until 1993. These missiles had a very short range—120 and 450 km.[6]

The use of these tactical weapons was then conceptualized. They were supposed to serve as an *ultime avertissement* ("final warning"). This final warning was intended to show the adversary the determination of the French through limited nuclear strikes on military targets. If, unfortunately, the adversary did not understand and stop, then, during the Cold War, this *ultime avertissement* would be followed by a massive strike on Soviet cities. The tactical weapons were later called "prestrategic," a term meant to imply that their use would be part of the strategic deterrence.

Understandably, these short-range weapons raised immense concern in Germany, since they were supposed to be used to stop the possible advance of Soviet ground forces toward France. After years of major controversies with the Germans (in particular on what form consultation with the Germans would take in case of a French decision to use the tactical weapons on German soil), the French devised a policy to use airborne missiles to send the final warning on the soil of the aggressor.

After the fall of the Berlin Wall in 1989, nuclear proliferation took precedence over past concerns. The new perceived threats originated from far-away countries with a lower level of armament. In 1993, the surface tactical missiles were withdrawn from the inventory, and the *ultime avertissement* was assigned to the 300-km range missiles based on aircraft.

French Nuclear Forces as of 2009

The current French nuclear forces are shown in Table 7.1. They comprise four aircraft squadrons (one carrier-based) and a submarine fleet, which has undergone modernization: the new class of submarines is much quieter than the previous class, quieter even than the background ocean noise. The Mirage and Super Etendard aircraft will be retired as the Rafale are introduced.

Missiles have also been modernized. The new M51 missile scheduled to replace the M45 in 2010 will have a range of 6,000 km with the nominal charge, and could reach 9,000 to 10,000 km if it carries fewer warheads. In 2015, the M51 missile will be modified to be able to carry the new TNO warhead (*tête nucléaire océanique*, oceanic nuclear warhead) that will replace the TN-75 warheads. In 2010, the ASMP missile (*à Air-Sol Moyenne Portée*: medium-range air-to-surface missile) was replaced by an advanced missile (ASMP-A) with a range of 500 km, better precision—10 meters—and the new TNA warhead (*tête nucléaire aéroportée*, airborne nuclear warhead). The TNO and TNA are the new generation of the so-called robust weapons. The last series of tests conducted in 1995–96 was precisely devoted to validating this concept.

French nuclear weapons have a lifetime of about twenty years. Robust warheads and simulation programs are the tools for the renewal of the nuclear warheads. The simulation program is intended to give the capacity to validate

TABLE 7.1

French Nuclear Forces, 2009

	Airborne Nuclear Force				
	Entry in service	Number of aircraft	Nuclear warheads	Type x yield (kt)	Range (km)
Land-based					
Mirage 2000 /ASMP	1988	60	50 TN-81	1 x 300	2,750
Rafale / ASMP-A	2009	40		1 x 300	500
Aircraft carrier					
Super Etendard	1978	24	10 TN-81	1 x 300	2,750
Rafale / ASMP-A	2010			1 x 300	500

	Submarine-based Nuclear Force			
SSBN	Entry in service	Number of missiles x type	Nuclear warheads type x yield (kt)	Range (km)
Le Triomphant	1997	16 x M45	6 TN-75 x (100–150)	6,000
Le Téméraire	1999	16 x M45	6 TN-75 x (100–150)	6,000
Le Vigilant	2004	16 x M45	6 TN-75 x (100–150)	6,000
Le Terrible	2010	16 x M51	6 TN-75 x (100–150)	9,000

new nuclear weapons at a cost 40 percent lower than the costs of the nuclear tests.[7] The simulation program includes a high-power laser, a radiography system (to analyze the dynamics of materials and study the non-nuclear parts of the weapon), and a parallel computing system. The Megajoule laser, which is being built in Le Barp near Bordeaux, will be equipped with 240 beams and will allow the study of the nuclear fusion processes. The first ignition and combustion experiments are expected in 2011. The simulation program will also study aging phenomena in the weapons, and work to insure the validity of certain parameters for robust warheads. Finally, this program aims to maintain scientific excellence and competence in nuclear weapon design for scientists who have never participated in real tests.

THE NEW INTERNATIONAL CONTEXT AND FRENCH "DISARMAMENT" MEASURES

After the discovery of the Iraqi nuclear program in the early 1990s, the risks of proliferation took precedence over past security concerns and induced France to implement several significant measures of armament reduction. France ratified the NPT in 1992, and in April 1992 President Mitterand announced a unilateral moratorium on nuclear testing. The moratorium initiative was conceived as a proposal to the other nuclear weapon states as a first step, to be followed by them, toward a comprehensive test ban. At the same time, however, CEA was initiating the development of the simulation program PALEN (Préparation à la limitation des essais nucléaires [Preparation for the Limitation of Nuclear Testing]), which is, as was stated by Mitterrand, dedicated to "obtain[ing] a full simulation that will enable the development of the weapons that [France] will need in the year 2010."[8]

Several other measures were decided at this time:

- Reduction of the alert level for the strategic forces;
- Early retirement, in 1992, of the short-range surface-to-surface Pluton missiles;
- Reduction of the short-range surface-to-surface Hadès missiles program, from 120 to 30 units, and a decision not to deploy them;
- Reduction of the number of new-generation nuclear submarines from six to five, and the staggering of the commissioning schedule; and
- Halting in 1992 the production of plutonium for nuclear weapons at the Marcoule separation plant.

However, President Mitterrand decided to maintain the surface-to-surface strategic M4 missiles of the Plateau d'Albion until 2005, the date at which they would be replaced by the M45 missile.

The two last years of the Mitterrand presidency were marked by a period of political "cohabitation." In 1993 a conservative majority was elected in Parliament, and in the mid-1990s recurrent discussions occurred on the need to adapt the nuclear deterrent to the emerging threats and to the increasing number of conflict zones. In February 1994 the Defense Committee of the French Parliament presented a report on military programming that supported a policy of extended deterrence, which would allow France to defend its vital interests with the possibility of limited and very precise nuclear strikes, a strategic choice that implied resuming nuclear testing and giving up the simple concept of deterrence of the weak to the strong.[9]

Mitterrand had converted to nuclear deterrence earlier in his political career, in the most Gaullist fashion. In the 1980s, faced with different modernization choices, he had clearly made a choice to "perfect the apocalypse" and to stick to the original deterrence concept.[10] In 1994 President Mitterrand gave a speech in Parliament in which he reaffirmed his views on the deterrence doctrine and opposed what he considered as "potential drifts away from the initial concept" and the emerging hypothesis according to which nuclear weapons could be used against "the weak or the mad." He denounced the "major heresy" that would lead to a doctrine of use: "Would it be necessary to come round to the use of so-called surgical strike, or even more picturesque, a decapitating strike, which could after all go down to the nuclear rifle? This seems to me a major heresy, and, in no circumstance, would I accept it." To remove this temptation, he limited the magnitude and the diversity of weapon systems.[11]

In May 1995, with Jacques Chirac elected president, the proponents of a resumption of nuclear testing gained a sympathetic listener in the Elysée. Following the final round of five tests, Chirac decided on the following measures:

- Support for the Comprehensive Test Ban Treaty with a zero yield. France ratified the treaty in April 1998;
- Irreversible dismantlement of the test site in Mururoa, completed in 1998;
- Ratification of the Pelindaba and Roratonga treaties in 1996;
- Dismantlement of the ground-launched nuclear missiles on the Plateau d'Albion, decided in 1996;
- Definitive retirement of the Hadès missile (the last one was dismantled in 1997);

- Abandonment of the alert level;
- Reduction in the number of submarines permanently at sea to one;
- An end to the production of highly enriched uranium for nuclear weapons in the enrichment facility of Pierrelatte;
- Dismantlement of the production plants in Pierrelatte and Marcoule; and
- Reduction of French strategic forces to 350 weapons.

In Cherbourg in March 2008, in a speech presenting *Le Terrible*, the fourth nuclear ballistic missile submarine of the second generation, scheduled to enter service in 2010, President Sarkozy announced further reduction measures: the total number of nuclear weapons would be reduced to fewer than 300. For the airborne component, the number of nuclear weapons, missiles, and aircraft was to be reduced by one-third (to forty Rafale aircraft, which are currently being produced). This measure came in a time of budgetary restraint: according to the Ministry of Defense, there will be a deficit of 30 billion Euros in the defense budget between 2009 and 2013, if the current rate of spending is maintained.[12]

In his speech, the French president also made a prominent call to "the eight nations in the world which have declared they have conducted nuclear tests"—a way to include North Korea but not Israel—for "the immediate launching of negotiations on a treaty to ban the production of fissile materials for nuclear weapons purposes, and to establish without delay a moratorium on the production of such materials" for "opening negotiations on a treaty banning short- and intermediate-range surface-to-surface missiles."[13] And, as a measure of transparency, international experts from forty countries were invited in September 2008 to see for themselves the effective dismantlement of the facilities in Marcoule and Pierrelatte.

In recent years French official speakers have frequently praised the example of France in the matter of nuclear disarmament.[14] It should, however, be underlined that none of these measures have altered the French nuclear stance, and the modernization programs continue. The reductions in numbers have been made in order to reach "strict sufficiency" for the French nuclear arsenal. Most of the disarmament measures appear to be for the purpose of rationalization—including financial rationalization. The short-range weapons were retired when it became obvious that their use was truly inconceivable. The moratorium and then the end of nuclear testing came when the French nuclear weapon community determined that it would be possible to continue the weapon development through the simulation program. The fissile material production centers were shut down when France had accumulated sufficient weapons-grade material for foreseeable future needs.[15] The opening up of the military fissile material production sites was a gesture to show the "French commitment to disarmament and transparency" before the NPT Review Conference in 2010 and the resumption of the work of the Conference on Disarmament in Geneva.

Arguably, the French disarmament measures are most welcome. Some of them are irreversible, in particular the dismantlement of the nuclear testing facility. France is the only country to have dismantled totally its nuclear test site, with no way to reconstruct it. Nevertheless, it should be underlined that all these measures have been taken unilaterally—and that in parallel, France is pursuing an extensive modernization program. As far as reductions are concerned, France refuses multilateral constraints.[16] In multilateral fora, France agrees to discuss only the CTBT and Fissile Material Cutoff Treaty (FMCT).

ADAPTATION TOWARD FLEXIBILITY

The positive changes in international security after the end of the Cold War were underlined in the 1994 White Paper (WP), but nuclear deterrence remained—and still is—the basis of French defense policy and a major element of French independence. The 1994 WP noted that new scenarios involving regional powers must be envisaged, and rejected any mix-up between deterrence and use, but nevertheless reaffirmed the *ultime avertissement*.[17] The more powerful enemy that French nuclear forces were supposed to deter had vanished, but scenarios justifying a "strictly sufficient" (but nevertheless significant and modernized) nuclear force proliferated. To address the diverse threats to vital interests in a changing world, with threats of varying degree of danger and coming from different regions, France's strategy is to implement an "adapted" response, with the possibility to strike selectively with means which are made more flexible in order that their use would be credible.

French authorities realized that nuclear deterrence aimed at Russia was no longer sufficient, and the doctrine was adjusted to take Asia into account. The new missiles have a range greater than 9,000 km. At the end of the 1990s and the beginning of the 2000s, prompted by a discussion of a new nuclear doctrine in the United States and nuclear proliferation–related events (the Indian and Pakistani nuclear tests, undetected proliferation in Iraq, the North Korean crisis), President Chirac once again described nuclear deterrence as having the most important role in French security policy.[18]

President Chirac gave a major speech in January 2006. He insisted that the deterrence principles underlying French nuclear doctrine had not changed:

"There is no question, under any circumstances, of using nuclear means for military purposes during a conflict." But a few words later, he added: "This formula should not, however, allow any doubts to persist about our determination and capacity to resort to our nuclear weapons."[19] The ambiguity is clear.

Several scenarios have been spelled out for the role of nuclear weapons:

1. As "life insurance" to deter the big powers, in particular China.
2. To deter the regional powers, the "proliferators," from threatening French vital interests with weapons of mass destruction—not only nuclear weapons.[20]
3. To deter state-sponsored terrorism.[21]
4. To deter more limited threats. The question of protecting the right of French troops to intervene outside of French territory and to resist blackmail was mentioned by the chief of the defense staff, Général Henri Bentégeat.[22] Of course the stakes would be limited. France's survival would not necessarily be at stake, so to be credible the threat to use nuclear weapons should be adapted to the level of nuisance.

France has always maintained ambiguity on the definition of vital interests, as she considers that to do so enhances deterrence, which is necessary in order to "preserve the freedom of assessment and action" of the authorities.[23] The vital interests are not specified in detail, nor is the frontier between strategic and vital interests.[24] In his January 2006 speech, President Chirac, however, broke with this tradition, stating that the list includes "safeguarding our strategic supplies and the defense of allied countries,"[25] and the defense minister added a few days later that the "list goes beyond the European Union."[26]

In his 2008 Cherbourg speech, President Sarkozy remained vague in the definition of vital interests and gave fewer details than his predecessor, but he did not contradict him:

> Our nuclear deterrence protects us from any aggression against our vital interests emanating from a state—wherever it may come from and whatever form it may take. Our vital interests, of course, include the elements that constitute our identity and our existence as a nation-state, as well as the free exercise of our sovereignty. My responsibility, as Head of State, is to assess their limit at all times, for in a changing world they cannot remain static.[27]

There is some dissent: General Lucien Poirier, one of the main thinkers on the French deterrence concept, maintains that the vital interests should be defined very strictly, and that they are limited to the protection of the "national space."[28] General Poirier disagrees with the present stance of ambiguity on the nature of the vital interests, and asserts that the only ambiguous element should be the time when it is considered that vital interests are threatened.

A major inflection in the deterrence concept and in the adaptation of the means was announced by President Chirac in 2001 and was clarified in 2006.[29] French policy is to deter regional powers, not by an anticipated threat against populations, but by a precise threat to destroy the major government, army, or even economic centers of a country. The nuclear forces have been configured accordingly; for example, the number of nuclear warheads has been reduced on some of the missiles.[30] This reduction was explicitly made to increase the credibility of the use of the weapon.[31] Decided very discreetly, the change was implemented in 2003.[32]

French authorities, such as the Ministry of Defense and the chief of the defense staff, are convinced that these limited and precise strikes would involve very limited collateral damage.[33] As expressed by the chief of the defense staff: "The credibility of our threat against these regional powers implies that the population losses be kept limited if we want that our adversary takes it into consideration. . . . [In] western public opinions, it would be unimaginable to announce that, in retaliation to a missile which killed one thousand persons in Paris, we decide to strike a regional power killing millions of people. To be able to destroy centers of power, we possess very precise weapons with a variable yield to avoid collateral damages, without having built miniaturized weapons."[34]

This argument is now enshrined in the most recent white paper, now called "White Paper on Defense and National Security," which was published in June 2008. Among the adapted responses, the white paper adds also the ability "to paralyze an adversary's capacity for action."[35]

This credible use, consisting in the capacity to strike precisely with weapons of a lower yield, has a concept attached: the *ultime avertissement*, now also called the *avertissement nucléaire*. Officially it is argued that the long-lived concept of *ultime avertissement* remains essential to avoid locking the president into a two-prong alternative: everything or nothing. A limited strike such as the *ultime avertissement* seems to be the major element of a flexible response. In 2006, Minister of Defense Alliot Marie emphasized the fact that the *ultime avertissement* is at "the core of the deterrence doctrine."[36] On the link between the *ultime avertissement* and ultimate deterrence, General Bentégeat explained:

> A reason why it is imperative to think in terms of *ultime avertissement* is that, toward regional powers, it may be necessary to restore deterrence. If they have not understood that nuclear deterrence can hit the core of their vital interests, it is necessary to make them understand in one way or in another, and nothing can better do it than the *ultime avertissement*.[37]

The *ultime avertissement* could consist of limited strikes with nuclear-equipped ASMP missiles from aircraft or a strike with a strategic missile with a reduced number of warheads launched from a submarine. Or the final warning could instead be an electromagnetic pulse produced by a nuclear explosion in the high atmosphere. In October 2006 General Bentégeat explained that the explosion of a nuclear weapon at an altitude of several tens of kilometers would create an electromagnetic pulse resulting, "within a definite radius," in the destruction of all electromagnetic and computing devices, "without any blast or radioactive effect on the ground."[38] The threat of such a use would represent, among all the possibilities for *ultime avertissement*, the least destructive mode.

Although the authorities always stress that such a flexible use of a nuclear weapon does not mean a lowering of the nuclear threshold, the discourse remains very unclear, including on such points as the possibility of preventive strikes or the modalities of the assessment of the hostile intentions of a potential aggressor, which could be misinterpreted. In his speech, Chirac was ambiguous, but a military decision-maker explained that with such an electromagnetic use for the nuclear weapon "one loses in deterrence but one gains in use."[39]

In any case, several important issues remain: instead of protecting anything, such a use—if really meant to protect the vital interests—would rather prove that deterrence had not worked. Nothing guarantees that the opponent would be convinced, unless this final warning were to annihilate him completely, as well as his army. The consequences of the *ultime avertissement* are in any case very difficult to assess, and there is a big risk that they may prove more catastrophic than the threat the warning is suppose to erase.

Thus, since the mid-1990s, there have been "major inflections" in the original French deterrence concept, shifts that have been justified by new perceived threats. The doctrine has been adapted in three major ways: deterrence of the "weak to the strong" has become the deterrence of the "strong to regional powers"; the anticity strategy has become anti–centers of power, with the main parameter being a modulated impact; and the vital interests have been expanded.[40] This was recognized by President Chirac in a rather ambiguous formulation: "Thus the principles underlying our deterrence doctrine remain unchanged, but the modalities of expressing this doctrine have evolved and keep evolving,"[41] and by many political and military figures.[42] These changes, which were decided very quietly in the late 1990s, have never been discussed publicly, including in the Parliament.

THE LACK OF PUBLIC DEBATE ON NUCLEAR MILITARY ISSUES

The main control over French nuclear affairs remained, and still remains, with the CEA. Such centralized control has facilitated the policy of secrecy. The relations between CEA and the government's leaders are very close, and CEA is the only body that gives advice to the government on nuclear weapons technology. For example, in May 1995, newly elected President Chirac asked CEA to make a report on the various possibilities to guarantee the long-term reliability of the French deterrent, and CEA prepared the decision to resume nuclear tests. Moreover, CEA regularly makes proposals on technological choices. This has been the case for the thermonuclear bomb, tactical weapons, and the MIRV, among others.

Beginning with de Gaulle's enthusiastic support for the deterrence force, there has been overall continuity of policy under every French president, with no reservation. The Socialist Party was opposed to the French nuclear deterrent until 1978, when it realized that Mitterrand could be elected president. The first political leader to change his mind on this issue was Michel Rocard, who was prime minister during the period 1988 to 1991. When he participated in the Canberra Commission, Michel Rocard became convinced of the necessity to get rid of nuclear weapons.[43] Such a rare event—a former French prime minister contesting the validity of maintaining a nuclear arsenal—went almost unnoticed in France.

Yet very recently a national *première* happened on the French scene. Four leading figures—two former prime ministers: one conservative, Alain Juppé, and one socialist, Michel Rocard; a retired Air Force general, Bernard Norlain, who had been chief of the military cabinet under two prime ministers, Chirac and Rocard; and a former defense minister, the socialist Alain Richard—published in a major newspaper a call for France to engage radically in the Global Zero process.[44] A leading French defense journalist reacted promptly: "For Paris, the only efficient measure presently consists in strengthening the antiproliferation measures, and there is little chance that the text written by the two former Prime Ministers would lead to any evolution."[45]

There is no reason to foresee any change in the official position. Apart from the "French Four," all the voices on the political or military scene—and in the media—argue in converging ways for a continuing deterrent, and there is no lack of extreme scenarios to justify this position. The nuclear weapon is still for France a "weapon of political status."[46] From the beginning, the nuclear weapon was primarily an instrument of independence and grandeur, rather than of pure military value. Although there have been some real shifts in the military value associated with the nuclear weapon, the argument of sovereignty and international status is even today of utmost importance. In 2008 the president stated that the nuclear force "is neither a matter of prestige nor a question of rank,"[47] but in many other instances, the nuclear weapon is referred to as a sign of global importance: a weapon "which sets the size of the international status of our country,"[48] which is also an "essential element of international status for our country, recognized by the NPT,"[49] making France "a nation which counts and is listened to on the international scene."[50] The nuclear force is also seen as an indispensable attribute of a permanent member of the UN Security Council and increases in importance with regard to a potential extension of the members.[51] And finally, in the eventuality of a decrease of the U.S. presence in Europe, the role of the French nuclear force could be enhanced.[52]

In French decision-making circles, it is assumed that nonproliferation policies and nuclear deterrence are not contradictory and that, as a matter of fact, they reinforce each other.

> [D]iscouraging a potential adversary, deterrence contributes to non proliferation, and the French refusal of a no-first use stance is part of this logic. . . . Adopting a *tous azimuth* deterrence, France exercises indirectly a conflict prevention action outside its borders, contributes to reinforce security in France and in Europe. . . . Since nuclear weapons will never be eradicated from the planet, non proliferation actions do not aim at prohibiting it, but to insure compliance in the Non Proliferation Treaty, which limits its possession to a restricted club of five countries.[53]

For many officials, the best argument to oppose the thesis that it is the lack of disarmament which drives proliferation, is that proliferation continued in the 1990s, while the nuclear powers were "disarming" and that this, by itself, is a proof that disarmament is not a good strategy to promote nonproliferation.[54]

The January 2007 *Wall Street Journal* op-ed and the recent declarations by President Obama in April 2009 have forced some reactions and comments in

France on the possible elimination of nuclear weapons. Essentially, the comments unanimously reassert the need for a French nuclear deterrent.[55] In a recent paper, for example, two retired diplomats, Rose and Debouzy, argue that it would be dangerous not to maintain the status quo.[56]

The reluctance of French officials to openly discuss the possible abolition of nuclear weapons is mirrored by the fact that any public discussion on nuclear deterrence is still taboo in France. Voices that challenge the soundness of the nuclear deterrence policy exist but are seldom heard in France, in part because of self-censorship of the media. It may happen that some rather quiet voices speak in favor of the elimination of nuclear weapons, but they are swiftly ridiculed by members of the establishment. Michel Rocard restated in 2008 his stance in favor of the elimination of nuclear weapons.[57] The answer was: "One is left confused by so much thoughtlessness."[58] The October 2009 op-ed by Juppé, Norlain, Richard, and Rocard has not led to any debate.

There is also very little debate on the tools of nuclear deterrence or the modernization program. In the UK, the Trident modernization programs did eventually lead to extensive public discussions. In France, by contrast, the weapons modernization programs have proceeded in relative secrecy until the test phase. Some members of the military establishment would prefer to allocate funds to conventional armaments better adapted to the present tasks rather than to the nuclear program, especially in a period of financial scarcity,[59] but this kind of debate may occur only behind closed doors.

It is therefore surprising that regrets concerning the lack of debate are sometimes echoed in official fora,[60] from those who should foster, or at least authorize, the debate.[61] The chief of the defense staff regrets that "[t]he debate about nuclear deterrence is currently quite poor."[62] The fact is that France is unwilling to provide information on the nuclear deterrent, which is a "nontopic."[63] One clear example is the collision between a UK and a French nuclear submarine which occurred in February 2009. The French Navy initially claimed the submarine had been in a collision "apparently with a container."[64] The real reason for the damage of the French submarine was only revealed after the UK made the collision public. A responsible official from the French Ministry of Defense states: "In France, deterrence is reserved to a club of big priests. The Fifth Republic system is based on the idea that the Parliament should not debate about strategic questions, which are the prerogative of the executive."[65]

French authorities always insist that there is a consensus on nuclear deterrence. A political consensus has existed since 1978, when the Left came round to the French deterrent; all the political parties, apart from the Greens, do not question this issue. But even in political circles, it is a consensus by lack of information and therefore lack of debate. There cannot be any public consensus, since the public is not informed.

CONCLUSIONS

In the four decades of its existence, the French nuclear program and posture have undergone major changes in form and in justification.

French authorities consider it irresponsible to argue that nuclear disarmament and nonproliferation are two sides of the same coin. On the contrary, the general motto is that "deterrence constitutes still today the most efficient strategy to oppose [proliferation] or at least to protect from it."[66] The September 2009 declaration of the French president at the United Nations reaffirms this position.[67] One might argue that nuclear proliferation gives France the best motive for a modernization of its arsenal and eases the task of justifying its weapon developments.

The changes in the international context, in domestic politics, and in the modernization programs have led to significant drifts in posture, which are not acknowledged as such by the French decision-makers or "official" analysts. France points out that, in the past and most recently in 2008, it has made cuts in its nuclear forces and structures. These measures, however, have not had and do not have logical corollaries in shifts in French nuclear doctrine. On the contrary, the unilateral armament reduction measures have been accompanied by modernization measures designed to render the arsenal more efficient, more precise, more accurate, and longer lasting. This cannot be explained simply by the inertia of decade-long programs, since the threshold for use has explicitly been lowered with the introduction of the new technology. The trend has been to substantially lower the threshold for triggering the use of nuclear weapons. A strict dividing line between deterrence and use, and the obvious development of a more versatile arsenal, are hardly compatible.

Nuclear weapons now can be given missions that conventional weapons could also fulfill with far less collateral damage. Most decision-makers have stated that the modernized weapons are not battlefield weapons; nevertheless, they are made more and more usable. Moreover, as the official view seems to be that the collateral damage would be minimal, it is undisputable that the taboo against use of the weapons is weakened. While some military officers have argued that even a surgical strike would have indiscriminate effects,[68] the nuclear taboo is even more weakened when the use of nuclear weapons is conceived as a mean to "paralyze the capacity of action of the opponent." It cannot be excluded that the use of nuclear weapons to produce an electromagnetic pulse would push France toward a preventive strike.

This risk is aggravated by the fact that there is hardly any public information and no real debate in France on nuclear military matters or choices. The general public is not aware of the nuclear policy in general or of the potential shifts in the French nuclear posture. The general public is not at all prepared for the eventuality of such decisions as launching the *ultime avertissement*, and even less for the possible reactions from adversaries. If there is no public debate, maybe one reason could also be the fact that "one should have the courage to speak in terms of Hiroshimas not only in the camp of the adversary but also in our own."[69] All this for the sake of a paradoxical logic.

It is often said in France that the two major nuclear powers, Russia and the United States, should take the lead. Their huge arsenals are of course a main concern, but new studies of a limited nuclear exchange have shown that any country equipped with some dozens of weapons poses a global threat.[70] Therefore any move toward real disarmament by those countries with small arsenals would have important consequences in reducing the danger of their use and in delegitimizing nuclear weapons. An example of such a move happened when South Africa gave up its nuclear armament, although its arsenal was very limited. This led to the entry into force of the Pelindaba Treaty.

The middle nuclear powers, France and the UK, could take several short-term measures on their own initiative without waiting for agreement between Russia and the United States:[71]

1. The calls for the elimination of nuclear weapons seldom express the logical conclusion of their assertions—that is, that it is not possible to convince other countries that nuclear weapons are not in their interest if the nuclear doctrines and weapon system modernization programs are not changed accordingly. France and the UK should publicly renounce their first-use policy, specify what they consider to be their vital interests, and renounce the modernization of their warheads and missiles. France should dismantle the airborne component, which is the essential element of the *ultime avertissement*, and decrease further the number of weapons placed on submarines.

2. A verifiable elimination of nuclear weapons is a critical element of a nuclear weapon–free world. Britain and a non-nuclear weapon state, Norway,

have begun a collaboration on developing new technologies, methods, and procedures. France, as well as other countries, both nuclear and non-nuclear weapon states, should join in this endeavor.[72]

3. There is no alternative to global multilateral negotiations on complete nuclear disarmament. France and Britain should put the issue of a Nuclear Weapon Convention on the international agenda now. In a first step, France and Britain should convene a conference to study all aspects—technical and political—of the design of this convention, considering a time horizon in the range of years and not decades for the conclusion of the convention. The organization of this conference should be open, and participation as wide as possible should be encouraged: at least all nuclear-equipped states, as well as the countries having civilian nuclear ambitions, should participate. Last but not least, the conference should provide for the meaningful participation of members of the civil society, including independent scientists and experts.

The dialog on Nuclear Zero should move away from its Western-centrism and consider the security assurance needs of the other countries. Outside Europe and the affluent West there is a widespread feeling that the West wishes to use its military force to politically dominate the world, and that it analyzes and reacts to the world developments only according to its narrow and short-term interests and those of its allies in order to maintain its economic superiority and secure its access to strategic supplies. Some countries, such as Iran or Brazil, may feel threatened, as they possess important natural and energy resources that they want to protect.

Moreover, the unwillingness of the nuclear powers to implement their own commitments does not give them any international legitimacy to require new constraints from other countries, such as more intrusive inspections or possible limitations in national development or access to sensitive but permitted technologies, such as uranium enrichment. The variable norms in nuclear policies between "friendly" and "unfriendly" proliferators can only lead to bitter feelings in the populations of other countries, as well as their governments, which may, with the support of their people, refuse control measures, such as the International Atomic Energy Agency (IAEA) Additional Protocol, or may lead to policies that reduce transparency. Western leaders should realize that only multilateral agreements that are global and truly nondiscriminatory have a chance of bringing stability in the long run.

NOTES

I would like to thank Catherine Kelleher and Judith Reppy for their editorial assistance and General (ret.) Bernard Norlain for his interesting comments on an earlier draft. Any errors that remain are my responsibility.

1. Ordonnance no. 45-2563 du 18 octobre 1945 portant création du Commissariat à l'énergie atomique (CEA).

2. "Intervention de M. François Mitterrand, Président de la République, sur la politique de défense de la France et la dissuasion nucléaire," Paris le 5 mai 1994, at http://discours.vie-publique.fr/notices/947007300.html.

3. Ibid.

4. Jean-Damien Pô, "Les moyens de la puissance. Les activités militaires du CEA, 1945–2000." Ed. Ellipses marketing, Paris, 2001.

5. Pierre Billaud and Venance Journé, "The Real Story behind the Making of the French Hydrogen Bomb," *Nonproliferation Review* 15, no. 2 (2008): 353–72.

6. White Paper on Defense, 1972, at http://www.vie-publique.fr/documents-vp/livre_blanc_1972.shtml, indicates that conventional weapons were closely associated with nuclear weapons on the battlefield in case the Soviet forces would march toward Western Europe.

7. Sénat 2005, avis 77, at http://www.senat.fr/rap/a04-077-4/a04-077-48.html.

8. "Intervention de M. François Mitterrand."

9. Pô, "Les moyens de la puissance," p. 219.

10. See http://www.vie-publique.fr/chronologie/chronos-thematiques/politique-defense-loi-programmation-militaire-autre-1994-2007.html.

11. "Intervention de M. François Mitterrand."

12. Alain Ruello "Ces milliards qui manquent à la Défense," *Les Echos*, 16 Juillet 2007.

13. President Sarkozy, Cherbourg, 2008 at http://www.acronym.org.uk/docs/0803/doc09.htm.

14. NPT Prepcom Conference, New York, 4–15 Mai 2009, speech by Eric Danon, French ambassador to the CD.

15. According to Charles Million, French defense minister (1995–97), "France has a fissile material stock sufficient for the next fifty years," and "beyond these fifty years, we will know how to recycle the materials currently employed in our nuclear weapons." Quoted in Global Fissile Material Report 2008, "Banning the Production of Fissile Materials for Nuclear Weapons: Country Perspectives on the Challenges to a Fissile Material (Cutoff) Treaty," p. 15.

16. Présentation devant l'Assemblée nationale, par M. François Léotard, ministre de la défense, du projet de loi de programmation militaire 1995–2000, 24 mai 1994, at http://www.vie-publique.fr/chronologie/chronos-thematiques/politique-defense-loi-programmation-militaire-autre-1994-2007.html.

17. White Paper on Defense, 1994, at http://lesrapports.ladocumentationfrancaise.fr/BRP/944048700/0000.pdf, p. 52–57.

18. Speech by President Chirac at the Institut des Hautes Etudes de Défense Nationale, 8 June 2001, at http://discours.vie-publique.fr/notices/017000120.html. "I am convinced that in the long run our security will rest on three fundamental and complementary pillars: respect for the rule of law, the modernity and Europeanization of our defense capability, and permanence of nuclear deterrence. . . . "[O]ur security is and will be guaranteed first and foremost by nuclear deterrence. This is true today and will be even more so tomorrow. . . . Nuclear deterrence is above all an important factor of global stability."

19. Speech by President Chirac during his visit to the Strategic Air and Maritime Forces at Landivisiau/L'Ile Longue, 19 January 2006, at http://www.cedoc.defense.gouv.fr/-Politique-de-defense-Strategie-.

20. President Sarkozy, Cherbourg, 2008.

21. President Chirac, speech, 2006; Audition de Mme Michèle Alliot-Marie, Ministre de la Défense, sur la dissuasion nucléaire française, Commission de la Défense Nationale et des Forces Armeés, Compte Rendu N° 21, Mercredi 25 janvier 2006, at http://www.assemblee-nationale.fr/12/cr-cdef/05-06/c0506021.asp#TopOfPage.

22. "Dissuasion," Henri Bentégeat, in Défense nationale et sécurité collective, n°8–9, août–septembre 2004, p. 11.

23. White Paper, 1994, p. 24.

24. Ibid., p. 25.

25. President Chirac, speech, 2006.

26. Audition de Mme Michèle Alliot-Marie, 2006.

27. President Sarkozy, Cherbourg, 2008.

28. Lucien Poirier: "Je crois en la vertu rationalisante de l'atome," *Le Monde*, 27.05.06.

29. Général Bentégeat, in "Rapport d'Information sur le rôle de la dissuasion nucléaire française aujourd'hui," Serge Vinçon, Sénat, octobre 2006, at http://www.senat.fr/rap/r06-036/r06-0361.pdf, p. 24.

30. President Chirac, speech, 2006.

31. Audition de Mme Michèle Alliot-Marie, 2006. "The French President has underlined the fact that our country has made more flexible its capacities of action and has now the possibility to target decision centers of a possible aggressor, avoiding in this way an overspread of fallout which might make us hesitate." [Le Président de la République a souligné que notre pays a assoupli ses capacités d'action et a désormais la possibilité de cibler les centres de décision d'un éventuel agresseur, évitant ainsi les retombées trop générales susceptibles de nous faire hésiter.]

32. Laurent Zecchini, "La guerre nucléaire propre," *Le Monde*, 2 March 2006.

33. Alliot-Marie, 11 janvier 2005, quoted in Isabelle Lasserre, "La France modernise sa dissuasion nucleaire," *Le Figaro*, 14 janvier 2005.

34. "La dissuasion nucléaire: quel rôle dans la défense française aujourd'hui?" Sénat, Rapport d'information n° 36 (2006–7) de M. Serge VINÇON, fait au nom de la commission des affaires étrangères, déposé le 24 octobre 2006, at http://www.senat.fr/rap/r06-036/r06-0363.html.

35. The French White Paper on Defense and National Security (2008), at http://www.defense.gouv.fr/content/download/134828/1175142/version/1/file/LivreBlancGB.pdf, p. 162.

36. Audition de Mme Michèle Alliot-Marie, 2006.

37. Bentégeat, in "Rapport d'Information," p. 29.

38. Ibid.

39. Zecchini, "La guerre nucléaire propre."

40. Audition de Mme Michèle Alliot-Marie, 2006.

41. President Chirac, speech, 2006.

42. Capitaine de Frégate Guillaume Martin de Clausonne (now in charge of the Barraduca project at the Commandement of the Marine Corps), "Ouvrons le débat sur la dissuation nucléaire, La Tribune du Collège Interarnées de défense," October 2006. Galy-Dejean, 2006, at http://www.assemblee-nationale.fr/12/cr-cdef/05-06/c0506021.asp#TopOfPage.

43. Michel Rocard, a son of Yves Rocard, one of the very few scientists in favor of a French nuclear weapon from the very beginning. Report of the Canberra Commission on the abolition of nuclear weapons, preface to the French edition, Editions Odile Jacob, 1997.

44. "Pour un désarmement nucléaire mondial, seule réponse à la prolifération anarchique, Alain Juppé, Bernard Norlain, Alain Richard, Michel Rocard," *Le Monde*, 14 octobre 2009.

45. Jean Guisnel, "Alain Juppé et Michel Rocard en faveur d'un désarmement nucléaire mondial, y compris pour la France," *Le Point*, 14 Octobre 2009.

46. Le général d'armée Jean-Louis Georgelin, chef d'Etat-major des armées, "22/10/08: 50e anniversaire de la direction des applications militaires du commissariat à l'énergie atomique," at http://www.defense.gouv.fr/ema/commandement/le_chef_d_etat_major/interventions/discours/22_10_08_50e_anniversaire_de_la_direction_des_applications_militaires_du_commissariat_a_l_energie_atomique.

47. President Sarkozy, Cherbourg, 2008.

48. Louis Gautier, conseiller à la Cour des comptes, ancien conseiller Défense du Premier ministre, *L'avenir de la dissuasion française*, Intervention prononcée lors du colloque L'avenir de la dissuasion française du 10 juillet 2006, at http://www.fondation-res-publica.org/L-avenir-de-la-dissuasion-francaise_r27.html.

49. Xavier Pintat, rapporteur pour avis de la commission des affaires étrangères, de

la defense et des forces armées du Sénat, le 24 novembre 2004. "Projet de loi de finances pour 2005: Défense-Nucléaire, espace et services communs," at http://www.senat.fr/commission/etr/etrg041129.html#toc4.

50. Alliot-Marie, "La France modernise sa dissuasion nucleaire," 14 janvier 2005.

51. "La propulsion nucléaire, un savoir-faire indispensable à la souveraineté nationale," Michel Picard, avec la collaboration de Bruno Tertrais, Fondation pour la Recherche Stratégique, 30 juin 2006, p. 12, at http://www.frstrategie.org/barreFRS/publications/rd/RD_20060630.pdf. In the hypothetical situation of an increase in the number of permanent members of the UN Security Council, maintaining a nuclear force would allow France to preserve its greater weight relative to the non-nuclear newcomers (for example Germany or Japan), p. 13.

52. Ibid., p. 12.

53. Clausonne, "Ouvrons le débat sur la dissuation nucléaire."

54. "Intervention prononcée" par Eric Danon, chef de la délégation française, 6 Mai 2009, NPT Prepcom, at http://www.un.org/disarmament/WMD/Nuclear/NPT2010Prepcom/PrepCom2009/statements/2009/04May2009/04May2009.

55. Francis Gutmann, "Nécessité de la dissuasion," DéfenseIHEDN, n°140 Juillet–Août 2009.

56. François de Rose and Olivier Debouzy, "Eliminer les armes nucléaires?" *Commentaires* 126 (Eté 2009).

57. Michel Rocard, "Oui à un second porte-avions financé par le nucléaire," *Le Figaro*, 12 juin 2008.

58. Dominique David, "Non, Monsieur Rocard, le porte-avions n'est pas la France," *Le Figaro*, 19 juin 2008.

59. Laurent Zecchini, "Revisiter la dissuasion nucléaire," *Le Monde*, 27 october 2004.

60. "La dissuasion nucléaire" at
http://www.senat.fr/rap/r06-036/r06-0363.html.

61. Paul Quilès, "France Inter," quoted in "The Reactions to the Speech by Jacques Chirac on the Eventual Cases of Nuclear Response," Nouvelobs.com, January 20, 2006. A former defense minister "regrets that the debate never materialized on this issue [of the deterrence adapted to present circumstances] not in the Parliament, nor in any other place."

62. Bentégeat, "Dissuasion," p. 11.

63. Heisbourg quoted in Zecchini, "Revisiter la dissuasion nucléaire."

64. Cahal Milmo, "So, Admiral, What Have You Got to Say about the Nuclear Submarine Crash?" *The Independent*, 17 February 2009.

65. Zecchini, "Revisiter la dissuasion nucléaire."

66. Clausonne, "Ouvrons le débat sur la dissuation nucléaire."

67. The 4th United Nations General Assembly, United Nations Security Council

Summit on Nuclear Non-Proliferation and Nuclear Disarmament—speech by Nicolas Sarkozy, President of the Republic, to the United Nations Security Council, New York, 24 September 2009.

68. Clausonne, "Ouvrons le débat sur la dissuation nucléaire."

69. Ibid.

70. See the research results of Alan Robock and Brian Toon at http://climate.envsci.rutgers.edu/nuclear/.

71. Venance Journé, "Towards Disarmament: What Role for Middle Nuclear Powers?" August 2008, World Scientific Publishing Co. Pte. Ltd., Singapore, Science and Culture Series, International Seminars on Nuclear War and Planetary Emergencies, 40th Session.

72. UK-Norway initiative presentation, at http://www.armscontrolverification.org/2009_05_01_archive.html.

8 Challenges for U.S.-China Strategic Stability in the Obama Administration

Jeffrey Lewis

Speaking in Prague on April 5, 2009, President Barack Obama committed the United States to seeking what he described as "the peace and security of a world without nuclear weapons." Obama omitted any mention of China in this speech, as he did in an earlier speech on the campaign trail. Yet a world without nuclear weapons rests, in no small part, on whether the administration can succeed in creating a stable strategic relationship with China. Moreover, each step in the ambitious agenda he outlined on the road to zero—deeper reductions in warheads and stockpiles, Senate ratification of the Comprehensive Test Ban Treaty, and a new treaty that verifiably ends the production of fissile materials—requires a more sustained engagement with China than is currently in place.

Some in Washington are concerned that deeper U.S. and Russian reductions will spark a Chinese "sprint" to numerical parity with the United States. Others see extended deterrence, particularly its ability to assure Japan, as the most difficult problem in U.S. nuclear strategy. Still others view a crisis over the status of Taiwan as the only probable scenario for a deliberate nuclear exchange involving the United States.

So far, the administration has shown little evidence that it understands the necessity of a fundamental transformation in the U.S.-China strategic relationship, let alone the challenges in attempting such a transformation. The 2010 Nuclear Posture Review maintains the fundamental ambivalence toward China's status as a nuclear power. If the president seeks a world without nuclear weapons, he must find a way to transform the U.S.-China strategic relationship. This chapter sketches out the challenges posed by ongoing strategic modernization in the United States and China, past efforts to manage strategic stability between the two countries, and a modest agenda for the Obama administration. The fundamental question is whether the United States will accept, as a fact, the reality of China's deterrent or seek to negate that deterrent through the development of more sophisticated strategic capabilities, including missile defenses and conventional strike.

CHINA'S STRATEGIC MODERNIZATION

China and the United States maintain nuclear forces that are extremely different in size, posture, and policy. China's nuclear stockpile is probably a few hundred nuclear weapons.[1] About half of its nuclear weapons are "operationally deployed" for use with ballistic missiles, with the warheads stored separately.[2] The remainder of the stockpile is in storage. China has issued a pledge to "never at any time or under any circumstances be the first to use nuclear weapons." Some observers claim, however, that there is ambiguity in its no-first-use pledge, pointing to statements in military writings criticizing no first use as inflexible or statements by academics expressing skepticism that the pledge would hold in extremis. To be clear—there is no ambiguity in the official statements. China, as a matter of policy, has sought bilateral and multilateral no-first-use agreements.

China is modernizing its strategic forces, largely through the deployment of solid-fueled ballistic missiles. In the 1980s, it focused on developing solid-fueled, mobile ballistic missiles to replace its first generation of ballistic missiles. Although it deployed the first of these new missiles, the DF-21, beginning in the early 1990s, flight testing on the DF-21 continued through the 1990s, and China did not begin large-scale deployments in earnest until around 2000. The first brigades of road-mobile variants—the DF-31 and the DF-31A—became operational in 2007 and 2008, respectively.

China is also developing a submarine-launched variant of the DF-31, called the JL-2, and has put to sea a new class of ballistic missile submarines, one of which was on display during a fleet review in Qingdao in April 2009. The Office of Naval Intelligence believes China may build as many as five of the new submarines to replace its lone Xia-class SSBN, which is not believed to be operational. China appears to have rather limited capabilities for communicating with submarines at sea and probably has not established operational practices for conducting deterrent patrols. The United States expected the JL-2 missile to become operational in 2010, but it failed its final round of flight tests and the future of the program is uncertain.

The growth in China's ballistic missile arsenal is not confined to its nuclear forces. It has also developed new conventionally armed solid-fuel short-range ballistic missiles, the DF-11 and DF-15, which are deployed in very large numbers near Taiwan. China has also deployed a conventional variant of the DF-21, the DF-21C, which is also the basis of a conventionally armed antiship ballistic missile. (The DF-21 may also be the basis of China's hit-to-kill interceptor tested against an orbiting Chinese satellite in January 2007 and in an anti–ballistic missile mode in January 2010.) Finally, China has also deployed a new land-attack cruise missile—the ground-launched DH-10—as part of a broad effort to acquire ground-, air-, and sea-launched cruise missiles.[3]

This process of replacing liquid-fueled ballistic missiles with solid-fueled ballistic and cruise missiles underpins China's ongoing strategic modernization. Although many observers have linked the deployment of the DF-31 and DF-31A to recent U.S. missile defense deployments, it is important to keep in mind that these programs date to the mid-1980s and were to have been completed many years ago.

Some observers worry that these developments could result in a dramatic increase in the number of Chinese nuclear weapons, as well as an abandonment of China's no-first-use posture. This is part of a concern that China is moving toward a posture that might be called "limited deterrence." The idea that China might move away from a minimum deterrent to a posture that more closely resembles that of the United States is long-standing: the theme of moving toward greater operational flexibility appears in early analyses of China's nascent nuclear doctrine by RAND's Alice Langley Hsieh.[4] In the late 1980s, the term "limited deterrence" began to populate military journals and books from scholars associated with the Chinese Academy of Military Sciences (AMS), National Defense University, General Staff Department, and Second Artillery. Some scholars anticipated China would move toward this posture, which would permit it to use its strategic forces in limited nuclear war–fighting roles. Beijing was expected to significantly increase the size, mobility, flexibility, and diversity of Chinese strategic forces. Others anticipated that China would abandon its no-first-use pledge.

Is China's deterrent evolving away from what a senior Chinese official once described as "the minimum means of reprisal"? It seems clear that China will increase the size of its nuclear forces—for example, it appears to have established new brigades to operate the DF-31 and DF-31A, rather than converting existing units. How much that indicates about China's deterrent posture, however, is an open question. It remains to be seen whether China will increase the number of nuclear warheads as much as current U.S. intelligence community predictions—which anticipate very large increases in Chinese nuclear forces to respond to U.S. missile defense efforts—project. In 2001, the U.S. intelligence community asserted that the number of Chinese warheads capable of reaching the United States could grow to 75 to 100 by 2015.[5] In 2006, the National Air and Space Intelligence Center warned that the number of Chinese nuclear warheads that could reach the United States "could expand to well over 100 in the next 15 years."[6]

Such an expansion would require not merely the production of additional missiles and nuclear warheads. In discussing U.S. estimates that China might deploy as many as 200 ICBMs, Ken Allen and Maryanne Kivlehan-Wise caution that we need to be mindful of the organizational requirements of such a transformation. "From an organizational perspective, an increase from the current 18–20 ICBMs to 200 would mean increasing the number of brigades from the existing two to about twenty brigades," they write. "If this were the case, the PLA would most likely have to create several new bases with multiple brigades per base, acquire all of the requisite equipment, and train the necessary enlisted and officer force. The question remains whether this is realistic."[7]

A force of more than a hundred ICBMs, deployed on both road-mobile and submarine-launched ballistic missiles, seems more consistent with a small, retaliatory force rather than a limited war–fighting capability. The most important measure is probably the operational patterns of these forces. By all indications, Chinese nuclear warheads are not normally mated to their missiles. Robert Walpole, then National Intelligence Officer for Strategic and Nuclear Programs, stated in 1998 that "China keeps its missiles unfueled and without warheads mated."[8] The warheads are stored at nearby, but separate, bases.[9] Press reports of Chinese mobile ballistic missile exercises, carried by the Xinhua News Agency, indicate that nuclear warheads would be mated in the field to mobile ballistic missiles before launch, similar to the procedure used by Soviet "Mobile Technical Rocket Bases" (PRTB in Russian) stationed in East Germany and elsewhere during the Cold War.[10] Anecdotal evidence from public descriptions of Chinese exercises and doctrinal materials suggest that Chinese forces expend considerable effort training to conduct retaliatory missions in the harsh environment after a nuclear strike.[11]

It would seem likely that once its ballistic missile submarines become operational, China will deploy them to sea with nuclear warheads, as do France, the United Kingdom, and the United States. On the other hand, there are alternative models. Russia, for instance, does not maintain "continuous at sea deterrence"—the practice of keeping at least one submarine on combat patrol at all times. In recent years, the number of Russian ballistic missile submarine patrols—probably conducted for training purposes—detected by the United States Navy has varied widely. Just as China seems reluctant to send mobile launch companies into the field with nuclear weapons, it may choose not to maintain continuous at-sea deterrence, despite the expectations of those in the United States and elsewhere.

Indeed, Chinese officials seem to view placing forces on alert as an important signaling measure. The 2009 National Defense White Paper makes clear that, in a crisis, China would place its nuclear forces in a state of alert. This echoes an earlier document that describes alert operations to demonstrate will—what it calls "counter-nuclear deterrence"—as an important phase in nuclear operations.

CHALLENGES FOR U.S.-CHINA STRATEGIC STABILITY

Chinese posture is extremely different from that of the United States. The U.S. nuclear stockpile is believed to number about 5,000 nuclear weapons. About 1,000 of these warheads—those on silo-based missiles and submarines at sea—are on "day-to-day" alert. These are the most ready of a larger "operationally deployed" force of 2,200 warheads which includes warheads on submarines and in storage at bomber bases and which can be brought to a generated alert over the course of days. These numbers are decreasing, as the United States and Russia continue the process of negotiated reductions.

Like China, the United States is making significant changes in its strategic forces. As part of the "new triad," the United States has pursued ballistic missile defense capabilities and conventional strike. It has deployed ground-based midcourse interceptors in Alaska, and it is pursuing a number of conventional strike capabilities, initially on modified D-5 submarine-launched ballistic missiles carried by Ohio-class submarines. These capabilities are pointedly not constrained by the U.S.-Russian strategic arms control regime, nor by any other legally binding instrument.

China is not the primary driver of these changes—although they are deeply disconcerting to some Chinese strategists. Similarly, these changes are not the primary drivers of China's development of solid-fueled ballistic missiles, which is a long-standing effort that predates both the mid-1990s decline in U.S.-China relations, as well as recent developments of current missile defense and conventional strike systems. This is not to suggest that missile defense and other aspects of U.S. strategic modernization have no effect on Chinese decisions, or vice versa. China has developed and flight-tested a sophisticated suite of penetration aids for the DF-21 and DF-31 family of ballistic missiles.[12] Some Chinese specialists have argued that China may increase the number of nuclear warheads capable of reaching the United States, rather than simply replacing the DF-4 and DF-5 on a one-to-one basis.[13] But the essential feature of U.S. and Chinese forces is that, unlike U.S.-Soviet forces during the Cold War, they are decoupled. The two sides do not engage in the kind of day-to-day deterrent operations that characterized the Cold War relationship between the United States and Russia. Chinese missiles remain in their garrisons or silos, with the warheads in storage, and it has conducted only a single patrol of its ballistic missile submarine, with rather disappointing results.

Yet this could change. The ongoing modernization of both Chinese and U.S. strategic forces could create the kind of escalatory dynamics that characterized the most dangerous moments of the Cold War, raising the prospect of a serious crisis between two nuclear-armed nations with vastly different historical, cultural, and strategic outlooks.

The United States and China have experienced several tense crises in recent years, arising from the operation of military forces in close proximity to one another. In 2001, a Chinese fighter jet collided with a U.S. EP-3E reconnaissance aircraft, killing the Chinese pilot and forcing the EP-3E to land on Hainan Island. China detained the crew for eleven days, while the United States and China negotiated the return of the crew and the aircraft. More recently, in March 2009, the United States Navy announced that "five Chinese vessels shadowed and aggressively maneuvered close to the USNS *Impeccable* in the South China Sea." Although the *Impeccable* was described as an "oceanographic ship" that was "conducting routine operations in international waters," the Chinese viewed the ship as conducting surveillance for antisubmarine warfare activities. Although the *Impeccable* was operating well within the boundaries of international law, the Chinese actions may have been motivated by a desire to protect sensitive submarine operations in the area. In a third incident, in June 2009, a Chinese submarine accidentally collided with a sonar array being towed by a U.S. destroyer.[14]

These three incidents illustrate that U.S.-Chinese forces, operating in close proximity to one other during a crisis, face serious strategic stability challenges.

Based on press reports of exercises, in a crisis China would disperse mobile ballistic missiles and fuel missiles in fixed sites.[15] How would American policy-makers react, especially if its own forces were placed on alert? The history of U.S. alert operations suggests that alert operations have an inherent escalatory potential. In studies of the four U.S. DEFCON-3 or higher alerts, Scott Sagan found that orders were frequently misunderstood or ambiguous events misinterpreted to confirm the sense of crisis and concluded that "keeping the alert at the desired level will be extremely difficult, and the degree of further grave escalation uncertain."[16] The inherent risk is captured by President Kennedy's sardonic remark, upon learning that a U2 had strayed over Soviet airspace during the Cuban Missile Crisis: "There's always some son-of-a-bitch who doesn't get the message."[17]

One can imagine the potential for escalation if, for instance, Chinese missile submarines put out to sea during a crisis. U.S. attack submarines would surely attempt to tail them. What would happen if, in a crisis, two submarines collided? Or if the Chinese submarine suffered a crippling accident, like the torpedo explosion that sank the Russian submarine *Kursk*? Would Chinese policy-makers, in the midst of a tense atmosphere, be able to distinguish the loss of contact with submarines from early efforts to eliminate their deterrent? How would U.S. policy-makers react if China appeared to prepare mobile ballistic missiles that could perform antisatellite missions? Or antiship DF-21D missiles that, externally, are identical to China's nuclear-armed DF-21 and DF-21As? It is impossible to predict. But the recent history of U.S.-Chinese crisis stability is not encouraging.

Mechanisms for Dialogue

Recognizing these issues, recent Democratic and Republican administrations have pressed to expand military-to-military exchanges. The United States and China have begun a formal dialogue on strategic issues in recent years. In 2005, former secretary of defense Donald Rumsfeld visited the headquarters of the Second Artillery. In 2008, Secretary Gates announced that the United States and China had established a hotline linking the Department of Defense and the Chinese Defense Ministry and initiated talks between their two militaries on nuclear issues.

These are important steps, but they are limited in scope. The Second Artillery is an important factor in Chinese strategic policy, but they are first and foremost "operators" who are responsible for handling ballistic missiles. The

General Armaments Department—which is responsible for the ballistic missile program and the entire nuclear complex—is probably a more important voice, particularly on the issue of modernization. The United States has had rather less access to the nuclear weapons complex, since the laboratory-to-laboratory exchange program was shuttered in the 1990s.

The United States and China also have a Strategic and Economic Dialogue (SED). Initially conducted between the Treasury Department and the Ministry of Finance, Secretary of State Hilary Clinton has pushed to make the dialogue a Strategic *and* Economic Dialogue, serving as a co-chair with Treasury Secretary Timothy Geithner, and changing the acronym from SED to SAED to reflect the dual nature. At the undersecretary level, the United States and China have conducted four rounds of a bilateral U.S.-China security dialogue, with the most recent having occurred in June 2008 between Acting Undersecretary of State John Rood and Vice Minister He Yafei. This dialogue is the principal forum for arms control discussions, although the agenda includes a wide variety of other issues including nonproliferation concerns.

A Note on Laboratory to Laboratory Exchanges

In 1994, the United States and China initiated laboratory-to-laboratory exchanges.[18] The exchanges were ended after allegations of Chinese espionage leveled in the Cox Report. In 2005, the United States government sought to revive the laboratory-to-laboratory exchange program. Having felt that previous exchanges were mischaracterized by opponents, the Chinese side insisted that the United States provide a letter that included the written assurance that laboratory-to-laboratory exchanges during the 1990s had been "legal and mutually beneficial." Although some officials within the Department of Energy pressed to issue China this assurance, others in the Bush administration successfully opposed the measure. The Obama administration has yet to revive cooperation, despite encouraging statements similar to those made in recent years.

Informal Exchanges

In lieu of formal contacts, the U.S.-China relationship is sustained by a multitude of so-called Track II dialogues—the term deriving from "Track I" channel of official government-to-government discourse. There are currently a number of such discussions organized by academic institutions. Bridging political, cultural, and linguistic divides is a difficult task. The ongoing policy dialogue between the United States National Academies of Science Committee on International Security and Arms Control (CISAC) and the Chinese Scientists

Group for Arms Control (CSGAC) is probably the oldest, continuous "Track II" dialogue. The CISAC-CSGAC group completed a joint *Nuclear Security Glossary* of terms commonly used in their dialogue which illustrates some of the challenges. The document is an impressive achievement, all the more so for the challenges that confronted the authors over a number of phrases. For example, Chinese participants objected to including the term "limited deterrence" out of concern that it might suggest China's nuclear posture was changing along the lines outlined above. U.S. participants pointed to the literature discussed earlier to suggest that it deserved inclusion. The phrase—有限威慑 (*yǒuxiàn wēishè*)—was eventually included, with explanations like "there is no consensus on the definition" and "in some descriptions it refers to France's nuclear deterrent."[19]

AN AGENDA FOR COOPERATION

There is real danger that ongoing modernization in both countries could gradually couple the two countries' nuclear forces, creating an analogous situation to the dangerous force interactions that characterized U.S. and Soviet nuclear forces during the Cold War. The prospect of entanglement is driven by the differing perceptions in Beijing and Washington. American observers worry that China will increase the size of its nuclear forces to seek parity with the United States, undermining extended deterrence. When China deploys road-mobile missiles, the United States sees this as threatening its ability to come to the aid of allies in the region. When the United States deploys missile defenses, Chinese leaders view this as an effort to negate China's deterrent. As both sides undertake essentially technology-driven improvements to a defensive capability, they become more deeply entangled. Avoiding this outcome requires that both countries understand their shared interest in maintaining strategic stability, including the viability of China's deterrent as well as the U.S. extended deterrent in Asia.

The concern that China might seek numerical parity is embedded in the loose idea that the United States should maintain a nuclear force that is "second to none." In practice, this means that the United States should maintain operationally deployed strategic forces that are at rough parity with Russia and therefore several factors larger than the worst-case estimate for Chinese forces. There is a real fear among American policy-makers that substantial reductions in U.S. operationally deployed strategic forces would tempt China to "sprint" to numerical parity—quickly increasing the number of nuclear-armed ballistic missiles, much as it did with conventionally armed short-range ballistic missiles near Taiwan over the past decade. As the United States and Russia explore further bilateral reductions, the prospect of larger Chinese forces has become a "floor" for deep reductions.

There is little evidence, however, that Chinese officials view numerical parity as an important concept, having lived with a numerically inferior deterrent for decades. Moreover, substantial increases in force size would, as noted above, require a fundamental transformation of the Second Artillery and, presumably, the nuclear navy. These changes are possible, of course, but they would likely occur over a very long time-frame with substantial indications.

Because China maintains ambiguity about what one Chinese observer called "operational information and armament capabilities"—technical information about the size and capability of China's nuclear forces—China has not taken steps to reassure the United States that it would welcome significant reductions. Indeed, most Chinese observers express disbelief that China would seek parity and note that China's forces are so small that it makes little difference if the United States reduces from 2,200 to 1,500 warheads. It is difficult for many Chinese to contemplate placing even general constraints on the modernization of the forces, given current disparities in force size.

Within China, there is a real sense that the United States seeks to negate China's deterrent. Chinese officials are quite worried about the long-term implications of missile defense and conventional strike on their deterrent. Although one frequently hears U.S. commentators indicate that the purpose of China's nuclear forces is to discourage U.S. involvement in a crisis over Taiwan, Chinese officials and academics continue to describe their deterrent in terms of an existential safeguard to prevent the United States from using the threat of a nuclear attack to coerce China.

This reflects a fundamental difference in conception: many U.S. officials and academics think about the utility of nuclear weapons in terms of use. This is not surprising—popular mythology in the United States is that the use of two nuclear weapons against Japan brought the Second World War to its conclusion. Chinese interlocutors on the other hand tend to emphasize the role of nuclear weapons in coercion. This reflects China's experience with U.S. nuclear threats during the Korean War. Two Chinese scholars—Li Bin and Nie Hongyi—are particularly direct about this difference in conception and its implications:

> General offense-defense theory and classic arms control theory are the same in assuming a nation selects behavior based solely on the magnitude of its interest. This is a bit different than the reality of strategic weaponry. Classic arms con-

> trol theory predicts that when a nuclear country is going to lose a conventional war and does not worry about nuclear relation, the possibility [of] saving the situation with a nuclear attack is great. But the Korean, Vietnam and Afghan wars all demonstrate that this prediction does not reflect actual conditions in international society. The theory of the nuclear taboo in constructivist theory postulates a norm in international society against the use of nuclear weapons, a norm known as the nuclear taboo. Under the conditions of this nuclear taboo, just because a country has the ability to carry out a preemptive nuclear attack does not mean they can carry out this type of nuclear attack at will. However, the existence of the nuclear taboo does not prevent a nuclear weapon state from using the superiority of its nuclear weapons to engage in coercion. Consequently, the most direct result of a strategic imbalance is nuclear coercion.[20]

The difference is an important one; consider the case of a no-first-use pledge. Many Americans describe such a pledge as a hollow promise, noting that a president retains, irrespective of such pledges, the right of *belligerent reprisal.* On the other hand, if the primary utility of nuclear weapons is coercion rather than actual use, forswearing first-use does constrain a leader's "use" of the weapons in a political context.

As a result, Chinese arguments about strategic stability are rooted in overall questions about the political relationship rather than force-exchange ratios. Central to this is the pursuit of a mutual deterrent relationship, enshrined in a bilateral no-first-use pledge. China sought such an assurance in the 1990s, resulting in the so-called nontargeting agreement signed by presidents Bill Clinton and Jiang Zemin.

Whereas American officials tend to regard such pledges as meaningless—and call into question the sincerity of the Chinese pledge—Chinese observers believe that the political significance of the gesture is the important thing, and it could result in visible changes to U.S. posture that would be reassuring to Beijing. The precise formulation is perhaps not so important, one senior official told me: "The important thing is that you say it." The Chinese side, in the bilateral exchange in 2008, renewed their interest in a no-first-use pledge, without success.

The reluctance of the United States to make such a statement demonstrates how far the United States and the rest of the world remain from the goal of the elimination of nuclear weapons. Despite the president's vision in Prague, the United States continues to rely on nuclear weapons for a number of missions beyond the fundamental purpose of deterring and, if necessary, responding to nuclear attacks. The 2010 Nuclear Posture Review (NPR), despite its claim to reduce reliance on nuclear weapons, does not represent a sharp break with past U.S. nuclear weapons policies.

In some cases this is not unwelcome. The NPR, for example, embraces strategic stability in the U.S.-China relationship. Yet the implications of this statement are not articulated, in part reflecting ambivalence within the United States. When Acting Undersecretary Rood was unwilling to state that the United States does not seek to negate China's deterrent, he was accurately reflecting the lack of consensus about China's deterrent that has continued into the Obama administration. This debate is often characterized by the question of whether China is a "little Russia" or a "big rogue"—with the implication being that Russia is to be deterred, while a rogue (like North Korea) is to be defended against. The text of the NPR compares China to Russia, but does not commit to the implication of that comparison.

The NPR leaves open the possibility of a fundamental transformation in the strategic relationship of the two countries, but the Obama administration appears reluctant to move further. In part, the careful wording of the NPR appears intended to leave open some options, while not taking on a debate that might undermine prospects for Senate ratification of the U.S.-Russia New START treaty. Many in the Bush administration argued strongly that the United States should *not* accept China's deterrent. In 2001, Undersecretary of Defense Doug Feith claimed that "it is not the case" that the United States and China have a mutual deterrent relationship, adding that "we should not import into our thinking about China the cold war concepts of mutual assured destruction."[21] Similarly, deputy secretary of defense Paul Wolfowitz, in a draft report to the secretary of state (later leaked to the *Washington Times*), explained that the United States "should make it clear that it will not accept a mutual vulnerability relationship with China."[22] This view remains a political reality in Washington.

Yet "mutual vulnerability" is a particularly unflattering description of what many regard as a simple fact: that China and the United States each have a significant military capability to threaten the security of the other. Another view in Washington is that this is not a policy choice, but rather a fact. A recent Council on Foreign Relations Task Force, co-chaired by William Perry and Brent Scowcroft, captured this sense by noting "that mutual vulnerability with China—like mutual vulnerability with Russia—is not a policy choice to be embraced or rejected, but rather a strategic fact to be managed with priority on strategic stability."[23]

Yet despite the wildly divergent perceptions in Beijing and Washington, each government is preoccupied with essentially the same concern—that the other party does not respect the status quo. An understanding, therefore, needs to state clearly what aspects of the status quo each party values and seeks to preserve. For the United States, it is assurance that China does not seek strategic parity or to undermine U.S. security commitments—above all else to Japan. For China, it is that the United States does not seek to negate China's deterrent or conduct "nuclear blackmail" like that Beijing believes it endured in the 1950s.

NOTES

1. Declassified documents from the 1990s place classified estimates of the total stockpile, including a small stockpile of aircraft-delivered gravity bombs, between 200 and 250 warheads. See, for example, *China's Nuclear Weapons Testing: Facing Prospects for a Comprehensive Test Ban*, Office of Scientific and Weapons Research, September 30, 1993, p. 1; and "China Seeking Foreign Assistance to Address Concerns about Nuclear Stockpile under CTBT," *Proliferation Digest* (March 29, 1996): 38 (released under the Freedom of Information Act).

2. According to unclassified U.S. intelligence assessments, China "has over 100 warheads deployed operationally on ballistic missiles. Additional warheads are in storage." *Proliferation: Threat and Response*, Office of the Secretary of Defense, 1997. The intelligence community continues to describe the Chinese nuclear stockpile in this manner. See, for example, DIA director Michael Maples's statement in 2006 that "China currently has more than 100 nuclear warheads." Lieutenant General Michael D. Maples, U.S. Army Director, Defense Intelligence Agency, "Current and Projected National Security Threats to the United States," statement to the Senate Armed Services Committee, February 28, 2006.

3. On Chinese ballistic missile developments, see *Annual Report to Congress: Military Power of the People's Republic of China 2008*, Department of Defense, 2008; and *Ballistic and Cruise Missile Threat*, National Air and Space Intelligence Center, August 2006.

4. Alice Langley Hsieh, "China's Nuclear-Missile Programme: Regional or Intercontinental?" *China Quarterly* 45 (January–March 1971): 85–99.

5. "CIA National Intelligence Estimate of Foreign Missile Developments and the Ballistic Missile Threat through 2015," hearing before the International Security, Proliferation, and Federal Services Subcommittee of the Committee on Governmental Affairs, United States Senate, 107th Congress, second session, March 11, 2002, S. Hrg. 107-467.

6. *Ballistic and Cruise Missile Threat*, National Air and Space Intelligence Center, Wright-Patterson Air Force Base, Ohio. March 2006.

7. Kenneth Allen and Maryanne Kivlehan-Wise, "Implementing the Second Artillery's Doctrinal Reforms," in *China's Revolution in Doctrinal Affairs*, ed. James Mulvenon and David Finkelstein (Alexandria, VA: Center for Naval Analysis, 2005), p. 179.

8. Robert D. Walpole, National Intelligence Officer for Strategic and Nuclear Programs, speech at the Carnegie Endowment for International Peace, September 17, 1998, at http://www.cia.gov/cia/public_affairs/speeches/1998/walpole_speech_091798.html. *Operational Studies* implies this arrangement by defining the "missile base group" as "two or more missile bases and warhead bases." See *Operational Studies* [*Zhanyi xue*] (Beijing: National Defense University, 2000), ch. 14, p. 1. For a description of Chinese operating practices, see *Strategic Missile Tidbits* (1995), p. 3, at http://www.armscontrolwonk.com/file_download/4/DOD_Strategic_Missile_Tidbits.pdf.

9. For an account of China's centralized system of warhead storage, see Mark Stokes, *China's Nuclear Warhead Storage and Handling System*, March 12, 2010, at http://project2049.net/documents/chinas_nuclear_warhead_storage_and_handling_system.pdf.

10. PRTBs are described in Richard Clarke, *Your Government Failed You* (New York: Ecco, 2008), pp. 102–3. Chinese press reports of mobile ballistic missile exercises are described in Li Bin, "Tracking Chinese Strategic Mobile Missiles," *Science and Global Security* 15, no. 1 (2007): 11–30.

11. *Operational Studies* [*Zhanyi xue*].

12. See *Current and Projected National Security Threats to the United States*, Hearing before the Select Committee on Intelligence of the United States Senate, S. Hrg. 107-597 (February 6, 2002), p. 321; and *Country Profiles: China* (Ballistic Missile Defense Organization Countermeasure Integration Program, April 1995), pp. 12–18. China also has the capability to place multiple warheads on its older, liquid-fueled DF-5 ICBMs, although it has not yet done so.

13. For example, Sun Xiangli has disputed the notion that "the number of weapons that make up a limited nuclear force is immutably fixed. In fact, the required size for such a capability is a dynamic quantity relating to the nuclear arsenal's survivability. For instance, one guide to the size required of China's nuclear force is to be able to mount a nuclear strike that can penetrate an enemy's missile defense system after surviving a first strike." Sun Xiangli, "Analysis of China's Nuclear Strategy," *China Security* no. 1 (Autumn 2005): 23–27.

14. "U.S.-China Naval Incidents-Updated June 12, 2009," *War and Conflict Journal*, weblog, at http://warandconflictjournal.com/2009/06/u-s-china-naval-incidents-updated-june-12-2009/.

15. For example, one exercise is described in Dong Jushan and Wu Xudong, "Build New China's Shield of Peace," *Beijing Zhongguo Qingnian Bao* (July 1, 2001), FBIS-CPP-2001-0703-000119.

16. Scott D. Sagan, "Nuclear Alerts and Crisis Management," *International Security* 9, no. 4 (Spring 1985): 136.

17. Scott D. Sagan, *Limits of Safety: Organizations, Accidents, and Nuclear Weapons* (Princeton: Princeton University Press, 1993), pp. 117–18.

18. For a history of the program, see Nancy Prindle, "Report: The U.S.-China Lab-to-Lab Technical Exchange Program," *Nonproliferation Review* 5, no. 3 (Spring–Summer 1998): 111–18.

19. *English-Chinese, Chinese-English Nuclear Security Glossary* (Washington, DC: National Academies Press; and Beijing: Atomic Energy Press, 2008), p. 33. Chinese participants also objected to the inclusion of the phrase "assassin's mace" or 杀手锏 (*shāshǒujiǎn*), which some U.S. analysts assert is a key strategic concept. The Chinese participants, in interviews with the author, strongly objected to such a characterization, treating the term as a colloquial metaphor, much as English speakers use "silver bullet" or "trump card." The resulting definition states that an "assassin's mace" is a "type of metal weapon" before noting its use in a metaphorical context.

20. Li Bin and Nie Hongyi, "An Investigation of China-U.S. Strategic Stability," *World Economics & Politics* 2 (2008): 13–19, translated by Gregory Kulacki (李彬, 聂宏毅, "中美战略稳定性的考察" 世界经济与政治 2 (2008): 13–19. English translation available at http://www.ucsusa.org/assets/documents/nwgs/Li-and-Nie-translation-final-5-22-09.pdf.

21. *Administration's Missile Defense Program and the ABM Treaty*, hearing before the Committee on Foreign Relations, United States Senate, S. Hrg. 107–10 (July 24, 2001), p. 32.

22. Secretary of State International Security Advisory Board (ISAB) Task Force on China's Strategic Modernization, *China's Strategic Modernization*, undated draft (c. 2008).

23. William J. Perry and Brent Scowcroft, Chairs, Charles D. Ferguson, Project Director, *U.S. Nuclear Weapons Policy*, Independent Task Force Report No. 62 (New York: Council on Foreign Relations, 2009), p. 45.

REGIONAL CONSEQUENCES

9 Europe, Nuclear Disarmament, and Non-Proliferation: What Next?

Nadia Alexandrova-Arbatova

PARADOXICAL LINKAGE

Generally speaking, Europe, in its pure European dimension—the European Union—could survive and retain its international position as an influential economic and political center of power without nuclear weapons. Having adopted its WMD Strategy in 2003, the European Union (EU) has taken steps to become a more effective and coherent actor in the policy fields of nuclear nonproliferation and disarmament. The EU recognizes that nonproliferation, disarmament, and arms control remain indispensable elements of cooperative security among states. Further, while acknowledging the considerable nuclear arms reductions that have taken place since the end of the Cold War, especially by two EU member states, the EU recognizes that there is a need for an overall reduction of the global stockpile of nuclear weapons in accordance with Article VI of the Non-Proliferation Treaty (NPT), in particular by those with the largest arsenals. The EU welcomes the reductions in deployed nuclear weapons brought about under START and the Moscow Treaty, and stresses the need for more progress in structurally reducing these nuclear arsenals through appropriate follow-on processes and the like.[1]

Though well known, these principles cannot be very useful in practical terms because Europe's ability to influence nuclear disarmament is rather limited, while proliferation challenges have a strong impact on its nuclear posture and reliance on nuclear weapons. Herein lies a paradoxical linkage between Europe's position on nuclear weapons, nuclear disarmament, and nuclear proliferation.

FOUR LEVELS OF INFLUENCE

Europe, however, is not homogeneous. We can single out four groups of states with a different say and role in nuclear disarmament: the two nuclear haves (the UK and France); those European countries that host the U.S. tactical nuclear weapons (TNW) (Germany, Belgium, the Netherlands, Italy, and Turkey); the group of NATO states without nuclear weapons; and the European neutral states (Sweden, Finland, Austria, Ireland, Malta, and Cyprus) that are EU members, and Switzerland, which is a nonaligned state.

The Nuclear Haves

The United Kingdom and France can be singled out as positive examples in certain aspects of nuclear disarmament. The UK has ratified the Comprehensive Test Ban Treaty (the CTBT) and halted production of fissile materials for weapons purposes. It has announced that it will reduce its stockpile of operational nuclear warheads from 200 to 160 and the number of nuclear-armed submarines from four to three. Unlike all other nuclear-armed states, the UK bases its nuclear deterrent only at sea, and has no land- or air-based nuclear weapons.

France has also signed and ratified the CTBT, and shut down and dismantled its facilities for the production of fissile materials for explosive purposes and its nuclear testing facilities. The French president has asked China to sign and the United States to ratify the CTBT and asked for transparency measures among the five permanent Security Council members. He called for the abolition of short- and medium-range surface-to-surface missiles and strongly supported negotiations on the Fissile Material Cut-Off Treaty (FMCT).[2] In March 2008, President Sarkozy announced that France was further reducing its nuclear arsenal so that it would be left with "fewer than 300 nuclear warheads."[3] The French nuclear reduction plans are partly driven by budgetary constraints, but also stem from a revaluation of what minimum capabilities France needs to uphold nuclear disarmament. Some political analysts believe that Sarkozy's new reduction plans aim to create legitimacy for the unquestioned nuclear deterrence strategy and to defuse criticism of the French distaste for the idea of totally eliminating nuclear arsenals.

Certainly, there are differences between the two countries. In the UK the domestic political debate is very lively, while in France it does not exist at all. In 2006 the British government made a decision to extend the life cycle of the Trident system by twenty years into the 2040s. The government decided to upgrade and renew the warheads and missiles, and to replace the submarines. The official budget estimate for the replacement is 30 billion GB pounds. Now this expensive decision needs to be implemented. Opponents of this decision debate the value of nuclear weapons in the twenty-first century, the opportunity costs of nuclear modernization, and the impact of the decision on arms control as a whole.[4] Politicians from most of the parties represented at Westminster continue to ask questions on all aspects of British nuclear policy, from practical aspects of the Trident program such as costs, infrastructure, and deployment, to the government's stance on arms control and disarmament. In response to the budget crisis facing the British government, prime minister Cameron announced in October 2010 that a decision on the start of construction of new submarines would be delayed to "about 2016."

Unlike France, the UK has in many ways taken the lead among the recognized nuclear weapons states in embracing the objective of a nuclear weapons–free world.[5] But in practical terms there is no difference between the two European nuclear haves. The British position is, "Let us seek to create a world in which nuclear weapons do not need to play a role, but until then, sustain a deterrence force available for a second strike." Nicola Butler wrote in her 1999 article "Nuclear Disarmament Issues in the UK Parliament: More Questions than Answers": "Although at the time, the Labour Government's Strategic Defence Review broke new ground in the disarmament process, especially in the area of transparency, some sections of it are now increasingly being used to justify a 'business as usual' approach to arms control and disarmament."[6] This is particularly clear in the UK's rejection of a no-first-use policy and its reiteration of a nuclear posture based closely on an unchanging NATO nuclear doctrine. The UK's own rejection of a no-first-use policy is also linked to NATO's policy—as former defence secretary Geoff Hoon stated in 2005: "A policy of no first use of nuclear weapons would be incompatible with our and NATO's deterrence."[7]

The French position can be reduced to the formula that "we need nuclear weapons regardless of what other states do." As President Sarkozy has pointed out in one of his interviews, "[T]he value of nuclear weapons is deterrence. As far as I know at the moment there's no emergency, France's nuclear strategy and nuclear doctrine are [based on the protection of France's] vital interests. If France's vital interests were threatened, then, at that point, like all the other French presidents who have preceded me, I would be able to consider the use of nuclear weapons."[8]

With regard to nonproliferation the United Kingdom clearly holds a special position within the EU. Being "three in one"—a trustworthy partner of the U.S., a leading member of the EU, and an influential nuclear weapon state—the UK is doomed to play a contradictory role in the EU. Analyzing the British nonproliferation policy, Rebecca Johnson strikes a rather skeptical note on how well the UK government was able to reconcile these different roles. In her view, in 2005 London had only low expectations for a substantive outcome of the NPT Review Conference from the beginning: "Its principal objective was to avoid open and damaging conflict that would further weaken the regime or exacerbate U.S. isolation."[9]

Like the other EU countries, France is very concerned about nuclear proliferation, and President Sarkozy has already singled out Iran as a threat, noting that Teheran "is increasing the range of its missiles while there are serious suspicions over its nuclear programme. European security is at stake."[10] But France's aversion to the idea of eliminating all nuclear arsenals undermines the core bargain of the NPT, which makes the treaty a weaker basis for insisting that others not acquire these weapons.[11] Furthermore, France played a negative role in the 2005 Review Conference (RevCon), where it sided with the United States and demanded removal of any reference to 13 Steps from the concluding conference documents.

What is really worrisome is that with the removal of the fear that any nuclear weapon use would escalate to a global catastrophe, all nuclear weapon states have become much more arrogant, irresponsible, and "easygoing" in contemplating the initiation of actual combat employment of nuclear weapons to perform various military missions. Great Britain, France (and China) are declining to undertake any limitation of their nuclear forces through arms control treaties, alleging that they lag far behind the two major nuclear powers. They are implementing planned long-term modernization, and, in the case of China, a quantitative buildup of nuclear arsenals. Both France and Great Britain have in their official nuclear doctrines (and so, allegedly, in operational planning) selective options for nuclear strikes, which usually implies first or preemptive/preventive attacks. The French position vis-à-vis nuclear weapons still builds upon the rather conservative nuclear doctrine presented by President Jacques Chirac in January 2006. Chirac understood deterrence as part of a preventive strategy: in his view, deterrence could also be used against state sponsors of terrorism.[12] The UK admits nuclear deterrence against other threats, such as from biological or chemical weapons, and has declined to give promises of no first use. So, in addition to traditional perceptions of nuclear deterrence as a main security pillar, the nuclear weapons states (NWS), including the UK and France, have adopted new approaches to nuclear weapons that lower the threshold for potential use of their nuclear arsenals, blur the distinction between nuclear and conventional wars, and introduce new categories of potential enemies (including nonstate organizations).[13]

States Hosting U.S. Nuclear Tactical Weapons

Under NATO nuclear-sharing arrangements, an estimated 170 to 450 tactical nuclear weapons remain deployed in five NATO non-nuclear-weapon states (Belgium, Germany, Italy, the Netherlands, and Turkey) and in the United Kingdom, which also possesses an independent nuclear arsenal. Canada and Greece have ended their participation in nuclear sharing. According to several sources, the United States has withdrawn its nuclear weapons from the RAF Lakenheath air base seventy miles northeast of London, and from Ramstein Air Base in Germany, but without making an official announcement.[14] Why NATO and the United States chose to keep these major withdrawals secret is a big puzzle. As Hans M. Kristensen rightly pointed out, "[T]he explanation might simply be that 'nuclear' always means secret, that it was done to prevent a public debate about the future of the rest of the weapons, or that the Bush administration just doesn't like arms control. Whatever the reason, it is troubling because the reductions have occurred around the same time that Russian officials repeatedly have pointed to the U.S. weapons in Europe as a justification to reject limitations on Russia's own tactical nuclear weapons."[15]

Though the predominant part of public opinion in the affected countries is in favor of the withdrawal of the U.S. tactical nuclear weapons from European soil,[16] the official position, most vividly represented by Germany before its last election, is that Atlantic solidarity, as well as the fair sharing of burdens, requires European allies to make a contribution toward nuclear participation. NATO must reevaluate nuclear deterrence when the Allies negotiate a new strategic concept to adapt the alliance to a new security environment.[17] By withdrawing from their nuclear sharing arrangements, countries hosting U.S. TNW would damage the mechanism of joint deterrence and cut an important link between the United States and European defense policies. The nuclear weapons are also viewed as a more credible deterrent toward a conventional opponent. Too, a complete withdrawal of U.S. nuclear weapons from Europe could weaken extended deterrence and possibly lead to further proliferation. In Europe, an end to the nuclear umbrella might cause Turkey to reconsider its status as a non-nuclear-weapon state.[18] This last argument does not hold water because the nuclear umbrella did not prevent the UK and, particularly, France from going nuclear. The presence of the U.S. TNW in Turkey would not contain Ankara's decision to join the nuclear club, if such a decision were taken. It would mean radical changes in Turkey's domestic political landscape, and in this case Turkey itself would try to get rid of the U.S. TNW. Before the release of NATO's new Strategic Concept on November 18, 2010, there were expectations that considerable debate about the value of TNW to the alliance would somehow be reflected in the decisions of the Lisbon summit. The final document, however, did not call for withdrawal of the TNW, as some had urged, so the status quo remains unchanged.

The question of U.S. tactical nuclear weapons in Europe will remain topical because the current Tornado fighters are to be replaced within the coming decade by Eurofighters, which are not yet capable of carrying nuclear bombs.[19] Germany is in a unique position among NATO members in that it alone has a coalition agreement that asks to negotiate TNW withdrawal and is the sole state that has not taken a decision to procure a nuclear-capable replacement for its dual-capable aircraft. The German government has repeatedly stated that it has no intention to certify the Eurofighter in a nuclear-capable role. The main reason for this position is the wish to protect the interests of European industry. The Eurofighter consortium consists of Airbus, through its parent European Aeronautic Defense and Space Co. (EADS), which is dominated by France and Germany, BAE in Britain, and Finmeccanica in Italy. The Eurofighters are estimated to cost $131 million each, so the projected total cost of 236 fighters would be around $30.9 billion, and the entire program as it was originally envisaged would cost $81.2 billion. EADS fears the loss of commercial proprietary information, should U.S. technicians get access to the Eurofighter during certification procedures. Apparently, the German government has assured industry that no such access will be granted. The United States, on the other hand, has little interest in certifying the Eurofighter in a nuclear role because this would create a competitor to the Joint Strike Fighter as a dual-capable aircraft.[20] Besides Germany, two other countries hosting TNW—the UK and Italy—and Spain have committed to buying the 236 combat aircraft between them. But some European defense analysts are now predicting that all four countries may agree to purchase only 112—less than half the number originally envisaged.[21]

In the absence of transparency about TNW, many European experts emphasize that NATO should begin discussions on a new Strategic Concept that will have to provide a rationale for maintaining nuclear deterrence and explain military requirements following from a new nuclear doctrine. Like the NWS nuclear postures, the rationale for the U.S. TNW in Europe remains as it has been for many years, in spite of all the radical changes in the international relations after the end of bipolarity. Domestic debate on the future of U.S. TNW involving parliamentarians, pressure groups, budgets, and public opinion in the host member states may provide an important catalyst for the United States and NATO members to discuss the future of U.S. nuclear sharing in Europe.

Part of the international strategic community believes that progress on Russian tactical nuclear weapons would be more likely if there were further reductions in U.S. tactical weapons in NATO countries, a change in NATO nuclear policy, or a change in plans for deployment of ballistic missile defenses (BMD) in Europe. Many European governments would support such a plan, even though some of the new Eastern European NATO members see Russian resurgence as a reason to continue the deployment. As Lukasz Kulesa, a Polish researcher, has pointed out, "The gravest danger of any move to eliminate U.S. nuclear weapons from Europe, from the perspective of Central Europe, would be to create the impression that NATO has gone 'soft' where its primary function of defending the territories of the member states is concerned. Therefore, such a move would probably need to be counteracted by a set of decisions giving credible reassurance on the value of NATO's Article V. These should include first and foremost the affirmation of the function of the strategic nuclear forces as the supreme guarantee of security of the Allies."[22]

The minority in the international strategic community emphasizes that unilateral measures are not sufficient, that they can represent only the first step and have to be replaced by a formal treaty. The treaty will have to include data exchange and verification provisions. It is a key lesson learned from the TNW reductions in 1991 under the informal Bush-Gorbachev agreement. As Nikolai Sokov has pointed out, "[U]nlike START I (which was signed only two months before the dramatic breakthrough on TNW), which includes elaborate provisions on data exchange and verification, the unilateral statements contained nothing in this regard. The numbers of TNW each side had in 1991 remained unknown; they were not even disclosed at confidential briefings the sides held in the aftermath of the parallel statements. The U.S. side apparently did not know that TNW had been already removed from the majority of republics. The share of warheads slated for elimination and those moved to storage remained unknown as well. The process of elimination of warheads is still completely closed."[23]

The EU/NATO Members without Nuclear Weapons

This group of states is eclectic, since it includes countries like Greece, which has already got rid of U.S. nuclear tactical weapons, and those new member-states that might be willing to host the U.S. TNW. At present there is no indication of a plan to extend the deployment of U.S. nuclear weapons in Europe or to modify the present nuclear bases. Also there is no indication that the United States is engaging the new NATO members in drafting all the necessary bilateral agreements that would prepare for the peacetime deployment of U.S. tactical nuclear weapons in host countries. Nevertheless, the NATO countries have refused to make any commitment that would exclude new nuclear weapons deployments and relieve legitimate Russian worries with regard to NATO's extension. On the contrary, the new NATO members declared or implied that they could "only accept full membership" and would not take any commitment in advance that "some specific weapons on their soil" should be excluded.[24]

The supreme guarantee of the security of the Allies is provided by the strategic nuclear forces of the Alliance. Regarding NATO nuclear forces, the 1995 "Study on NATO's Enlargement" emphasizes that "new members will share the benefits and responsibilities from this in the same way as all other Allies in accordance with the Strategic Concept. New members will be expected to support the concept of deterrence and the essential role nuclear weapons play in the Alliance's strategy of war prevention as set forth in the Strategic Concept."[25] There are no zones of different nuclear security within the alliance, no different classes of membership. This applies despite the politically binding reassurance of NATO in the NATO-Russia Founding Charter of 1997 that no nuclear weapons will be deployed in the respective states, and that no infrastructure for the deployment of nuclear weapons will be maintained and no new infrastructure for such weapons will be constructed.

This position is closely related to the debate on a Nuclear Weapon Free Zone in Central and Eastern Europe, which might include three Baltic States (Estonia, Latvia, and Lithuania), the Czech Republic, Poland, Slovakia and Hungary, Romania, Bulgaria, former Yugoslav states, and three former Soviet Republics (Belarus, Moldova, and Ukraine). Over the years there have been a number of proposals to establish nuclear weapon–free zones (NWFZs) in Europe. However, due to Cold War politics none of the proposals (Poland in 1958, Finland in 1963, Romania in the 1970s) were successful. The possibility of establishing a NWFZ in Europe opened up as the former Warsaw Pact and Soviet States collapsed. In July 1996 Belarus and Ukraine called for a Central and Eastern

European NWFZ. But the idea gained little support from other states. Several countries in the area, notably those that aspired to join NATO, opposed the proposal. Poland at the 1998 NPT Preparatory Committee (PrepCom), in a letter addressed to the chairman of the PrepCom on behalf of nine of the key states (Bulgaria, Croatia, the Czech Republic, Hungary, Poland, Romania, Slovakia, the former Yugoslav Republic of Macedonia, and Slovenia) which would comprise such a zone, opposed the idea as "incompatible with our sovereign resolve to contribute to, and benefit from the new European security architecture."[26]

At the same time it would be unfair to put the bulk of responsibility only on the new NATO members. Proposals for NWFZ in Europe are receiving increasing support from a range of sources, including governments, academic communities, NGOs, and parliaments in Europe. In April 2007 the European Parliament adopted "A Comprehensive Approach towards Nuclear Disarmament," and called European governments to promote nuclear disarmament and to encourage the establishment of Nuclear Weapon Free Zones in Europe as a stepping stone toward global nuclear abolition. These could include a Central European NWFZ and a Northern Europe Arctic NWFZ. However, the main nuclear haves oppose the establishment of NWFZs in strategic regions in which they currently deploy or wish to retain the option to deploy nuclear weapons. In 1995, the U.S. government published its own criteria for the establishment of a NWFZ, highlighting the right of states parties to grant or deny the passage of nuclear-capable ships and aircraft of nonparty nations, and the validity of rights recognized under international law, such as the freedom of navigation and overflight, the right of innocent passage, and the right of archipelagic sea lanes passage.

The concept of NWFZs prohibits the use of nuclear weapons by NWS against any state of the zone. For this purpose, the existing treaties include protocols which obligate the nuclear-weapon states (China, France, Russia, United Kingdom, and the United States) to give negative security guarantees to states in the NWFZ. The United States is particularly reluctant when it comes to granting such guarantees to NWFZ. France, Russia, and the United Kingdom generally accept the UN principles for establishment of NWFZs. They make their decisions to support individual NWFZs on a case-by-case basis. China is the only NWS that has officially rejected the first use of nuclear weapons and has pledged not to use nuclear weapons against any non-nuclear-weapon states or member of a NWFZ.[27]

Summing up, despite all difficulties with regard to TNW and NWFZs, some steps can be taken by Russia and the United States if political relations are favorable. In the first stage, Russia and NATO could accept mutual obligations not to deploy TNW in Central and Eastern Europe. This zone would include the territory of the NATO member countries that came into this organization after the end of the Cold War, as well as Belarus and other post-Soviet states located in Europe, and Russia's Kaliningrad region. Full absence of TNW is much easier to control than its quantitative limitation. The next step—and there is some progress in the area of reduction and limitation of general purpose conventional forces in Europe—could be an agreement about a complete relocation of Russian and American TNWs to their national territories and their placement exclusively at centralized storage facilities beyond the deployment areas of troops and arms.[28]

The EU Neutral States and Switzerland

Ireland, Sweden, Finland, Austria, Malta, and Cyprus are strong proponents internationally for nuclear disarmament and nuclear weapon limitations. Throughout the years, they have advocated a nuclear test ban, nonproliferation of nuclear weapons, de-alerting of nuclear arsenals, and also a ban on nuclear weapons. All of them have ratified the Comprehensive Nuclear Test Ban Treaty. Through the EU Common Security and Defense Policy, non-nuclear member states inevitably become involved in the nuclear debate, though their role remains very limited. Ireland and Sweden are part of the New Agenda Coalition (NAC), which was launched in Dublin in June 1998, with a Joint Declaration by the Ministers for Foreign Affairs of Brazil, Egypt, Ireland, Mexico, New Zealand, South Africa, Sweden, and Slovenia, the latter of which subsequently left the coalition. In 2000, NAC was instrumental in crafting a breakthrough in the NPT Review Conference. It put together a historic agreement outlined in the 13 Steps, in which the nuclear weapons states affirmed, in accordance with Article VI of the NPT, that nuclear disarmament can and should proceed independently of general disarmament, that the nuclear powers have a responsibility to work together on "an unequivocal undertaking" to eliminate their arsenals, and that thirteen relatively simple steps could help rid the world of nuclear weapons quickly, verifiably, and irreversibly.

Sharing a strong preference for linking nonproliferation issues to nuclear disarmament, the European neutral states identified the insertion of a clear reference to previous calls for nuclear disarmament by the NWS into the final document as its principal policy goal during the RevCon 2005 (it did not happen) and stressed the need for a "carefully crafted balance of the NPT's three pillars: non-proliferation, disarmament and peaceful use." Not surprisingly, they see the rather modest ambitions of the EU on disarmament as one of the principal shortcomings of its common policy during the conference.

Switzerland's position on nuclear disarmament and nuclear arms control is based on several principles. First, Switzerland is in favor of the complete elimination of all weapons of mass destruction and attaches great importance to protection based on international law. Consequently, it has adhered to all relevant treaties and is a member of all relevant organizations and institutions. Second, Switzerland supports all multilateral efforts for disarmament and arms control which aim at concrete results. Third, regardless of the specific substance of the various agreements, Switzerland holds the view that these agreements must meet several criteria. They should be universal, nondiscriminatory, verifiable, and legally binding.[29]

For Switzerland, the NPT represents the sole legally binding instrument of global scope intended to promote nonproliferation and nuclear disarmament and thus a key tool for international peace and stability. Switzerland emphasizes the NPT is based on three mutually reinforcing pillars (namely nonproliferation, disarmament, and peaceful uses of nuclear energy), and that the stress currently placed on nuclear proliferation should not lead to neglect of the other two pillars of the NPT, including nuclear disarmament. In its view the overwhelming majority of the non-nuclear-weapon states have fully respected their commitments, and the problems of our time are due to the nuclear-weapon states and to only a very small number of other states.

Switzerland was the last holdout against the U.S.-India nuclear deal. "The draft initiative for nuclear cooperation between India and the United States raises fundamental questions about the future of the nuclear non-proliferation system based on the NPT. This project of de-regulating nuclear cooperation contrasts with various proposals put forward recently to adopt even more restrictive measures formulated recently regarding access to sensitive technologies of the nuclear fuel cycle. It is Switzerland's view that the right to cooperation and access to sensitive technologies remains dependent on adherence to the NPT and on strict application of all of the Treaty's provisions."[30]

Though the neutral states are limited in their potential to influence nuclear disarmament, which is closely related to the nuclear policies of NWS, they objectively create a favorable international environment for this process.

FACTORS SHAPING EUROPE'S NUCLEAR POSTURE

Three factors will be shaping Europe's position on nuclear disarmament: first, Russia-West relations; second, proliferation risks; and third, the attitude of the Obama administration toward nuclear disarmament and nuclear weapons. Here are three scenarios to provoke thought.

A Threat from the East

The Caucasus crisis resulted in unprecedented flare-up of tensions in Russia-West relations. It has raised concerns about the repetition of this scenario in Ukraine. No doubt, a big conflict over Ukraine, which would involve Russia and NATO, would increase Europe's reliance on nuclear weapons. It would result in a new Germany-like divide in Europe and a new confrontation. NATO would smoothly come back to its traditional missions. The neutral European states, at least Sweden and Finland, would cease to be neutral and join NATO. In that case, there would be further proliferation of U.S. tactical nuclear weapons in Europe. The United States–Europe linkage would become stronger, and there would be a new nuclear burden-sharing arrangement within NATO. The latter would require integration of the British and French nuclear forces. Ukraine could become a new proliferation candidate in Europe and, unlike other cases, the West would support it.

A Threat from the South: Proliferation Risks

If Russia-West relations improve but proliferation risks remain high, the question of the integration of European nuclear forces will remain topical for Europe, but it could be resolved outside NATO in the European security and defense policy (ESDP) context. The contrast to the first scenario is clear. In the absence of any threat from the East, the United States–Europe nuclear linkage will become irrelevant, and the U.S. tactical nuclear weapons will be withdrawn from Europe because currently they threaten only Russia. Under this scenario a need for European integrated nuclear forces (built upon the British and French nuclear arsenals, with the participation of other EU member-states in the nuclear decision-making process) could be justified with regard to new proliferation candidates. Europe would not be able to rely only on the U.S. commitments as it did in the times of bipolarity. Even in the Cold War, there was concern in Europe formulated by French president De Gaulle that "Americans would not trade New York for Paris." It is all the more so now, since the USSR as a military opponent was a much more credible threat to U.S. and European interests than the new proliferation candidates.

U.S. officials have said a missile defense system on European soil is crucial for protecting both North America as well as the rest of NATO against a missile attack from Iran or North Korea. Depending on whether an enemy missile is aimed at Europe or the United States, different "rules of engagement" could govern the launch of NATO and U.S. missile defense interceptors, all under the auspices of the American commander. The concern of many European NATO nations about the initial U.S. plans was two-fold: They objected to the idea that a U.S. missile defense system could make some member countries more secure than others (an idea they believe would go against the very basis of the alliance); and they were keenly against the idea of the countries hosting U.S. missile defense assets developing a relationship with Washington that would transcend that of any other European NATO nation.[31]

Under the best scenario EU and Russia could cooperate on BMD in Europe and, what is more important, on air defense, because unlike the United States, the EU countries and Russia can be easily reached with air dynamic vehicles (cruise missiles, or civilian or military aircraft) from the territories of the so-called rogue or failed states.

The U.S. Factor

The U.S. position on arms control under the Obama administration and the U.S. foreign policy at large will be crucial for Europe's nuclear posture. The devil-may-care attitude of the Bush administration toward arms control dealt a heavy blow to nuclear disarmament. Nowadays there is a growing understanding that the United States and Europe will have to cooperate with Russia in areas where they have "common objectives and common ground," especially on nonproliferation, to include reduction of the global nuclear arsenal, security of nuclear materials, and challenges such as North Korea and Iran.[32] At the same time the Russian liberal political elite is fearful that under domestic pressures President Obama will put forward the worst possible combination of security initiatives—new proposals on arms control, which are badly needed to fill the security vacuum in the Russia-U.S. strategic relations, but also a renewal of the U.S. commitments to the previous policy of NATO's enlargement. If this happens, the latter will discredit the former and remove all hopes for a breakthrough in the Russia-West relations and the nuclear disarmament process as well.

Not only U.S. disregard for arms control during the George W. Bush administration has negatively affected nuclear disarmament and nonproliferation. The 1999 NATO military operation backed by the United States in Kosovo, the war in Iraq, the U.S. withdrawal from the Anti-Ballistic Missile (ABM) Treaty, and its first BMD plans in Europe strongly affected the international context of nonproliferation. The main lesson learned by the so-called rogue states from U.S./NATO military operations during the last decade is that only nuclear weapons would help them to avoid a repetition of the Yugoslav and Iraq experience. North Korea withdrew from NPT almost on the morrow of the U.S. withdrawal from the ABM Treaty, which deprived the United States of any moral right to criticize Pyongyang's decision. And if the United States had not withdrawn from the ABM Treaty and not blocked the Comprehensive Test Ban Treaty and the Fissile Materials Cut-Off Treaty, North Korea (and potentially Iran in the future) would have had not just one barrier to overcome, but three (the NPT, the CTBT, the FMCT) in trying to acquire nuclear weapons.[33]

The way the United States implemented its antiterrorist strategy after 9/11 and conducted its military operations brought about dissatisfaction among U.S. allies. After the September 11th terrorist attacks and the superbly executed operation in Afghanistan, the United States returned to unilateralism in an even more exacerbated form. The United States invaded Iraq (on an invented pretext and without UN authorization) and planned to go further by "reformatting" the entire Greater Middle East to fit its own economic, political, and military interests.[34] Generally speaking, the Iraq controversy was about more than "just" Iraq. It was representative of the new crisis of traditional Atlanticism which made Europe a hostage to U.S. policy. Though the diplomatic damage of the Iraq controversy to the Euro-Atlantic relationship has been partly repaired, in Europe there remains a fear that for the United States NATO is just a means to influence and engage Europeans in its foreign policy preferences, first and foremost with regard to so-called states of concern.

The EU recognizes that the conflict with Iran is critical for the future of the NPT and for the EU's ability to speak with one voice and act coherently in the area of nonproliferation policy. For many observers, the hope was that the initiative of three influential EU countries, backed by the community as a whole, could work as a model case for "effective multilateralism." However, the key conclusion of the expert community is that the "EU-3" failed to play the role of a mediator between the United States and Iran "because both parties viewed the European Union as a buffer and a potential coalition partner vis-à-vis the other."[35]

Furthermore, the EU countries were concerned that Russia's dissatisfaction with the U.S. initial BMD program in Europe (which is regarded by Moscow as an open-ended process alongside the NATO enlargement process) reduced the chance for international cooperation, including Russia, on Iran. Just as bad, that BMD program sent a wrong signal to Iran, which interprets the U.S. BMD system as a de facto recognition of its nuclear status.

The role of President Barack Obama, with regard to the most urgent security challenges can be effective and positive only if he is ready to really change the substance of U.S. foreign policy, recognizing the mistakes of his predecessor and presenting a new foreign policy concept. It is very promising that President Obama has already singled out a "move toward a nuclear free world" as one of the administration's key objectives. Strengthening the NPT regime is the second key objective for the new administration. Other encouraging news is the successful negotiation of the New START treaty, designed to further reduce and limit strategic weapons. At their April 2009 meeting, presidents Obama and Medvedev announced, "We committed our two countries to achieving a nuclear free world, while recognizing that this long-term goal will require a new emphasis on arms control and conflict resolution measures, and their full implementation by all concerned nations. We agreed to pursue new and verifiable reductions in our strategic offensive arsenals in a step-by-step process, beginning by replacing the Strategic Arms Reduction Treaty with a new, legally-binding treaty."[36] With all the importance of this statement, it is just the beginning of a truly amicable U.S.-Russia relationship, and there are still a number of serious disagreements between them which will be shaping their cooperation on arms control.

Nonetheless, nuclear security and nonproliferation are areas that the Obama and Medvedev administrations should find most amenable to pressing the reset button on. Central to this radical change was the growing recognition that attempts to pressure Russia into toeing the U.S. line had failed; a new tactic was needed. The U.S. decision to withdraw plans for the BMD system in Poland and the Czech Republic was met with optimism in the Kremlin, and the efforts of the Obama administration were not wasted. Russia and the United States reached a new agreement on Afghanistan. The previous agreement allowing for the transportation of nonlethal supplies to Afghanistan was supplanted by an agreement that allowed NATO forces to use Russian airspace to transport troops and arms. Echoing that decision President Bakiyev stated in his 9/11 memorial address that Kyrgyzstan would allow the United States to continue using Manas Air Force base for logistical operations in the fight against terror. Beyond this, Russia has showed that it will be inclined together with the United States to take a harder line on sanctions against Iran.

WHAT NEXT?

General and complete nuclear disarmament is a noble goal, though it seems at present very distant and unrealistic. However, this goal is crucial for creating a general framework for arms control negotiations. As mentioned above, at current force levels European nuclear weapons cannot be an obstacle to nuclear zero during the early stages of disarmament; no doubt, the primary responsibility here rests with Russia and the United States. Nevertheless, the fact that the European nuclear states hold the view that nuclear weapons are still indispensable, even as they support new disarmament and arms control negotiations, undercuts their credibility. From this point of view, there is little difference between the UK, which accepts the idea of nuclear disarmament as a final goal, and France, which avoids any explicit mention of abolition of nuclear weapons. The very fact that their disarmament credibility rests on their propensity to see the elimination of nuclear arms as a future option—one day, but not now—creates legitimacy for nuclear weapons expenditures to a domestic audience, which in turn creates an image of a "drug addict"-like nuclear weapons dependency to the outside world.

Certainly, it should be recognized that the future of NPT lies not only in the responsibility of the nuclear weapons states. Nuclear disarmament by the NWS, including the UK and France, will not lead a determined proliferation candidate to stop its programs. Iran's or North Korea's intentions are guided not by the lack of disarmament but by their regional strategic considerations, considerations of prestige, or those of regime survival. However, reliance on nuclear weapons is the soft spot of any NWS nonproliferation approach. Unless sincere efforts are made by the nuclear weapons states to eliminate their stockpiles under international agreement, other countries are also likely to acquire nuclear weapons, which means that it will more difficult to prevent the spread of nuclear weapons to "rogue regimes" or nonstate actors.

Furthermore, one cannot ignore the fact that around forty new countries, including two of the declared nuclear powers, France and China, joined NPT at the same time as intensive nuclear disarmament talks and real reductions in stockpiles of nuclear weapons were taking place (INF Treaty, SALT-1, SALT-2, the START III Framework Treaty, the ABM limitation agreements, the CTBT, and unilateral reductions of tactical nuclear weapons by the United States and the USSR/Russia).[37] Put simply, nuclear disarmament creates a favorable international context for nonproliferation.

Efforts by the great powers to maintain their nuclear arsenals are still largely based upon the strategy of mutual nuclear deterrence. Therefore, more attention and efforts should be devoted to reconsidering this strategy and the existing nuclear doctrines that allow very flexible approaches to using nuclear weapons.

Though in principle Europe cannot oppose nuclear disarmament within a reasonable time frame, there is a problem of asymmetry. Since the UK and France lag far behind the U.S. and Russian nuclear arsenals, the European nuclear haves cannot issue demands of equal standing. From this point of view, radical reductions of the U.S. and Russian nuclear arsenals could upgrade Europe's role in the process of nuclear disarmament. Another factor, which would increase Europe's involvement in this process, would be the integration of European nuclear forces. Like it or not, European integration in this sphere is an objective process in Europe's postbipolar evolution. It would provide ESDP with blood and flesh, and end Europe's dichotomy in the security sector. In the absence of a well-founded and clear demarcation between the military components of the EU and NATO, this dichotomy will continue to be a major obstacle to creating a well-functioning ESDP.

European integration in the nuclear field is already going on, although it is not very visible. Since the early 1990s, bilateral dialogue and cooperation mechanisms have existed between the UK and France in the nuclear field, and in November 2010 they signed a treaty to share facilities for research on nuclear stewardship technologies. Since the early 1990s there has been a general consensus among politicians and commentators about "Europeanizing" (giving a European dimension to) the French nuclear deterrent, taking into account the collective interests of the EU members when making nuclear decisions.[38] On several occasions (in 1995, 2006, and 2008) France invited Germany to participate in joint nuclear decision-making. The French efforts have been politely rejected by Berlin because in the eyes of the German political elite the idea of a concerted deterrence is not in accordance with Germany's perceptions of ESDP, which should be directed primarily toward crisis management and the postconflict evolution of weak states. But the EU dichotomy embodied in the artificial division of labor between NATO and ESDP cannot last forever. As Bruno Tertrais argues, "In the short run nothing would preclude a solemn and explicit affirmation by London and Paris that their two nuclear forces protect the EU countries."[39]

There is no clear position on whether a single European voice on the nuclear issues would be good. An integrated European nuclear force, however, would make Europe a more visible player in the nuclear debate. The EU parliamentarians and high-ranking officials have already pointed out that the issue of nuclear weapons and the future of the NPT could not be excluded from the Common Foreign and Security Policy (CFSP). In 2008 the EU foreign ministers endorsed new lines for EU action to combat the proliferation of weapons of mass destruction and their delivery systems. The overriding goal of the plan is to achieve greater coordination within the EU.

Integration of the British and French nuclear forces in the EU context would be a crucial element in achieving consensus among the great powers on specific nonproliferation issues and cases, since the "threshold" countries are increasingly coordinating their policies and are playing on the divisions between the five NWS. For the time being, the EU context is very important for consultations on new verification instruments and confidence-building measures to be discussed in the UN Conference on Disarmament among the P5 or G8. A single European voice would be decisive for reconsidering the existing NATO strategy of nuclear deterrence (including the presence of U.S. TNW on European soil), which needs to be updated to postbipolar realities. And under the best scenario in the strategic relations between Russia and the United States, Europe at a certain stage can become part of arms control negotiations. One cannot but agree with Javier Solana, European Union High Representative for the CFSP, who said in his keynote speech in the European Parliament: "The world badly needs more progress on nuclear disarmament. With new thinking in the major countries and also in the countries which can experience the temptation of nuclear armament, progress is possible. The task of political leaders is to set a sense of direction and to build trust among the key players. That is a task for many people, including in the European Union."[40]

NOTES

1. See consilium.europa.eu/cms3_fo/showPage.asp?id=1125&lang=en.

2. Bruno Tertrais, "France and Nuclear Disarmament: The Meaning of the Sarkozy Speech," *Proliferation Analysis*, 1 May 2008, at www.carnegieendowment.org/publications/index.cfm?fa=view&id=20090&prog=zgp&proj=znpp.

3. George Perkovich and James M. Acton, "Abolishing Nuclear Weapons," *Adelphi Paper* 396 (London: IISS, 2008), p. 20.

4. See www.atlcom.nl/site/english/nieuws/wp-content/AP%202008%20nr.%204%20Riecke.pdf.

5. Perkovich and Acton, "Abolishing Nuclear Weapons," p. 21.

6. Nicola Butler, "Nuclear Disarmament Issues in the UK Parliament: More Questions than Answers," *Disarmament Diplomacy* 38 (June 1999), at http://www.acronym.org.uk/dd/dd38/38ukparl.htm.

7. "Campaign for Nuclear Disarmament—No to NATO," at www.cnduk.org/index.php/campaigns/no-to-nato/no-to-nato.html.

8. French president Nicholas Sarkozy on "Nuclear Weapons and Missile Defence" (7–8 June 2007) at www.acronym.org.uk/docs/0706/doc21.htm.

9. "The EU's Emerging Role in Nuclear Non-Proliferation Policy—Trends and Prospects" at www.euractiv.com/en/security/eu-emerging-role-nuclear-non-proliferation-policy-trends-prospects/article-148386.

10. See www.thaindian.com/newsportal/world-news/irans-nuclear-pursuits-threat-to-europe-sarkozy_10029973.html.

11. Perkovich and Acton, "Abolishing Nuclear Weapons," p. 20.

12. "The EU's Emerging Role in Nuclear Non-Proliferation Policy—Trends and Prospects," 15 November 2005, updated Thursday, 17 November 2005, at http://www.euractiv.com/en/security/eu-emerging-role-nuclear-non-proliferation-policy-trends-prospects/article-148386.

13. Alexei Arbatov, ed., *At the Nuclear Threshold* (Moscow: Carnegie Moscow Center, 2007), p. 94.

14. See www.fas.org/blog/ssp/2008/06/us-nuclear-weapons-withdrawn-from-the-united-kingdom.php.

15. Ibid.

16. Some 76 percent of the German population thinks that Germany should get rid of U.S. tactical nuclear weapons deployed in Germany. Similar numbers were reflected in a 2006 Greenpeace poll, which found that 69 percent of the citizens in nuclear deployment states supported a nuclear weapons–free Europe. This included 88 percent in Turkey, 71 percent in Italy, 65 percent in Belgium, 63 percent in the Netherlands, and 56 percent in Britain. See www.gsinstitute.org/pnnd/pubs/Tactical_nukes.pdf.

17. *White Paper 2006* on German Security policy and the future of the Bundeswehr, Federal Ministry of Defence.

18. Summary of interview with Karl Heinz Kamp, head of Unit Foreign Policy, Konrad-Adenauer-Stiftung, Berlin, 15 February 2007.

19. See Otfried Nassauer, "50 Jahre Nuklearwaften in Deutschland," *Aus Politik und Zeitgeschihte*, no. 21 (2005).

20. See www.frstrategie.org/barreFRS/publications/rd/RD_20080129.pdf.

21. "Analysis: European Defence Contracts," at www.breitbart.com/article.php?id=upiUPI-20090429-181803-2953&show_article=1.

22. Lukasz Kulesa, "Reduce US Nukes in Europe to Zero, and Keep NATO Strong (and Nuclear). A View from Poland," at https://www.carnegieendowment.org/files/2009npc_kulesa.pdf.

23. See www.acronym.org.uk/dd/dd21/21tactic.htm.

24. See www.uspid.org/sections/02_Books_Documents/Proceedings/none_cast97/cotta.html.

25. See www.nato.int/docu/basictxt/enl-9505.htm.

26. See www.fas.org/nuke/control/cenwfz/index.html.

27. See cns.miis.edu/nwfz_clearinghouse/.

28. A. Arbatov and V. Dvorkin, *Beyond Nuclear Deterrence: Transforming the U.S.-Russian Equation* (Washington, DC: Carnegie Endowment for International Peace, 2006), pp. 141–62.

29. See www.ippnw.ch/content/pdf/monte_veritas/friedrich.pdf.

30. See www.icanw.org/files/Switzerland.pdf.

31. See cndyorks.gn.apc.org/yspace/articles/bmd/nato_planning_europe_shield.htm.

32. See euobserver.com/9/26863.

33. Arbatov, *At the Nuclear Threshold*, p. 100.

34. Alexei Arbatov, "Moscow-Munich: A New Framework for Russian Domestic and Foreign Policies," *Moscow Carnegie Center Working Papers*, no. 3 (2007), p. 14.

35. See www.euractiv.com/en/security/eu-emerging-role-nuclear-non-proliferation-policy-trends-prospects/article-148386.

36. Statement from Obama, Medvedev, "Political Hotsheet—CBS News," at www.cbsnews.com/blogs/2009/04/01/politics/politicalhotsheet/entry4909175.shtml.

37. Arbatov, *At the Nuclear Threshold*, pp. 98–99.

38. Bruno Tertrais, "The Last to Disarm? The Future of France's Nuclear Forces," p. 266, at cns.miis.edu/npr/pdfs/142tertrais.pdf.

39. Ibid.

40. "European Proposals for Strengthening Disarmament and the Non-Proliferation Regime," speech by EUHR Solana at www.europa-eu-un.org/articles/en/article_8354_en.htm.

10 Israel's Nuclear Future: Iran, Opacity, and the Vision of Global Zero

Avner Cohen

INTRODUCTION

It is often said that while we don't know which nuclear weapons state will disarm first, we do know which will disarm last. That country is Israel.

Israel's nuclear past hints at that direction. Israel's father-founder, David Ben Gurion, dreamt about the bomb almost since Israel was born. By the end of its first decade Israel had initiated its nuclear weapons project. Less than a decade later, on the eve of the 1967 war, Israel assembled its first nuclear devices.[1]

Israel's determined drive to the bomb stems from its historical consciousness and geopolitical situation. Today it reflects the avowal "Never Again" in reaction to the Holocaust, the most formative event in modern Jewish history. A few years ago Israeli columnist Ari Shavit suggested thinking of the bomb as "a glass greenhouse" that shields Israel in the Middle East. It has been Dimona—the site of Israel's prime nuclear facility—that allowed Israel to grow and prosper despite the hostile environment.[2] This metaphor highlights how most Israelis view the bomb, as the nation's sacred insurance policy.

Israel is a major stakeholder in the global nuclear order. Not only is Israel the world's sixth nuclear weapons state, but it signed (with the United States as a cosigner) an "exceptionalist bargain" with the bomb.[3] Since its birth the Israeli bomb has remained opaque, unacknowledged. The policy, known as "nuclear opacity," has been at the core of Israel's exceptionalist bargain: Israel has neither confirmed nor denied its possession of nuclear weapons, but rather committed "not to be the first to introduce nuclear weapons." Opacity (in Hebrew, *amimut*) is Israel's distinct and unique contribution to the nuclear age.

Not surprisingly, Israelis are skeptical about the old-new vision of a world without nuclear weapons. Israeli leaders have remained publicly mute on the matter—Israeli leaders ignored President Obama's Prague speech as if it had no relevance to their country—but privately they dismiss the vision as unrealistic, in fact, naive and dangerous. Israelis do not believe in either the feasibility or desirability of the vision.

At the bottom, Israelis cannot conceive of *themselves* dismantling their nation's sacred national insurance. Israel's policy of nuclear opacity is designed to safeguard this view. One of its functions it to keep Israel exceptional and to ensure that Israel would not be engaged in any practical talk about nuclear disarmament.

For the last decade Israel's focus in nuclear matters has been Iran. From an Israeli perspective, any conversation on the nation's nuclear future starts and ends with one subject only, Iran. Israelis will have a hard time elevating themselves above the horizon of Iran, and their own policy of opacity, even to consider the vision of a world without nuclear weapons.

ISRAEL AND THE IRANIAN NUCLEAR CHALLENGE

Israel's intense response to Iran reveals much about Israel's own predicament. The consensus within Israel is that the advent of a nuclear Iran—and a great deal depends on how exactly one defines this phrase—would pose a threat Israel has never yet faced, a hostile state in the region in possession of nuclear weapons. The phrase Israeli leaders often use to characterize the gravity of that eventuality is "existential threat."[4] Until his election to become Israel's prime minister in early 2009, Benjamin Netanyahu often used this phrase, implying that Israel must be committed to preventing a nuclear Iran, preferably with cooperation with others, but if necessary, on its own.[5] Since his election, however, Netanyahu hardly ever uses this phrase in his public speeches, but Uzi Arad, his national security advisor, recently defined the goal of preventing an Iranian bomb as an "existential imperative."[6] Mossad chief General Meir Dagan—whose organization has the overall responsibility to prevent a nuclear Iran—maintained that if and when Iran were to develop nuclear weapons, "this [would be] a significant existential threat to the state of Israel."[7]

The reference to "existential threat" is based on the linkage Israelis make between two key elements: first, the Iranian regime and its pursuit of a nuclear-weapons capability, and second, its extreme ideological hostility toward Israel, in particular its rejection of Israel's legitimacy as a state. On the first, despite some uncertainty, Israeli assessments depict Iranian strategic intentions and capabilities as aiming at full nuclear weapons capability, even if those assessments are occasionally amorphous and hesitant on matters of political tactics.[8] Israeli assessments of Iran tend to be more alarmist than assessments by others.[9] For example, the November 2007 U.S. National Intelligence Estimate (NIE) on Iran, which concluded that Iran halted its overt nuclear weaponization work in 2003, was strongly disputed by Israel's national assessment.[10] Recent revelations on the Iranian nuclear program, especially the "white paper" report prepared by the IAEA-International Atomic Energy Agency (IAEA), as well as the discovery of the new enrichment facility near Kum, have given more credence to the Israeli assessment.[11]

There is an abundance of evidence of the Iranian government's extreme hostility toward Israel. This has been true since the Islamic revolution, but it became more pronounced and explicit after the 2005 election of Mahmoud Ahmadinejad as president of Iran. Ahmadinejad's statements mean, for Israelis, a return to the old pan-Arab discourse about the destruction of the Zionist entity, a discourse that hardly exists anymore in the Sunni Arab world (some would argue due, in part, to the existence of the Israeli bomb). The difference between the anti-Israeli rhetoric in Ben-Gurion's era and today is that now, for the first time, such threats are voiced by a president of a state that is seriously pursuing a nuclear weapons capability. Moreover, Ahmadinejad's rhetoric is combined with increasing Iranian involvement in other parts of the Middle East, most visibly though Hezbollah in Lebanon and Hamas in the Gaza strip.

In Israeli eyes the Iranian nuclear threat does not lie in the risk that Iran may be utterly irrational and might one day drop the bomb over Israel. Most Israeli strategists agree that it is nearly inconceivable that Iran would attack Israel out of the blue with nuclear weapons because Iranians must be aware of the catastrophic consequences of such a suicidal act.[12] The risk of a nuclear confrontation between Israel and Iran might arise, instead, from misperceptions and miscalculations during a conventional crisis. Israel would also need to face the possibility (however low) of an accidental or unauthorized nuclear launch by Iran and the risk that nuclear weapons might leak or be transferred by Iran to nonstate actors. In the Israeli view, an Iranian bomb could profoundly change the entire political dynamics in the Middle East. As Uzi Arad put it, "[We] cannot live with a nuclear Iran because a nuclear Middle East would not be the same as the Cold War nuclear stalemate. A nuclear Middle East would become a multi-nuclear Middle East, with all that entails."[13]

Specifically, Israelis perceive three areas of great concern. The first is that nuclear weapons could exacerbate concerns about other aspects of Iran's foreign and defense policies by inducing more risk-prone and aggressive strategies. Nuclear Iran would pressure the Palestinians and possibly other Arab states (for example, Syria) to take hard-line positions, and would encourage Palestinian society to adopt more extreme positions that would stimulate terrorism and make peace negotiations with Israel even more difficult than in the present situation. Furthermore, a mutual assured destruction (MAD) deterrent situation between Israel and Iran could be exceptionally unstable due to the asymmetry in size and population between Iran and Israel. Mutual hostility and the lack of communication between the two states further increase the danger.[14]

The second concern is that a nuclear Iran, especially if Iran is a declared nuclear state, could ignite a cascade proliferation effect in the entire Middle East.[15] A dangerous nuclear Iran would defy the global nuclear order that is based on the Nuclear Nonproliferation Treaty (NPT) regime, and be a direct threat to the subtle nuclear order that currently exists in the Middle East under the veneer of Israeli nuclear opacity. One thing is sure: a nuclear Iran would be the end of Israel's benign nuclear monopoly in the region.

The third is the social and psychological impact that a MAD-like balance of terror with Iran might have on the Israeli public and its psyche. Some Israeli public figures who push the politics of the Iranian scare (such as former deputy minister of defense Ephraim Sneh, columnist Ari Shavit, and academic historian Benny Morris) argue that Iran might be able to "wipe the Zionist state off the map" without actually dropping the bomb. The mere existence of the Iranian bomb, or the fear that Iran has the bomb, they declare, might lead Israelis to leave Israel for a friendlier place where their very existence would not be threatened. After the Holocaust, Sneh argues, Jews would have no stomach to live in the shadow of an Iranian bomb, another Holocaust. Those who had the means to leave would leave.[16] Benjamin Netanyahu has pushed this line of reasoning to its ultimate limit by explicitly introducing the Holocaust into the discussion about Iran, and drawing an analogy between President Ahmadinejad and Hitler.[17]

ISRAEL'S DILEMMAS VIS-À-VIS IRAN

The closer Iran is perceived to the bomb, the more Israel will have to redefine its own bargain with the bomb, including opacity. Israel would be forced—in a sense, it already has been forced—to decide whether and how to respond to this eventuality. As Iran crosses one technological barrier after another, and as its enrichment program is increasingly a fait accompli, those policy dilemmas for Israel are more acute. Stripped to their conceptual essentials, they are as follows.[18] The first dilemma stems from the Israeli decision-making process itself and the politics surrounding it, domestically and internationally. The Israeli government would have to decide whether and when it should articulate its red lines about a nuclear Iran, or leave them loose and not fully defined, as they are now. In parallel, Israeli leaders would have to decide how much they are willing to discuss the threshold with others, especially with the United States. Specifically, since any deal with Iran would entail some "compromise"—a word former prime minister Olmert used in this context—Israel would have to find a way to convey to its close allies, especially the United States, what kind of compromise it would accept.[19] How to define those red lines and how to communicate them to others are extremely sensitive matters.[20]

Israeli assessments have determined that Iran has been and is involved with various aspects of nuclear weaponization, but Israeli concern over the Iranian nuclear program focuses on its fissile material (currently uranium enrichment) capability. In the past, when Israeli intelligence officials used the phrase "point of no return," it generally meant the point at which Iran would have mastered centrifuge technology. In the wake of criticisms from inside and outside the Israeli intelligence community that the phrase "point of no return" is conceptually flawed and makes little political sense, it was dropped.[21] Israel now uses the phrase "technological threshold." In his July 2009 interview, Arad referred specifically to this terminological/definitional issue:

> The point of nuclear no-return was defined as the point at which Iran has the ability to complete the cycle of nuclear fuel production on its own; the point at which it has all the elements to produce fissionable material without depending on outsiders. Iran is now there. I don't know if it has mastered all the technologies, but it is more or less there. However, the term "no-return" is misleading. Even if Iran has fissionable material for one bomb, it is still at a low grade of enrichment. And if it wants to conduct a test, it will not have even one bomb. It follows that Iran is not yet nuclear and not yet operational. Serious obstacles still lie in the way. The international community still has enough time to make it stop of its own volition.[22]

Once the "technological threshold" was achieved, it would be very difficult for intelligence agencies to nuance the exact status of the Iranian nuclear program. The Israeli intelligence community strongly rejected the implicit definition in the U.S. NIE of November 2007 that weaponization activity is the defining feature of a nuclear-weapons program.[23] Israeli red lines relate rather to the enrichment program, not to weaponization. One wonders to what extent Israel assesses Iran's nuclear program by doing a reverse mirroring of its own nuclear history.

The second dilemma Israel may face is whether and how to act—and non-action is also a kind of action—if Iran crosses those red lines. So far Iran has continued to defy the will of the Security Council on the matter of enrichment, mastering the enrichment technology to the industrial level. If the international community either proves itself powerless to enforce those Security Council resolutions, or reaches a deal with Iran that places it too close to attaining the bomb, Israel would face a difficult decision: either follow that lead, and ultimately have to accept a situation of a de facto nuclear Iran (by Israeli definition); or take independent action and forestall the Iran nuclear program. This would amount to a fundamental strategic choice between prevention and deterrence. It would test Israel's commitment to the 1981 Begin Doctrine: the commitment to take preventive action, including military action, against any hostile neighbor in proximity to the bomb.[24]

Israeli leaders consider this challenge highly sensitive, and little has been leaked from the behind-the-scene deliberations. After Minister Shaul Mofaz warned in June 2008 that Israel could not accept a nuclear Iran—implying military action would be necessary—he was criticized.[25] Against this official mute policy, it was shocking that former prime minister Ehud Olmert, in his final interview before departing from office in late September 2008, dismissed openly as "megalomania" any thought that Israel should or would attack Iran on its own to halt its nuclear program: "Part of our megalomania and our loss of proportions is the things that are said here about Iran. We are a country that has lost a sense of proportion about itself."[26] It is the international community, and not Israel, which should deal with the Iranian nuclear issue.

Of course, if Iran overtly acquired nuclear weapons and clearly signaled its intent by withdrawing from the NPT, it would simplify Israel's choices and create more international support for preemption. In addition to a decision about taking military action, Israel would have to decide whether to change its own nuclear policy; that is, whether to adopt an overt deterrence policy and to bring opacity to an end. There were indications Prime Minister Netanyahu entertained this case seriously at one time. Notwithstanding the common wisdom in Israel that, if Iran tested a weapon, Israel would have to follow suit in some fashion, there are reasons to believe that Israeli policy- makers would still see more benefit in not testing and letting Iran bear the brunt of international opprobrium. In any case, Israeli reaction to Iran's possibly leaving the NPT or even testing a device is not automatic.

Apart from the need to overcome a domestic impulse to trade an eye for an eye, an overt weapons posture by Iran would simplify Israel's options for deterrence and containment. At a minimum, Israel would make sure that the Iranians had no doubt about its ability to devastate Iran in retaliation, including with its sea-based assets. Israel would also seek to strengthen its missile defense and pursue civil defense measures as a means of deterrence by denial. On the diplomatic front, it would amplify efforts to sanction Iran and to deny it all trade that could assist its weapons capabilities.

Another longer-term dilemma involves deterrence, arms control, and containment. If prevention ultimately fails and a new kind of nuclear regime is inevitable in the Middle East, how should Israel respond to the making of such a regime? During the height of the Cold War, as the world learned to live under the balance of nuclear terror, as in mutual assured destruction, the theory and practice of arms control were developed to provide measures of stability and robustness. But those dialogues took place against the explicit and declared presence of nuclear weapons. Would it be possible to have such an arms-control dialogue in a context of opacity on both sides? How would it be possible to maintain conversations about nuclear weapons when neither side had introduced nuclear weapons?

There are the political costs of diplomatically engaging Iran, for which there is almost no current domestic constituency in Israel. But there are other difficulties, as well—for example, such a dialogue would be perceived as accepting, and thereby legitimizing, Iran's nuclear capability. On the surface, as long as President Ahmadinejad remains in power in Tehran, the issue of engagement is moot, since anti-Zionism is so central to the Iranian hardliners' worldview.

If prevention fails, it is unlikely that Israelis at present would look to arms control as a solution. In the face of a nuclear-capable and hostile Iran, the feasibility of changes in opacity would be unlikely. In theory, Israelis may prefer having zero nuclear-armed countries in the Middle East compared to there being two. But given Iran's record and its anti-Israel posture, Israelis would not trust Iran to comply with disarmament measures. Part of the difficulty would stem from the traditional view of nuclear disarmament in the Middle East, which is based solely on the vision of a nuclear weapons–free zone (NWFZ).

But the NWFZ vision is really only a vision, and thus is not anchored in the current political reality of the Middle East. For Israel, a NWFZ is conditioned on peaceful relations among all the members of the zone, something that does not appear possible under the current regime in Tehran.

Still, under different political circumstances in Iran, with a different governing group, this might be an opening for a new regional grand deal. If and when leaders are willing to think "outside the box," there are other ideas, discussed below, about measures of arms control, disarmament, and nonproliferation which are compatible with the region as it is.

THE IRONY OF OPACITY

In February 2007 Ali Larijani, then the secretary general of Iran's Supreme National Security Council and the head of its nuclear negotiating team, declared that Iran's nuclear program is at present for peaceful purposes, but as far as the future is concerned, he continued, nobody knows what is in store. If Iran is threatened, everything is open. It was difficult not to see an intriguing historical resemblance between his statement in 2007 and what Prime Minister Ben Gurion told President Kennedy in their meeting in May 1961.[27] Israel then, like Iran now, was in the midst of an ambitious national nuclear initiative designed to create a nuclear-weapons option, but not yet with a good idea of how far it could push the envelope. Like Israel in the early- to mid-1960s, Iran today seems to be committed to obtaining nuclear-weapons capability, but in spite of their determination, they probably have no idea how far they will be able to push.[28]

At a minimum, Iran seems to want to position itself very close to the weapon threshold by maintaining a large-scale enrichment capability (albeit keeping enrichment at a low level) while creating a certain ambiguity as to its weaponization activities. The Iranian political leadership may look at nuclear Israel today and hope that they could do likewise. But in reality, even apart from the 1969 Nixon-Meir political deal that relieved Israel from any inhibition about going nuclear, it will be more difficult for Iran to achieve a "bomb in the basement" posture. Only by massive deception—say, by building large-scale undeclared enrichment facilities (the recent discovery of the facility near Kum may be a case in point)—can Iran achieve a bomb in the basement while still within the NPT.

The worry over Iranian enrichment at industrial-scale capacity, what Israeli intelligence refers to as the "technological threshold," is not that it can lead to an ambiguous bomb in the basement, but that large-scale, low-enriched uranium (LEU) enrichment capabilities can create dangerous "breakout" scenarios: they quickly could be reconfigured into a highly enriched uranium (HEU) mode of production, thereby giving little warning time to the international community. And, of course, if Iran were to withdraw from the NPT, that would also be a clear sign of nonpeaceful intent. Under safeguards, it is a so-called breakout, not a bomb in the basement, which is the main worry. In contrast, Israel has never been under safeguards, so nuclear weapons under opacity have been an option.

Nevertheless, Iran may reconstruct its own posture of nuclear opacity through modalities different from but functionally similar to those used in Israel. The political differences between an actual "bomb in the basement" and Iranian "industrial production" are not that significant for a country that chooses the strategy of opacity. It would be opacity, even though not an Israeli-like opacity. In any case, the opacity can be intensified, as it is difficult to locate activity related to weaponization or even undeclared enrichment facilities.

This brings us back to the following question: how should Israel react to the emergence of an opaquely nuclear Iran? I noted earlier that much depends on what we really mean by "nuclear Iran," and it is time to explicate that. Based on this analysis, as long as Iran remains within the boundaries of the NPT there will probably never be a "nuclear Iran," insofar as that means an Iran with actual nuclear weapons, even undeclared à la Israel. In this respect, a great deal of the Israeli discourse on nuclear Iran is rooted in scare politics. It says more about the Israeli psyche than about Iran.

It is likely that we will face a different sense of nuclear Iran, in which Iran develops a full latent nuclear-weapons capability opaquely, under the guise of its peaceful program within the NPT, and this ultimately would blur the difference between possession and nonpossession. In fact, all signs are that Iran has already adopted that modality. This type of opacity—call it "latent opacity"—would be politically convenient for Iran, precisely because Iran is a signatory to the NPT. It is also an extremely flexible modality, politically and technologically, because it rests on true ambiguity about intentions and capabilities. Any explicit weaponization activities may remain concealed, opaquely disguised, or even put on hold.

It would allow Iran to gain a great deal of political advantage by having an advanced nuclear-weapons capability, extracting elements of deterrence and prestige out of it. At the same time, it would allow Iran to maintain friction with the world within the parameters of its legal claims under the NPT. Iran would continue to claim that its nuclear program is merely peaceful and that it has a right under the NPT to have access to the entire nuclear fuel cycle; at the same time, Iran would spread rumors that it is on the verge of possessing weapons (or maybe even has a bomb in the basement), and therefore it should be considered a de facto nuclear state, just as Israel is an undeclared nuclear state.

Iran's choice of opacity would be a political challenge for the international nuclear system, but a far greater challenge to Israel, which was the first and only country to use opacity as a nuclear posture. There is an important difference between Israel and Iran: Israel's opacity succeeded as an international phenomenon because the world—in particular the United States—decided to accept its maintaining such a policy in preference to all other options. Israel received an implicit exemption from the international community, which closed its eyes to the nuclear issue for political, legal, and even ethical reasons unique to Israel. Iran's choice of latent opacity, in contrast, would come under radically different circumstances. The world has explicitly expressed its opposition to anything resembling a nuclear program in Iran.

Herein lies the real challenge for all: at what point in time should Israel and the international community remove the mask of opacity and insist on calling a spade a spade? When should the world start to call the Iranian capability a virtual bomb? Is it preferable to remove the mask from Iranian ambiguity and to call it by name, or is an opaque Iran preferable to an openly nuclear Iran? At what point in time should we insist on international nuclear accountability? And what will be the future of Israeli ambiguity in such a world? These are questions that until now have hardly been asked, but they demand a great deal of thinking, both worldwide and in Israel.

Israelis tend to see the conflict with Iran in dichotomous terms: either take a sharp action against Iran—preferably some sort of military action or naval blockade—or accept living with a nuclear Iran. This is a bad dilemma, but Israelis see no way out of it. Given Israel's own opacity, it appears that Israel would be cautious to "out" nuclear Iran prematurely. While one must presume that Israel is preparing itself for the eventuality that Iran one day may be openly nuclear, Israelis agree that these preparations should be done under the veil of opacity. There is a strategic consensus in Israel that Israel should stick to opacity as long as it can; that is, as long as Iran itself clings to its own declaratory "peaceful" mode. The Iranian situation commands caution and makes any change in opacity—even minor change—more resistible. Opacity is not only the safest public posture, especially during times of strategic uncertainty, but it is also in itself a firewall against change.

THE ROBUSTNESS OF OPACITY

I noted earlier that Israeli nuclear thinking focuses now almost entirely on the Iran issue. Everything else about the future of Israel's nuclear policy awaits the resolution of the Iranian nuclear issue. Israelis now have little interest in or patience for discussing other issues related to the global nuclear order. One could make this point even stronger. The Iranian nuclear situation adds another incentive for Israel to remain conservative in its nuclear policy, to stick to its opacity policy without changing an iota. Israelis believe that their country has little to gain and much to lose in ending opacity, including possibly sparking regional nuclearization and unraveling of the NPT regime.[29] Most important, Israelis believe that the world wants them to continue with their opacity.

There are three fundamental issues that Israel must consider: opacity's strategic value, alternatives to it, and the role of opacity within the international system. The conventional wisdom in Israel (but also in the United States) strongly favors opacity based on all three counts. On the first issue, Israelis believe that opacity is still beneficial to Israeli security for the same reasons that existed forty years ago: opacity provides the country existential deterrence and allows the international community to live with a nuclear Israel. Moreover, it allows the international community to treat Israel as an exceptional case without saying so explicitly. On the second issue, there is even stronger consensus that opacity has no feasible alternative. On the third issue, the United States, and along with it much of the international community, supports the practice of opacity because they agree with the Israelis that there is no realistic alternative to it. Indeed, at the present time, there is no pressure on Israel to consider changing the bargain. Underlying these three judgments is the most important conceptual presumption: the equivocation between opacity as a declaratory posture and Israel's ability to possess the bomb.

At present, the delicate battle of wills between Iran and the international community over the nuclear issue is a work in progress, and it is impossible to tell how this impasse will be sorted out—by way of sticks, carrots, or anything in between. For now, Israel (with tacit support from many within the international community) is anxious to contain the Iranian problem without allowing any outside links, regional or global. This means that as long as the Iranian nuclear issue remains unresolved, Israel will be reluctant to change its own posture, especially on the issue of opacity.

THE FMCT ISSUE[30]

The Fissile Materials Cutoff Treaty (FMCT) is a prominent element on the Obama administration's nuclear roadmap. Israelis see the FMCT issue as incompatible with their national interest, and from more than one angle. For Israel, there is a unique dimension: whether (and how far) the FMCT is compatible with Israel's long-standing commitment to opacity.

The FMCT idea, first proposed in the early nuclear age, resurfaced after the end of the Cold War. In September 1993, in a speech before the United Nations, President Bill Clinton proposed a "multilateral convention banning the production of fissile materials for nuclear explosives or material outside international safeguards."[31] Two months later the UN General Assembly adopted resolution 48/75L calling for the negotiation of a "non-discriminatory, multilateral and international effectively verifiable treaty banning the production of fissile material for nuclear weapons or other nuclear explosive devices."[32] In March 1995, the Geneva-based Conference on Disarmament (CD) established an ad hoc committee to carry out this mandate.

Despite its reservations, Israel joined the General Assembly consensus resolution and participated in the negotiations in the CD. Israel, however, kept a low profile, calculating that it would be wiser to let others impede the negotiating process. The strategy proved correct until the summer of 1998 when, due to the consensus rule, Israel's joining the consensus became essential. By early August 1998, after China, India, and Pakistan joined the consensus, Israel was the last holdout in the CD. It was in those days of mid-August 1998 that the otherwise friendly Clinton administration exerted the harshest pressure it had ever used against any Israeli government.

Even though no draft treaty was on the horizon, Israeli prime minister Benjamin Netanyahu recognized that an FMCT, any FMCT, might have profound long-term implications for the future of Israel's opacity issue. Under intense pressure from Washington, however, Israel joined the consensus, but it also let it be known that Israel would oppose the treaty. In two letters and several conversations with the president, Netanyahu wrote Clinton, "We will never sign the treaty, and do not delude yourselves—no pressure will help. We will not sign the treaty because we will not commit suicide."[33] Netanyahu's concerns were premature. During the (second) Bush administration, disagreements over the scope and purpose of the FMCT, and over linkages to other arms control issues, stalled the negotiations for nearly a decade.[34]

Throughout the 1990s Israel was vague, even secretive, about its reservations and concerns about the FMCT. It appears that its underlying but unstated reasons for opposition to the FMCT involve both political and technical considerations. Central to both was a perceived conflict between the FMCT and opacity.

Politically, the main Israeli concern is that an FMCT would be the first stage in a slippery slope pushing Israel toward premature nuclear disarmament. The Arab states would argue that an FMCT should not be a substitute for the establishment of a NWFZ in the Middle East, and should not legitimize Israel's nuclear monopoly, something the Arab states could never accept. Hence, the Israeli fear is that the Arab states would "pocket" Israel's agreement to an FMCT as the first practical step toward the establishment of a nuclear weapons–free zone in the Middle East and use it as a platform to exert further pressure on Israel to disarm.

Technically, it would also be difficult for Israel to maintain opacity under an FMCT, especially if the FMCT contained provisions for credible verification. Although the shutdown of Israel's Dimona reactor, which presumably was used to produce plutonium for its weapons program, could be verified remotely, it is known that the reactor is also used to produce tritium via neutron irradiation of lithium-6 targets.[35] Because tritium has a relatively short half-life—12.3 years—shutting down the reactor would eventually lead to a degradation of the tritium-boosted weapons in Israel's arsenal. While Israel could continue to produce tritium as a party to the FMCT, it would have to agree to verification to ensure that the reactor was not also being used to produce plutonium. It is not clear that this could be accomplished without intrusive on-site inspections that would compromise opacity.[36]

During the second Bush administration Israel made its objections to the FMCT explicit and linked them to the Iranian nuclear issue. These objections reflect Israel's old guiding principles on matters of arms control and disarmament: first, the nuclear issue has to be negotiated in a regional framework and in close linkage to the political situation; and second, the FMCT does not address Israel's grave concerns about the deficiencies of the NPT.

Out of these general principles, one can articulate the two specific Israeli objections to the FMCT:

1. The global objection: an FMCT allows the operation of both uranium enrichment and reprocessing facilities as long as the products are used for os-

tensibly peaceful purposes, not weapons. However, even if the safeguards to detect possible diversion of these fissile materials to weapons are credible, they cannot prevent breakout, and they would provide a convenient rationale for the acquisition of expertise and technology that would facilitate the construction and operation of clandestine enrichment and reprocessing plants.

2. The regional objection: the only avenue for nuclear disarmament in the Middle East is via the regional NWFZ route, not the FMCT. Such a route could be initiated only in the context of a comprehensive peace process, where the peace issue is the primary driver, not the nuclear issue.

Israel sees an FMCT as a net loss, requiring constraints on its nuclear activities which could erode the benefits of opacity, while giving virtually no gain to Israel—especially in constraining Iran—in return. The FMCT has no direct application to an Iran that claims that its enrichment activities are legitimate under the NPT, directed to peaceful purposes. Furthermore, Israel views any international attention to its own nuclear program as a dangerous distraction from the urgent need to focus on the threat of Iranian nuclearization.

But this Israeli position may become more problematic in the coming years. The Obama administration is committed to reversing the Bush administration's nuclear status quo. The FMCT is now a real item in President Obama's nuclear disarmament vision. In his historic speech in Prague in April 2009, he declared the need for a treaty that "verifiably ends the production of fissile materials intended for use in state nuclear weapons."[37]

An FMCT in the Middle East is not likely to be a viable near-term prospect. But one can still ask whether there is anything else that Israel could do, apart from military action against Iran, to lessen the dangers of nuclearization in the region and possibly to contribute ultimately to a satisfactory diplomatic deal with Iran (but surely not under the regime that we have today in Iran). Israel's answer is in the negative. At present Israel vehemently resists any linkage—legal or otherwise—between the two nations' nuclear programs; there is no connection between Natanz and Dimona.

Israel is legally right. In reality, however, for many people such a linkage is not only commonsensical, but also desirable. Some analysts argue that the dichotomy that Israel seems to advance, "either accept nuclear Iran or bomb Iran before" is a deceptive one.[38] Bombing Iran would most likely guarantee that Iran would depart from the NPT and turn openly toward the bomb. The only way to prevent a nuclear Iran is for Iran itself to make the strategic decision that its own interest is not to have the bomb. At this point Israel would have to decide about its own strategic preference: does Israel prefer an open nuclear deterrence with Iran over a situation in which Israel accepts the linkage in order to establish a regional arms control scheme? The answer to this dilemma is not a simple one, but it is worth debating.

CONCLUSION

It is time to consider the Israeli nuclear case against the broader nuclear global context, both the vision of a world without nuclear weapons and the renewed interest in nuclear power. This historical junction could pose long-term challenges for Israeli nuclear policies, in particular to its commitment to the policy of opacity.

It is plain that there is major tension, indeed conflict, between the logic of nuclear abolition and Israel's concept and practice of opacity. First, the movement to global nuclear zero must apply to all nuclear weapons states, those under the NPT and those outside the NPT. There can be no exceptions. But at present Israel has no interest whatsoever in nuclear disarmament. Second, the logic of global zero assumes at least minimum transparency about nuclear status: all nuclear weapons states must self-declare. Nuclear acknowledgment must be a norm; acknowledgment and declaration precede verification and global zero. For the short and mid term, the global buzz about a world without nuclear weapons—a talk that Israelis view as naive and unfeasible—will only strengthen the Israeli consensus behind opacity. While Israelis may understand "theoretically" the long-term linkage between horizontal and vertical proliferation, they hardly see the issue as applying to Israel, surely not now, before the Iranian nuclear issue is resolved. Israel would adopt a long "wait and see" attitude, reluctant to make any visible commitment that would go beyond its own past verbal commitment to a NWFZ. It is likely that Israel would even tighten the practice of its opacity policy as a firewall to ensure that no external political pressure could force Israel to support the disarmament vision prematurely.

Israelis believe that the policy of opacity, and the U.S. support behind it, will ensure Israel's exceptional status, at least for the short and mid term. In general, Israelis view the vision of a world without nuclear weapons in a very similar fashion to the way they view their own official vision of a NWFZ in the Middle East. Both are essentially just verbal diplomacy, a vision for a far-into-the-future world that cannot be achieved in our lifetime.

For the longer run, however, a great deal depends on how the Iranian nuclear issue is finally resolved, and the state of the Arab-Israeli conflict. As long as Israel sees itself facing existential threats, or even the possibility of existential threats, it is unthinkable that it would be willing to disarm from its national insurance policy, its nuclear deterrent. It is unrealistic to expect that Israel could move toward a vision of nuclear disarmament unless a just and durable peace is achieved and established. A just and durable peace in the region is a necessary condition for a nuclear-free Middle East.

But one could also conceive of another long-term scenario. If a nuclear renaissance in electric power production were to become a reality in the Middle East, and if there were to be significant progress on the Arab-Israeli peace process front, it is also conceivable that, under certain political conditions, Israel would be interested in cooperating in the establishment of a regional framework of nuclear control. After all, as I pointed out earlier, probably only under a larger regional arrangement is there a chance to persuade Iran to give up its nuclear ambitions. Given the Israeli interest in preventing diversion of nuclear material and expertise that could be used for weapons, one could conceive of an Israeli interest in cooperating with others on creating a new structure of mechanisms for nuclear control, in particular, banning "sensitive technologies." Such cooperation could be seen as part of a roadmap toward a NWFZ in the region. A new system of nuclear control might also apply to Israel's own facilities, and in this case it would surely have an impact on opacity. This could be a true first step toward the establishment of a NWFZ in the Middle East.

If there is a real lesson that the Israeli nuclear case generates for the vision of a world without nuclear weapons, it is about the close linkage of nuclear weapons to major regional conflicts. Until these conflicts can be resolved, it is unlikely that regional nuclear weapons states will be willing to disarm.

NOTES

1. For a detailed account of Israel's nuclear history, see Avner Cohen, *Israel and the Bomb* (New York: Columbia University Press, 1998).

2. Ari Shavit, "Dimona," *Ha'aretz Friday Magazine*, December 12, 1999.

3. I elaborate on the notion of "nuclear bargain" in my book *The Worst Kept Secret: Israel's Bargain with the Bomb* (New York: Columbia University Press, 2010).

4. International Institute for Strategic Studies, *Nuclear Programmes in the Middle East: In the Shadow of Iran* (London: IISS, 2008), 136–38.

5. On Netanyahu's views on the gravity of the "Iranian threat," see Ronen Bergman, *The Secret War with Iran* (New York: Free Press, 2008), pp. 343–44.

6. Ari Shavit, "There Is No Palestinian Sadat, No Palestinian Mandela," interview with Uzi Arad, *Ha'aretz*, July 11, 2009, at http://www.haaretz.com/hasen/spages/1099064.html.

7. "Mossad: Iran Will Have Nuclear Bomb by 2014," *Ha'aretz*, June 16, 2009. I should note, however, that other Israeli leaders—among them even Minister of Defense Ehud Barak, as well as the current opposition leader and former foreign minister, Tzipi Livni—have been reluctant to use this phrase, insisting instead that Israel is the strongest military power in the region and could protect itself under any circumstances.

8. Former Prime Minister Ehud Olmert highlighted this outlook in a public speech in Herzelya in early January 2007: "For many long years, we have followed Iran's efforts to acquire nuclear weapons, in the guise of a civilian nuclear program. They are working through secret channels in a number of sites spread out across Iran," at http://www.pmo.gov.il/NR/exeres/C672BEFF-A736-42A0-83F5-6907958ADCBA,frameless.htm?NRMODE = Published).

9. For a mainstream Israeli analysis of these concerns, see Ephraim Kam, "A Nuclear Iran: What Does It Mean, and What Can Be Done," *Memorandum* no. 88 (Tel Aviv: Institute for National Strategic Studies, 2007), at http://www.tau.ac.il/jcss/memoranda/memo88.pdf.

10. National Intelligence Council, "Iran: Nuclear Intentions and Capabilities," National Intelligence Estimate, November 2007, at http://www.dni.gov/press_releases/20071203_release.pdf. For a dissenting Israeli view of the November NIE, see Bergman, *Secret War with Iran*, esp. pp. 338–40, 346–49.

11. "How Secrecy over Iran's Qom Nuclear Facility was Finally Blown Away," *The Times Online*, September 26, 2009, at http://www.timesonline.co.uk/tol/news/world/middle_east/article6850325.ece.

12. Yet some Israelis question whether the current religious leadership of Iran could be deterred at all by nuclear weapons, given their views on Israeli and Shi'ite religious beliefs, and Israeli concerns that such beliefs could have an impact on Iranian leaders' sense of rationality.

13. Shavit, "There Is No Palestinian Sadat." Of course, with Israel's nuclear weapon, there is already a nuclear Middle East, something that Israel's policy of opacity does not acknowledge.

14. This point was central in Prime Minister Ehud Olmert's Herzliya speech in January 2007 (see note 8) .

15. Some Israeli leaders, such as Prime Minister Netanyahu, believe that Israeli deterrence must be fully explicit and crystal clear. In Netanyahu's words: "Against lunatics, deterrence must be absolute, perfect, including a second strike capability. The crazies have to understand that if they raise their hands against us, we'll put them back in the Stone Age" (quoted in Bergman, *Secret War with Iran*, p. 344).

16. Cam Simpson, "Israeli Citizens Struggle amid Iran's Nuclear Vow," *Wall Street Journal*, December 22, 2006.

17. In a speech on November 2006, Netanyahu claimed, "It's 1938 and Iran is Germany. And Iran is racing to arm itself with atomic bombs. Believe him and stop him." "Netanyahu: It's 1938 and Iran Is Germany," *Ha'aretz*, November 14, 2006.

18. The substance and much of the style of this section are taken from my contribution, "Israel: Nuclear Monopoly in Jeopardy," in International Institute for Strategic Studies, *Nuclear Programmes in the Middle East*.

19. Ehud Olmert, "Prime Minister Ehud Olmert's Address at the 2007 Herzliya Conference," Prime Minister's Office, January 24, 2007, at http://www.pmo.gov.il/PMOEng/Archive/Speeches/2007/01/speechher240107.htm.

20. Chuck Freilich, *Speaking about the Unspeakable: U.S.-Israeli Dialogue on Iran's Nuclear Program*, Policy Brief no. 77 (Washington, DC: Washington Institute for Near East Policy, 2007), at http://www.washingtoninstitute.org/templateC04.php?CID=284.

21. I was one of the critics of this phrase. See Avner Cohen, "Point of No Return?" *Ha'aretz*, May 17, 2005.

22. Shavit, "There Is No Palestinian Sadat."

23. National Intelligence Council, "Iran: Nuclear Intentions and Capabilities," National Intelligence Estimate, November 2007.

24. Shlomo Nakdimon, *First Strike: The Exclusive Story of How Israel Foiled Iraq's Attempt to Get the Bomb* (New York: Summit Books, 1987).

25. "Mofaz Criticised over Iran Threat," BBC News, June 8, 2008.

26. Ethan Bronner, "Olmert Says Israel Should Pull Out of the West Bank," *New York Times*, September 29, 2008.

27. On the Kennedy–Ben Gurion 1961 meeting, see Cohen, *Israel and the Bomb*, pp. 131–32.

28. There are also important historical differences in the nuclear situation of the two countries. Technologically, today it is far easier to acquire nuclear weapons than it was in the early- to mid-1960s, when only four countries had such weapons. Politically, however, there is a nuclear nonproliferation regime, whose legal and normative core is the NPT, which did not exist then. Apart from its bilateral political pledges to the United States, Israel was sovereign, in terms of law and international norms, and thus free to pursue its nuclear ambitions, although surely in an opaque way. Dimona has never been under anything like international IAEA safeguards. All Israel had to deal with were bilateral site visits whose ground rules it controlled. This ended with the Nixon-Meir deal in 1969. Ultimately, there was nothing illegal, or even improper, about going nuclear opaquely. This is not the case with Iran today. Iran is an NPT signatory; that is, it has a legal obligation not to develop nuclear weapons. Iran is also under the IAEA safeguards system and under today's verification technology. Of course, to the extent that Iran may have undeclared secret enrichment facilities—a most severe violation of its obligation under the NPT/IAEA—technology is incapable of detecting such activity.

29. This possibility became even more explicit with the Arab League announcement on March 6, 2008, that if Israel acknowledged it had nuclear weapons, Arab states would collectively withdraw from the treaty.

30. This section draws on a larger paper coauthored with Marvin Miller and commissioned for the International Panel on Nuclear Materials (IPFM). The paper appears in IPFM, *Banning the Production of Fissile Materials for Nuclear Weapons: Country Perspective on the Challenges to a Fissile Material Cutoff Treaty*, a companion volume to Global Fissile Material Report 2008, pp. 27–33, at www.fissilematerials.org.

31. President William Jefferson Clinton, "First Address to United Nations," United Nations General Assembly, September 23, 1993.

32. United Nations General Assembly, 48th Session, Resolution 75, "General and Complete Disarmament," December 16, 1993, at http://www.un.org/documents/ga/res/48/a48r075.htm.

33. Aluf Benn, "The Struggle to Keep Nuclear Capabilities Secret" (in Hebrew), *Ha'aretz*. September 14, 1999. See also Avner Cohen and George Perkovich, "The Obama-Netanyahu Meeting: Nuclear Issues," Carnegie Endowment for International Peace, May 14, 2009.

34. "Fissile Materials Cut-off Treaty," Reaching Critical Will, at http://www.reachingcriticalwill.org/legal/fmct.html.

35. Quoted in Benn, "The Struggle to Keep Nuclear Capabilities Secret."

36. Ibid.

37. White House, "Remarks by President Barack Obama in Prague," April 5, 2009, at http://www.whitehouse.gov/the_press_office/Remarks-By-President-Barack-Obama-In-Prague-As-Delivered/. Furthermore, Obama's vision is not entirely a partisan vision. Senator John McCain has also endorsed a vision of a world without nukes, in which FMCT plays an important role.

38. Mark Fitzpatrick, *The Iranian Nuclear Crisis: Avoiding Worst-Case Scenarios*, Adelphi Paper 398 (International Institute for Strategic Studies, November 2008).

11 Iran Policy on the Way to Zero

Jill Marie Lewis with Laicie Olson

The international community can eliminate the nuclear threat that Iran's pursuit of nuclear energy and weapon technology poses by ridding the world of all nuclear weapons, associated technology, nuclear material, and bomb-making knowledge. In short, if nuclear weapons are disinvented, the threat of a nuclear Iran, and the greater threat of nuclear terrorism, will vanish. Disinventing nuclear weapons is not possible in the near future, but it could be possible to reduce Iran's perceived need for a nuclear deterrent.

Several variables make Iran's nuclear case a great challenge: Iran's threat perception, difficulties in developing U.S. policy that curbs Iran's nuclear progress, loopholes in the Nuclear Nonproliferation Treaty (NPT), and Iran's divided theocracy. Policies implemented under the Bush administration, which combined threats, sanctions, and incentives, failed to convince Iran to freeze a program that now could be used for nuclear energy or for weapon production.

Solving Iran is not only a necessary step toward zero, but also essential to maintaining zero. A policy solution to Iran will be needed to sustain a future nuclear weapons–free world, since a nuclear weapon in such a world would be the ultimate deterrent. President Obama's administration and the international community at large face many challenges as they work toward curbing the proliferation of nuclear weapons and in particular preventing Iran from becoming a nuclear weapon state.

IRAN'S NUCLEAR PROGRAM

As an important ally of the West during the Cold War, Iran's drive toward a nuclear capability began as early as the 1950s. The capability was fueled by the United States and Europe. With no plans to enrich or reprocess nuclear material, the construction of nuclear facilities and Shah Pahlavi's plans for the construction of twenty-three nuclear reactors by the 1990s were of no threat to the West.[1]

The 1979 revolution brought Iran's program to a near halt. Scientists fled the country, and the West stopped exporting supplies to it. The popular Supreme Leader Ayatollah Khomeini announced his objection to a nuclear program and the development of nuclear weapons. Khomeini stopped most of the construction on Iran's twin nuclear reactor plant at Bushehr, which was being built by a West German company, on the grounds that such things were wasteful Western projects.

A decade later, however, in response to an Iraqi threat, Iran restarted its nuclear program.[2] Iran felt the threat from Iraq growing as that nation broke the Geneva Protocol and used chemical weapons on hundreds of thousands of Iranians during the 1980–88 Iran-Iraq War. This threat to Iran increased when the international community (in particular the United States) tolerated Iraq's use of chemical weapons and tried to prevent Iran from importing chemical precursors.[3] It increased even more when Iraq restarted its nuclear program (bombarded in 1981 by Israel).

Iran tried to acquire chemical weapons in response to Iraq's chemical weapon use, and began a nuclear weapons program in response to Iraq's growing nuclear capability.[4] Not long after Iraq began to rebuild its nuclear program, Supreme Leader Khomeini reversed his decision to freeze Iran's nuclear program. Iran signed contracts with Argentina, Russia, and China to build the program.[5] In 1984 Iran secretly contacted Pakistan's Abdul Qadeer Khan to buy centrifuge designs,[6] and in 1987 it received information on how to mold highly enriched uranium into hemispheres for the core of a nuclear weapon.[7]

Importing centrifuge technology from Khan's Market, from 1989 to its discovery in 2002, Iran developed a covert enrichment program at Natanz in central Iran. When the program was exposed in 2002, the International Atomic Energy Agency (IAEA) began to explore Iran's case of noncompliance with its safeguards agreement, agreed to as part of Iran's NPT commitment, and the United States began to lobby members of the IAEA Board of Governors to send Iran's case to the United Nations Security Council.

In June of 2003, at the request of the United States, IAEA Director General Mohamed El Baradei presented a report on Iran's nuclear program to the IAEA Board of Governors. This prompted the board to pass a September 2003 resolution requiring Iran to freeze all work at Natanz, cooperate in full with the IAEA inspectors, and sign the Additional Protocol, or face UN Security Council action. Iran did not obey, and in October, the case went to the Security Council and the first UN Security Council Resolution reproving Iran's nuclear program passed.

IAEA inspections and reports have continually raised questions on a military dimension to Iran's program. A January 2006 IAEA report states that Iran showed the agency more than sixty documents containing drawings, specifications, and supporting documentation dating from the early- to mid-1980s which had been handed over by intermediaries. "Among these was a 15-page document describing the procedures for the reduction of UF6 to metal in small quantities, and the casting of enriched and depleted uranium metal into hemispheres, related to the fabrication of nuclear weapon components," reads the IAEA report.[8]

By February 2009 Iran clearly had built a dual-use (nuclear energy and weapons) program.[9] Iran could use its stock of low-enriched uranium to make nuclear fuel or enrich it to bomb grade to put in the core of a nuclear weapon.[10] According to Iran, this capability will only be used for energy production, since the production and use of nuclear weapons runs up against the overarching cultural, religious, and ideological concerns of the leaders that took over after the revolution.[11] Supreme Leader Khamenei issued a fatwa on the production, stockpiling, and use of nuclear weapons, forbidding them under Islamic law.[12] Yet this ideological reasoning does not explain why Iran continued procurement of dual-use technology after 1991, began to conceal construction of additional enrichment plants from the IAEA, and began to enrich uranium to 20 percent U-235 in 2010.[13]

In 2009, President Barack Obama went public with intelligence on another hidden enrichment facility, located in Qom (approximately 100 miles southwest of Tehran). Built in secret, the Fordow Fuel Enrichment Plant (FFEP) was embedded in a mountain close to a Revolutionary Guards base with air defense. Although Iran has indicated that the decision to build the FFEP was made in the second half of 2007, the IAEA reports that "extensive information from a number of sources" indicates that design work for the facility began as early as 2006.[14] Concealing portions of its atomic complex underground, Iran's peaceful intentions are brought into question.

Pushing its dual use capabilities up a notch are Iran's plans to enrich uranium to higher grades. According to a February 10, 2010, IAEA report, Iran told the agency that it would begin to enrich its stock of low enriched uranium (now at approximately 4 percent U-235) to 20 percent U-235.[15] Iran stated that it had run out of the 20 percent enriched uranium needed to produce medical isotopes. U.S. officials stated that this was a "transparent ploy."[16] On February 8, 2010, Iran requested that the agency be present for a transfer of 10 kg of low-enriched uranium (LEU) from Natanz's Fuel Enrichment Plant (FEP) to its Pilot Fuel Enrichment Plant (PFEP), but started test feeding the pilot centrifuges before the IAEA arrived on February 10. A February 18 IAEA report confirmed that Iran had reached enrichment levels of up to 19.8 percent U-235 and had transferred approximately 1,950 kg of its stocked LEU to the pilot plant's feed station.[17] Enriching uranium from its natural state of 0.7 percent U-235 to approximately 4 percent U-235 is technically a much larger challenge than enriching from 4 percent to 20 percent.[18] Likewise, the move from 20 percent to 90 percent (bomb grade) will be even easier and faster for Iran if it chooses to do so.

Allowing Iran to be at the brink of nuclear weapon production leaves its options open. Some nations involved in negotiations with Iran strongly believe that Iran already intends to build a bomb, and they continue seeking ways to end the nation's nuclear advancements.[19] France, the United Kingdom, and the United States persist in their demand that Iran freeze all nuclear enrichment activities. Even if Iran's intent is peaceful today, several variables could change its intent in the future. These include: stronger threats from the West, an attack from Israel, or even larger internal unrest that leads Iranian hardliners to build a bomb. It could also be a combination of these things that change Iran's intentions.

IRAN'S THREAT PERCEPTION

One variable that could influence Iran's intentions and perceived need for a nuclear deterrent capability is its threat perception. In more recent years, Iran's Iraqi threat was replaced by the United States and Western U.S. allies, especially Israel. Former president George W. Bush labeled Iran part of an "axis of evil" and set up two carrier strike groups, with strategic lift capabilities, in the Strait of Hormuz in front of Iran. The Bush administration made it clear that they were there to deter Iran.

The Obama administration still deploys a strike group and an amphibious assault ship next to Iran's waters. The carrier strike group, the USS *Dwight D. Eisenhower*, has 6,900 troops on board, a guided-missile cruiser, and two guided-missile destroyers. The USS *Boxer*, the amphibious assault ship, has around 6,750 U.S. troops on board. This ship is designed to put troops on the ground and can assault from water to land. It can carry several types of helicopters, Harrier jets, and anti–submarine warfare equipment. Thousands of U.S. troops sit in two of Iran's bordering countries. As of October 2009 there were 124,000 U.S. troops in Iraq and over 60,000 in Afghanistan. As troop numbers decreased in Iraq under the Obama administration, they increased in Afghanistan. Lack of dialogue between the United States and Iran raises the threat that Iran perceives from the United States. U.S.-Soviet relations in the 1980s were easier to manage, since there were constant bilateral dialogue and fewer unknowns.

A policy of sanctions adds stress to U.S.-Iran relations, and increases Iran's perception of a threat from the United States. To persuade the nation into freezing its nuclear activities, both the Bush and Obama administrations tried policies that put sanctions on Iran's critical oil and gas markets. On September 30, 2009, Secretary of State Hilary Clinton warned Iran, "If we don't get the answers that we are expecting, and the changes in behavior that we are looking for, then we will work with our partners to move for sanctions." On January 28, 2010, the Senate passed the Comprehensive Iran Sanctions, Accountability and Divestment Act of 2009. The bill authorizes state and local governments to divest from local companies involved in critical business with Iran, and sanctions companies supporting Iran's import of refined petroleum products. This policy has done little to persuade Iran to curb its nuclear activity. Rather, to lessen the strain of sanctions on government activities, in 2007 Iran increased its refining capacity and enacted a more effective rationing program, significantly decreasing Iran's reliance on foreign petroleum products.

NOT MUCH NEW FROM OBAMA ON IRAN

The Obama administration spoke early on of a change in the U.S. approach to Iran, but little seems to have actually changed. The EU3 (France, Germany, and the United Kingdom) and the P5+1 (once joined by China, the United States, and Russia) attempted several times to entice Iran into freezing its nuclear program with an incentive package, but a U.S.-enforced precondition of a freeze on Iranian program work has always prevented substantive negotiations from taking place. Signifying a possible change in this policy, President Obama said in Cairo on June 4, 2009, that "there will be many issues to discuss between our two countries, and we are willing to move forward without preconditions."[20]

Nevertheless, the administration is still demanding that Iran prove its peaceful intent through a freeze in nuclear activities, and is even continuing a threat of force if Iran fails to cooperate. On February 21, 2010, General David Petraeus stated that the United States had not ruled out military strikes on Iran and that "no one" could claim that the United States and the rest of the world had not given Iran every opportunity to resolve the issues diplomatically.[21]

During his campaign and early on in his term, President Obama said he was willing to engage Iran, unlike the Bush administration. Now, the Obama administration defines its dual track strategy as different from President Bush's, but it sounds virtually the same. "We've pursued a dual track strategy of economic sanctions and engagement," said Obama's deputy secretary of state, Jim Steinberg, on October 6, 2009, at a congressional hearing on Iran. "They [the P5+1 partners] specifically reaffirmed the dual track, meaning that we are offering negotiations to Iran; but should Iran not be able to meet the terms of those negotiations, we are prepared to sanction them further," said Under Secretary of State for Political Affairs Nicholas Burns for President Bush in September 2007.[22]

It may not be that Obama's offers are all "talk," but that Iran's June 2009 election debacle left U.S. policy-makers with little to work with. After Iranian hardliners cracked down with brute force on peaceful election protests, the Obama administration put little effort into engaging Iran without preconditions. Minus one possible LEU deal brewing with Iran, the current U.S. administration is left following basically the same policy as the Bush administration.

The only truly new initiative coming out of the Obama administration was a proposal to provide Iran with 20 percent enriched uranium, which it needs to keep its Tehran Research Reactor (TRR) running. Iran's LEU at an approximate level of 4 percent would be transferred to a participating country (possibly France) for further enrichment and fuel fabrication, and shipped back to Iran for use in the TRR. Not only would this deal take away Iran's need to further enrich uranium, but it would also remove the majority of Iran's LEU stockpile from the country, increasing the time it would take Iran to build a bomb. Fearing again (as it did with the Russian proposal) that its LEU would be stuck outside its borders, Iran has since backed out of the deal, offering instead an even exchange of its 4 percent LEU for 20 percent enriched uranium on Iranian soil. It is still to be seen if Obama's team can keep this deal alive and prevent Iran from continuing its plan to produce its own TRR fuel.

Obama's appointees may also be slowing the possibility of real change in

U.S.-Iran policy. Although President Obama is trying to take the focus off state sponsors of terror and put it on America's gravest threat to security—terrorism—some of his appointees are still giving priority to their battle of the rogues. President Obama is careful not to claim that Iran has already decided to go for a bomb, but rather, leaves room for diplomacy in his public overtures on Iran. In his April 2009 speech in Prague, the president said that Iran had "yet to build a bomb" and that there was time to influence Iran's intent. In order to influence that intent, the president said we would engage Iran based on "mutual interests and mutual respect," and "support Iran's right to peaceful nuclear energy." We want "Iran to take its rightful place in the community of nations, politically and economically," he said.

Obama's vision sounds quite different from that of one of his appointees, Dennis Ross. Ross was Obama's Middle East envoy, picked to implement policy on Iran at the State Department. In 2009 he was moved to the National Security Council, where he is advising the president more regularly. In November 2008, Ross published an article in *Newsweek* claiming that the United States needed to put greater economic pressure on Iran to hit its "profound economic vulnerabilities."[23] Like the former Bush administration, he demonized Iran and said that "everywhere you look in the Middle East today, Iran is threatening U.S. interests and the political order."[24] He did not lay out room for diplomacy to convince Iran not to go for a bomb, but said that "Tehran clearly wants nukes for both defensive and offensive purposes."[25]

The Bush administration's Iran policy did nothing to prevent Iran from achieving its nuclear weapon break-out capability; if Obama's very similar strategy also allows Iran's program to advance, Iran could soon have a nuclear weapon capability.

U.S. NONPROLIFERATION AND DISARMAMENT POLICY

Dramatic change in the U.S.'s own nuclear posture and policy could influence Iran and other non–nuclear weapon states, but like change in U.S.-Iran policy, major change in this area is not coming quickly. As both dual-use nuclear fuel cycle technology and terrorism spread, leaders of nuclear weapon states recognize the qualitatively different threat that nuclear weapons represent today and the increasing chance of their use. This new and increasing threat impelled the United States in 2009, and other nuclear states, to commit to steps toward a world free of nuclear weapons. "I state clearly and with conviction America's commitment to seek the peace and security of a world without nuclear weapons," said President Barack Obama in his 2009 Prague speech.[26] Obama warned the international community of going back to an arms race; he said:

> There are those who hear talk of a world without nuclear weapons and doubt whether it's worth setting a goal that seems impossible to achieve. But make no mistake: We know where that road leads. . . . Let us bridge our divisions, build upon our hopes, and accept our responsibility to leave this world more prosperous and more peaceful than we found it.

Although President Obama said this goal would not be achieved in his lifetime, he laid out steps in Prague that the United States could take toward it. Steps included: a new nuclear arms reduction agreement with Russia, U.S. ratification of the Comprehensive Nuclear Test Ban Treaty (CTBT), negotiation of a verifiable fissile material cut-off treaty, and the establishment of a new framework for civil nuclear cooperation. Obama also spoke of Iran's nuclear case. He said his administration would engage Iran with respect and support its right to peaceful nuclear energy, but it was up to Iran to allow for "rigorous inspections" and prove its peaceful intent, or it would face "increased isolation" and "international pressure."

Taking the steps toward zero laid out in Prague could slightly reduce the chance that Iran builds a bomb in contravention of its NPT commitments. Such steps could strengthen the value of the NPT bargain by proving a U.S. commitment to its NPT Article VI (nuclear disarmament) obligations and reduce any perceived nuclear threat from the United States. However, U.S. nuclear policy will have little effect on nuclear programs in Iran and other non–nuclear weapon states until the majority of the Prague steps are taken, including changes made to U.S. nuclear posture to reduce the chance that U.S. nuclear weapons will ever be used.

Rather than decreasing the threat of a nuclear attack on Iran from the United States, the latest U.S. Nuclear Posture Review (NPR), released after the Prague speech, heightened Iran's fears. The April 2010 NPR reserves the right for the United States to use nuclear weapons on states in noncompliance with their NPT commitments. The NPR states, "[T]he United States is now prepared to strengthen its long-standing 'negative security assurance' by declaring that the United States will not use or threaten to use nuclear weapons against non-nuclear weapons states that are party to the NPT and in compliance with their nuclear non-proliferation obligations."[27] The Iranians may contest their compliance status in international fora, but they know for certain that the United States views them in noncompliance with their NPT nonproliferation obligations, and therefore still a target for U.S. nuclear attack. Iran took the NPR as an overt threat of nuclear attack. On May 5, 2010, President Ahmadinejad came to the first day of the NPT Review Conference and stated that "under the NPR, some States [including Iran] have been threatened to be the target of a pre-emptive nuclear strike."[28]

GLOBAL NONPROLIFERATION EFFORTS

Iran is a complex case, more complex than North Korea. The international community might have had an easier time with North Korea if the NPT's Article X (withdrawal clause) provided for penalties in response to a nation's withdrawal. Iran cannot be solved simply by strengthening U.S. nonproliferation policy and closing the NPT's loopholes. Iran did not choose complete isolation from the international community by going straight for a bomb and withdrawing from the NPT; rather, it built an enormous enrichment facility and continues to fight for it, citing Article IV of the NPT, which gives non–nuclear weapon states the right to nuclear technology for peaceful use. Iran also has a more diverse political system than North Korea. This system includes reformers who will fight to stay out of international isolation and condemnation, and conservatives who will fight for Iran's nuclear ascendancy. Strengthening U.S. nonproliferation policy and the NPT will help solve the Iran problem, but it is only one part of the solution. The Iranian nuclear problem will only be solved through comprehensive negotiations that meet a vast variety of Iranian and Western concerns.

Global Steps toward Zero

It is unlikely that steps toward zero, as laid out in President Obama's Prague speech, will affect non–nuclear weapon states like Iran until all nuclear weapon states are on the road toward zero. President Obama did say that arms reduction negotiations with Russia would "set the stage for further cuts, and we will seek to include all nuclear weapons states in this endeavor." It is unlikely, however, that other nuclear weapon states will join in nuclear disarmament negotiations before the United States and Russia reduce their stockpile totals to levels closer to 500 total warheads; that is, numbers closer to the stockpiles of the smaller nuclear weapons states.

There are no near-term plans for the United States and Russia to include their total stockpiles in a disarmament treaty. The New START is the latest arms reduction treaty between the United States and Russia (the world's leading nuclear weapon holders). Signed in April 2010, the treaty will bring each deployed arsenal down to 1,550 strategic warheads and 700 delivery vehicles, but nondeployed warheads are not included in this treaty.

Even if there were the will and a way to disarm to 500 total U.S. strategic and nonstrategic weapons, it would take the United States a minimum of two presidential terms (that is, eight years), possibly more, to accomplish the drawdown. Core defense policies from nuclear doctrine to highly technical weapons programs will have to be changed, and the entire U.S. weapons complex reimagined.[29] Hazardous nuclear waste will have to be safely dealt with and Congress convinced to change the focus of work for thousands of scientists and employees at U.S. national laboratories.

Also slowing and complicating the global shift toward zero is the fact that several nuclear weapon states do not partake in the NPT regime. North Korea withdrew from the treaty, and Israel, Pakistan, and India were never members. Israel's arsenal is not even officially recognized, so getting them involved in negotiations toward zero could be a great challenge. According to Iran, only if Israel enters the disarmament movement will its own nuclear decisions be affected. It submitted ten of the approximately forty working papers to the NPT Preparatory Committee (PrepCom) Meeting in New York in 2009. It stated in several of its working papers the importance of establishing a nuclear weapons–free zone (NWFZ) in the Middle East, reminding states that it was the first country in the Middle East region to initiate the idea in 1974.[30] Iran consistently refers to Israel as an obstacle to NPT success. If concrete steps were taken by NPT parties toward the realization of a NWFZ in the Middle East, it could reduce the probability that Iran would build a bomb. The United States is willing to mention the importance of taking steps toward a NWFZ in the Middle East, and said so at the 2009 NPT PrepCom and the 2010 NPT Review Conference. However, it is a very sensitive topic with a tight ally, and it is very doubtful the United States is prepared to aggressively push for its implementation. Without strong U.S. support for the NWFZ, it will not come about any time soon.

It looks as if a real Nuclear Weapons Convention (prohibiting the use and threat of use of nuclear weapons, as well as providing a phased program for total elimination)[31] between all nuclear weapon states is not on the horizon, but even if it were, would it decrease or increase a non–nuclear weapon state's aspiration to build a bomb? Some experts say that such a convention would decrease Iran's need for a nuclear security assurance, but others believe it would raise the value of a nuclear deterrent to a state like Iran, since an Iranian bomb in a world without any other nuclear weapons would provide the ultimate deterrent. In any case, states are not yet near consensus on a nuclear weapon convention. At the 2009 PrepCom meeting in New York, the final consensus document started out with the mention of such a convention, but it was quickly negotiated out of subsequent drafts by NPT state parties.[32]

Spreading Peaceful Use Technology

President Obama set the stage to pursue disarmament policies that will strengthen the NPT, but there are other multilateral initiatives in play that could weaken their positive effect. Many non–nuclear weapon states perceive new initiatives by nuclear weapon states to facilitate the spread of nuclear power while curbing the spread of enrichment and reprocessing technology to be working against their NPT Article IV (peaceful-use) rights. A late 2008 U.S. Congressional House Committee report instructed the Energy Department to continue to foster relations with countries with advanced fuel-cycle capabilities (that is, Britain, France, and Japan), but not with those that do not have them.[33]

This approach is fostering distrust in the NPT system, and could be weakening Iran's (and other non–nuclear weapons states') commitment to the regime. The former Bush administration pursued such an approach with the launch of the Global Nuclear Energy Partnership (GNEP) in 2006. GNEP initially required partner nations receiving fuel services to "forgo their own investments in enrichment and reprocessing technologies." President Bush outlined the original purpose of GNEP's international component in his speech at the National Defense University on February 11, 2004:

> The world's leading nuclear exporters should ensure that states have reliable access at reasonable cost to fuel for civilian reactors, so long as those states renounce enrichment and reprocessing. Enrichment and reprocessing are not necessary for nations seeking to harness nuclear energy for peaceful purposes.[34]

GNEP is one of several fuel cycle initiatives proposed in the international community since 2005. Russia, Germany, Japan, and the United Kingdom also proposed initiatives to better manage the spread of sensitive fuel cycle capabilities. Rather than curbing the spread of enrichment and reprocessing technology, initiatives like GNEP may have provoked a number of nations to announce new policies to resuscitate dormant or launch new nuclear energy and enrichment programs. As soon as the United States launched GNEP, several nations made clear that they would not give up their inalienable right to nuclear technology as granted to them under Article IV of the Nuclear Nonproliferation Treaty.

The Obama administration is trying hard to change the original vision President Bush laid out for GNEP. U.S. diplomats have changed the tone of GNEP consensus statements, inserting whenever possible the idea that GNEP looks to help non–nuclear weapon states gain access to their nuclear rights under the NPT, not take them away. Negotiations are even taking place to change GNEP's name to something that a broad variety of states agree on. At the writing of this chapter the name International Framework for Nuclear Energy Cooperation is being strongly considered to replace GNEP. Still, the original GNEP vision is hard to wipe from memory in key non–nuclear weapon states, and turning GNEP into a useful international framework for progress continues to be an uphill battle.

President Obama has emphasized that fissile material, which can be produced at Natanz, poses the greatest threat to U.S. security, not nuclear weapons. He promised to secure fissile material around the globe in four years. It is "the dangers posed by nuclear proliferation and nuclear terrorism" that "animate President Obama's call for a new direction and new momentum in pursuit of nuclear disarmament," said U.S. ambassador Marguerita Ragsdale at the NPT PrepCom, May 6, 2009, in New York.[35]

The prioritization of managing the spread of sensitive fuel cycle technology over nuclear disarmament could weaken Iran's, and other non–nuclear weapon states', commitment to the NPT. Claiming that Iran's nuclear program blocks nuclear states from fulfilling their NPT disarmament commitment could also weaken Iran's NPT nonproliferation commitment. Assistant Secretary of State for Verification, Compliance, and Implementation Rose Gottemoeller delivered a statement to the NPT PrepCom in New York on May 5, 2009, stating that her "delegation would like to note how important stopping the spread of nuclear weapons is, to give the nuclear weapons states confidence that further reductions in these weapons can be made without undermining international peace and security."[36] Two days later, U.S. ambassador Ragsdale said that "it is also essential that the vast majority of states who are parties fully comply with its [NPT] provisions.... [U]nfortunately we know that some Parties—Iran and North Korea—have broken the Treaty's rules."

The United States laid out the argument at the 2009 PrepCom that Iran is blocking NPT progress and the abolition movement. Iran's NPT delegation called this a "continued unbalanced and discriminatory approach," and stated that the real threat to international peace and security is that the United States and other nuclear weapon states are "uncommitted to Article VI [nuclear disarmament], and still threatening peace and security."

According to Iran, clamping down on the spread of sensitive fuel cycle technology raises the value of such technology. Iran claimed that the way in which the United States cracked down on peaceful-use technology in the past forced them to go to Pakistan's black market for nuclear fuel supplies. "Access of developing countries to peaceful nuclear materials has been continuously denied to the extent that they have had no choice than to acquire their requirements for peaceful uses of nuclear energy, including medical and industrial applications, from open markets, [and] intermediaries," said Iranian ambassador Ali Asghar Soltanieh on May 8, 2009, at the PrepCom. Iran also views restrictions on nuclear energy technology as a "grave injustice" against their NPT rights. At the NPT Review Conference in 2010, President Ahmadinejad added:

> One of the gravest injustices committed by the nuclear weapon states is equating nuclear arms with nuclear energy. As a matter of fact, they want to monopolize both the nuclear weapons and the peaceful nuclear energy, and by doing so impose their will on the international community.[37]

In no way do U.S. efforts to strengthen nonproliferation policy globally give Iran the justification to pursue a dual use nuclear program, but Iran believes they do, or at least uses this as an excuse for its noncompliance with IAEA safeguards requirements. Recent U.S. efforts to make GNEP a more equal opportunity venture and efforts to insert more language at the NPT on a non–nuclear weapon state's right to nuclear energy will help counter Iran's claims. Nevertheless, Iran is a complex case that cannot be solved by U.S. and global nonproliferation policy alone.

NPT Outsiders

Also affecting Iran's nuclear decisions and negotiations are non-NPT member states Pakistan, India, and North Korea. As nuclear-armed Pakistan becomes more and more unstable, the possibility of a jihadist takeover increases. If Pakistan becomes a recognized safe haven for al Qaeda and other terrorist groups, it will threaten Shia Iran and likely encourage an expansion of the Iranian nuclear program.[38] Meanwhile, India signed a nuclear trade agreement with the United States in 2006, reversing thirty years of U.S. law that prohibited the United States from trading nuclear technology with states outside the NPT regime. Some experts say that the India deal set a good example for Iran, proving that if a state follows the rules and does not proliferate, it could gain greater access to the Western market.[39] Other experts fear that the U.S.-India nuclear agreement has undermined the NPT regime and forced non–nuclear weapon states like Iran to doubt the value of the NPT bargain. Iran will continue to use the U.S.-India deal as proof that the NPT regime is unfair.

How the international community deals with the North Korean case could also affect Iran's future nuclear decisions. North Korea illegally withdrew from the NPT, built six to eight nuclear bombs, and tested two. So far, North Korea has faced only reprimands and sanctions for its actions. Iran is watching this situation closely. North Korea is a staunch supporter of Iran's program, and reportedly provided Iran with technical advice and technology for its nuclear and ballistic missile programs. If North Korea continues to get away with being a nuclear weapon state, Iran may itself choose sovereignty and a nuclear deterrent over peaceful integration in the international community. President Obama called in Prague for "real and immediate consequences for countries caught breaking the rules." It will be up to his administration to find ways to work with NPT members to close the NPT loophole that allowed North Korea, without immediate consequences, to withdraw from the NPT and, while a party, to use technology toward a nuclear weapon capability. Iran's choice to go nuclear and drop its NPT membership will likely be influenced by the international community's future success or failure on redefining the NPT's withdrawal clause.

IRAN'S LEADERSHIP STRUGGLE

U.S. and Western influence on Iran's nuclear choices in the near future will be negatively impacted by the fragile state of the current Iranian regime. To change the goals of Iran's nuclear program prior to June 2009, the West could have convinced the single most powerful figure in Iran at the time, Supreme Leader Khamenei.[40] Khamenei was likely the only Iranian in the political system who held enough power to change Iran's nuclear intentions, yet after the contentious presidential elections of June 2009, Khamenei may no longer have enough control over all factions of Iran's system to effect a change in Iran's nuclear program goals.

In the wake of the June 12, 2009, presidential elections, tens of thousands of Iranians took to the streets to contest the election of the incumbent conservative, Ahmadinejad, in the largest occurrence of street protests and rioting since the 1979 Iranian Revolution. Reformist leader Mir-Hussein Mousavi ran against Ahmadinejad and continues to lead the opposition, dubbed the "green movement" in honor of the *mowj-e-sabz*, or "green wave," a symbol of Mousavi's campaign. On June 19, 2009, the supreme leader publicly allowed the Basij army, an arm of the Revolutionary Guards, to beat down the ongoing protests. In the days that followed, tear gas, guns, and water cannons were used.

Hundreds of protestors, Iranian journalists, human rights lawyers, and reformist politicians have since been beaten and jailed. Pictures of blood-stained young students killed by the Iranian government are posted all over the internet. Millions of Iranians who were once protesting election results were even more enraged by the government's violent crackdown. The green movement morphed from its inception as a political campaign, to a campaign to annul the presidential election, and finally, more broadly, into a movement to restore the civil liberties promised by the 1979 Islamic Revolution. President Obama is careful to express only moral support for Iranians fighting for their civil rights, so as not to lend credence to the government's assertion that the movement is a foreign-inspired plot to foment a "velvet" or "color" revolution. Until Iran's regime changes or settles down, it will be very hard to engage them on sensitive nuclear issues.

CONCLUSION

In light of Iran's current political instability, it is hard to foresee what the real impact of any new U.S. or multilateral policy would be on Iran. A central goal of any new policy should be to decrease the threat Iran perceives from the West and reduce the chance that the nation will build a nuclear weapon as a security assurance. The world is not ready to eliminate nuclear weapons tomorrow, and even if it did, it is unclear if global zero would increase or decrease the value to Iran of building a bomb. In any case, until a less antagonistic and more diplomatic Iranian regime comes to power, any hope to positively influence Iran's nuclear ambition is lost. This problem is complex, and not solvable in a short book chapter, but it is clear that a solution to the question of Iran will be necessary to achieve the goal of a nuclear weapon–free world and sustain it.

NOTES

This chapter was completed in the September 2009, before the principal author began her current position in the U.S. government, and updated since by Laicie Olson, Center for Arms Control and Nonproliferation.

1. Sharon Squassoni, "Iran's Nuclear Program: Recent Developments," *Congressional Research Service*, November 23, 2005, Order Code RS21592.

2. For more on Iran's response to Iraq's nuclear program, see Mahdi Obeidi, *The Bomb in My Garden* (Hoboken, NJ: Wiley and Sons, 2004), p. 65.

3. Millions of Iranians were affected by the September 1980 to August 1988 Iran-Iraq War; 220,000 Iranians were killed and 500,000 injured (40,000 prisoners of war were taken). Today, there are still 60,000 Iranian survivors that are registered to receive treatment for chemical weapon exposure, according to Dr. Shahriar Khateri, International Relations director for the Society for Chemical Weapon Victim Support: "Acute and Chronic Health Effects of Chemical Weapons: Lessons Learned from the Iranian Survivors," presentation in Washington, DC, May 8, 2008. For details on President Reagan's secret tolerance of Iraq's use of chemical weapons, see Patrick E. Tyler, "Officers Say U.S. Aided Iraq in War Despite Use of Gas," *New York Times*, August 18, 2002.

4. Iran failed to persuade the international community to impose sanctions on Iraq for its violations of the 1925 Geneva Protocol, and in response acquired its own chemical weapon stockpile; see Tyler, "Officers Say U.S. Aided Iraq." For Iran's response to the restart of Iraq's nuclear program, see Dilip Hiro, "Why Iran Didn't Cross the Nuclear Weapon Road," *YaleGlobal*, December 11, 2007.

5. For more on Iran's contracts with Argentina and China, see Taylor and Francis Group, Lucy Dean, *The Middle East and North Africa* (New York: Routledge, 2003), p. 410; "The China-Iran Nuclear Cloud," *Middle East Defense News*, July 22, 1991; and Jack Boureston and Charles D. Ferguson, "Schooling Iran's Atom Squad," *Bulletin of the Atomic Scientists* 60, 3 (2004): 31–35.

6. Bruno Tertrais, leading French nuclear expert, at Fondation pour la Recherche Stratégique, on Iran's program, email interview with author, May 26, 2009.

7. For a report citing Iran's acquisition of nuclear weapon drawings, see International Atomic Energy Agency, "International Atomic Energy Agency Report on Iran," GOV/2006/15, February 27, 2006.

8. "International Atomic Energy Agency Report on Iran," International Atomic Energy Agency, GOV/2006/15.

9. To see Iran's achievements by this time, see: "International Atomic Energy Agency Report on Iran," GOV/2009/8, February 19, 2009.

10. With no previous experience in making a nuclear weapon, experts estimate that it could take from six months to two years for Iran to do so.

11. Gregory F. Giles, "The Islamic Republic of Iran and Nuclear, Biological, and Chemical Weapons," in *Planning the Unthinkable*, ed. Peter Lavoy, Scott Sagan, and James Wirtz (Ithaca, NY: Cornell University Press, 2000).

12. "Iran Holder of Peaceful Nuclear Fuel Cycle Technology," Iran's Statement at IAEA Emergency Meeting, August 10, 2005, available at http://www.fas.org/nuke/guide/iran/nuke/mehr080905.html.

13. Ibid.; on Iran procuring dual use technology after 1991, see Tertrais email interview.

14. Reported in "Implementation of the NPT Safeguards Agreement and Relevant Provisions of Security Council Resolutions 1737(2006), 1747(2007), 1803(2008) and 1835(2008) in the Islamic Republic of Iran," GOV/INF/2010/10, February 18, 2010.

15. Ibid., GOV/INF/2010/2, February 10, 2010.

16. "Obama Official: Iran Medical Isotopes Claim a 'Transparent Ploy,'" *The Cable*, March 17, 2010.

17. Ibid.; GOV/INF/2010/10.

18. To understand how it is easier to quickly move from 4 percent to 20 percent enrichment, see Jeffrey Lewis's post on *ArmsControlWonk.Com*, "Iran to Enrich 20 Percent LEU," February 9, 2010, *ArmControlWonk.Com*.

19. Although a 2007 U.S. National Intelligence Estimate (NIE) states that Iran stopped weaponization work in 2002, the NIE proves that Iran had, and could still have, a weaponization capability. "Iran: Nuclear Intentions and Capabilities," National Intelligence Estimate, U.S. National Intelligence Council, November 2007.

20. "Obama Egypt Speech," *Huffington Post*, June 4, 2009.

21. Jay Deshmukh, "Iran to 'Hide Nuclear Plants inside Mountains," *AFP*, February 22, 2010.

22. James B. Steinberg, Opening Statement before the Senate Banking, Housing and Urban Affairs Committee, October 6, 2009. Nicolas Burns's statement of September 28, 2007 can be found at http://merln.ndu.edu/archivepdf/iran/State/92953.pdf.

23. Dennis Ross, "Iran: Talk Tough with Tehran," *Newsweek*, November 29, 2008.

24. Ibid.

25. Ibid.

26. Remarks by President Barack Obama, Czech Republic, Prague, April 5, 2009.

27. Nuclear Posture Review Report, *U.S. Department of Defense*, April 2010.

28. Statement by Iranian president Mahmoud Ahmadinejad, May 3, 2010, Nuclear Nonproliferation Treaty Review Conference, United Nations, New York.

29. See the chapter by Judith Reppy in this book.

30. Report submitted by Iran to the NPT Preparatory Committee Meeting, "Establishment of a Nuclear Weapon Free Zone in the ME," April 21, 2009, NPT/CONF.2010/PC.III/PC.7.

31. The Lawyers Committee on Nuclear Policy, text of the "Convention on the

Prohibition of the Development, Testing, Production, Stockpiling, Transfer, Use and Threat of Use of Nuclear Weapons and on Their Elimination," April 1997.

32. To view the drafts of the Draft Recommendations to the 2010 NPT Review Conference during negotiations toward a consensus document at the 2009 NPT Preparatory Committee Meeting, see "PrepCom *Almost* Falls Apart," blog post from the Nuclear Nonproliferation Treaty Preparatory Conference in New York, Physicians for Social Responsibility, May 14, 2009.

33. Energy and Water Development and Related Agencies Appropriations Act, 2009, H.R. 7324, U.S. House of Representatives.

34. President George W. Bush, "President Announces New Measures to Counter the Threat of WMD," remarks by President George W. Bush at Fort Lesley J. McNair, National Defense University, February 11, 2004.

35. Jill Parillo, "Iran vs. the United States at the PrepCom," *Physicians for Social Responsibility*, May 8, 2009, available at http://www.psr.org/nuclear-weapons/blog/iran-vs-the-united.html.

36. This and the following three quotations are from notes taken by author at the event.

37. Statement by Iranian president Mahmoud Ahmadinejad, May 3, 2010, Nuclear Nonproliferation Treaty Review Conference, United Nations, New York.

38. Bruce Riedel, "Pakistan's Nuclear Weapons: Averting the Worst," Brookings Institution, May 27, 2009, available at http://www.brookings.edu/opinions/2009/0506_pakistan_riedel.aspx.

39. Stephen Cohen in a talk, "The U.S.-India Nuclear Agreement," at the Brookings Institution, Washington, DC, July 30, 2008.

40. Akbar Ganji, "The Latter-Day Sultan," *Foreign Affairs* 87, no. 6 (November/December 2008): 45–66.

12 India and Nuclear Zero

Waheguru Pal Singh Sidhu

INTRODUCTION

As the country that claims to have given the world the concept of "zero," India has a particular affinity toward this number. However, when it comes to the issue of nuclear zero, this affinity is found wanting. Today India professes to support the concept of nuclear zero without having zero nuclear weapons. However, this has not always been the case.

Until at least 1974 (when India tested a nuclear "device") and possibly the mid-1980s (when India covertly built nuclear weapons), India did vociferously support nuclear disarmament without having any nuclear weapons of its own. Subsequently, even though it developed nuclear weapons, New Delhi continued to advocate complete nuclear disarmament within a time-bound framework, at least until 1998, when it conducted a series of tests and declared itself to be a nuclear weapon state. More recently, even as India declared its intentions to create a minimum credible deterrence, it also pursued attempts to reduce nuclear dangers from existing nuclear weapons on the one hand, while also working toward the complete elimination of all nuclear weapons on the other. Thus, India's nuclear disarmament policy has become closely intertwined with its nuclear armament policy and vice versa, and to understand India's approach to nuclear disarmament in general and global zero in particular it is essential to examine the weapons program.

This chapter begins with a historical overview of India's nuclear weapon program through its four phases. It also examines India's efforts at global disarmament since its independence in 1947. The next section looks at India's efforts to reduce nuclear dangers at the regional level through a series of confidence-building measures with Pakistan and China. The final section draws the linkages between the weapons program and the disarmament effort, and argues that the window of opportunity for engaging India in global zero is rapidly closing. The chapter will identify the driving forces behind the present and future weaponization program, as well as the drivers toward nuclear disarmament: politics, technology, the military, and—above all—Indian strategic notions, including its perception of the emerging global order, and targeting dogmas.

HISTORICAL OVERVIEW OF INDIA'S NUCLEAR WEAPON PROGRAM

The rationale behind India's nuclear weapon program was complex and was driven partly by external security concerns and partly by internal drivers, which included the scientific community, the political leadership, and the military, as well as New Delhi's perception of its place in the world order based on the possession of nuclear weapons. India's nuclear weapon program has evolved in four distinct phases: the "weapon option" phase (from the establishment of the Atomic Energy Commission in 1947 to the first nuclear tests in 1974); the "un-weaponized" phase (from 1975, when India virtually slowed down, if not halted, its march toward weaponization, to around the mid-1980s, when the decision to weaponize the option was made); the "non-weaponized deterrence" and "recessed deterrence" phase (from the covert development and fabrication of nuclear weapons and their delivery systems in the mid-1980s to the overt nuclear tests in May 1998); and the present "credible minimum deterrence" phase (since May 1998).[1]

Weapon Option Phase

There is near unanimity among students of India's nuclear program that the option to make weapons was built into the program from its inception in the late 1940s, and that both India's first prime minister, Jawaharlal Nehru, and Homi Jehangir Bhabha, the chief of the Indian Atomic Energy Commission, were its principal architects.[2] This built-in ability to weaponize came to be known as the "weapon option." Although the exact origin of the phrase "weapon option" is elusive, it appears to have been coined by Nehru. Interestingly, the move toward establishing this ability was embarked on well before there was any perceivable nuclear threat to India. By the time of China's first nuclear test in 1964, India had an implicit policy of keeping open the "weapon option." This option became viable in 1965, when India had completed construction of the 40 MW CIRUS plutonium production reactor and the Trombay plutonium reprocessing plant, and drew up plans for the Subterranean Nuclear Explosion Project (SNEP).[3] Prime Minister Lal Bahadur Shastri, who had succeeded Nehru, gave the go-ahead to SNEP in November 1965. However, following the sudden deaths of Shastri and Bhabha in 1966, SNEP was shelved. It was revived by Prime Minister Indira Gandhi only in the form of the "peaceful nuclear explosion" (PNE) in 1974, when India tested but did not weaponize its nuclear capability for at least another decade.

Un-weaponized Phase

A few years before the 1974 nuclear tests, the annual report of the minister of defense noted the Chinese trend of developing "ballistic missiles with nuclear warheads" and estimated that China had stockpiled about 150 nuclear and thermonuclear weapons, with a capacity of producing forty weapons of 20 kilotons annually. The report seemed particularly concerned about the medium-range ballistic missiles (with a range of up to 3,200 km), which when operational were "capable of reaching targets in India from launching bases in Tibet."[4] Thus, after 1974 and with the growing threat posed by the Chinese nuclear arsenal, there was a security case to enhance India's nuclear weapon capability. This capability, however, was curtailed for a number of organizational and political reasons. Although the scientists were eager to go ahead with further developments of the nuclear arsenal, including the development of a thermonuclear capability, and were, reportedly, given the "go-ahead" to conduct preliminary work, the technical capacity to do so was drastically reduced. Following the 1974 nuclear test the availability of fissile material went "from one to zero." This was partly on account of the sharp international reaction, especially from Canada, which had provided the CIRUS reactor on the strict understanding that it would be used only for "peaceful purposes," and partly on account of the closure of the Trombay plutonium separation plant for refurbishment. This was coupled with a feud that had broken out between Raja Ramanna (the chief architect of the 1974 nuclear device) and Homi Sethna (the head of the Indian Atomic Energy Commission) in their contest to control the organization. The feud paralyzed the "bomb-makers" at the Bhabha Atomic Research Centre.[5] Finally, Prime Minister Gandhi, who had been a supporter of the program, became increasingly distracted by political challenges in the late 1970s and was eventually voted out in 1977. The new prime minister, Morarji Desai, a staunch Gandhian, ensured that during his tenure the weapon option remained "un-weaponized."

However, even during this period of "un-weaponization," several steps were taken that were to strengthen the weapon option in coming years. First, in 1977, work began on a new 100 MW plutonium production reactor, originally called R-5 but subsequently named "Dhruva." This reactor was a scaled-up version of the original CIRUS reactor and had the added advantage of not being under safeguards and, therefore, not vulnerable to sanctions.[6] On August 8, 1985, Dhruva attained criticality but encountered start-up problems; it attained full power only on January 17, 1988. Second, although Prime Minister Desai was instrumental in keeping the option "un-weaponized," in 1978 he approved the purchase of Jaguar aircraft, which could be designed to carry India's first generation of nuclear weapons. Finally, the return of Indira Gandhi as prime minister in 1980 saw not only a move to resume nuclear tests in 1982, but also the launch of an ambitious Integrated Guided Missile Development Programme, which was tasked to develop at least two nuclear-capable missiles: the Prithvi and the Agni.[7] However, despite growing evidence that Pakistan was well on its way to acquiring a nuclear weapon capability, nuclear tests were shelved at the behest of Prime Minister Gandhi and never revisited until her assassination in 1984. In the absence of precise evidence, there is only the speculation that Indira Gandhi changed her mind primarily on account of pressure by the United States and, perhaps, the absence of a perceived clear and present nuclear threat.

This weaponless state did not necessarily reflect an "Indian" way of deterrence, but came about because India's latent nuclear capability was not immediately translated into a weaponized deterrent. The delay was produced by the slow development of India's technological capability to build nuclear weapons and missiles; the exclusion of the military from the nuclear weapon program (which remained exclusively in the hands of civilian scientists and technocrats); and the absence of a clear and present nuclear danger to India's security until the 1980s. This phase lasted at least until the early 1980s if not 1988, when the decision to weaponize appears to have been made.[8]

Recessed Deterrence Phase

After 1974, but more evidently since the premiership of Rajiv Gandhi in 1985, when a formal decision to weaponize without conducting further tests appears to have been taken, India developed a missile-based delivery system for its covert arsenal of nuclear weapons and started to adopt a deterrence policy, without actually deploying nuclear weapons. Scholars have described this situation as "recessed deterrence" or "non-weaponized deterrence" or even "existential deterrence."[9] "Non-weaponized deterrence," in which a country has the basic components of a deliverable nuclear weapon but chooses not to weaponize these components, provides the best explanation of this period. This phase continued until the nuclear tests of 1998, which ushered in the phase of "minimum credible deterrence." While the various "nuclear" crises of the 1980s did provide a compelling rationale for weaponization, there is no doubt that weaponization was possible only because the fruition of the scientific and technological capabilities coincided with the will of the political leadership to covertly cross the nuclear Rubicon.

May 1998 and Minimum Credible Deterrence

The Indian tests of May 1998 (followed in quick succession by the Pakistani tests), while critical for India's autonomy of action, raised three primary challenges. First, India attempted to justify its de facto right to bear nuclear arms and also to provide some element of de jure recognition of this right. Second, it wished through its declarations and actions to portray and prove itself as a responsible member of the exclusive nuclear weapon club. Thus, soon after the tests, India declared its desire to create a "minimum credible deterrence," but also offered a qualified "no-first use guarantee." In a curious move soon after the tests India also offered to join the Nuclear Non-Proliferation Treaty (NPT), but only as a nuclear weapon state. India also readily agreed to provide negative security guarantees for proposed nuclear weapon free zones in its vicinity.[10] This move was not entirely altruistic: it was aimed at acquiring de facto recognition of India as a nuclear weapon state. Similarly, India, followed by Pakistan, declared a unilateral moratorium on further nuclear tests. Third, given the level of hostility with Pakistan and the rudimentary nature of the nuclear arsenals, there was fear that the region might become the flash point (accidental or deliberate) for a nuclear exchange. This concern was highlighted by the 1999 Kargil intrusions. While the reasons behind the Kargil confrontation need not concern us directly here, it is important to note that both Islamabad and New Delhi showed a willingness to manage the crisis and prevent a dangerous increase in tension (even though democracy in Pakistan might have become the hapless victim of this success).[11]

Similarly, while both India and Pakistan have conducted missile tests to validate delivery systems for their nuclear weapons, this has not led to an open-ended arms race. Moreover, so far, neither India nor Pakistan has deployed or put their nuclear forces on hair-trigger alert, and both are keen on nuclear stability. Soon after the Kargil crisis on August 17, 1999, India unveiled a draft nuclear doctrine.[12] This doctrine categorically stated India's quest to establish a "minimum credible deterrent." Almost three years later New Delhi also elaborated its nuclear command and control structure.[13] These doctrinal developments were a direct result, not necessarily of the clear and present nuclear threat, but of a compromise between the three key actors in the nuclear decision-making process: the political leadership; the nuclear and defense scientific establishment; and the armed forces.

Doctrine and Deployment

India's present nuclear doctrine emphasizes a strong civilian control of the nuclear arsenal through the "nuclear command authority" headed by the prime minister. This civilian control is further buttressed by a "divided control" of the nuclear arsenal between the nuclear scientists (who have control of the warheads) and the military (who possess the means of delivery). In addition, during peacetime the nuclear arsenal is in a state of de-alert (where the warheads are separate from the delivery systems) and the nuclear forces are not deployed in an operational mode. The declared Indian doctrine also calls for a no-first-use posture, which notes that the nuclear arsenal can be used in response to a nuclear "attack on Indian soil, or an attack on Indian forces anywhere." This no-first-use guarantee has also been qualified with the caveat that India might launch a nuclear attack in response to a chemical or a biological attack against it.[14]

India's no-first-use doctrine by implication also rationalized the need for a survivable second-strike nuclear triad (composed of aircraft-delivered, land- and sea-based missiles). Whereas by all accounts India possessed only an air-deliverable capability when the nuclear doctrine was unveiled in 1999, the launch of the INS *Arihant* nuclear-armed submarine in July 2009 has provided all the key elements for the nuclear triad.[15] Although it is still years if not a decade before the triad will be fully operational, India's quest for a minimum credible deterrence appears to be nearing fruition. Nonetheless, many experts who have looked at this arsenal and doctrine have displayed skepticism of India's actual use, or deterrence credibility.

Interestingly, although India has not signed either the NPT or the Comprehensive Test Ban Treaty (CTBT), nor is it a member of any other international restriction agreement such as the nuclear suppliers group or the missile technology control regime, the 1999 doctrine calls for nuclear abolition, clearly indicating the linkage between nuclear weapons, doctrine, and disarmament.

INDIA'S GLOBAL NUCLEAR DISARMAMENT EFFORTS

Like India's nuclear weapon program, its global disarmament policy has also evolved in four distinct phases: the complete nuclear disarmament phase (from 1947 till the time of the first Chinese nuclear test in 1964); disarmament diplomacy coupled with the quest for nuclear guarantees and the nuclear disarmament abstinence phase (from 1964 till India's rejection of the Nuclear Non-Proliferation Treaty in 1968, and from then until the mid-1970s during which India virtually abstained from engaging in nuclear disarmament efforts); the continuing call for nuclear disarmament coupled with the building up of the nuclear armament phase (from the mid-1980s to the overt nuclear tests in May 1998); and the "reducing nuclear dangers" to "devalue to discard" phase (since May 1998).

Complete Nuclear Disarmament Phase

Prime Minister Nehru, who was the chief architect of building India's nuclear weapon capability, was also responsible for constructing India's global nuclear disarmament efforts. Nehru's personal aversion of nuclear weapons was evident as early as 1946, when he called the bomb "a symbol of evil."[16] He was horrified at the destructive power that these weapons were capable of unleashing. Following the March 1, 1954, "Bravo" test on the Bikini Atoll—the biggest U.S. hydrogen bomb ever tested, with a yield of 15 megatons and fallout that spread worldwide—Nehru introduced the first UN General Assembly resolution calling for a comprehensive test ban of nuclear weapons, a precursor to the CTBT negotiated in 1996. Nehru also commissioned the world's first public study of the effects of nuclear weapons, which was published in 1956.[17]

While championing the cause of global nuclear disarmament, Nehru was also categorical about India not building nuclear arms itself. For instance, speaking in parliament in the debate on the department of atomic energy in 1957, Nehru vowed, "[We] have declared quite clearly that we are not interested in making atom bombs, even if we have the capacity to do so. . . . I hope this will be policy of all future governments."[18] In a similar debate in 1963 Nehru reiterated the "no-bomb" policy and argued: "On the one hand, we are asking the nuclear powers to give up their tests. How can we, without showing the utter insincerity of what we have always said, go in for doing the very thing which we have repeatedly asked the other powers not to do?"[19]

Nehru's assertion was endorsed in the active diplomatic role that New Delhi played in the Eighteen Nation Disarmament Committee (ENDC), the forerunner to the present-day conference on disarmament (CD) in Geneva, to ensure the successful negotiation of the Partial Test Ban Treaty (PTBT), which banned nuclear tests in the atmosphere, underwater, and in outer space, and entered into force in 1963. Interestingly, India lamented the limitations of the PTBT in the UN General Assembly in October 1963 in that it did not ban underground tests and called for continued efforts to achieve a CTBT.[20] Around this time India also supported other General Assembly resolutions that sought general and complete disarmament, especially the prohibition of nuclear and thermonuclear weapons, as well as resolutions that called for a suspension of all nuclear tests.

Thus, according to K. D. Kapur, Nehru's "genuine concern about the horrors of nuclear menace, his conviction in the peaceful uses of nuclear energy which should never be used for military purposes, normative and moralistic overtones emanating from the country's commitment to non-alignment, and his commitment to nuclear disarmament [resulted in a] high profile and diplomatically active role in disarmament negotiations in the 1950s and 1960s."[21] Of course, the absence of any nuclear threat to India—direct or perceived—might also explain the zealous idealism with which New Delhi pursued the cause of global nuclear disarmament.

Nuclear Disarmament and Security Guarantees

The Indian defeat at the hands of China in the 1962 Sino-Indian border war, coupled with the first Chinese nuclear test at Lop Nor in 1964, not only dealt a severe blow to the Indian national psyche, but also established the perception of a nuclear threat from a more formidable and now nuclear neighbor. The emerging alliance between China and Pakistan, with whom India had already fought one war and was about to face another, accentuated the potential nuclear threat from Beijing. These developments posed a serious dilemma to the traditional idealistic approach that India had adopted toward global nuclear disarmament.

In response to the new scenario India embarked on three approaches: first, to participate in global nuclear disarmament negotiations that would target all nuclear weapons in general, but Chinese nuclear weapons in particular. Second, to simultaneously seek nuclear guarantees from other nuclear powers (albeit through the UN) against China. Third, as discussed in the previous section, to embark on its own nuclear weapon program to deter China's growing capabilities. Clearly, these three approaches were in contradiction to each other and posed a challenge to India's quest for global nuclear disarmament. For instance, by seeking nuclear guarantees against other nuclear weapon states (especially China), even through the UN, India was forced to tacitly accept the presence, possession of, and protection by nuclear weapons.

As part of the first approach India took an active part in proposing the principles of the NPT in the ENDC in 1965. However, its hopes of having an NPT that would lead to the elimination of all nuclear weapons, especially those in the hands of China, were soon dashed, and New Delhi argued that the treaty was discriminatory and created a class of "nuclear haves" and a class of "nuclear have-nots." Subsequently, India sought to at least have security guarantees provided to non-nuclear states under the UN auspices. The Kosygin Proposal submitted in February 1966 by the Soviet Union to provide "negative security" guarantees might have alleviated the Indian concerns, but it was subsequently withdrawn, leaving India with no credible guarantee for its security.[22] By 1967, although India continued to participate in the NPT negotiations, it became disillusioned at the "imposed exercise in non-armament of unarmed countries" and that there was no real effort to "deny prestige to possession of nuclear weapons." Privately, Prime Minister Indira Gandhi did not want to accede to the NPT on the grounds that "with China at her back, and Pakistan lurking on the sidelines, she saw no alternative but to keep open her option on the production of nuclear weapons."[23]

Thus, when the draft of the NPT was submitted to the UN General Assembly in April 1968, India voted against it and categorically refused to sign the treaty. India's detailed critique of the NPT included its failure to prevent vertical proliferation, its inability to ensure a step-by-step approach toward nuclear disarmament, its discriminatory nature, and the lack of any security guarantee to the non-nuclear weapon states, which was a quid pro quo for accepting the treaty.[24]

India's quest for security guarantees fared even worse outside the ENDC negotiations. Given its nonaligned status and inherent abhorrence to military alliances such as NATO (which had provided security guarantees to all its members), India was reluctant to get assurances from only one camp. On the other hand, military alliances like NATO were unwilling to provide a nuclear security umbrella to nonmembers such as India. India's preferred position, of multilateral guarantees ideally under the UN banner or from nuclear weapon states on both sides of the Cold War divide, was a nonstarter. Consequently, India gave up its quest for seeking nuclear guarantees and resumed its nuclear weapon program.

Nuclear Armament and Disarmament

From 1968, when New Delhi rejected the NPT, through 1974, when it carried out its nuclear test (which became the target of many multilateral nonproliferation instruments, such as the Nuclear Suppliers Group), India was noticeably absent from the international disarmament arena. In 1978, four years after conducting its first nuclear test, India presented a resolution at the UN General Assembly which stated that the use of nuclear weapons violated the UN charter, was a crime against humanity, and should therefore be prohibited pending nuclear disarmament. The resolution, like most General Assembly resolutions, was adopted but not enforced. In 1982, while Prime Minister Indira Gandhi was contemplating a second round of nuclear tests, she also proposed a five-point program of action to the Second Special Session of the UN General Assembly (UNSSOD-II) which included the "negotiation of a binding convention on the non-use of nuclear weapons, a freeze on nuclear weapons . . . , the immediate suspension of all nuclear weapon tests, and negotiations addressed to the task of achieving a Treaty on GCD [General and Complete Disarmament] within an agreed time-frame."[25] It was only in May 1984 that India joined the "Six Nation Initiative" (along with Argentina, Greece, Mexico, Sweden, and Tanzania) with the stated objective of promoting the CTBT and nuclear and general disarmament. The initiative took place against the backdrop of the second Cold War and the concerns of a limited nuclear war being contemplated between the two superpowers. The appeal of May 1984 may have contributed to the Reykjavik summit in 1986, although there is no evidence of a direct correlation. India may have joined this initiative for two reasons: first, with the Soviet intervention in Afghanistan in 1979, the Cold War had come to India's doorstep, and this may have been an effort to indirectly address that concern. Second, the close ties between India and Sweden at this time, evident in the personal friendship between Indira Gandhi and Olof Palme, may also have played a role in India's joining the initiative. The initiative was superseded by the 1986 Reykjavik summit between Gorbachev and Reagan.[26]

However, in November 1986, in the wake of the failure of the October Reykjavik summit, Rajiv Gandhi and President Gorbachev signed the "Joint Declaration of Principles of a Nuclear-Weapon-Free and Non-Violent World," "echoing many of the themes relating to general and complete disarmament, including a proposal for the elimination of nuclear weapons 'before the end of the century' and for the progress toward a 'nuclear-weapon free civilization.'"[27] This declaration was short on details and almost served as a consolation for the failure of Reykjavik. Interestingly, this was probably the only time that one of the two nuclear superpowers had issued a joint declaration with a purportedly non-nuclear weapon state, although in reality India was already on its way to creating its covert nuclear arsenal.

In June 1988, by which time India had already developed an operational nuclear arsenal, Rajiv Gandhi unveiled his Action Plan at the Third UN Special Session on Disarmament (UNSSOD-III). The grandiose plan sought to eliminate all nuclear weapons by 2010 in three distinct stages. The plan called for a binding commitment from all nations to eliminate nuclear weapons in a fixed time frame; participation of all nuclear weapon states in the process of nuclear disarmament, while ensuring other countries also took part in the process; the need to demonstrate tangible progress at each stage; and changes in the doctrines, policies, and institutions to sustain a world free of nuclear weapons.[28]

In presenting the plan, Rajiv Gandhi made two noteworthy statements that for the first time revealed the inherent tension between India's own nuclear weapon aspirations, as well as its desire to contribute to nuclear disarmament. The first statement asserted: "Left to ourselves, we would not want to touch nuclear weapons. But when tactical considerations, in the passing play of great power rivalries, are allowed to take precedence over the imperative of nuclear non-proliferation, with what leeway are we left?" This was, perhaps, the first public declaration of India's intention to build nuclear weapons and an attempt to link New Delhi's emerging arsenal with the failure of global nonproliferation and disarmament.

The second statement noted India's desire to use the Action Plan to "replace the NPT, which expires in 1995. This new Treaty should give legal effect to the binding commitment of nuclear weapon States to eliminate all nuclear weapons by the year 2010 and of all non-nuclear weapon States to not cross the nuclear weapons threshold."[29] Although the Rajiv Gandhi plan, unlike previous Indian initiatives, provided elaborate details of the various stages for the negotiations, it was simply too ambitious and revealed a naivety about the scope and scale of the challenges that would have to be addressed to rid the world of tens of thousands of nuclear weapons. Consequently, the plan could not be taken seriously by any of the nuclear weapon states, particularly the superpowers.

The last Indian contribution to nonproliferation and disarmament before New Delhi conducted its *Shakti* series of tests and declared itself to be a nuclear weapon state in 1998 was its participation in the CTBT negotiations. Here India played an active role between 1994 and 1996, right up to the time that the treaty neared completion and bumped up against the reality of India's untested nuclear arsenal. At that stage India, which had initially proposed such a treaty in 1954, felt compelled to block it at the Conference on Disarmament in Geneva. It was left to Australia to resurrect it in the UN General Assembly.

Reducing Nuclear Dangers

Soon after the May 1998 nuclear tests there was a discernible shift in India's approach to nuclear disarmament. While New Delhi still espoused the cause of complete nuclear disarmament in a time-bound framework, there was now a greater emphasis on ensuring that existing nuclear weapons were properly managed so as to reduce the danger posed by them. The first indication of this was the introduction of the "Reducing Nuclear Dangers" resolution in the UN General Assembly in fall 1998. Since then, this resolution has been presented annually. This resolution was buttressed by another one, which sought to establish a "Convention on the Prohibition of Use of Nuclear Weapons."[30]

This shift became even more evident when India introduced a working paper in the UN General Assembly in 2006 "to build a consensus that strengthens the ability of the international community to initiate concrete steps towards achieving the goal of nuclear disarmament." This working paper, which drew heavily from the 1988 Rajiv Gandhi Plan, had three key components: first, the reaffirmation of a commitment to complete elimination of nuclear weapons; second, efforts to reduce the salience of nuclear weapons; and third, measures to reduce nuclear dangers. These were elaborated in the following seven measures:

- Reaffirm commitment to complete elimination
- Reduce salience of nuclear weapons
- Measures to reduce nuclear dangers and accidents
- Global "no-first-use" agreement
- Universal nonuse against non-nuclear states
- Convention to prohibit use or threat of use
- Negotiate Nuclear Weapon Convention

Not surprisingly, given India's own nuclear weapon status, five of these seven measures did not address the elimination of nuclear weapons, but their responsible possession by states. Although much more in line with the reality on the ground, this was a marked departure from India's earlier principled stand toward unqualified complete nuclear disarmament. Increasingly, India is unlikely to lead but is more likely to follow the lead of other nuclear weapon states, and "a serious initiative for elimination by leading nuclear weapons states, with the United States taking the lead, would be welcomed by India."[31]

For its part, India is well content to continue the slow-paced modernization of its nuclear arsenal as well as its nuclear-use doctrine, while seeking to convince other nuclear weapon states to first devalue and then discard their nuclear weapons. Indian scholars have elaborated the necessary steps to ensure "attitudinal devaluation" (by targeting the belief of nuclear deterrence; redrafting nuclear doctrines to restrict the role of nuclear weapons; and reinvigorating multilateral measures); "actual devaluation" (through a no-first-use policy; banning the use or threat of use of nuclear weapons; halting nuclear modernization; and restricting delivery systems); and "accessorial devaluation" (including building a safeguards regime and related verification technologies and dealing with delinquents).[32] This approach also indicates that India no longer expects a rapid path to nuclear disarmament (as envisaged in the Rajiv Gandhi plan, which sought the complete elimination of all nuclear weapons within a twenty-two-year time frame) and sees instead a slow, step-by-step approach.

While promoting a devalue and discard approach for nuclear weapons held by states, India, given its own experience with transnational terrorism, has taken a more strident stance on the issue of nuclear weapons and nonstate actors, especially terrorist groups. Following the adoption of UN Security Council Resolution 1540 in 2004, India enacted the Weapons of Mass Destruction (WMD) Act in June 2005 to strengthen the existing legislative and regulatory mechanisms for exercising controls over WMDs and to ensure that they do not fall into the hands of terrorist groups. India has also offered its assistance to other countries in implementing Resolution 1540.[33] Primarily because of its concerns over the use of nuclear weapons and materials by terrorist groups, India also actively participated in the first nuclear security summit hosted by President Barack Obama in April 2010 and strongly endorsed both the communiqué and the work plan. Another reason for India's participation in the summit was that it makes no reference to the NPT and is considered to be the start of an effort to establish a new nuclear order.[34]

Bilateral versus Multilateral

India has approached the issue of nuclear disarmament only at the multilateral level, while rejecting regional measures. The only exception to this is the Bangkok Treaty, which calls for a Southeast Asian nuclear weapons–free zone. Perhaps New Delhi supports this treaty because it acknowledges India's nuclear weapon status and also reassures key allies in a critical region. At the bilateral level, India has undertaken a series of nuclear confidence-building measures since its covert weaponization in the mid-1980s which, strictly speaking, are not arms control or disarmament measures, although they do address India's nuclear capability.

Prominent among them are the following three agreements with Pakistan:

- The 1991 non-attack on nuclear facilities agreement, which calls for the two countries to exchange a list of nuclear facilities annually on the understanding that all the facilities listed will not be attacked by the other side. In doing so the two countries are sharing with each other the most sensitive information, information that they are unwilling to share even with their own people.
- The 1999 and 2005 prenotification of ballistic missile tests agreement under which each side is obliged to inform the other side before conducting a test. India and Pakistan are only the second pair of countries (after the United States and Russia) to have such an agreement.
- The 2007 agreement on reducing the risk from nuclear weapon accidents.

India also has one similar agreement with China. The 1996 Sino-India Confidence-Building Measures in the Military Field along the Line of Actual Control calls on the two sides to take a series of steps to reduce tensions and the prospect of accidental conflict. The steps include: the reduction of specific categories of armaments (including missiles); prohibition of exercises involving a division (15,000 or more); a no-fly zone for combat aircraft; and exchange of information on natural disasters and diseases.

All of these bilateral agreements are compatible with India's multilateral approach to disarmament in that they do not contradict each other but, in fact, complement each other. However, the 2005 Indo-U.S. civil nuclear agreement, which came to fruition in 2008, is the exception and contradicts India's multilateral approach. The Indo-U.S. agreement calls, in the first instance, for a separation of the Indian civilian and military nuclear programs. This was followed by an agreement between New Delhi and the International Atomic

Energy Agency (IAEA) which would put all fourteen Indian civilian nuclear reactors under IAEA safeguards, followed by another special arrangement with the Nuclear Suppliers Group (NSG) to allow its members to supply nuclear fuel for India's civilian reactors. Predictably, this effort to establish Indian exceptionalism proved to be contentious both within India and outside. One school, pejoratively referred to as the "nonproliferation ayatollahs," argues that such a deal, which rewards actions that blatantly challenge the nonproliferation norm, would not only allow India to expand its nuclear arsenal but further undermine the already battered NPT regime.[35] Another equally vocal school asserts that the Indo-U.S. deal is not only essential to facilitate India's participation in the global nonproliferation regime, but is also essential to ensure the relevance of the existing regime and to strengthen it further.[36] In either case, it is evident that ad hoc approaches, which promote the exceptional rather than the universal, are likely to be regarded with great suspicion and, consequently, unlikely to be smoothly integrated with the global regime.

CONCLUSIONS

India's approach to nuclear disarmament in general and nuclear zero in particular has evolved over a period of time, and has been closely linked to its own nuclear weapon program. When New Delhi was not pursuing nuclear weapons its approach was earnest, devoted, and unequivocal. However, once it began its nuclear weapon program in the run-up to the NPT negotiations, India's approach became much more cautious, considered, and equivocal. This pattern became even more evident in the run up to the CTBT. Noted Indian scholar Rajesh Rajagopalan observes: "As the non-proliferation order tightened, with the NPT being extended indefinitely and the CTBT threatening to eliminate an Indian nuclear option, various Indian governments sought to slip the noose by conducting nuclear tests."[37] Since the nuclear tests of 1998 India's approach has shifted priority from disarmament per se to devaluing the weapons, with disarmament becoming an increasingly distant goal. More recently, in the wake of the Indo-U.S. nuclear deal, which establishes Indian exceptionalism through positive discrimination rather than a universal, nondiscriminatory approach, New Delhi's credentials as a champion of multilateralism are likely to be increasingly questioned.

The pessimistic explanation for this evolution is that India was never serious about disarmament and that this was merely a hypocritical ploy to divert attention from its desire to stay outside the NPT regime while building its nuclear arsenal. Another, slightly more charitable, explanation argues that India's approach was "because no serious cost-benefit analysis has been undertaken by the government of the implications of nuclear disarmament on India's security interest."[38] Consequently, India has consistently miscalculated on disarmament.

Whatever the explanation, as the revived debate on the credibility of India's nuclear arsenal (especially the hydrogen bomb) has shown,[39] there is a very narrow window of opportunity to effectively engage New Delhi on the benefits of supporting nuclear zero. Pressure is growing to resume testing. Once the window closes, India will have earned the dubious distinction of having uninvented zero.

NOTES

1. See Waheguru Pal Singh Sidhu, "Evolution of India's Nuclear Doctrine," Centre for Policy Research, Occasional Paper No. 9 (April 2004). These phases are slightly different than the three phases suggested by George Perkovich, indicating that such "phaseology" is likely to remain arbitrary and divergent, although with some overlap. Perkovich's first phase begins in 1948 and ends in 1974, while his second phase runs from 1975 to 1995 "and was marked by singular self-restraint in not conducting further nuclear tests and deploying a nuclear arsenal." The third phase starts from 1995 and "led to the 1998 nuclear tests." Perkovich does not designate a new phase for the post–May 1998 period, but simply notes that the "trajectory of Indian nuclear policy remains uncertain." See George Perkovich, "What Makes the Indian Bomb Tick," in *Nuclear India in the 21st Century*, ed. D. R. Sar Desai and Raju G. C. Thomas (New York: Palgrave, 2002), p. 26.

2. See Bharat Karnad, *Nuclear Weapons & Indian Security: The Realist Foundations of Strategy* (New Delhi: Macmillan, 2002); George Perkovich, *India's Nuclear Bomb: The Impact on Global Proliferation* (Berkeley: University of California, 1999); Itty Abraham, *The Making of the Indian Atomic Bomb: Science, Secrecy and the Postcolonial State* (London: Zed Books, 1998); Peter R. Lavoy, "Learning to Live with the Bomb: India and Nuclear Weapons 1947–1974," Ph.D. dissertation, University of California, Berkeley, 1997; Waheguru Pal Singh Sidhu, "The Development of an Indian Nuclear Doctrine since 1980," Ph.D. dissertation, University of Cambridge, February 1997; and Zafar Iqbal Cheema, "Indian Nuclear Strategy 1947–1991," Ph.D. dissertation, University of London, 1991.

3. The "CIRUS" reactor is a Pressurized Heavy Water Reactor (PHWR) based on the Canadian Deuterium Uranium (CANDU) design and is an acronym for Canada-India Reactor. The "US" was added when the United States provided the initial supply of heavy water for the reactor. This reactor "went critical" in July 1960. The Bhabha Atomic Research Centre's plutonium plant began reprocessing fuel from the CIRUS research reactor in 1964 with a 30 tons/year operating capacity. See "India" country profile on

the Nuclear Threat Initiative website, at http://www.nti.org/e_research/profiles/India/Nuclear/2103_2603.html. See also Perkovich, "What Makes the Indian Bomb Tick," p. 29.

4. Ministry of Defence (MOD) *Annual Report* 1970–71 (New Delhi: Government of India, 1971), pp. 1–2. Curiously, the report discounted the possibility that Chinese nuclear weapons were "an effective means of political blackmail."

5. Author's interview with a nuclear scientist associated with the 1974 nuclear test.

6. David Albright and Mark Hibbs, "India's Silent Bomb," *Bulletin of the Atomic Scientists* (September 1992), at http://www.thebulletin.org/14. Another account indicates that the preliminary planning phase for this new reactor began in 1973.

7. The Prithvi was a single-stage, liquid-fueled missile with a 1-ton throw-weight and a range of 40 to 150 kilometers. Subsequently, a 250-kilometer version was also developed. The original two-stage Agni was designated a "technology demonstrator" and used both solid and liquid fuel. It was designed to carry a 1-ton payload to targets up to 2,500 kilometers away, although its first tests did not reach beyond 1,500 kilometers. See Andrew Koch and Waheguru Pal Singh Sidhu, "Subcontinental Missiles," *Bulletin of the Atomic Scientists* (July/August 1998), at http://www.thebulletin.org/issues/1998/ja98/ja98koch.html; and Anand Parthasarathy, "For a Weapons Delivery System," *Frontline* (6–19 June 1998), at http://www.frontlineonnet.com/fl1512/15120340.htm.

8. At a seminar on "India's Nuclear Doctrine" held at the Centre for Policy Research on 5 May 2003, the Director of the Institute for Defence and Strategic Analyses, K. Santhanam, hinted that the formal decision to weaponize India 's nuclear capability was taken some years before 1988, which had come to be regarded as the year of weaponization.

9. For "recessed deterrence," see Air Commodore Jasjit Singh, "Prospects for Nuclear Proliferation," in *Nuclear Deterrence: Problems and Perspectives in the 1990s*, ed. Serge Sur (New York: United Nations Institute for Disarmament Research, 1993), p. 66; for "non-weaponized deterrence," see George Perkovich, "A Nuclear Third Way in South Asia," *Foreign Policy* 91 (Summer 1993): 86; for "existential deterrence," see Devin Hagerty, "Nuclear Deterrence in South Asia: The 1990 Indo-Pakistani Crisis," *International Security* 20, no. 3 (Winter 1995/96): 87.

10. During the late July 1999 Singapore meeting of foreign ministers of ASEAN, China announced that it had decided to sign the protocol to the SEANWFZ (Southeast Asian Nuclear Weapon Free Zone) Treaty (Treaty of Bangkok). India, too, announced that it would "endorse" the treaty and was ready to sign the protocol, but it was noted that, according to Article 3 of that instrument, this is open to signature only by the five recognized nuclear-weapon states. See "Non-Proliferation Developments," *PPNN Newsbrief* 47 (3rd Quarter 1999): 1.22.

11. General Pervez Musharraf's coup against Prime Minister Nawaz Sharif was to some extent the result of the differences between the two over the Kargil conflict. See

Waheguru Pal Singh Sidhu, "In the Shadow of Kargil: Keeping Peace in Nuclear South Asia," *International Peacekeeping* 7, no. 4, Special Issue on Managing Armed Conflict in the 21st Century (Winter 2000): 189–206.

12. See "Draft Report of the National Security Advisory Board on the Indian Nuclear Doctrine," at http://www.meadev.gov.in/govt/indnucld.htm.

13. See Vishal Thapar, "India's N-Command in Place," *Hindustan Times*, 5 January 2003; Rajat Pandit, "Nuke Command Set Up, N-Button in PM's Hand," *Sunday Times* (India), 5 January 2003; and Waheguru Pal Singh Sidhu, "A Strategic Mis-step?" *The Hindu*, 13 January 2003.

14. See "Draft Report of the National Security Advisory Board on the Indian Nuclear Doctrine"; and Thapar, "India's N-Command in Place."

15. See W. P. S. Sidhu, "This Doctrine Is Full of Holes," *Indian Express*, 8 September 1999; "PM Launches INS Arihant in Vishakapatnam," and "INS Arihant to Take Long Time to Become Operational: Experts," *Press Trust of India*, 26 July 2009.

16. K. D. Kapur, *Nuclear Non-Proliferation Diplomacy: Nuclear Power Programmes in the Third World* (New Delhi: Lancer Books, 1993), p. 292.

17. *Nuclear Explosions and Their Effects* (Delhi: Publications Division, Ministry of Information & Broadcasting, Government of India, 1956).

18. *Lok Sabha Debates*, vol. III, no. 8 (24 July 1957): 4954.

19. G. G. Mirchandani, *India's Nuclear Dilemma* (New Delhi: Popular Book Services, 1968), p. 23.

20. Kapur, *Nuclear Non-Proliferation Diplomacy*, p. 296.

21. Ibid., p. 303.

22. Ibid., p. 299.

23. U.S. Embassy, New Delhi, Airgram A-540 to Department of State, "Canadians Warm GOI on NPT" (12 December 1967), Secret, National Security Archives.

24. K. Subrahmanyan, "India's Attitudes towards the NPT," SIPRI *Nuclear Proliferation Problems* (Stockholm: MIT Press, 1974), pp. 259–60.

25. See B. M. Udgaonkar, "India's Nuclear Capability, Her Security Concerns and the Recent Tests," *Current Science* (Bangalore), 1999, at http://www.ias.ac.in/currsci/jan25/articles20.htm.

26. See "1986: Reykjavik Summit Ends in Failure," at http://news.bbc.co.uk/onthisday/hi/dates/stories/october/12/newsid_3732000/3732902.stm.

27. See Sergio Duarte, "Keynote Address," in *Towards a Nuclear Weapon Free World*, ed. Manpreet Sethi (New Delhi: Knowledge World, 2009), p. 9.

28. For details of the plan, see Rajiv Gandhi, "A World Free of Nuclear Weapons," in *Towards a Nuclear Weapon Free World*, pp. 141–49.

29. Ibid.

30. See introduction of the resolution "Reducing Nuclear Danger," statement by Mr. Rakesh Sood, PR to Conference on Disarmament, on 19 October 2000, at http://www.

un.int/india/ind341.htm, and introduction of the resolution "Convention on the Prohibition of the Use of Nuclear Weapons," statement by Mr. Rakesh Sood, PR to Conference on Disarmament, on 17 October 2000, at http://www.un.int/india/ind342.htm.

31. See Rajesh M. Basrur, "Indian Perspectives on the Global Elimination of Nuclear Weapons," in *Unblocking the Road to Zero*, ed. Barry Blechman (Washington, DC: Stimson Center, March 2009), p. 18.

32. See Manpreet Sethi, "Approach to Nuclear Disarmament: Devalue to Discard," in *Towards a Nuclear Weapon Free World*, pp. 88–97.

33. See the statement by Ambassador Manjeev Singh Puri, Deputy Permanent Representative of India to the United Nations, at the open debate on the agenda item "Briefings by Chairs of the Subsidiary Bodies of the Security Council" in the chamber of the UN Security Council in New York on 13 November 2009.

34. See W. Pal Sidhu, "Towards a New Nuclear World Order," *Mint*, 3 May 2010.

35. See Kaushik Kapistalam, "Nuclear Hypocrisy and Hot Air Proliferation," *Bharat Rakshak Monitor* 6, no. 6 (May–July 2004); Praful Bidwai, "The 'Ayatollahs' Are Here," *Frontline* 22, no. 23 (5–18 November 2005); and A. Vinod Kumar, "Nobel Laureates Pitch In against the Indo-US Nuclear Deal," *IDSA Strategic Comments* (19 June 2006).

36. Ashley Tellis, "Atoms for War? U.S.-Indian Civilian Nuclear Cooperation and India's Nuclear Arsenal," *Carnegie Report*, June 2006; C Raja Mohan, "As Complicated as 1, 2, 3," *Indian Express*, 13 July 2007; and K. Subrahmanyam, "To PM, Sonia, Advani," *Indian Express*, 10 May 2008.

37. Rajesh Rajagopalan, "Nuclear Non-Proliferation: An Indian Perspective," Friedrich Ebert Stiftung Briefing Paper 10, October 2008, p. 3.

38. Ibid., pp. 4–5.

39. See K. Santhanam, "On the Yield of the Thermonuclear Device Tested in May 1998," *South Asian Strategic Forum*, 18 September 2009; Siddhartha Varadarajan, "'Fizzle' Claim for Thermonuclear Test Refuted," *The Hindu*, 28 August 2009; and W. Pal Sidhu, "Does India Really Need the H-bomb?' *Mint*, 8 September 2009.

ISSUES AND CONSTRAINTS

13 Fissile Materials and Disarmament: Long-term Goals, Short-term Steps

James M. Acton

VERIFYING ZERO: AN OVERVIEW

For the abolition of nuclear weapons to be feasible, a necessary condition is international confidence that compliance with an abolition agreement can be ensured. Verification has an important part to play in convincing the leaders of nuclear-armed states and their allies, domestic political opponents, and potentially skeptical publics that the benefits of disarming outweigh the risks. But it cannot accomplish that task by itself. In addition to being able to detect violations reliably and in a timely manner, the international community would also need to be able to act upon them quickly and effectively. Attenuating the security threats that drive nuclear weapons acquisition is yet another part of the challenge. The multifaceted task of building confidence that states intend to remain in compliance with a treaty is a central element of the disarmament challenge. It is important to acknowledge from the outset that the technical approaches discussed in this chapter are vital, but still only one part of the overall challenge.

Two distinct phases can be discerned in the task of verifying nuclear disarmament.[1] During the transition to zero, states would want confidence that all nuclear weapons were being eliminated and all fissile material was being placed under appropriate international safeguards. Once this had been accomplished, ongoing verification of all remaining nuclear activities would be necessary to detect any attempts at rearmament.

Ironically, we probably have a clearer conception of the ongoing verification that would be needed to detect rearmament in a nuclear weapons–free world than of the scheme required to verify the elimination of nuclear weapons in the first place. Safeguards against rearmament would involve verifying the nondiversion of nuclear material in declared civilian facilities, and also that no state was conducting undeclared nuclear activities. This is essentially the task performed by the International Atomic Energy Agency (IAEA) today—at least in non–nuclear weapon states that have an Additional Protocol in force.[2] In a nuclear weapon–free world, however, such safeguards would presumably need to be applied to all states, including the former nuclear-armed states. Moreover, before dismantling their last nuclear weapons, the nuclear-armed states would also probably need to be convinced that these safeguards were considerably more effective than they are today. For this reason, some have suggested that traditional safeguards may need to be augmented by eliminating the most proliferation-sensitive nuclear activities or by placing them under some kind of international or multinational control. Nevertheless, there has been extensive research into safeguards for civilian nuclear activities, and a large body of experience has already been built up in applying them.

Verifying the transition to zero presents more of a challenge. As with all arms-reduction treaties, a key task would be to verify that declared weapons were being dismantled as claimed. Where nuclear weapons are concerned, this process would be complicated by the existence of classification rules that prevent international inspectors from viewing warheads directly or using most, if not all, standard measurement techniques for assaying fissile material. Largely because of this, no previous nuclear-arms control treaty has placed verified limits on warheads. Nevertheless, in expectation of future arms-control treaties that do concern warheads, there has been extensive research into the problem.[3] Originally, this research was confined to U.S. and Russian national labs, but it is now being conducted more broadly. Although there are a number of technical challenges still to be overcome, it seems likely that, with enough effort, adequate solutions can be found.

Ultimately the toughest verification challenge would be to ensure that no nuclear-armed state has retained any undeclared stockpiles of fissile material, whether in the form of nuclear weapons or not. It involves "proving a negative"—that is, verifying the absence of something.[4] The challenge with this, of course, is that it is impossible to check each and every conceivable hiding place for illicit material, and there is always the possibility that something might have been stashed in a place that hasn't been inspected. In the case of fissile material the challenge is exacerbated by the ease of shielding its radioactive emissions, making it undetectable at anything more than a few meters.

Fortunately, there is a solution to this problem—at least at a conceptual level. In theory, the inspectorate could uncover undeclared material by first verifying a state's declaration of the quantity of fissile material it had produced and used. Then inspectors would compare the amount of material that a state ought to have (its estimated inventory) to the amount it actually did have (its measured holdings). If a state had declared all its fissile material to inspectors, these two quantities should be equal. If, on the other hand, a state had secreted some nuclear material away, its estimated inventory would be larger than its current holdings. In practice, there are inevitably uncertainties associated with estimating the quantity of fissile material produced and used by a state and with measuring its current holdings. Consequently, the amount of material that ought to be present would never be exactly equal to the amount actually measured, and there would be no way of knowing whether any discrepancy was due to measurement errors or diversion. If the difference were smaller than the amount needed to produce a nuclear weapon, this might not matter much. However, if the difference were larger (as the following analysis shows it would be), the international community might worry that the state in question had secreted away a militarily significant quantity of fissile material—and this could prove a barrier to abolition.

ESTIMATING PAST PRODUCTION

The first step in the verification process would be for the nuclear-armed states to submit comprehensive declarations detailing the complete history of their fissile material production programs for each weapons-usable fissile material (that is, not just uranium-235 and plutonium-239, but also uranium-233, neptunium-237, and possibly others). The declarations would include detailed information on current holdings of these materials.

The inspectorate might be able to build some confidence in the veracity of information on past production by checking the records for internal consistency, as well by as subjecting them to traditional forensic analysis (that is, checking that the paper and ink are of the right age, and so forth). Such analysis has its limitations, however. Records are often incomplete or erroneous.[5] Moreover, the move from paper to computer records in the past decade or two has had the side effect of making it significantly easier to doctor them. States' records, by themselves, would be insufficient for the inspectorate to verify the veracity of their declarations.

"Nuclear forensics" provides an independent means of reconstructing fissile material production by examining the physical evidence left by the production techniques.[6] For instance, the majority of plutonium for weapons programs was produced in so-called graphite-moderated reactors. All graphite contains very small quantities of impurities. During reactor operation, some of these impurities capture neutrons to form isotopes that are not naturally occurring. By measuring the abundance of these "activation products" it is possible to estimate the total quantity of plutonium produced in the reactor.[7] This method is known as GIRM—the graphite isotope ratio method.

GIRM has the potential to reduce the uncertainty in the amount of plutonium produced in a reactor significantly—to about 5 percent, in fact. Moreover, it has been validated successfully in a field trial.[8] In 1995–97 it was applied to the Magnox reactor at Trawsfynydd in the UK, which was then being decommissioned. It was estimated that the total quantity of plutonium produced in this reactor was 3.63 ± 0.19 MT—an error of about 5 percent. This is a formidable technical achievement. Nevertheless, even this uncertainty represents sufficient material for about twenty nuclear weapons in a state with some experience of weapons design. Moreover, GIRM does nothing to reduce any uncertainty in the amount of plutonium that a state actually separated from the spent fuel.

Graphite-moderated reactors are, however, not the only means for producing fissile material. Heavy water–moderated reactors account for the remaining eleven out of forty-five reactors that have been used to produce plutonium for weapons programs. Moreover, the vast majority of weapons-origin fissile material is high enriched uranium. No equivalent forensic techniques exist for estimating fissile material production in either heavy water–moderated reactors or enrichment facilities. Even if such techniques were developed it would not be possible to apply them in all cases because a number of enrichment plants are being, or have been, disassembled.

MEASURING CURRENT HOLDINGS

Although not as severe, there are also uncertainties associated with measuring a state's holdings of fissile material. Any measurement is accompanied by some uncertainty. Where large quantities of nuclear material are concerned, the cumulative effect of uncertainties on multiple measurements can be significant, leading to a noticeable difference between the amount of fissile material that is calculated to be present and the amount that is actually measured. In IAEA terminology this difference is known as material unaccounted for (MUF). As mentioned above, the problem is that it can be impossible to determine whether MUF is due to measurement errors or the diversion of nuclear material.

The existence of MUF is a source of controversy leading some to question the effectiveness of today's IAEA safeguards system.[9] Whether or not criticisms are valid, MUF is inevitable. As British Nuclear Fuels, for instance, pointed out in a press release (following some media controversy about MUF at Sellafield):

> These uncertainties exist in all industrial processes, for example the gold industry experiences the same thing when extracting gold from ores—the amount recovered never precisely matches the amount estimated in the ore.
>
> No nuclear material has been stolen. Figures change from year to year. Negative numbers do not mean material has disappeared; positive numbers don't mean material has been created.[10]

An idea of the likely magnitude of the MUF associated with nuclear weapons programs can be found in recent UK and United States efforts to account for the material in their fissile material production programs.[11] Both states calculated how much plutonium and HEU they ought to have (shown in row 1 of Table 13.1) and measured the amounts they actually did have (shown in row 2). The MUF (the difference between these two figures) is shown in row 3. In the case of UK it is negative because the UK found more material than it thought would be present. In the case of the United States, the MUF would be enough for about 1,000 warheads.

In fact, from the perspective of international inspectors, there would be an even bigger source of uncertainty. Some of the material in the UK and United States inventories would be unavailable for verification. For instance, it would be impossible to accurately verify the quantity of material used in nuclear tests—even if the state that conducted the tests knew those quantities accurately. Row 4 of the table shows a *lower bound* for the amount of "material unavailable for verification" (MUV) based on the quantities estimated to have been used in tests. In fact, the MUV would probably be much larger because some of the material in the UK and United States inventories was burned in reactors, lost in waste streams or decayed—and, again, verifying such losses to any accuracy would prove impossible.

TABLE 13.1

Calculated and Measured Quantities of Fissile Material in the UK and U.S. Military Stockpiles

	UK		U.S.	
	Pu (MT)	HEU (MT U)	Pu (MT)	HEU (MT U-235)
Amount recorded in inventory	3.22	21.64	102.3	623.5
Measured holdings	3.52	21.86	99.5	620.3
Material unaccounted for	–0.29	–0.22	2.8	3.2
Material unavailable for verification	>0.2	>0.6	>3.4	>10

SOURCE: This table originally appeared in George Perkovich and James M. Acton, *Abolishing Nuclear Weapons*, Adelphi Paper 396 (London: Taylor and Francis, Ltd., 2008), ch. 2, reprinted by permission of the publisher.

THE BOTTOM LINE

These various sources of error—both in estimating past production and in measuring current holdings—would make it impossible for an inspectorate to definitively prove that a disarming state had not retained a clandestine stockpile of fissile material containing a few percent of its total holdings. In the case of the United States or Russia this would be sufficient for literally thousands of warheads.

Although this conclusion seems (and indeed is) rather pessimistic, it does *not* necessarily imply that nuclear disarmament is infeasible. In fact, on one previous occasion the IAEA did succeed in convincing the international community that a state had completely eliminated a homemade nuclear arsenal and placed all of its fissile material under international safeguards. The state in question was South Africa, and the lessons from verifying the elimination of its nuclear weapons program are potentially instructive.[12]

Starting in 1979, South Africa manufactured six nuclear weapons and an uncompleted seventh. All of these devices used high enriched uranium. In 1990 South Africa made the decision to disarm. It dismantled these weapons and, in 1991, acceded to the Nuclear Non-proliferation Treaty (NPT) and submitted its "initial declaration" to the IAEA. This document detailed its holding of fissile material.

For all the reasons discussed above, verifying the completeness of this declaration proved a significant challenge. The results of "technical" verification activities were inconclusive; that is, the IAEA could not rule out the existence of a clandestine stockpile of HEU sufficient for one or more nuclear weapons.

The strongest conclusion that the IAEA director-general was able to reach was that "having regard to the uncertainties normally associated with data of this nature, it is reasonable to conclude that the uranium-235 balance . . . of the pilot plant is consistent with uranium feed."[13]

Nevertheless, that uncertainty did not lead to states questioning South Africa's good faith or intentions. Part of this success (but by no means all of it) was due to South Africa's open and transparent behavior, beyond any legal requirement: it provided inspectors with a comprehensive history of its nuclear program, gave them all relevant records, and provided them with access to all facilities, materials, and personnel. It cooperated fully to resolve any discrepancies that did arise. This transparency did *not* reveal information that allowed the IAEA to definitively rule out the existence of clandestine HEU; rather, it convinced the inspectors on the ground, as well as outside observers, that South Africa had nothing to hide. South Africa provides a clear example of how transparency can help substitute for unavoidable deficiencies in technical verification.

Applying this model to today's nuclear-armed states would certainly be a tremendous challenge and, it is necessary to acknowledge, may not be possible. They have produced much more fissile material than South Africa. More important, they could have much more reason to cheat. The goodwill shown to South Africa after the end of apartheid cannot be ignored either. But, equally, it would be wrong to dismiss the relevance of the South Africa model. What should be tried is more than just a "one off" verification attempt in which the nuclear-armed states are submitted to a single, intensive round of verification. Rather, a slower and more gradual process should be envisaged in which the nuclear-armed states gradually become more transparent about their fissile material and are proactive in finding ways to build confidence in the veracity of their claims. Over time, if no irresolvable evidence emerges to contradict these claims, states might be much more willing to tolerate uncertainties associated with verifying fissile material.

One important element in such a confidence-building process would be a verified fissile material cut-off treaty (FMCT), including stocks. Such a treaty would involve the nuclear-armed states declaring existing stocks of fissile material and submitting them—presumably as they became excess—to some kind of verification. Because the nuclear-armed states would still retain their nuclear weapons as a hedge, a fissile material cut-off treaty would require less stringent verification than a treaty eliminating nuclear weapons. However, if stocks were successfully verified (and it may be a gradual process that is only possible as stocks are declared excess) and if, in the following years, no irresolvable evidence came to light that any state had failed to declare all of its stocks, the international community would be presented with a much more promising "baseline" from which to contemplate the complete elimination of nuclear weapons. That said, the prospects for including stocks in a fissile material cut-off treaty are very poor.[14] An FMCT treaty that did not include them would still be a worthwhile and important step—but not nearly as significant if elimination is the ultimate goal.

Unfortunately, even though negotiations on an FMCT in the Conference on Disarmament have now commenced, a fissile material cut-off treaty cannot be considered a short-term goal. The remainder of this chapter sketches out the first steps that could be taken by the nuclear-armed states in a confidence-building process. Non–nuclear weapon states should be willing to publicly recognize them as meaningful steps toward zero.

In the short term it is necessary to recognize that greater transparency about capabilities by China, India, Israel, and Pakistan could be detrimental to disarmament efforts by stimulating a competitive reaction from their adversaries.[15] A confidence-building process must be tempered by this concern while working to build relations that are conducive to greater transparency.

COMPILING NUCLEAR HISTORIES

As mentioned above, one of the most significant challenges to be faced in the long term is that states' own records of their nuclear programs are incomplete, either because they were never kept in the first place (especially in the early days of nuclear weapon programs) or because they have been lost or destroyed. Records are important, not just as evidence to support declarations, but also because making them available to inspectors is a powerful sign of good faith (à la South Africa). Conversely, the failure to produce the records requested by inspectors could be interpreted as an indication that a state had something to hide, even if it were genuinely because the state was unable to produce the records in question.

The failure of states to keep comprehensive records, along with the deaths of the first generation of personnel associated with many nuclear weapon programs, means that some information that would be useful for verification has been irretrievably lost. However, the nuclear-armed states should take action to avoid this situation deteriorating further. Specifically, they could appoint national commissions to compile comprehensive records of their nuclear programs by, among other steps, collecting documents and interviewing personnel. These records would *not* have to be made public in the first instance. States could reveal as much or as little of them as they felt able to. The crucial point is that by collecting this information—even if it were kept secret for the time being—states would be facilitating more robust verification further down the line. For this reason, the value of the exercise would be increased even further if the nuclear-armed states were to agree among themselves what information would be useful, as well as relevant standards for record keeping.

One objection to compiling nuclear histories (and indeed, some of the other verification measures discussed in this paper) is expense. The specific justification for compiling nuclear histories is that they provide a baseline against which measurement of current holdings can be measured and, further, that they are a very powerful confidence-building measure and hence provide value for money. More generally, however, there are various points to be made when analyzing the costs of verification. First, on the scale of nuclear weapon budgets, the costs of any verification activities are very modest. Second, the short-term costs of verification need to be compared against the long-term savings of reducing and eventually eliminating nuclear weapons. Third, many of the verification measures discussed in this paper, being directed toward improved accounting of fissile materials, also serve to prevent nuclear terrorism. They are therefore worth doing irrespective of disarmament goals.

FISSILE MATERIAL PRODUCTION HISTORIES

As described above, both the UK and the United States have published some details of their fissile material production histories and current holdings. To date, none of the other nuclear-armed states have done so—but they could and should follow suit. In general, the more information that was included, the more useful the declarations would become. In this regard, there is certainly scope for the UK and the United States to supplement their declarations. For instance, the UK gives quantities of HEU in terms of tonnes of uranium (thereby not distinguishing between material of different enrichment levels), whereas the U.S. declaration uses the somewhat more useful unit, tonnes of U-235. The UK could follow the U.S. lead in this regard, and both states could consider giving more details about the various enrichment levels of their HEU holdings. Nevertheless, it is important to point out that, in spite of these areas for further development, the UK and the United States are still ahead of the other nuclear-armed states merely by having published any data at all.

CIVILIAN NUCLEAR ACTIVITIES

Civilian plutonium and high enriched uranium are as important from the perspective of disarmament as military fissile material. After all, they are all weapons-usable (even if civilian plutonium is typically of a higher burn-up than military plutonium and hence less suitable for military ends).

One positive development in this regard is that since 1998, the five nuclear-weapon states (along with Belgium, Germany, Switzerland, and Japan) have published details of their civil plutonium holdings in so-called INFCIRC/549 declarations, as part of a larger IAEA project on managing civilian plutonium.[16] France and the UK (along with Germany) include civilian HEU holdings in these declarations. The other weapon states could emulate this. Moreover, India, Israel, and Pakistan could consider joining this initiative, which, because it relates to civilian and not military material, might be feasible.

This laudable initiative would be enhanced by placing more civilian nuclear material in the nuclear-weapon states under IAEA safeguards—a step that would help demonstrate the veracity of these declarations. All of the nuclear-weapon states have "voluntary offer agreements" with the IAEA.[17] These specify both the aim and scope of safeguards (which vary from state to state) and include a (confidential) list of the facilities that the IAEA is permitted to safeguard. These offers vary greatly in their comprehensiveness. At one extreme are the British and French offers, which apparently include every civilian facility (these are already subject to Euratom safeguards anyway); at the other extreme are the much more limited Chinese and Russian offers. A useful first step would be for China, Russia, and the United States to expand the scope of their voluntary offers.

In practice, because of severe budgetary constraints, the IAEA only safeguards a very small number of these facilities. Indeed, there is an ongoing discussion about whether three new gas centrifuge plants to be built in the United States will be safeguarded; the IAEA is reluctant to do so because of the cost. The nuclear-weapon states could consider, therefore, paying for the IAEA to safeguard more of their facilities. They should be prepared to meet the full costs of safeguards, including the costs of employing the extra inspectors required so that scarce inspection resources are not diverted from non–nuclear weapon states. The goal should be to place all civilian nuclear activities in the weapon states under safeguards, even if it may take years to accomplish.

FISSILE MATERIAL CONTROL INITIATIVE

A more comprehensive, multilateral framework for dealing with fissile material stocks, the Fissile Material Control Initiative (FMCI), has been proposed by special adviser to the U.S. Department of State Robert J. Einhorn. He describes it as follows:

> FMCI would be a voluntary, multilateral arrangement open to any country that possessed fissile material (whether safeguarded or not) and was willing to sign onto a set of agreed principles. The overall goals of FMCI would be to increase security, transparency, and control over fissile material stocks worldwide; to prevent their theft or diversion to non-state actors or additional states; and to move fissile materials verifiably and irreversibly out of nuclear weapons and into forms unusable for nuclear weapons.
>
> FMCI would establish an agreed set of guidelines that partners, as appropriate to their particular fissile material holdings, would be encouraged to follow. The guidelines would call on the partners:
>
> - to make regular declarations regarding their fissile material stocks by category;
> - to apply the highest standards of physical protection and accountancy to those stocks;
> - to declare regularly amounts of material they regard as excess to their weapons needs;
> - to place such excess material under IAEA safeguards as soon as practicable; and
> - to convert excess material as soon as possible to forms that cannot be used for nuclear weapons (e.g., by blending down HEU to low-enriched reactor fuel).[18]

Einhorn's premise is that it is very unlikely that stocks will be included in an FMCT because of the opposition of most of the nuclear-armed states. Accordingly, he argues that FMCI could make agreement on an FMCT more likely by helping to address the concerns of states that wished stocks to be included in an FMCT. I believe that this is correct and, moreover, that FMCI would also increase the likelihood of achieving an FMCT that included stocks by getting nuclear-armed states used to the type of verification and transparency measures that would be needed.

THE BIGGER PICTURE

This chapter is intended to give an overview of the challenges associated with the most difficult aspect of verifying the elimination of nuclear weapons—accounting for fissile material—and of how these challenges might be overcome. In the final analysis, however, the issue of whether states would be willing to accept the inevitable uncertainties of verification is an essentially and unavoidably political question. For this reason, this paper will close with a very brief exploration of the political question: how effective would verification need to be for the nuclear-armed states to disarm completely?[19]

The "classical" or Wiesner model of verification argues that as a state reduces the size of its nuclear arsenal in accordance with treaty commitments, the size of a violation by an adversary that would upset the strategic balance also decreases.[20] For instance, when the United States went about verifying the 1987 Intermediate Nuclear Forces Treaty it put in enough inspection effort to assure itself that the Soviet Union had retained no more than about fifty SS-20 missiles (even though the agreement required the Soviet Union to eliminate that type of weapon completely), because it deemed that a violation involving fewer than fifty missiles did not pose a military threat to the United States.[21] Had the United States possessed a smaller arsenal when the treaty was concluded, the size of a violation that it deemed to be militarily significant would have been smaller and correspondingly more inspection effort would have been required. This Wiesner model predicts that even a very small violation would be militarily significant in a nuclear weapon–free world, and, in consequence, almost perfect verification would be needed. If this model is correct, the prospects for disarmament are dim.

However, there has been little, if any, serious enquiry into the validity of the Wiesner model or its assumptions. At least three questions can be asked of this model:

- In a nuclear weapon–free world would the size of a militarily significant violation really be so small as to make effective verification infeasible? Or, in plainer terms, would the retention or creation of a very small nuclear arsenal actually upset the strategic balance?
- The Wiesner model implicitly assumes that the level of distrust between states remains unchanged during the verification process. But, would the implementation of a verification scheme that produced no irresolvable

evidence of cheating build states' confidence in each other's intentions and hence prevent spiraling demands for verification?

- Even if verification were perfect, effective enforcement would still be required. Could improvements in enforcement mechanisms therefore compensate for verification deficiencies?

There are no easy or obvious answers to any of these questions, but addressing them would help to assess how good verification needs to be. They therefore deserve as much attention as the mechanics of verification.

NOTES

Some of the material in this chapter draws upon George Perkovich and James M. Acton, *Abolishing Nuclear Weapons*, Adelphi Paper 396, ch. 2 (London: Taylor and Francis, Ltd., 2008), http://www.informaworld.com.

1. For a detailed discussion of verifying disarmament, see George Perkovich and James M. Acton, *Abolishing Nuclear Weapons*, Adelphi Paper 396 (London: Taylor and Francis, Ltd., 2008), chs. 2 and 3. This volume is available in George Perkovich and James M. Acton, eds., *Abolishing Nuclear Weapons: A Debate* (Washington, DC: Carnegie Endowment for International Peace, 2009), section 1, http://www.carnegieendowment.org/files/abolishing_nuclear_weapons_debate.pdf. See also Steve Fetter, "Verifying Nuclear Disarmament," Henry L. Stimson Center Occasional Paper 29, October 1996, http://www.stimson.org/wmd/pdf/fetter.pdf; Committee on International Security and Arms Control, National Academy of Sciences, *Monitoring Nuclear Weapons and Nuclear Explosive Materials: An Assessment of Methods and Capabilities* (Washington, DC: National Academies Press, 2005), at http://www.nap.edu/catalog.php?record_id=11265.

2. Contrary to popular belief, the IAEA's legal authority to verify the absence of undeclared nuclear material does not stem from the Additional Protocol, but from Article 2 of the Comprehensive Safeguards Agreement, which asserts "the Agency's right and obligation to ensure that safeguards will be applied . . . on *all* source or special fissionable material" (my italics) (IAEA, "The Structure and Content of Agreements between the Agency and States Required in Connection with the Treaty on the Non-Proliferation of Nuclear Weapons," INFCIRC/153 [Corrected], June 1972, http://www.iaea.or.at/Publications/Documents/Infcircs/Others/infcirc153.pdf). The Additional Protocol does, however, give the IAEA the practical tools it needs to be able to draw credible conclusions about the absence of undeclared nuclear material.

3. Office of Nonproliferation Research and Engineering, "Technology R&D for Arms Control," *Arms Control and Nonproliferation Technologies* (Spring 2001): 4–17, http://www.fas.org/sgp/othergov/doe/acnt/2001.pdf; Committee on International Secu-

rity and Arms Control, National Academy of Sciences, *Monitoring Nuclear Weapons and Nuclear Explosive Materials*, pp. 97–108.

4. For a discussion of the problem of "proving a negative," see John Carlson, "Safeguards in a Broader Policy Perspective: Verifying Treaty Compliance," paper presented to the conference on "Changing the Safeguards Culture," Santa Fe, NM (30 October–2 November 2005), www.asno.dfat.gov.au/publications/2005_santa_fe_policy.pdf.

5. See, for example, Thomas W. Wood, Bruce D. Reid, John L. Smoot, and James L. Fuller, "Establishing Confident Accounting for Russian Weapons Plutonium," *Nonproliferation Review* 9, no. 2 (Summer 2002): 134, http://cns.miis.edu/pubs/npr/vol09/92/92wood.pdf.

6. Steve Fetter, "Nuclear Archaeology: Verifying Declarations of Fissile-Material Production," *Science and Global Security* 3, nos. 3–4 (1993): 240–44, http://www.princeton.edu/sgs/publications/sgs/pdf/3_3-4Fetter.pdf.

7. In practice the measured quantity is actually the mass ratio between impurities and their activation productions.

8. Wood et al., "Establishing Confident Accounting for Russian Weapons Plutonium," pp. 130–31.

9. Henry Sokolski, ed., *Falling Behind: International Scrutiny of the Peaceful Atom* (Carlisle, PA: Strategic Studies Institute, February 2008), http://www.npec-web.org/Books/20080327-FallingBehind.pdf, ch. 5.

10. British Nuclear Fuels PLC, "Media Response: Publication of Materials Unaccounted For," 13 August 2005, http://www.bnfl.com/content.php?pageID=49&newsID=70.

11. U.S. Department of Energy, "Plutonium: The First 50 Years. United States Plutonium Production, Acquisition, and Utilization from 1944 through 1994," DOE/DP-0137, February 1996, http://www.fissilematerials.org/ipfm/site_down/doe96.pdf; U.S. Department of Energy, "Highly Enriched Uranium: Striking a Balance: A Historical Report on the United States Highly Enriched Uranium Production, Acquisition, and Utilization Activities from 1945 through September 30, 1996," draft, revision 1, January 2001, http://www.fissilematerials.org/ipfm/site_down/doe01.pdf; UK Ministry of Defence, "Historical Accounting for UK Defence Highly Enriched Uranium," March 2006, http://www.fissilematerials.org/ipfm/site_down/mod06.pdf; UK Ministry of Defence, "Plutonium and Aldermaston: An Historical Account," 2000, http://www.fas.org/news/uk/000414-uk2.htm.

12. For an account of denuclearization in South Africa, see Adolf von Baeckmann, Gary Dillon, and Demetrius Perricos, "Nuclear Verification in South Africa," *IAEA Bulletin* 37, no. 1 (1995), http://www.iaea.org/Publications/Magazines/Bulletin/Bull371/37105394248.pdf; and Darryl Howlett and John Simpson, "Nuclearisation and Denuclearisation in South Africa," *Survival* 35, no. 3 (Autumn 1993).

13. IAEA, "The Agency's Verification Activities in South Africa," GOV/2684 (8 September 1993), para. 29.

14. For a discussion of issues confronting the FMCT, see Jenni Rissanen, "Time for a Fissban—or Farewell?" *Disarmament Diplomacy* no. 83 (Winter 2006), http://www.acronym.org.uk/dd/dd83/83fissban.htm.

15. Perkovich and Acton, "Abolishing Nuclear Weapons," pp. 40–42.

16. "Guidelines for the Management of Plutonium (INFCIRC/549): Background and Declarations," Institute for Science and International Security (1 April 2004, revised 16 August 2005), http://isis-online.org/global_stocks/end2003/infcirc_549.pdf.

17. For a comprehensive description of IAEA safeguards in the nuclear weapon states, see International Panel on Fissile Materials, *Global Fissile Materials Report 2007* (International Panel on Fissile Materials, 2007), ch. 6, http://www.fissilematerials.org/ipfm/site_down/gfmr07.pdf.

18. Robert J. Einhorn, "Controlling Fissile Materials and Ending Nuclear Testing," paper presented to the conference on "Achieving the Vision of a World Free of Nuclear Weapons: International Conference on Nuclear Disarmament," Oslo (26–27 March 2008), http://disarmament.nrpa.no/wp-content/uploads/2008/02/Paper_Einhorn.pdf. See also Ivo Daalder and Jan Lodal, "The Logic of Zero: Toward a World without Nuclear Weapons," *Foreign Affairs* 87, no. 6 (November–December 2008): 86–90.

19. For a somewhat lengthier treatment of this issue, see Perkovich and Acton, "Abolishing Nuclear Weapons," pp. 49–52.

20. Allan S. Krass, *Verification: How Much Is Enough?* (London: Taylor and Francis for SIPRI, 1985), pp. 167–71.

21. Office of Technology Assessment, U.S. Congress, *Verification Technologies: Cooperative Aerial Surveillance in International Agreements* (Washington, DC: U.S. Government Printing Office, July 1991), p. 104, Box C-1, n. 1, http://www.princeton.edu/~ota/disk1/1991/9114/9114.PDF.

14 Nuclear Zero at the Weapons Laboratories

Judith Reppy

INTRODUCTION

The impact of nuclear zero on the nuclear weapons laboratories has been a neglected issue. But it should not be ignored: for decades nuclear weapons provided the rationale for the growth and continued support for national weapons laboratories in the nuclear weapons states (NWS). In addition to their work to develop successive generations of nuclear weapons, the laboratories have also made major contributions to nonproliferation policy—for example, through the development of verification technologies and participation in on-site inspections—and to the national science and technology base. Under the ongoing moratorium on nuclear testing, they are tasked with monitoring the stockpile of nuclear weapons, as well as supervising the disassembly of nuclear weapons that have been removed from national inventories. Presumably this technical work on verification and disassembly will be even more important during the transition to nuclear zero, even as the support for new nuclear weapons disappears.

The role of the laboratories has not been wholly benign, however. In the past the U.S. national laboratories have contributed to undermining support for arms control measures whenever the laboratory leadership judged those measures might lead to a lowered support for their institutions. For example, during the 1999 Senate debate on the Comprehensive Test Ban Treaty, the lab directors testified that they could not guarantee the long-term safety and reliability of the U.S. nuclear stockpile under a CTBT, although they had earlier said that, if fully funded for the Stockpile Stewardship Program (SSP), they could.[1] In January 2010 the directors wrote letters to the ranking minority member of the Armed Services Committee's subcommittee on strategic forces in which they asserted—contrary to a JASON report—that the SSP was not enough to guarantee the reliability of the nuclear weapons in their charge in future years.[2] Given the prestige traditionally accorded to the national laboratories in Washington, their position poses a real risk to the goal of nuclear zero.

The major nuclear weapons states all maintain laboratories dedicated to nuclear weapons, with varying degrees of civilian control, commercial involvement, and political engagement.[3] In every case, the early development of a nuclear weapon was the product of a high-priority secret program, working in most cases under considerable time pressure. With the passing of the years—particularly since the end of the Cold War—the urgency has faded, and the weapons complexes have become "normal" bureaucracies. Beyond these generalizations, however, they are diverse: the national laboratories have been shaped by their specific political cultures and positions in the international arena and their profiles differ in interesting ways.

NUCLEAR WEAPONS LABORATORIES IN THE MAJOR NUCLEAR WEAPONS STATES

United States

In the United States, the National Nuclear Security Administration (NNSA), a "semiautonomous" agency within the Department of Energy (DOE) is responsible for the development and production of nuclear weapons, while the Department of Defense provides the delivery systems. The nuclear weapons laboratories are Los Alamos National Laboratory (LANL), Lawrence Livermore National Laboratory (LLNL), and Sandia National Laboratories (SNL), which together had approximately 22,000 employees at the end of 2009.[4] There are an additional five manufacturing, assembly and disassembly, and testing facilities in the DOE nuclear weapons complex which will also be affected by going to zero, but they do not play a major role in research and development (R&D) activities.

Over the years the three major laboratories have diversified their research programs to include work on conventional weapons, alternative energy technologies, biomedical projects, and climate modeling, and—in recent years—homeland security. Nuclear weapons activities, however, still account for 85 to 90 percent of the total NNSA budgets for the three laboratories.[5] Other sources of income for the laboratories fall in the category of "Work for Others" (WFO), which covers contracts with non-NNSA parts of the Department of Energy, with other federal agencies such as the departments of Defense and Homeland Security, and with private companies. Sandia has been the most successful of the three laboratories in shifting away from a reliance on NNSA funding; as of 2009 approximately 50 percent of its budget came from other funders; Los Alamos, by contrast, reports only 15 percent WFO.[6]

In 1946, the creation of the Atomic Energy Commission established the principle that, in the United States, atomic energy, including both nuclear weapons and nuclear energy, would be under civilian control. This principle has been maintained ever since, through several bureaucratic reorganizations that led in 1977 to the creation of the Department of Energy (DOE) and in 1999 to the creation of the National Nuclear Security Administration (NNSA). Throughout the whole period, the weapons laboratories have been managed as government-owned, contractor-operated (GOCO) entities. For sixty years the contractor for LANL and LLNL was the University of California, but following a number of security incidents and other concerns, the DOE opened the contracts to outside bids in 2005–6. The current management teams at the LANL and LLNL are consortia of private corporations led by Bechtel Corporation and the University of California, with additional members from the private sector. SNL, which originated as the engineering arm of Los Alamos, was spun off in 1949 as a separate laboratory. It was managed by Sandia Corporation, which was a subsidiary of Western Electric (itself a subsidiary of AT&T) from 1949 until 1993, when the contract went to Martin Marietta (now Lockheed-Martin Corporation).

Russia

During the Cold War, the Soviet Union built up a vast scientific and industrial network for the design and manufacture of nuclear weapons. Much—but not all—of the work was carried out in closed "nuclear cities," whose very existence was for many years an official secret. The two major weapons laboratories, approximate counterparts to LANL and LLNL, were the All-Russian Scientific Research Institute of Experimental Physics (Arzamas-16) at Sarov, and the All-Russian Scientific Research Institute of Technical Physics (Chelyabinsk-70) at Snezhinsk.[7] The cities were literally sealed off from the rest of society through barbed wire and strict limitations on movement of residents and visitors. The nuclear weapons complex was under nominal civilian control in the Ministry of Medium Machine Building (1953–86) and then in the Ministry of Atomic

Power and Industry. Like other parts of the national security sector, residents of the nuclear cities enjoyed higher pay and special benefits, such as better health care.

With the end of the Soviet Union, the organization of the nuclear weapons complex underwent several changes. Responsibility for the complex was moved to a new Ministry for Atomic Energy (Minatom), which also had responsibility for nuclear energy. The main nuclear test site at Semipalatinsk was lost in 1991 when Kazakhstan became independent; the remaining site is Novaya Zemlya. In 2004 Minatom became Rosatom, and in 2007 the civilian nuclear activities were spun off to a joint-stock company.[8]

The closed nuclear cities suffered greatly during the hard times of the 1990s and lost substantial numbers of their professional staff. In recent years some of the closed cities have been opened up and been encouraged to diversify into civilian research, while others have simply been shut down.[9] The United States and Britain have each promoted collaborative projects between their nuclear scientists and their Russian counterparts, with the aim of promoting conversion to civilian work and preventing defections to clandestine nuclear programs in other countries, but the projects have faced bureaucratic hurdles and relatively few new jobs have been created. The restrictions under which the scientists live inhibit recruitment of new staff even though the remaining closed cities continue to enjoy special guarantees for government funding.[10]

United Kingdom

The nuclear weapons complex in the United Kingdom consists of the Atomic Weapons Establishment (AWE), with sites at Aldermaston and Burghfield. Originally nuclear energy and nuclear weapons were both part of the remit of the UK Atomic Energy Authority, but since 1973 the weapons establishment has been under the Ministry of Defence (MoD). In 1993, as part of the general move toward privatization in the Thatcher era, the management of AWE was converted to contractor operation, while ownership of the site remained with MoD. In late 2008 the government's one-third stake in the management consortium was sold to Jacobs, an American engineering group, so the consortium is now 100 percent American owned. The British government, however, maintains a golden share that allows it to intervene "if necessary."[11]

AWE faces problems of an aging infrastructure and the need to maintain a highly qualified work force in a period in which the number of technical graduates in the UK has been declining.[12] Besides a campaign to recruit a new generation of scientists, considerable investment in new facilities has been undertaken at Aldermaston, with more planned for the next ten years. This additional investment has been called into question, however, by the 2010 Defence & Security Cooperation Treaty between the UK and France, which assigns many of the stockpile stewardship activities planned for Aldermaston to a new joint laboratory in France.[13] In both countries the impetus for this new arrangement appears to have been the need to save money in a period of declining budgets.

A special characteristic of the UK nuclear weapons complex is its close ties to the U.S. program. Before the moratorium on testing, the UK performed most of its nuclear tests at the Nevada Test Site, and it relied heavily on the U.S. Polaris and Trident programs in building its submarine-based nuclear weapons system. According to news reports, AWE continues to cooperate with the U.S. national laboratories on certain weapons-based research projects.[14]

France

Unlike the other major nuclear states, France does not separate civilian nuclear uses from military uses at the highest level of government. From its inception, the French Atomic Energy Commission (CEA) has handled both civil and military nuclear programs in the same bureaucracy, and it currently employs about the same number of people (4,500) in each program.[15]

Overall, there is strong popular support for the nuclear sector. Nuclear energy plays a major role in France's energy sector, accounting for 78 percent of electricity production, and there has been substantial cross-subsidization between the military and civilian sectors. For example, in the past, civilian nuclear reactors produced weapons-grade plutonium for warheads; this ceased in the 1990s, when France halted all production of fissile material for weapons use.[16]

The Ministry of Defense funds research and development for nuclear weapons, but management of the program resides in the Military Applications Division of the CEA. There are a number of laboratories and production facilities in the complex, with the Centre d'Etudes de Limeil-Valenton near Paris serving as the central weapons design laboratory. Since signing the CTBT in 1996, France has relied on a simulation program for maintaining stewardship of its nuclear weapons and for designing replacement warheads in anticipation of the end of the service life of the current weapons.[17]

Because of the unitary administrative structure in France, a reduction in nuclear weapons work does not carry the same threat to organizational interests as it does in the United States and United Kingdom. Indeed, France has reduced the size of its nuclear arsenal and closed its nuclear weapons testing site without any noticeable domestic political or bureaucratic opposition, perhaps because the nuclear weapons establishment had secured what it needed during the last round of tests in 1995–96. The cuts in numbers and types of weapons do not, however, mean that France is likely to favor a move to nuclear zero unless there are major—and unlikely in the near term—changes in the international situation.[18] The investment in the design of new nuclear warheads suggests instead that, despite its rhetorical support for nuclear zero, the French government is operating on the assumption of a continued requirement for a nuclear deterrent force.

China

The nuclear weapons laboratories of China are part of a large, geographically dispersed nuclear weapons complex, with major concentrations in Mianyang (Sichuan Province), Subei (Gansu Province), and Haiyan County (Quinghai Province). The Chinese Academy of Engineering Physics (CAEP) and its many institutes in Mianyang constitute the leading laboratory, analogous to Los Alamos, Lawrence Livermore, and Sandia laboratories. According to the Congressional Research Service, the complex "appears" to be under military control;[19] other sources make it clear that there are numerous formal and informal links to the civilian sector, at least in the area of research and development.

In the early years of Chinese nuclear weapons development, the laboratories were granted an unusual degree of independence from normal bureaucratic control, and they developed fruitful relations across industries that normally would have been isolated from each other. The system that emerged was the leading sector of Chinese research and development, flourishing while R&D for conventional weapons and in the civilian sector fell behind. In the 1980s, the Chinese government adopted this R&D model more widely to spur innovation in a limited number of critical technologies, hoping to promote civilian technologies that would also benefit the military.[20]

This brief summary of the nuclear weapons research laboratories in the major nuclear powers suggests that broad similarity in the technologies under development has not been accompanied by institutional convergence. Instead, the relations between the labs and the rest of the defense establishment and between the labs and the civilian nuclear sector have evolved to reflect social and political cultures unique to each state. The rest of this chapter will focus on the U.S. case, but there is room to ask whether the same opportunities and constraints are operating in the other NWS and what the likely responses will be. For example, during the transition to zero all the NWS will want to be assured of the reliability and safety of their remaining nuclear weapons; they will require robust verification technologies to detect any defections from the nonproliferation regime; and they will face the challenge of retaining experienced personnel in a declining field.

THE U.S. NUCLEAR WEAPONS COMPLEX

A History of Patronage

The path to nuclear weapons began with basic scientific discoveries in the 1930s made by academic scientists in a number of countries. The development in the United States of weapons based on those discoveries was, however, a massive industrial effort, involving thousands of workers in mines, power plants, separation facilities, university physics laboratories, testing facilities, and, of course, Los Alamos, where the first atomic bomb was designed and built. In a few short years, an entire complex of laboratories and production facilities was created, along with a knowledge base that went far beyond the basic physics of nuclear fission.

The U.S. nuclear weapons complex experienced fairly steady growth until the end of the Cold War, when the sea change in the international situation brought about by the breakup of the Soviet Union called into question the whole raison d'être of the nuclear enterprise. Outlays for research and development for "atomic energy defense" declined in real terms by over 25 percent through 1995 before recovering gradually to the level of the late 1980s; since 2006 the funds have fluctuated around a slightly lower level.[21] The laboratories, especially SNL, have diversified into other areas, but the nuclear weapons activities continue to dominate at LANL and LLNL.

Following the 1992 test moratorium and in anticipation of a permanent comprehensive test ban treaty, the laboratories' role was redefined as one of stockpile stewardship. Stewardship is an elastic concept, but it typically includes maintaining the safety and reliability of a smaller stockpile of nuclear weapons into a distant future; dismantling excess warheads and disposing of nuclear materials; and in some versions, retaining a "rebuild" capability.[22] In January 1996 the DOE formally established the Stockpile Stewardship and Management Program (later the Stockpile Stewardship Program). Under the program every year the Department of Defense (DOD) and DOE jointly certify the arsenal as safe, secure, and reliable. The FY 2010 budget for this part of the SSP is $1.5

billion; an additional $1.6 billion is authorized for the science and engineering "campaigns" supporting the stewardship function.[23]

The laboratories rely on computer simulations and physical tests of non-nuclear components to support their judgments about the reliability of the weapons in the stockpile, and they maintain a capacity to refurbish and remanufacture components as needed. They also maintain a test readiness program as a hedge in case nuclear testing is ever again deemed necessary. In addition, in a move that was widely interpreted at the time as a quid pro quo for the support of the laboratories for the Comprehensive Test Ban Treaty, SSP included increased funds for science at the laboratories and the construction of expensive new facilities such as the National Ignition Facility at LLNL, and the Dual-Axis Radiographic Hydrodynamic Test facility. It is worth noting that these science facilities have yet to contribute to the directed stockpile work at the laboratories; that is, they have not been necessary for the annual certification of the stockpile.[24]

Nuclear weapons have often been touted as a cheap security guarantee ("more bang for the buck"), compared to the cost of a force posture based solely on conventional forces, but the sums are still staggering. Estimates of the cumulative resources devoted by the United States to the development and production of nuclear weapons between 1940 and 2005 run as high as $7.5 trillion (in 2005 dollars), or around $115 billion a year; Stephen Schwartz has estimated that nuclear weapons accounted for 29 percent of total defense spending between 1940 and 1996.[25] Most of this spending was in the DOD budget and went to develop and produce delivery systems, command and control systems, and defensive systems, including air defense and the various iterations of ballistic missile defense systems. The budget for the nuclear components of the weapons, which falls under the DOE, was only 7 percent of the total costs through 1996.[26] An update of these estimates for FY 2008 suggests a higher share for DOE in recent years: the total appropriations for nuclear forces and operational support were $29 billion, of which $22.5 billion was in the DOD budget and $6.6 billion in DOE. The grand total for 2008, including missile defense and deferred environmental and health costs, was $52.4 billion.[27]

Regional Impacts

The assets and activities of the U.S. nuclear weapons complex are not distributed evenly across the national economy. New Mexico is the geographical core of the complex; it also has the distinction of being the most research-intensive state in the country, as measured by the share of R&D spending in state domestic product, with 95 percent of its total R&D spending—public and private—coming from the federal government, and 75 percent of the total attributable to LANL and SNL.[28] In fiscal year 2008, the DOE spent $182.7 million directly on basic science research programs at LANL, LLNL, and SNL in addition to the funds appropriated for weapons activities.[29]

This pattern of spending has created specific constituencies based in the nuclear weapons complex and defense industry which will be negatively affected by a transition to a zero nuclear world. The defense industry can expect that its products will still be in demand: many, if not all, of the nuclear-capable systems, such as aircraft and missiles, are also produced in non-nuclear versions, and the satellites, communication systems, and radars will find a place in the conventional forces. The more specialized nuclear facilities, however, will be redundant. For example, the nuclear test facilities at the Nevada Test Site—now held in a state of suspended animation, ready to be reconstituted if nuclear testing were to resume—would lose any claim for DOE support, although the site would probably continue to be used for other activities. Depending on the decisions made for the transition period, other elements of the stockpile stewardship program would presumably be phased out over time, a future that would entail a downward trajectory in support for weapons activities at the national laboratories and possibly their elimination. It is likely that the laboratories will resist this possible future, as they have in the past.[30]

The Workplace

The weapons laboratories are a special kind of workplace. They are distinguished by their remote locations (no longer so remote for Lawrence Livermore and Sandia); the compartmentalization in the name of secrecy; the moral dilemma present in work on weapons of mass destruction; and the cultivated sense, especially in the early years, of being part of an elite group working for national security.[31] The same conditions that foster a strong sense of a special community make it difficult for scientists to leave the laboratories for other jobs; in particular, the secrecy requirements mean that many of their accomplishments are not recognized in the open literature.

A number of ethnographic studies of the national laboratories have delineated laboratory culture at the micro level.[32] These accounts make it clear that there is an internal politics in the laboratories along functional lines—weapons designers vs. production engineers, or experimentalists vs. theorists and computational experts—and also along the generational lines separating the older scientists from the younger generation, which has never participated in a nuclear test. The shift from the nuclear testing regime to reliance on computer simulations as the basis for credible deterrence was difficult for many of the scientists and engineers to accept; one consequence of it has been a rise in status of the computer modelers relative to experimental scientists.[33]

The laboratories' ability to fulfill their mandated security role depends strongly on success in recruiting and retaining talented scientists and technical workers. Even before President Obama affirmed the U.S. commitment to eventual nuclear disarmament, the problems of managing a declining enterprise were evident. Downsizing at LANL and LLNL has largely been accomplished through retirements without offsetting replacement, leading to an increase in the average age of the scientific workforce, even as the collective experience of the cold war scientists disappears. And more than creative scientists are needed: the tasks of dismantling surplus nuclear weapons during downsizing and remanufacturing uranium pits as part of the lifetime extension program require a workforce of trained engineers and technical workers. An additional problem is that these jobs are, in general, open only to U.S. citizens, while the pool of science and engineering graduates in the United States is 40–60 percent foreign born.[34]

The Role of the Labs in National Policy Debates

The internal politics of the laboratories as sketched above have not been closely linked to the "external" politics of formulating national policy with respect to nuclear arms control and disarmament, or even to a calculation of fluctuations in congressional support for the labs. Instead, the intralaboratory struggles have been about competing claims for credibility within the nuclear weapons community and—in another area of contention—about resistance to the micromanagement, as it is perceived, by NNSA. There is also frequent criticism from below of the changes made after the laboratory management contracts at LANL and LLNL were switched to for-profit corporations, changes that included shedding hundreds of jobs to offset the costs of the increase in the annual management fees and the loss of tax-exempt status.[35]

As with other institutions that rely on federal government funding, the top management of the laboratories engages directly with the Washington policy community. Policy positions are developed in consultation with DOE and DOD, and the laboratories also maintain their own representatives in the capital who serve as a source of information on issues affecting the labs. Laboratory leaders testify at congressional hearings, meet with agency and congressional staff, maintain contacts with advisory groups such as the Defense Science Board and JASON, and sponsor special events, like the fall 2009 Workshop on Nuclear Forces and Nonproliferation organized by LANL at the Woodrow Wilson International Center for Scholars. In these meetings they are able to make the case for the role played by the laboratories in guaranteeing the nuclear deterrent and, implicitly and explicitly, to argue for continued reliance on nuclear deterrence as the centerpiece of U.S. security policy. They deploy their prestige and expertise to promote particular policies—for example, in their support for the Reliable Replacement Warhead—and have a record of success in maintaining support for the labs' primary mission.[36]

Transformation Plans

Since the end of the Cold War, numerous commissions and task forces have considered the future of the U.S. nuclear weapons complex and issued their recommendations.[37] The issues at stake include the appropriate size for the complex, whether to maintain redundant weapons design capabilities in LANL and LLNL, replacement of aging infrastructure, and security and management issues. At a more fundamental level, however, the modernization questions are inseparable from the question of U.S. policy on nuclear weapons. They depend on the decisions about the size of the stockpile, whether new warheads should be developed to replace the current versions being maintained under the SSP, and the projected path to nuclear zero.

In December 2007, NNSA administrator Thomas D'Agostino announced a plan for "Complex Transformation." As adopted, the plan reduces the "footprint" of the nuclear weapons establishment by shutting down some redundant activities, while simultaneously investing in modernization of other facilities. This is the so-called modernization in place option; it avoids the near-term disruption of moving weapons activities to a central site, at the cost of maintaining all the existing sites for the foreseeable future. Under this plan, employment at the three weapons laboratories is projected to shrink by 20 to 30 percent beyond the cuts already taken in 2007–8. The laboratories will maintain their core functions, and competition between LANL and LLNL will continue.[38] NNSA explicitly rejected a "curatorship" alternative that would have implied the end of capabilities to design and develop replacement nuclear components and weapons.[39]

The Obama administration signed on to the Complex Transformation plan to the extent of increasing the NNSA budget for infrastructure in the FY 2011 budget to over $2.3 billion, and during the protracted negotiations in the Senate over ratification of the New START treaty, the administration pledged substantial additional funds for modernization of the weapon complex.[40] The Nuclear Posture Review of March 2010 explicitly states that the NNSA needs to recapitalize the aging infrastructure at the laboratories and to renew human capital.[41] Whether that decision is consistent with the path to nuclear zero depends, of course, on how long the transition is expected to take. There is no doubt that the current facilities at the labs pose safety and security risks that require attention, but much of the new money will be directed toward the controversial expansion of production capacity for plutonium pits.

Thus, the U.S. weapons complex in general, and the three national laboratories in particular, are on a path that will maintain an active program of research on nuclear weapons and a down-sized, but still considerable, capability to produce new nuclear weapons. The arguments for such a capability are rooted in a doctrine of continued dependence on nuclear weapons as a core element in national security; if that premise is granted, the decision to modernize old, inefficient facilities seems reasonable. The NNSA has acknowledged that a reduction in the size of the nuclear stockpile below 1,000 warheads "could result in a need to reassess the transformation options for the Complex," but it has chosen a plan that assumes no reductions beyond the figure of 1,700–2,200 deployed warheads which was agreed to in the Moscow Treaty of 2002.[42] By contrast, a commitment to nuclear zero would require a different set of decisions, both in the near term and, especially, in the longer term. The laboratories might be retained for reasons discussed in the next section, but the planned investment in new weapons production facilities would be dropped.

NUCLEAR ZERO AND THE TECHNOLOGY BASE

The weapons laboratories occupy a special position in the U.S. science and technology base: they are the largest recipients of federal funds for research and development, and they perform research in a number of scientific areas in addition to their primary focus on nuclear weapons research. Through its impact on the national laboratories, a move to nuclear zero will affect the national technology base; how great an effect is open to discussion. There are at least two perspectives that deserve attention:

1. The need for technical expertise in nuclear weapons during the transition to zero. Such expertise is necessary for maintaining the functionality of a diminishing stockpile of weapons, dealing with the dismantlement and disposal of the weapons taken out of service, and providing a robust verification regime. Maintaining large and modernized weapons laboratories, however, carries a proliferation risk. For example, dispersed sites for special nuclear materials and expertise arguably provide more opportunities for illegal diversion to other countries or nonstate actors.

2. The preservation of the physical and intellectual capital accumulated in the national weapons laboratories, which in this framing represents a national treasure that should be protected and made available for the national good. As noted above, the laboratories have a long history of supporting fundamental scientific research, and the facilities at the laboratories for computing, for example, are perhaps not available anywhere else.

The Laboratories' Role in the Transition to Zero

The transition to nuclear zero will require continued technical capabilities similar to those currently provided by the weapons laboratories; the obvious issue is how to guarantee that the necessary competence will remain available, while preparing for a world in which it will become irrelevant. The laboratories faced a similar situation at the end of the Cold War, with the same concerns about the threat of declining budgets, loss of scientific personnel to retirement or lay-offs, and lowered morale of the remaining work force.[43]

In the 1990s the labs were "saved" by the Stockpile Stewardship Program. The science component of the program and the promise of new infrastructure to support it were an important element in enrolling support in the labs for the CTBT because they served as a warrant that the laboratories would remain interesting places to do science.[44] Significantly, the charge for the SSP included a requirement to "[m]aintain the science and engineering institutions needed to support the nation's nuclear deterrent, now and in the future."[45] Note the unquestioned presumption of a permanent nuclear capability, a presumption that will not be an appropriate basis for policy-making during the transition to zero. While some have argued in favor of maintaining a "virtual" capability as a hedge, such a policy would undercut the possibility of gaining universal adherence to nuclear zero because other states would claim the same privilege.

SSP provided political cover for a substantial reduction in the number of U.S. nuclear warheads by offering reassurance that the remaining weapons in the stockpile were fully functional. As numbers decline to a few hundreds and then a few tens of warheads, however, the overall stewardship responsibilities will presumably shrink as well, albeit not uniformly. Verification technology will continue to be in demand for the foreseeable future—indeed, its importance will increase during the potentially unstable transition to zero—and the need will persist after zero, however "zero" is defined. A robust nuclear forensic capability would also be useful as a deterrent to clandestine developments.

It is not clear, however, that new technology is needed to provide these interim and long-term capabilities. Strengthened diplomatic and intelligence efforts and new confidence-building measures might well be more effective in managing the transition than investment in new technology. If further R&D at the weapons laboratories is deemed essential, then the political problems created by simultaneously promoting nuclear developments while preaching disarmament cannot be avoided.

There is a related problem that needs to be faced. So long as the laboratories are a repository of nuclear weapons knowledge, they represent a proliferation risk, the risk that the spread of technical knowledge about how to make nuclear weapons will lead to additional states acquiring them. Strenuous efforts to keep the secret of nuclear weapons during the Manhattan Project were nullified by the work of a few Soviet spies, and subsequent proliferators have all received help, either directly or through espionage, from existing nuclear weapons states.[46] The most recent example is the A. Q. Khan network, which transmitted technology for uranium enrichment to Iran, Libya, and North Korea before it was shut down in 2003.

With the publication of the Smyth Report in 1945, which made public the general principles of atomic weapons, it could truly be said that there was no longer any "atomic secret." Indeed, knowledgeable scientists understood what had been involved in constructing the bomb as soon as they heard of the attack on Hiroshima. How then to understand the high level of security classification maintained on all nuclear weapons knowledge, and the difficulty that would-be proliferators have had in acquiring the ability to build nuclear weapons? The answer to this apparent paradox lies in the considerable success that states have had in controlling access to fissile materials, along with the importance of specific technical knowledge, especially tacit forms of that knowledge. It is one thing to understand the principles of atomic fission, and another to master the technically difficult task of constructing a bomb.

Current proliferation threats from North Korea and Iran bear out the basic argument that it is difficult to produce a nuclear weapon, even when blueprints and contraband materials and components are available, but they also show that a determined regime can persevere and achieve a nuclear weapons capability.

Ironically, the effort that the national laboratories have made to counter the disappearance of tacit knowledge in the wave of retirements of senior scientists, by creating a more complete record of the historical tests and providing formal training programs to new hires, has served to maintain continuity of knowledge and make it available to more scientists, thus, implicitly, maintaining the paths open to proliferators.[47]

Preservation of the National Weapons Laboratories for Other National Goals

The major nuclear weapons states all have well-established national laboratories to provide the technical base for maintaining the weapons, a mission that, I have argued, will disappear in a nuclear weapons–free world. Many of the laboratories, however, also engage in research oriented toward the civilian sector, a mission that could be enhanced to justify maintaining the laboratories indefinitely, albeit with a revised mandate. The British nuclear complex, for example, has long-standing programs—not all of them successful—to transfer technology to the commercial sector.[48] Following the end of the Cold War, Russian and U.S. nuclear laboratories collaborated on civilian projects under a DOE program to support conversion to peacetime employment for Russian nuclear scientists. These programs and others like them are based on the proposition that military technologies can be "spun off" to benefit the civilian technology base, and they have a particular appeal during periods of declining funding for the nuclear mission.

Thus, today, the U.S. laboratories and their supporters emphasize the broad capabilities of the laboratories and argue that they deserve to be maintained with new rules that would allow them to interact more easily with other patrons besides DOE. This is the position taken in a recent report by the Stimson Center, *Leveraging Science for Security*.[49] A similar argument was put forward in 1993 by Hans Bethe, who argued that the nation should "redirect the nation's huge investment in the nuclear weapons laboratories towards research aimed at serious problems that we are sure to face as a society and in the global market place, but that universities and private industry do not have the resources to address."[50]

Historically, the labs' support for research with broad applicability to military and civilian goals was defended as a recruiting tool to attract top-level scientists to the laboratories. The general science programs are otherwise hard to justify in a mission-oriented agency because of their speculative nature: there is no guarantee of technical success in fundamental research and—even if successful—no guarantee that it will be relevant to the nuclear mission in the near term. If the nuclear mission disappears, the laboratories will lack the "fly wheel" (their phrase) which has provided the budgetary slack to cover the costs of their general science programs.

The laboratories have found it difficult to attract resources for projects that are not connected to the security mission. For example, the program for Cooperative Research and Development Agreements (CRADAs) with industry, which in the 1990s was promoted as a way to sustain the laboratories, has failed to live up to the early hype.[51] A major problem was the loss of congressional support after the Republicans took control of the House in 1995 and struck down any program that could be tarred with the label of industrial policy; another problem was the complex set of rules and rights that govern laboratory-industry interactions.[52] The "crown jewels" argument for continued support for the laboratories cannot be sustained if the jewels remain inside the laboratory walls.

In the current situation, the emphasis has been on reinventing the laboratories as national security laboratories with expertise in all kinds of weapons research. The Stimson Center's 2009 report makes the case for such a mission, supported through cooperative agreements with other agencies in the security sector—the Department of Defense, the Department of Homeland Security, and the CIA—and Sandia's success in reducing its dependence on NNSA funding shows that there is potential to increase sharply the role of Work for Others at the laboratories. It remains to be seen, however, whether the "Others" will be willing to include the long-term costs of laboratory infrastructure in their contracts. WFO has been typically in the form of short-term contracts, leading to a fragmentation of effort and difficult working conditions for scientists and engineers, who are forced to divide their time among numerous contracts.

The case for long-term support of the laboratories in a period of declining importance for the nuclear mission has, moreover, a serious weakness: the management problems that have plagued the laboratories for years. The recent history of safety incidents and security scandals do not—to put it mildly—inspire confidence. The insular laboratory workplace culture described above is at odds with the persistent tendency for DOE to manage ("micromanage," in the view of its critics) the laboratories from Washington.[52] Others point to the so-called cowboy culture of the laboratories as the reason why the DOE has added more and more layers of oversight.[54] The underlying tension between the two sides has been exacerbated by the series of security scandals involving lost or misplaced classified data and sloppy accounting practices.

The case of Wen Ho Lee, a physicist at Los Alamos who was charged with transferring nuclear secrets to China, only to have the case collapse after he had spent nine months in jail, is the most notorious. The furor over the mishandling of this case led a federal judge to apologize to Dr. Lee, and Congress to create the NNSA. Other scandals at LANL included the loss of two computer disks holding classified data in 2004 (eventually it was determined that the disks never existed, an outcome that drew further attention to the sloppy practices at the laboratory),[55] and a string of other security breaches involving mishandling of classified information.[56] These incidents precipitated the firing of one laboratory director, a stand-down in 2004 of several months at Los Alamos, and the opening of the management contracts at LANL and LLNL to corporate teams, a step that has proved deeply unpopular at the labs. Given this record, any argument to preserve the laboratories for their value to the national S&T base would need first to establish that the resources could not be better used elsewhere to accomplish the same mission.

CONCLUSIONS

A serious move to nuclear zero will have major implications for the U.S. weapons laboratories, as well as their counterparts in other nuclear weapons states. To the extent that the laboratories depend on their role in maintaining nuclear deterrence through stockpile stewardship programs or work on modernization programs, survival in their present form is unlikely in an era of nuclear disarmament. In the near term, the laboratories will be needed to provide guarantees for the reliability of the stockpile, to oversee the dismantlement of nuclear warheads, and to support verification technologies. The first two functions will, however, decline and eventually disappear during the drawdown to zero. The verification function will last longer, but in a zero nuclear world, when the problem will be detection of possible cheating, an international verification effort lodged in the IAEA or a successor agency would be a preferred solution because it would be more trusted than a capability based in a single state.

A roadmap could guide the transition to zero. How long is the long run? Is there a need to recruit and train another generation of laboratory scientists, or will the current cohort be sufficient? Is new knowledge needed to perform verification, or is current technology adequate? Related to these questions are the challenges of maintaining morale in organizations that are losing their main mission and of sustaining political support for the cost of running the laboratories during the transition period.

Are there alternative missions that would justify maintaining the weapons laboratories following abolition of nuclear weapons? In the UK, interest is strong in converting AWE into a laboratory for disarmament. The model is the conversion of Porton Down, the British chemical and biological weapons laboratory, to work only on defensive measures and support for international conventions, following the 1956 cabinet decision to stop development of offensive chemical and biological weapons.[57] In the ongoing debate over the future of the Trident, the government statement in summer 2009 that it would postpone signing the design contract for the new generation of submarines was accompanied by announcements of a new "centre of excellence" devoted to civil nuclear technology and of new funds for AWE's program of nuclear forensics.[58] These initiatives are consistent with a medium-term future for AWE as a laboratory supporting nuclear disarmament measures, but they do not answer the question for the long term when nuclear weapons have been abolished.

The U.S. laboratories might hope to expand their activities in the area of nuclear energy and nuclear forensics, but these would be unlikely to be funded at a level that would replace their weapons program funding. They face a daunting task if they seek to reinvent themselves as general purpose laboratories whose claim on the national budget would derive from their contributions to the civilian sector. The large sunk investment in scientific infrastructure is an argument in their favor, but there are many barriers to converting the laboratories to effective partners in commercial endeavors or even to expanding their participation in civilian-oriented government programs. The best prospect for the laboratories at present seems to expand WFO in the area of national security, accepting that such a change implies considerable changes in working conditions.

A serious commitment to nuclear zero would require laboratory leadership to prepare a long-term plan for phasing out nuclear weapons–related activities, with milestones to match political and technological developments, such as the entry of the CTBT into force, or the dismantlement of the last nuclear warhead. These milestones should be viewed as irreversible, and thus there would be no need for further modernization of the weapons complex. To argue that interim nuclear activities require continued modernization is to postpone the time when nuclear disarmament becomes an inevitable outcome, not just an aspiration.

NOTES

A version of this chapter first appeared in the July/August 2010 issue of the *Bulletin of the Atomic Scientists.*

1. Oliver Meier, "Verifying the CTBT: Responses to Republican Criticisms," *Disarmament Diplomacy* 40 (September–October 1999), at http://www.acronym.org.uk/dd/dd40/40verif.htm. See also Barb Mulkin, "The View from San Diego: Harold Agnew Speaks Out," *Los Alamos Science* 152 (Summer/Fall 1981): 154, at http://www.fas.org/sgp/othergov/doe/lanl/00326234.pdf.

2. William J. Broad, "Nuclear Labs Raise Doubts over Viability of Arsenals," *New York Times*, 27 March 2010.

3. This chapter describes the nuclear complexes of the Perm 5: the United States, Russia, the United Kingdom, France, and China.

4. U.S. Department of Energy, Office of Chief Financial Officer, *FY 2010 Congressional Budget Request*, vol. 1, Washington, DC (May 2009), pp. 535, 543, 559, at http://nnsa.energy.gov/management/documents/NNSA_Budget.pdf. Including contractors, students, and resident visitors would increase the total by approximately 5,000 employees.

5. U.S. Department of Energy, Office of Chief Financial Officer, "FY 2010 Congressional Budget Request, Laboratory Tables Preliminary" (2009), pp. 40–41; 44–46; 93–94, at http://www.cfo.doe.gov/budget/10budget/Content/Labandstate/FY2010lab.pdf.

6. Sandia National Laboratories, "Facts and Figures," at http://www.sandia.gov/about/faq; Los Alamos National Laboratory, "Fact Sheets," at http://www.lanl.gov.news.releases/index.html.

7. Sharon Weiner, "Preventing Nuclear Entrepreneurship in Russia's Nuclear Cities," *International Security* 27, no. 2 (Fall 2002), Table 1, pp. 130–31.

8. Jonathan Medalia, Shirley A. Kan, Paul K. Kerr, Carol Migdalovitz, Derek E. Mix, Mary Beth Nitikin, and Larry A. Niksch, "Nuclear Weapons R&D Organizations in Nine Nations," R40439 (Washington DC, Congressional Research Service, 2009), at http://www.fas.org/sgp/crs/nuke/R40439.pdf.

9. Dimitry Nikonov and Igor Khripunov, "The Rebirth of Russia's Closed Cities," *Bulletin of the Atomic Scientists* (web edition), 16 October 2008, at http://www.thebulletin.org/web-edition/features/the-rebirth-of-russias-closed-cities.

10. Ibid.

11. Ben Russell, "Secret Nuclear Sell-off Storm." *The Independent*, 20 December 2008.

12. Stuart Parkinson, "The Costs of Replacing Trident," *Physics World* (March 2007); Henrietta Wilson, "Renewing Trident: Can the UK's Atomic Weapons Establishment Cope?" *Disarmament Diplomacy* 88 (Summer 2008).

13. "UK–France Summit 2010 Declaration on Defence and Security Co-operation," 2 November 2010, at http://www.number10.gov.uk/news/statements-and-articles/2010/11/uk–france-summit-2010-declaration-on-defence-and-security-co-operation-5651.

14. Matthew Taylor and Richard Norton-Taylor, "US Using British Atomic Weapons Factory for Its Nuclear Programme," *The Guardian*, 9 February 2009.

15. Mycle Schneider, "Nuclear Power in France: Beyond the Myth," Report Commissioned by the Greens-EFA Group in the European Parliament (Brussels, December 2008), p. 8, at http://www.greens-efa.org/cms/topics/dokbin/258/258614.mythbuster@en.pdf.

16. See Venance Journé, Chapter 7, this volume.

17. Ibid.

18. Bruno Tertrais, "French Perspectives on Nuclear Weapons and Nuclear Disarmament," in *France and the United Kingdom*, ed. Barry Blechman (Washington, DC: Henry L. Stimson Center, 2009), pp. 1–22.

19. Medalia et al., "Nuclear Weapons R&D," p. 3.

20. Evan Feigenbaum, "Who's behind China's High-Technology 'Revolution'?" *International Security* 24 (Summer 1999): 95–126; Tai Ming Cheung, *Fortifying China: The Struggle to Build a Modern Defense Economy* (Ithaca, NY: Cornell University Press, 2009).

21. U.S. Office of Management and Budget, *The Budget for Fiscal Year 2009, Historical Tables* (Washington, DC: Office of Management and Budget, 2008), Tables 9.8 and 10.1, at http://www.gpoaccess.gov/usbudget/.

22. See Judith Reppy and Joseph Pilat, eds., *Defense Conversion and the Future of the National Nuclear Weapons Laboratories*, Cornell University Peace Studies Program Occasional Paper #18 (Ithaca, NY: Peace Studies Program, 1994), Panel I, "What Is the Nuclear Mission?"

23. 111th Congress, 1st Session, House of Representatives, "National Defense Authorization Act for Fiscal Year 2010," Conference Report to accompany H.R. 2647, Report 111-288, 7 October 2009, pp. 1137–39.

24. A. Fitzpatrick and I. Oelrich, "The Stockpile Stewardship Program: Fifteen Years On," Federation of American Scientists (April 2007), pp. 23–24, at http://www.fas.org/2007/nuke/Stockpile_Stewardship_Paper.pdf. The DOE reportedly called this "the anchor store approach," as in "Every shopping mall needs an anchor store." Stephen M. Younger, *The Bomb* (New York, HarperCollins, 2009), p. 183.

25. Stephen Schwartz, "The Costs of U.S. Nuclear Weapons," Issue Brief (Monterey, CA: James Martin Center for Nonproliferation Studies at the Monterey Institute of International Studies, 2008); Joseph Cirincione, "Lessons Lost," *Bulletin of the Atomic Scientists* 61 (November/December, 2005): 43–53.

26. Schwartz, "The Costs of U.S. Nuclear Weapons."

27. Stephen Schwartz, with Deepti Choubey, *Nuclear Security Spending Assessing Costs, Examining Priorities* (Washington, DC: Carnegie Endowment for International Peace, 2009).

28. National Science Foundation, National Science Board, *Science and Engineering Indicators 2008* (NSB 08-01; NSB 08-01A), Arlington, VA, 2008, Appendix Tables 4-23; 4-24, at http://www.nsf.gov/statistics/seind08/pdf_v2.htm#ch4.

29. U.S. Department of Energy, FY 2010 Congressional Budget Request.

30. Benjamin Sims and Christopher Henke, "Maintenance and Transformation in the U.S. Nuclear Weapons Complex," *IEEE Technology and Society Magazine* 27, no. 3 (Fall 2008): 32–38.

31. Hugh Gusterson, *Nuclear Rites: A Weapons Laboratory at the End of the Cold War* (Berkeley: University of California Press, 1996); Peter J. Westwick, *The National Labs: Science in an American System 1947–1974* (Cambridge: Harvard University Press, 2003).

32. Gusterson, *Nuclear Rites*; Laura McNamara, "Ways of Knowing about Weapons: The Cold War's End at the Los Alamos National Laboratory," Ph.D. dissertation, University of New Mexico, Albuquerque, NM, May 2001; Joseph Masco, "Nuclear Technoaesthetics: Sensory Politics from Trinity to the Virtual Bomb in Los Alamos," *American Ethnologist* 21, no. 3 (2004): 348–73; Sims and Henke, "Maintenance and Transformation."

33. This description applies mostly to LANL and LLNL. SNL were established as engineering centers and have been managed by the private sector from the beginning. By all reports, the laboratory culture at SNL is more open to industry collaboration than that of LANL and LLNL (Andrew Ross, private communication).

34. National Research Council, Committee on Prospering in the Global Economy of the 21st Century, *Rising above the Gathering Storm: Energizing and Employing America for a Brighter Economic Future* (Washington, DC: National Academies Press, 2007), p. 80.

35. See, for example, the comments on 31 August 2009 on the blog "LANL: The Rest of the Story," at http://lanl-the-rest-of-the-story.blogspot.com/2009/08/ltrs-lansees-employee-engagement.html. Similar comments can be found on "LLNL-The True Story," at http://llnlthetruestory.blogspot.com/2009_05_01_archive.html.

36. Sims and Henke, "Maintenance and Transformation."

37. These include the Galvin Report (1995); the Chiles Commission's *Report of the Commission on Maintaining United States Nuclear Weapons Expertise* (1999); the Secretary of Energy Advisory Board *Report of the Nuclear Weapons Complex Infrastructure Task Force* (2005); the Defense Science Board Task Force on Nuclear Capabilities (2006); and the Stimson Center report, *Leveraging Science for Security* (2009).

38. James Brosnan, "Nuclear Labs Face Workforce Cutbacks within 10 Years," ABQTrib.com (19 December 2007), at http://abqtrib.com/news/2007/dec/19/nuclear-labs-face-workforce-cutbacks-within-10-yea/.

39. U.S. Department of Energy, "Record of Decision for the Complex Transformation Supplemental Programmatic Environmental Impact Statement," *Federal Register*, 19 December 2008, 77651.

40. Mary Beth Sheridan and Walter Pincus, "Sen. Kyl Dampens Administration Hopes for Ratification of Arms Treaty," *Washington Post*, 16 November 2010.

41. "Administrator Highlights NNSA Role in Implementing Nuclear Posture Review in Congressional Hearing," *NNSA News*, 14 April 2010, at http://www.nnsa.energy.gov/2900.htm. Not surprisingly, that stance has been welcomed by the lab directors.

42. U.S. Department of Energy, NNSA, *Final Complex Transformation Supplemental Programmatic Environmental Impact Statement Summary*, DOE/EIS-0236-S4, October 2008, S-56–56; 3-72–3-75, at http://www.gc.energy.gov/NEPA/1017.htm. In fact, the new START treaty sets the number of deployed warheads for Russia and the United States at 1550 each.

43. Reppy and Pilat, eds., *Defense Conversion*, p. 18.

44. Ann Finkbeiner, *The Jasons* (New York: Viking, 2006), pp. 187–88.

45. U.S. Department of Energy, National Nuclear Security Administration, Nevada Site Office, "Stockpile Stewardship Program" (Las Vegas, NV: DOE/NV, 2004), at http://www.nv.doe.gov/nationalsecurity/stewardship. The National Defense Authorization Act for Fiscal Year 2010 raises preservation of the core intellectual and technical competencies in nuclear weapons to be the number one objective; 111th Congress, 1st Session, House of Representatives, "National Defense Authorization," Sec. 3111 (b).

46. Donald MacKenzie and Graham Spinardi, "Tacit Knowledge, Weapons Design, and the Uninvention of Nuclear Weapons," *American Journal of Sociology* 101, no. 1 (July 1995): 44–99.

47. McNamara, "Ways of Knowing about Weapons," pp. 267–74. A 2006 security case at LANL, in which classified documents from the nuclear weapons archiving project were found in an employee's home in the course of a drug bust, suggests that the danger is not merely theoretical. See Ralph Vartabedian, "Los Alamos Confirms Data Breach," *Los Angeles Times*, 26 October 2006, at http://articles.latimes.com/2006/oct/26/nation/na-lab26.

48. Graham Spinardi, "Aldermaston and British Nuclear Weapons Development: Testing the 'Zuckerman Thesis,'" *Social Studies of Science* 27, no. 4 (1997): 547–82.

49. Elizabeth Turpen, *Leveraging Science for Security: A Strategy for the Nuclear Weapons Laboratories in the 21st Century*, Henry L. Stimson Center, Report no. 71 (Washington, DC, March 2009). By contrast, the National Research Council, *Rising*, is skeptical of assigning the laboratories an S&T role beyond their core mission.

50. Reppy and Pilat, eds., *Defense Conversion*, Appendix A.

51. Andrew Lawler, "DOE to Industry: So Long, Partner," *Science* 274, no. 5284 (4 October 1996): 24–26; Rose Marie Ham and David C. Mowery, "Improving the Effectiveness of Public-private R&D Collaboration: Case Studies at a US Weapons Laboratory," *Research Policy* 26 (February 1998): 661–75.

52. Turpen, *Leveraging Science for Security*, Appendix III. In addition, the simple mechanics of cooperation are difficult because of the secrecy barriers. The proposed multi-million dollar "open campus" outside the fence at LLNL, intended to facilitate face-to-face collaboration with private business, is evidence of the problem. See Benjamin Pimentel, "Livermore Opens Its Doors to Outsiders, *Wall Street Journal*, 25 February 2010.

53. U.S. Department of Defense, Office of the Under Secretary of Defense for Acquisition, Technology, and Logistics, Defense Science Board Task Force on Nuclear Capabilities, *Report Summary* (Washington, DC, 2006). See also Turpen, *Leveraging Science for Security*, 22–25.

54. Ralph Vartabedian and Christine Henley, "Toxic Culture Brewing at Los Alamos Lab," *Los Angeles Times*, 26 July 2004. For a rebuttal, see Brad Lee Holian, "Is There Really a Cowboy Culture of Arrogance at Los Alamos?" *Physics Today* 57, no. 12 (2004): 60–61.

55. David Malakoff, "Security Safety Probe Shuts Down Los Alamos National Lab," *Science* 305, no. 5683 (23 July 2004): 462.

56. LANL: The Rest of the Story, "Another Security Breach at Los Alamos," 6 August 2007, at http://lanl-the-rest-of-the-story.blogspot.com/2007_08_01_archive.html. For a summary of problems at LLNL, see U.S. General Accountability Office, "Nuclear Security: Better Oversight Needed to Ensure That Security Improvements at Lawrence Livermore National Laboratory Are Fully Implemented and Sustained," GAO-09-321 (Washington, DC, March 2009).

57. T. Milne, H. Beach, J. L. Finney, R. S. Pease, and J. Rotblat, *An End to UK Nuclear Weapons* (London: British Pugwash Group, 2002), at http://www.pugwash.org/uk/documents/end-to-uk-nuclear-weapons.pdf.

58. Richard Norton-Taylor, "Trident Submarine Deal Delayed," *The Guardian*, 17 July 2009.

15 Is the Civil Nuclear Industry Relevant to Nuclear Disarmament?

Marco De Andreis and Simon Moore

INTRODUCTION

Over the last few years, there has been considerable talk all over the world about a revival of the civil nuclear industry. Before the financial collapse in late 2008, world economic growth had driven the price of fossil fuels to record heights. On top of that, evidence was mounting as to the impact of burning of fossil fuels on climate. The combination of these two factors made nuclear energy appear politically and economically palatable at a level unseen in two decades.

Unfortunately, nuclear power generation is related to nuclear proliferation, insofar as the fissile materials needed to have a controlled chain reaction in a nuclear reactor are the same as those needed for an uncontrolled chain reaction in a nuclear bomb.

With uranium the *degree of enrichment* (the proportion of the U-235 isotope, which is fissile, mixed in with the U-238 isotope, which is not) is very different: 0.7 percent in naturally occurring ores, around 3 percent for a reactor, around 90 percent for a bomb. But the technologies, and the attendant equipment to enrich it, are the same. This is the cause of the international concern about the Iranian nuclear program. Plutonium is a fission by-product and does not exist in nature, but once separated from spent nuclear fuel, it may be used to fuel a bomb as well as a reactor.

As a consequence, other things being equal, the more nuclear reactors are around, the more fissile materials are around, and the more difficult countering the proliferation of nuclear weapons becomes. Any expansion of civilian nuclear power generation therefore has a bearing on nuclear nonproliferation.

Global tendencies are the result of combining many individual decisions taken in different places under different sets of circumstances. Thus, to explore the nuclear revival issue, this chapter will look at some of the issues under debate around the world, showing what their impacts will be on the expansion of peaceful nuclear power and on nuclear weapons proliferation.

A WORLDWIDE NUCLEAR RENAISSANCE?

The growth prospects of the nuclear industry are a function of several factors. These factors—chiefly the economy, the environment, and security of supply—have their own peculiar way to change continuously and always stay the same. Let us briefly review the three factors separately.

The Economy

In mid-2008, after two decades of nuclear neglect, we appeared to be on the eve of a spectacular growth in the industry. World GNP was then growing at a historically unprecedented rate and world energy demand was rising with it. Demand for energy was driving up the price of fossil fuels: in July 2008 the price of oil reached $147 a barrel. At about the same time, Arjun N. Murti, an energy analyst for Goldman Sachs, made the headlines predicting a price of $200 "soon."[1] He was not the only one to do so.

High prices of fossil fuels make all other energy sources, including nuclear, more competitive. A historical problem for the nuclear industry—that of being highly capital intensive—appeared to have been overcome, because capital was abundant and competitive returns were assured as electricity generators sought to wean themselves off expensive fossil inputs.

In the space of a few months, these conditions evaporated. First, credit froze, with devastating, systemic consequences, and with little hope for substantial relief in the near term. World GNP growth turned negative in 2009, for the first time since the end of World War II. World trade also experienced negative growth. Most of the richest countries experienced their sharpest economic contraction of the last sixty years or so. Second, the price of oil plummeted: in December 2008 it had sunk to around $30 per barrel, despite a war in the Gaza Strip and the usual Christmas tinkering by Russia with its gas exports to Europe. Then it went gradually up to around $70 per barrel, where it stabilized. The price volatility of this most important commodity—that, among other things, drives the price of all fossil fuels—continues to complicate the kind of long-term economic calculations associated with the nuclear industry lead times.

On the other hand, the sharp economic downturn, the world over, has triggered, in most places, "stimulus packages" of public spending. In places where political and market conditions support it, taxpayer money could be directed to ensuring long-term energy supply security.

Aside from questions directly pertaining to the financial crisis, other perennial problems remain unresolved: How much does it cost to decommission a nuclear power plant? How much does it cost for long-term waste storage? Who will bear these costs? Governments (that is, taxpayers)? Utility firms (that is, consumers)? In Italy, households and firms cover nuclear decommissioning costs through a specific item in their electricity bills, as they have done since 1988. In excess of €9 billion has been collected so far, and this will go on well into the next decade and possibly beyond to the tune of €0.5 billion a year. Similar schemes are de rigueur elsewhere as a means to cover commissioning costs. "Customers of Georgia Power, a subsidiary of the Southern Co., will pay on average $1.30 a month more in 2011, rising to $9.10 by 2017, to help pay for two reactors expected to go online in 2016 or later."[2]

Ultimately, how the costs of a new fleet of nuclear generators will be distributed has not been clearly determined in many places. Roles for the government and the private sector both seem necessary, but the extent of each is a matter of hot political and economic debate.

The Environment

Nuclear power plants do not emit greenhouse gases, if one excludes the emissions linked to the construction phase. To the extent that global warming is a real and present danger the nuclear industry scores many points. Indeed, global warming is one of the strongest arguments behind the "nuclear renaissance." If a worldwide carbon pricing system (carbon tax or cap and trade) is ever realized, nuclear power should gain economic competitiveness over other, more carbon intensive generating methods as their price is raised by the policy intervention.

However, nonemission of carbon is perhaps not enough to grant the nuclear industry a certificate of environmental soundness. For the sake of the argument, let us assign zero probability to a major release of radioactivity from a nuclear power plant, either intentionally (terrorism) or unintentionally (accident). Even making this assumption, can one really define as "clean" the radioactive waste that is the inevitable by-product of the fission process? The amount of High Level Radioactive Waste (HLW) worldwide is currently increasing by about 12,000 metric tons every year. HLW includes radionuclides whose half-life is measured in tens of thousands, hundreds of thousands, and even millions of years. Mixed in the waste but chemically separable there is plutonium, a raw material for nuclear bombs.

Things are not going to get any better with more recent technology. The new, so-called third generation plus European Pressurised Reactor (EPR), built by the French company AREVA, was expected to produce less waste than its predecessors, for example. It turned out that, though less in volume and while generating substantially more power, its waste will be more radioactive than that produced by older reactors by a factor of seven, according to Greenpeace, and by 15 percent according to AREVA itself.[3]

No country in the world can claim to have solved the problem of permanent nuclear waste disposal. Most countries do not even know *where* to locate their disposal sites—the issue obviously triggers "NIMBY" concerns.

Take the U.S. site at Yucca Mountain, Nevada. President Barack Obama won in Nevada in 2008 with a pledge to "end the notion of Yucca Mountain." The Senate majority leader, Nevada Democrat Harry Reid, is a long-term opponent of the nuclear repository, and has repeatedly pledged to block any vote on the facility from taking place on his watch. Obama's 2010 budget made good on his electoral promise by cutting off most of the money for the project. The decision to abandon the Yucca site may cost the government billions of dollars in payments to the utility industry. On top of that, the $9 billion already spent on the site would be wasted.[4] Even if the site manages to survive this political barrage, its capacity—70,000 metric tons of HLW—will equal U.S. spent reactor fuel and military waste in "temporary" storage in 2010; in other words, the facility will be oversubscribed before it opens.

Security of Supply

As a general rule, the more diversified energy sources are, the more security of supply one has, especially if there are scarce domestic sources to rely on in the first place. Take Europe, for example. In 2005 the EU-27 import dependency was 57 percent for natural gas, 82 percent for oil, and 39 percent for coal. It is projected to climb to, respectively, 84 percent, 93 percent, and 59 percent by 2030.

The EU imports almost 100 percent of its uranium ore. But these are different sources (about half from Canada and Australia) than those for oil and gas (about half from Russia, Norway, and Algeria).[5] On top of that, the cost of uranium is a small fraction (a few percentage points) of the total cost of producing electricity, as opposed to fossil fuel generation, where variable (fuel) costs make up a much higher proportion of overall costs. What is true for Europe also applies wherever access to energy depends on imports. By helping to diversify both the fuel types needed for generation and the suppliers of those fuels, nuclear power helps solidify supply security.

EVIDENCE OF THE "NUCLEAR RENAISSANCE"

Talk of nuclear renaissance is abundant. However, as of 2010, action is far more scarce. Most plans remain at the approval and policy stage; little concrete has yet been poured. Still, after two decades which approximated stagnation for the industry, even this movement represents notable progress. In this section, we will highlight some of the policy innovations which have contributed to the evolution of the nuclear debate. We will seek to enhance these with examples from the different approaches being taken in different countries, the state of their respective domestic debates, and the possible impacts each of these decisions may have on the proliferation debate and global zero. As will be shown, these developments span the range from the largely innocuous to the highly controversial. This is not intended to be a comprehensive listing of all projects being planned around the globe—as much as anything else there is so much flux in the industry that such a listing would rapidly become obsolete. It should, however, provide a flavor of the range of perspectives on the topic.

Internationalization of Electricity Markets and the Impact on Nuclear Energy

Historically, electricity grids and the power plants that supplied them were national assets, often built and managed by national governments and with rare or nonexistent interconnection to neighbors. However, through deregulation in the 1980s onward, and the increasing internationalization of markets that occurred alongside, in many parts of the world electricity is now traded across borders. The European Union has made the development of European energy markets a priority. Annual trade between Canada and the United States exceeds 70 billion kWh.[6] Around the world, power plant projects are built with one eye on access to foreign consumers. This has implications for nuclear power as much as any other sector of the generating industry. It also reshapes some of the political questions which have shadowed nuclear power over the years.

Italy provides a useful example of this. It has no domestic nuclear power facilities, having abandoned its civilian nuclear program amid a campaign of public hostility to nuclear power in the late 1980s. Successive governments have refused to return to nuclear energy for two decades, until the government of Silvio Berlusconi, elected in May 2008, changed that course. Even so, though Berlusconi has promised to go back to nuclear power, no action has been taken within Italy. This does not mean, though, that Italian power consumers are not using nuclear energy. In fact, some 13 percent of Italy's total electricity consumption is imported from France, where it is predominantly nuclear-generated.

Nuclear links with neighboring France have flourished, filling the void left in domestic generation. The two dominant "national champion" firms, Enel in Italy and Electricité de France, have been heavily involved. The role of the European common energy market is thus of increasing importance to the Italian electricity sector. As the European Union has been pushing for more interconnection between historically separated national markets, so the French and Italian utilities have seen opportunities for increasing business across national boundaries. Buying nuclear power generated outside its territory has allowed the Italian government to tout its opposition to nuclear power while realizing many of its benefits in terms of reliable and modestly priced electricity (with the added benefit that French tax and rate-payers funded most of the original construction costs). Building new nuclear plants might divide those costs more equitably among consumers of whatever nationality, but could continue to work with France's comparative advantage in nuclear power. As Mycle Schneider reports, "France has a huge generating overcapacity, which it uses to export electricity to neighboring countries at cheap prices."[7]

The internationalization of electricity markets that this exemplifies affects the zero case in a few indirect ways. On the positive side, it is to be expected that the primary exporters of nuclear power would be the countries with an established track record in its production. These countries have histories of responsible behavior with regard to waste storage and control of nuclear materials. It is preferable to expand nuclear generation within these countries than to extend it to new locations with lesser expertise and experience. On the other hand, it does allow for the creation of a disconnect between public and government opinion and reality. Italian voters showed themselves to be strongly opposed to nuclear power in a number of referenda. Their wishes were largely responsible for the closure of Italian nuclear facilities. Yet they continue to consume nuclear-generated electricity every day. It is not at all clear how aware the electorate is of this, or of what their attitude would be were they to know. Allowing governments (and publics, to a lesser extent) to be publicly hostile to nuclear power, yet to condone and nurture its use, creates a hypocrisy on the issue that increases the distance between policy and action, and can weaken resistance to nuclear expansion in the future.

Small Reactors

Technological breakthroughs in reactor design are beginning to pose new questions for policy-makers, and have implications for the nonproliferation debate. Among the most groundbreaking developments could be the commercial rollout of small or self-contained reactors. Designed to be transportable by rail or truck, these smaller reactors have the potential to be a low-cost entrant into the nuclear generation market.

Their commercial advantage derives from their ability to be manufactured effectively on a production line, rather than having to be built bespoke on site. They will be faster to produce, able to be sited away from large sources of water because of their use of air-cooling systems, and able to be attached to developing grids unsuited to the vast outputs of conventional nuclear power plants (NPP). They need refueling less frequently, and so operate for far longer stretches without shutting down. According to U.S. Nuclear Regulatory Commission spokesman Michael Mayfield, they are also safer than large reactors, generating less heat and having fewer moving parts susceptible to failure.[8] Their low cost is also inherently less risky for utilities than staking huge sums on the success of one large NPP.

Small power plants undoubtedly have the potential to spread nuclear technology to places where it has been technically, economically, or politically unfeasible previously. However, when combined with fuel-cycle work provided by the supplier, they can minimize the need to transfer the most sensitive technologies—centrifuges for enrichment and facilities for reprocessing or recycling.

The ability of small plants to operate in lower-capacity electricity grids opens up nuclear technology to a host of previously untapped countries. Westinghouse is making this a deliberate marketing strategy, hoping to sell its "Iris" reactor to the 80 percent of the world's grids that cannot cope with larger units.[9] Logically, these are countries with no major history of nuclear activity. Demanding a smaller workforce and with support provided by the vendors, small reactors also reduce the expertise barrier to operating nuclear generators.

By reducing the necessity to develop domestic nuclear capabilities, small reactors help limit the required transfer of technology to countries seeking to harness this source of energy. This is particularly helpful, from a nonproliferation perspective, when it means sensitive fuel-cycle processes can occur under the auspices of established nuclear operators. There are enough of these around that they should, theoretically, be able to avoid trapping the new nuclear power states in a dependency relationship. The avoidance of this dependency has been one justification, in the past, for states to develop their own capacities. Since this is where the greatest risk of weapons-related proliferation exists, any steps that can be taken to minimize this concern should be implemented.

Done correctly, small reactors should be an example of a technology which facilitates the spread of peaceful nuclear technology, as sought by many nations under what is seen as a guarantee of Article VI of the Nuclear Non-Proliferation Treaty. With suitable support networks, and a competitive commercial market that mitigates against dependency issues, they can be rolled out without necessitating expansion of more troubling fuel-cycle technologies.

Waste Storage

As nuclear power reemerges, the question of waste handling once again must be addressed. Grand solutions (such as the U.S. Yucca Mountain repository or proposals for an international waste storage site) have foundered in the face of local opposition. "Temporary" solutions such as cask storage at the generating sites have evolved into quasi-permanent methods as alternatives fail to emerge. Ensuring the secure and safe handling of waste materials remains a high priority for firms and governments in the nuclear sector.

Finland is leading the way with construction of the world's first geological repository at Onkalo, near the Olkiluoto nuclear facilities where AREVA's first EPR-design reactor is also being constructed. It intends to relocate all its nuclear waste to Onkalo from on-site storage facilities once the waste has cooled sufficiently to be moved (in itself a forty-year process) and has been encased in steel, copper, and clay. Unlike other planned geological storage facilities, including the ill-fated Yucca Mountain project, the local population at Onkalo is heavily dependent on nuclear power and supportive of its use.[10] Replicating its potential elsewhere might be more difficult without similar public acceptance.

The U.S. firm General Atomics is offering a very different method for waste handling. Rather than simply storing nuclear waste and avoiding the expense of reprocessing, they believe that they can build small reactors, similar to those described above, which would use the waste products from normal reactors as their fuel. By reusing existing waste (there is enough for 3,000 such reactors, according to the company's estimates), the reactors would reduce the volume and toxicity of the waste stockpile while producing usable power. This approach is, however, far from implementation. Safety procedures and regulatory approval remain to be worked out, and the high temperatures necessary to run smaller reactors pose difficult engineering challenges. Nonetheless, the notion that nuclear by-products may have some utility, and are not just "waste" to be destroyed or removed as far from civilization as possible, is a healthy change of mindset that could produce more advances in the future.[11]

Another alternative witnessing something of a revival in interest is Mixed Oxide fuel (MOX). Using plutonium from spent reactor fuel and/or from decommissioned weapons mixed with uranium isotopes, MOX has been utilized in Europe (especially France and the UK) for many years. It has been a desirable technology with policy-makers because of its ability to reduce the quantities of waste left over from either conventional nuclear power generation or from military activities. Nevertheless, until recently, the United States has not developed a MOX program. That changed as the result of the 2000 agreement between the United States and Russia to decommission 34 tons of surplus plutonium. With the geological storage option embroiled in political wrangling, the Department of Energy began the construction of a MOX manufacturing plant at Savannah River, South Carolina. It hopes to sell the MOX to nuclear generating utilities for use in reactors converted for MOX use. Once MOX has been through the fuel-cycle, it is unsuitable for reuse or reprocessing. After that, it must be put into storage as with other spent fuels.

Improvements in dealing with nuclear waste would be a huge boon to the nuclear power industry and the nonproliferation movement. Safer, more secure methods of disposing of or reusing nuclear by-products that avoid the creation of extra plutonium should be welcomed by all sides.

An International Fuel Bank

The possibility of an international fuel bank for peaceful nuclear purposes has been bandied about in some circles for a long time. However, the controversy surrounding the Iranian nuclear program has propelled the idea back to the forefront. As the most likely operator and administrator of such a program, it is not particularly surprising that the International Atomic Energy Agency (IAEA) has been one of the strongest proponents of such a system, with Kazakhstan touted as a potential host.[12] The IAEA sees in the idea an opportunity to uphold the organization's objective of spreading peaceful uses of nuclear technology, while removing the risk of proliferation. As the editors of a special edition of *Daedalus* dedicated to the issue of nuclear power and proliferation explain, "Any fuel-cycle arrangement or agreed norm that limits the spread of enrichment and reprocessing technology will greatly circumscribe the proliferation risks associated with expanded nuclear power."[13]

Before we proceed with an investigation into the future of multilateral arrangements for addressing the fuel cycle on an international basis, it should be recognized that bilateral arrangements of a similar nature have been taking place for many years. The Soviet Union (and later Russia) handled enrichment and reprocessing duties for plants in the Eastern bloc where the host was unwilling or unable to take them on, and is uniquely placed to offer full front- and back-end fuel cycle services to customers. Britain and France have sold similar reprocessing services, mostly to Western European operators. Other countries too have carved out niches in the specialized and reasonably lucrative market for responsible handling of nuclear fuel. As a result, a multilateral version will have to overcome not only the political obstacles to its realization, which are not inestimable, but also the economic interests of those being well served by the current market's operation. This covers most commercial operators, especially those in developed democracies with legacies of respectable nuclear conduct. It is less well suited to countries where nuclear technology is seen as a matter of national prestige, where it is feared that outsourcing part of the fuel cycle (such as enrichment) will diminish the esteem in which their nuclear program and their technological development is held.

Of course, countries intent on breaking nonproliferation rules are those with the least interest in international systems, but those the international community is most eager to see bound by them. Iran has shown little but disdain toward proposals of the kind described in detail by Abbas Maleki, that it relinquish its enrichment capabilities in favor of a guaranteed supply stream of low-enriched uranium that can be used as reactor fuel but not further enriched to weapons grade.[14]

The problem with most proposals boils down to the fact that the countries that would deem them acceptable would be well behaved in any event, while potential proliferators will continue to disregard them. With other options constrained, as in the case of Iran, by elements of the international community and the UN Security Council unwilling to harden sanctions or impose additional retaliation, the proposals will have no effect on a determined proliferator. A number of the initiatives that Pierre Goldschmidt, former Deputy Director General and Head of the Department of Safeguards at the IAEA, highlights in his contribution to the special issue of *Daedalus*—multilateral fuel procurement arrangements, multinational enrichment facilities, multilateral fuel supply guarantees, and the "Russian initiative to establish a reserve of low enriched uranium (LEU) for the supply of LEU to IAEA for its member states"—all may have merit as commercial propositions and as guarantees of supply security for fledgling nuclear generators willing to obey the attached conditions.[15] However, they would seem to have little or no impact on a country that has decided that nuclear weapons, not nuclear power, are its objective. Goldschmidt's harshest recommended sanction is to prohibit military equipment sales and cooperation with a proliferator, showing a commendable concern for the welfare of the general public of the noncompliant country, but also showing the hesitancy common when ardent nonproliferation supporters are faced with a determined transgressor.

CONCLUSIONS

What is the foreseeable future of the nuclear industry worldwide?

According to Mycle Schneider, author of the "World Nuclear Industry Status Report," it is not very vibrant.[16] The number of operating nuclear reactors in the world is decreasing: there were 439 in 2008 in thirty-one countries, five fewer than five years before. Total installed capacity—372 gigawatts in 2008—is slightly increasing, however, thanks to technical improvements or "uprating" at existing plants. This corresponds to about 14 percent of the world's commercial electricity, or less than 6 percent of the commercial primary energy.

Estimating "the number of plants that would have to come online over the next several decades simply to maintain the same number of operating plants around the world," Schneider reaches the conclusion that "70 reactors (in addition to the 20 now under construction with a scheduled start-up date) would have to be planned, completed and started up by 2015—one every month and a half—and an additional 192 units over the subsequent decade—or one every 18 days." He believes this is highly unlikely, if not impossible. Schneider's conclusions are that "contrary to the public's perception and the industry's efforts, nuclear power will continue its long-term decline rather than move toward a flourishing future revival."

Several other sources reach similar conclusions. In 2003, a group of Massachusetts Institute of Technology faculty issued a study on the "Future of Nuclear Power" that advocated an increased recourse to nuclear energy in order to mitigate global warming. The last sentence of the 2009 update of that report, issued in May 2009, reads: "The sober warning is that if more is not done, nuclear power will diminish as a practical and timely option for deployment on a scale that would constitute a material contribution to climate change risk mitigation."[17]

Even IAEA notes with concern that "[t]he industrial capacity of nuclear suppliers has generally decreased over the past 20 years. Not only are there fewer reactor designers and less reactor choice, but there are also fewer architect engineers and project management organizations with experience in implementing large nuclear projects . . . . [These difficulties] . . . may constrain growth plans even in some countries with established nuclear programs."[18]

This review shows that an expansion of nuclear power will not significantly alter the dynamics of the nonproliferation and arms reduction debates. Countries willing to behave responsibly can continue to be expected to do so; countries that are determined to break nonproliferation protocols will be able to find ways to do so. Technical and policy innovations should help make nuclear power easier and more affordable for responsible actors; there is little sign, though, that they will be able to stop irresponsible ones. North Korea and Iran have shown that the route to the bomb now goes through the NPT and the access it grants to nuclear technology, rather than around it. These cases also show that it does not take hundreds of new nuclear power plants to shake the foundations of the nonproliferation regime. One or two reactors may suffice.

NOTES

1. See L. Story, "An Oracle of Oil Predicts $200-a-Barrel Crude," *New York Times*, 21 May 2008.

2. J. Kanter, "Not So Fast, Nukes," *New York Times*, 29 May 2009.

3. See J. Kanter, "Rebound of Nuclear Plants Raising Worries over Waste," *International Herald Tribune*, 31 January 2009.

4. See M. L. Wald, "Nuclear Waste Challenge Resurfaces," *International Herald Tribune*, 6 March 2009.

5. Commission of the European Communities, *An Energy Policy for Europe*, COM (2007) 1 final, 10.1.2007, at http://ec.europa.eu/energy/energy_policy/doc/01_energy_policy_for_europe_en.pdf.

6. Energy Information Agency, http://www.eia.doe.gov/emeu/cabs/Canada/Electricity.html.

7. M. Schneider, "2008 World Nuclear Industry Status Report: Western Europe," *Bulletin of the Atomic Scientists*, 19 September 2008.

8. R. Smith, "Small Reactors Generate Big Hopes," *Wall Street Journal*, 18 February 2010.

9. Ibid.

10. J. Kanter, "A Permanent Home for Nuclear Waste?" *New York Times*, 28 May 2009, at http://www.nytimes.com/interactive/2009/05/22/business/energy-environment/20090528_NUCLEAR/index.html.

11. R. Smith, "General Atomics Proposes a Plant That Runs on Nuclear Waste," *Wall Street Journal*, 22 February 2010.

12. J. Weisman and M. Champion, "Kazakhstan Offers Nuclear Fuel Deal to US," *Wall Street Journal*, 5 April 2009.

13. S. Miller and S. Sagan, "Nuclear Power without Nuclear Proliferation?" *Daedalus* 138, no. 4 (Fall 2009): 15.

14. A. Maleki, "Iran's Nuclear File," *Daedalus* 139, no. 4 (Winter 2010): 108–9.

15. P. Goldschmidt, "Multilateral Nuclear Fuel Guarantees & Spent Fuel Management," *Daedalus* 139, no. 4 (Winter 2010).

16. See M. Schneider, "2008 World Nuclear Industry Status Report: Global Nuclear Power," *Bulletin of the Atomic Scientists*, 16 September 2008.

17. The 2003 MIT report and its 2009 update are available at http://web.mit.edu/nuclearpower.

18. *International Status and Prospects of Nuclear Power* (Vienna: International Atomic Energy Agency, 2008), p. 3. For more analysis, see S. Squassoni, *Nuclear Energy: Rebirth or Resuscitation*, Carnegie Endowment for International Peace, http://www.carnegieendowment.org/files/nuclear_energy_rebirth_resuscitation.pdf.

16 Nuclear Abolition or Nuclear Umbrella? Choices and Contradictions in U.S. Proposals

Matthew Evangelista

Deterrence continues to be a relevant consideration for many states with regard to threats from other states. But reliance on nuclear weapons for this purpose is becoming increasingly hazardous and decreasingly effective.
—George P. Shultz, William J. Perry, Henry A. Kissinger, and Sam Nunn, "A World Free of Nuclear Weapons," *Wall Street Journal*, January 4, 2007

Although not suited for every 21st century challenge, nuclear weapons remain an essential element in modern strategy.
—*National Security and Nuclear Weapons in the 21st Century*, White Paper, U.S. departments of Defense and Energy, September 2008

The subtitle to Stanley Kubrick's 1964 film classic, *Dr. Strangelove*, is "How I Learned to Stop Worrying and Love the Bomb." This black comedy, starring Peter Sellers in three different roles, depicted a world gone crazy with exaggerated fears and far-fetched strategies for coping with them—most notoriously the Doomsday Machine, a Soviet device to launch nuclear Armageddon automatically in the event of a perceived attack from the United States. The film's main conceit stems from the fact that the Doomsday Machine could not serve its purpose of deterring such an attack, because the Soviet leaders neglected to tell their U.S. counterparts of its existence. In this respect *Dr. Strangelove* distilled an element of real-world nuclear politics: just two years earlier the actual Soviet leadership had kept secret the presence of Soviet nuclear weapons in Cuba, rendering them incapable of deterring U.S. action, and instead triggering a serious international crisis. Kubrick's work, considered a masterpiece of comic invention, reflected reality in other respects. The script was in fact based on the musings of professional nuclear strategists, many housed at the

RAND Corporation in Santa Monica, California. One may hesitate to claim that the RAND strategists *loved* the Bomb, but they certainly found it useful for the wide range of tasks, related to U.S. foreign and security policy, about which they worried.[1] Others—members of the public, citizens and leaders of foreign countries, scholars, and intellectuals—worried more about the Bomb itself, in particular, the proliferation of nuclear weapons in the arsenals of the so-called superpowers and of the arcane strategies for their use. They advocated nuclear arms control and disarmament and changes in strategy, such as pledges of "no first use" and the de-alerting of nuclear systems, intended to forestall the doomsday scenario depicted in Kubrick's movie.

The current situation resembles the era of *Dr. Strangelove* in two regards. There are still people who express concern about the dangers of nuclear proliferation—mainly to countries without existing nuclear arsenals and to terrorist groups—and there are still people who harbor ambitious objectives for the use of nuclear weapons. And some people, including many proponents of the long-term goal of a nuclear-free world, appear to do both: they are worried about the Bomb, but, for certain purposes, they continue to love it.

In the first decade of the twenty-first century the call for nuclear disarmament and a move toward "nuclear zero" has come from an unlikely source: four former U.S. officials—William Perry, Sam Nunn, George Shultz, and Henry Kissinger—with close ties to the Cold War nuclear strategists. Indeed Kissinger, the most famous member of the foursome, was a long-time consultant to RAND and the author of an early influential work of nuclear strategy, which advocated a prominent role for nuclear weapons in the defense of Western Europe.[2] One cannot say that such former U.S. officials have become worried about nuclear weapons only recently, however. They always expressed concern about *other* countries' nuclear weapons—particularly those of the Soviet Union, sometimes those of China, and, however briefly, even those of France. But the policies they pursued in the furtherance of their understanding of U.S. foreign and security interests suggested that they were not worried about *U.S.* nuclear weapons. Rather they valued those nuclear weapons as central to resolving U.S. security problems, and they developed strategies for nuclear use in a wide range of contingencies. Many of those contingencies—such as deterrence of an attack against European allies or discouraging China from settling its dispute with Taiwan by force—remain a part of U.S. military policy, and, as such, they pose a major barrier to nuclear disarmament.

The key element that prompted the four former officials to launch their nuclear disarmament initiative was a worry that "the deadliest weapons ever invented could fall into dangerous hands," as they put it in the opening paragraph of their *Wall Street Journal* article of January 15, 2008, a year after they announced their original appeal in the same newspaper.[3] The implication is that nuclear weapons have been in safe hands since their invention in 1945, even though those hands dropped atomic bombs on Hiroshima and Nagasaki, killing tens of thousands of innocents; came close to nuclear war over Cuba in 1962; put nuclear weapons on high alert during the 1973 Middle East War; and blundered into numerous hair-raising accidents and mistakes in handling nuclear weapons, some as recently as 2007, others in the distant past—their occurrence discovered in formerly secret documents and through interviews.[4] Even aside from the military use and near-use of nuclear weapons since 1945, the process of mining and enriching uranium, creating plutonium, manufacturing the weapons components, and testing the weapons in the atmosphere and underground posed life-threatening risks to many thousands of people and devastated the natural environment. None of this seemed to worry the custodians of the nuclear arsenals, who gave every indication of having instead come to Love the Bomb—as long as it seemed to them to enhance U.S. security.

Now they worry, because the Bomb could fall into dangerous hands and put U.S. security at risk. As the second paragraph of the 2008 *Wall Street Journal* article explains, paraphrasing the one a year earlier, "[W]ith nuclear weapons more widely available, deterrence is decreasingly effective and increasingly hazardous."[5] In releasing his administration's *Nuclear Posture Review* in April 2010, President Barack Obama articulated the same concerns. The review, he argued, "recognizes that the greatest threat to U.S. and global security is no longer a nuclear exchange between nations, but nuclear terrorism by violent extremists and nuclear proliferation to an increasing number of states."[6] The main concern of the former officials and the current president is, not surprisingly, for the effectiveness of U.S. deterrence. Rhetorically eliding "U.S. and global security," as the president did, will not convince everyone that they are the same thing. And as long as the initiative for a nuclear-free world gives priority to U.S. security, it will not make much of an impression on states that aspire to obtain nuclear weapons, let alone on terrorist groups, which are presumably undeterred by the traditional remedy of nuclear retaliation.

In the pages that follow, I describe the barriers to achieving nuclear disarmament posed by U.S. policy. They include: (1) that, despite changes announced by President Obama, the United States continues to depend on the threat of nuclear retaliation—often called "extended deterrence" or the quaintly nonsensical "nuclear umbrella"—to serve a wide range of security concerns; and (2) that the "nuclear zero" initiative provides no way of addressing the security concerns of the countries to which it is intended to deny nuclear weapons. Although the first steps toward nuclear zero seem promising—working with Russia and the other members of the nuclear club in the framework of traditional arms control to reduce their arsenals—even here there are serious difficulties. U.S. policy toward ballistic missile defense and the expansion of the North Atlantic Treaty Organization risk undermining cooperation with Russia and limits the possibilities for Russian reductions in nuclear weapons.

Even if these first steps are successful—convincing the acknowledged nuclear-weapon states to begin the process of disarmament—what would be the next steps in the absence of cooperation by the aspiring nuclear-weapons states, such as Iran and North Korea? Stopping those states from acquiring or accumulating nuclear weapons would then require coercive measures such as economic sanctions or military action. The nuclear-free initiative begins to look like a ploy by the dominant nuclear powers to rally support for such measures without seeming too hypocritical. The second part of the chapter takes up this issue by considering U.S. objectives in pursuing nuclear zero.

The third part of the chapter draws on historical experiences to suggest some alternative means to move toward nuclear disarmament by connecting the nuclear predicament to the broader security environment. The end of the Cold War in Europe came when the rationale for deployment of nuclear weapons disappeared. Initiatives on the part of the Soviet Union—such as unilateral reductions in its offensively oriented armed forces and political liberalization within the Soviet bloc—removed the threat of major conventional war in central Europe. Thus it was no longer necessary for the United States to pose the risk of nuclear escalation to deter such a war. Scholars and activists had prepared the groundwork for the changes that ended the Cold War arms race by explicitly proposing initiatives that would take account of the links between conventional and nuclear war. Prospects for a successful "nuclear zero" initiative will also need to take account of the links between nuclear weapons and broader security concerns—not only for the nuclear "haves," but also the nuclear "have-nots" and the nuclear "wannabes."

The end of the nuclear arms race between the United States and the Soviet Union is owed not only to the material changes, such as withdrawal of Soviet armed forces from central Europe, but also to ideational ones. The top leadership in the two countries—most notably Ronald Reagan and Mikhail Gorbachev—endorsed concepts such as "common security," where one side's security does not come at the expense of the other's. They publicly expressed their antipathy to nuclear weapons. Their views reflected widespread public revulsion and alarm at the prospect of nuclear war. Nuclear disarmament will become easier to achieve if leaders of the countries that have deployed nuclear weapons actively contribute to stigmatizing their possession and use—the focus of the final part of the chapter. To do so, they will have to face the contradictions in their existing strategies and make a choice between keeping their nuclear umbrellas and pursuing nuclear abolition.

THE PURPOSES OF NUCLEAR WEAPONS

Before considering how to get rid of nuclear weapons, we should review why they exist. The common answer is "deterrence," and the common follow-up question is "how much is enough?" to achieve it. When we think about nuclear weapons, however, the most important question should not be "how many?" but "what for?" We typically think of deterrence as the threat of retaliation with nuclear weapons by one country to forestall a nuclear attack by another. This is only one narrow category of deterrence, however, and it usually requires an adjective to specify its constrained role: *limited*, *minimum*, *finite*, or *existential* are the ones often attached. Beyond this limited purpose for nuclear weapons, the United States has pursued many far more ambitious ones. One of the most important purposes of U.S. nuclear weapons has been to deter war against U.S. allies or military conflict that implicates U.S. interests abroad but does not pose a threat of nuclear attack against the United States itself. Such purposes typically fall under the designation *extended deterrence*. Without addressing head-on the purposes of U.S. possession and planned use of nuclear weapons, many of the well-meaning discussions about how to reduce nuclear arsenals are beside the point. Experts who write about such topics as "redefining deterrence" without posing the question "deterrence of what?" are missing a key element of the picture.[7]

If we consider the history of nuclear weapons and U.S. policy we can see that from the beginning the United States deployed nuclear weapons for purposes that went far beyond the deterrence of a nuclear attack against itself. The United States developed the first atomic bombs during World War II initially in response to fears that Nazi Germany would do so. In that respect the new weapons might have been considered a deterrent to Germany's prospective use. But Germany was defeated before it developed a nuclear weapons capability. Following the end of the European war, the U.S. government used two atomic weapons against the Japanese cities of Hiroshima and Nagasaki in August 1945. Their purpose was not deterrence, but actual *use* in the service of what later became known as "compellence"—dropping the bombs was intended to compel the Japanese authorities to surrender quickly and perhaps to influence the policy of the Soviet Union.[8]

For the next four years, the United States held an atomic monopoly, and following the first Soviet atomic test in August 1949 it continued to maintain a monopoly on "deliverable" weapons into the early 1950s. By definition U.S. development, production, and deployment of atomic weapons during this period served not to deter the threat of nuclear attack by other countries—because no other countries could mount such an attack—but a variety of other purposes. The United States deployed "atomic-capable" B-29 bombers to Europe during the Berlin Crisis, for example, to signal resolve to the Soviet Union. It developed a worldwide system of air bases, planned already during the later stages of World War II (and without a specific postwar enemy in mind), and eventually used it to surround the USSR with nuclear-armed aircraft.[9] One of the purposes was to deter the Soviet Union from starting a war. U.S. leaders during the late 1940s justified monopoly possession of nuclear weapons as a counter to what they claimed was a Soviet superiority in conventionally armed forces poised to pour across the borders of the USSR in pursuit of worldwide military conquest. The security of Western Europe was a particular focus of concern. Even though declassified documents have made it clear that U.S. analysts and political figures overestimated the strength of Soviet forces in the immediate postwar era, perceptions of Soviet conventional superiority served as a justification for a U.S. policy of extended nuclear deterrence—the threat of U.S. nuclear attack against the Soviet Union to deter that country from invading Western Europe.[10]

Much of the subsequent development of U.S. nuclear strategy and weapons was premised on the need to bolster the credibility of extended deterrence—for example, to allay doubts that the United States would risk global nuclear devastation to protect its European allies. To that end, the United States deployed thousands of so-called tactical nuclear weapons into Europe starting in the early 1950s. But U.S. nuclear weapons had roles to play beyond Europe as well. In the early 1980s, for example, following the Iranian Revolution and the Soviet invasion of Afghanistan, the United States made increasingly explicit threats to escalate to the level of nuclear war in the event that a hostile power seeking militarily to deny U.S. access to oil supplies could not be defeated by conventional forces.[11] In the Pacific region, the United States has deployed nuclear weapons and employed nuclear threats for a variety of purposes over the decades: to influence China's policies toward Taiwan, to deter North Korean aggression against the South, and—however chimerical—to bolster the prospects for U.S. success in its disastrous war against Vietnam.[12]

To the extent that the United States still relies on nuclear weapons for a range of purposes associated with extended deterrence, it will be harder to move toward a nuclear-free world. Historically the U.S. Department of Defense has accorded nuclear weapons both a deterrent role and a "war-fighting" role in the event of military conflict. As late as May 2009 a doctrinal document from the U.S. Air Force, for example, stressed the importance of using nuclear weapons as a deterrent against countries suspected of developing chemical or biological weapons.[13] In April 2010, President Obama rejected this particular role for nuclear deterrence, when he declared that "we will not use or threaten to use nuclear weapons against non-nuclear weapons states that are party to the Nuclear Non-Proliferation Treaty and in compliance with their nuclear non-proliferation obligations."[14] Even limited to nuclear-armed states, and countries such as Iran and North Korea, which the United States does not consider to be in compliance with the NPT, U.S. military policy for nuclear war is still ambitious. Perhaps battle plans will change in response to Obama's commitment "to reduce the role of nuclear weapons in our national security strategy." But as it stands, the Pentagon intends to use nuclear weapons not only at the "strategic" level against countries that have attacked the United States, but also "in support of theater objectives" during an ongoing military conflict. Such use would have both military and political objectives, as the U.S. Air Force's doctrinal statement describes: "While the use of nuclear weapons will affect an ongoing engagement between friendly and enemy forces, their use should also be designed to help achieve the political goals of the operation." The document claims that "the law of armed conflict does not expressly prohibit the possession or use of nuclear weapons," and although "the destruction wrought by nuclear weapons can be immense," it can also "be tailored and limited for a particular scenario."[15]

For many decades, such U.S. plans for "tailored" and "limited," as well as massive, use of nuclear weapons have coincided with an inhibition on the part of U.S. leaders actually to resort to nuclear war—something Nina Tannenwald has described as the "nuclear taboo."[16] The political reluctance to launch a nuclear attack rests uneasily with the detailed military planning for doing so. The political commitment to *use* nuclear weapons in defense of allies rests uneasily with the goal of a nuclear-free world, even if Obama limited that commitment to defense of allies menaced by a nuclear-armed state.

As former and current U.S. leaders endorsed "nuclear zero," they still maintained and frequently reiterated a commitment to deter attacks against U.S. allies by threat of nuclear retaliation. That commitment is captured in the expression "nuclear umbrella," which so readily trips off the tongues of both supporters and opponents of moving toward a nuclear-free world. In a May 2009 article in the *Wall Street Journal*, for example, William Perry, a signatory of the original call for zero nuclear weapons, wrote with two other former U.S. officials that "an effective strategy to reduce nuclear dangers must build on five pillars: revitalizing strategic dialogue with nuclear-armed powers, particularly Russia and China; strengthening the international nuclear non-proliferation regime; reaffirming the protection of the U.S. nuclear umbrella to our allies; maintaining the credibility of the U.S. nuclear deterrent; and implementing best security practices for nuclear weapons and weapons-usable materials worldwide."[17] In a response in the same newspaper the following month, Richard Perle, a former Defense Department official, and Republican senator Jon Kyl criticized President Obama's commitment to a nuclear-free world for, among other things, its effect on "allies who may one day lose confidence in our nuclear umbrella."[18]

The criticism of Obama was misplaced. The U.S. president has regularly reasserted his country's commitment to use nuclear weapons to deter attacks against various countries, and some of his fellow Democrats have proposed additional commitments. In June 2009, for example, Senator John Kerry, chair of the Senate Foreign Relations Committee, suggested in an interview with London's *Financial Times* that "Israel should be included under the U.S.'s nuclear umbrella."[19] That same month, at a summit meeting in Washington, DC, with South Korean president Lee Myung-bak, Obama reaffirmed that the U.S. security commitment to the Republic of Korea included a nuclear component. As the Korean president put it at the joint press conference, "President Obama reaffirmed this firm commitment towards ensuring the security of South Korea through extended deterrence, which includes the nuclear umbrella." Both presidents vowed that North Korea should not be allowed to possess nuclear weapons.[20] To illustrate the possible consequences of the U.S. commitment to use nuclear weapons in defense of South Korea, and to deny those weapons to its northern neighbor, the *Korea Times* accompanied its article about the summit meeting with an illustration titled "Possible US Nuclear Umbrella Scenario." It depicted a map of the Korean peninsula, with B-52 bombers, F-117 "stealth" bombers, carrier-based aircraft, tactical nuclear-armed missiles, and 155 mm artillery pieces all carrying out a nuclear attack on a spot on the map not too far north of the border between North and South Korea.[21] Whether or not the illustration reflected accurately what weapons the United States might use in a nuclear attack in the region, it represented a rare depiction of the meaning of the anodyne expression "nuclear umbrella."

The dual approach of pursuing nuclear disarmament while issuing commitments of extended deterrence and expanding the "nuclear umbrella" constitutes official U.S. policy. In his speech in Prague in April 2009, announcing his administration's support for a nuclear-free world, President Obama, for example, promised simultaneously to "reduce the role of nuclear weapons in our national security strategy" and extend the nuclear deterrent to the Czech Republic as a member of NATO: "Make no mistake," he cautioned. "As long as these weapons exist, the United States will maintain a safe, secure and effective arsenal to deter any adversary, and guarantee that defense to our allies—including the Czech Republic."[22] He repeated nearly the same words a year later when releasing the Nuclear Posture Review.

President Obama explicitly connected the U.S. commitment to defend the Czech Republic, including with nuclear weapons, to the North Atlantic Treaty: "NATO's Article V states it clearly: An attack on one is an attack on all. That is a promise for our time, and for all time." During the last year of the Bush administration, especially following the military conflict between the Russian Federation and the Republic of Georgia in August 2008, the issue of extending NATO membership to Georgia and to Ukraine came to the fore. To the degree that the Obama administration pursues the expansion of NATO to those two countries, both of which border Russia, it will further complicate the prospects for nuclear disarmament. Would the United States and its allies be tempted to resurrect the arcane system of extended deterrence that characterized NATO's Cold War nuclear strategy, with its various "steps" along the "escalation ladder" to achieve "escalation dominance," and its thousands of "tactical" nuclear weapons deployed on European soil?

This is the sort of situation for which the term "Strangelovian" was coined—and today's situation is not so different, given the purposes that nuclear weapons continue to fulfill in U.S. security policy, despite official endorsement of a nuclear-free future. Especially in the wake of Obama's speech in Prague, however, numerous observers began to call into question the role of tactical nuclear weapons stationed in Europe, and, in some cases, the merits of extended nuclear deterrence.[23] In announcing the Nuclear Posture Review in April 2010, Obama chose not to address the weapons in Europe, promising instead to consult with U.S. allies about them.[24]

U.S. INTEREST IN A NUCLEAR-FREE WORLD

In Obama's Prague speech the president described U.S. interest in preventing further countries from developing nuclear weapons and stressed the importance of the Nuclear Non-Proliferation Treaty. "The basic bargain," he claimed, "is sound: Countries with nuclear weapons will move towards disarmament, countries without nuclear weapons will not acquire them." But he stressed the need for better enforcement measures for countries in the latter category: "We need real and immediate consequences for countries caught breaking the rules or trying to leave the treaty without cause." Specifically, "[V]iolations must be punished." Even more specifically, "[We] must stand shoulder to shoulder to pressure the North Koreans to change course" and deal with the "real threat" posed by "Iran's nuclear and ballistic missile activity." Finally, he argued, "[We] must ensure that terrorists never acquire a nuclear weapon," a possibility that he described as "the most immediate and extreme threat to global security."

Thus, the Obama administration's motives for seeking a nuclear-free world echo those of the original proposal from Perry, Nunn, Shultz, and Kissinger. Unlike them—and in a rare, if not unprecedented, acknowledgment for a U.S. president—Obama allowed that "as the only nuclear power to have used a nuclear weapon, the United States has a moral responsibility to act." Although Obama claimed, at another point in his speech, that "moral leadership is more powerful than any weapon," his administration remains concerned about nuclear weapons in dangerous hands. It is intent on denying such weapons to North Korea, Iran, and terrorist groups. But his critics have wondered how initiatives on the way to a nuclear-free world, such as U.S. ratification of the Comprehensive Nuclear Test Ban Treaty, would achieve that goal. Would U.S. ratification of the test ban treaty make North Korea, Iran, or al Qaeda any less interested in obtaining nuclear arms?[25]

A key argument that proponents of nuclear zero summon is that taking such near-term initiatives helps address the fact, as Perry, Nunn, Shultz, and Kissinger wrote, that "non-nuclear weapon states have grown increasingly skeptical of the sincerity of the nuclear powers" in their commitments under the Non-proliferation Treaty to move toward nuclear disarmament.[26] The problem is—as Kyl, Perle, and other critics point out—that professions of U.S. sincerity are unlikely to dissuade Iran or North Korea (let alone al Qaeda) from their nuclear ambitions. By ratifying the Comprehensive Test Ban and even negotiating deeper reductions with Russia, the United States could render its position less hypocritical on the matter of nuclear disarmament, but that will not be enough to achieve the main goal that motivates the nuclear zero initiative: the fear of nuclear weapons in the hands of "irresponsible" states or groups.[27] Moreover, to the extent that U.S. security policy still relies on nuclear weapons for a variety of purposes—not least to threaten (deter) states such as North Korea and Iran—that policy will still be seen to embody a double standard. Critics will understand the U.S. rhetorical commitment to a nuclear-free world, and even the intermediate steps in that direction, as a means to summon an international consensus to punish the states that refuse to go along.

The crux of the matter is that the United States pursues two contradictory paths to reducing the threat of nuclear weapons in "dangerous hands." The first is embracing nuclear disarmament as a long-term goal. The second is maintaining nuclear weapons and nuclear deterrence until that goal is achieved. In an interview with the *New York Times*, President Obama made the point with characteristic clarity: "We will retain our deterrent capacity as long as there is a country with nuclear weapons."[28] Thus, in Obama's lights, the last step to a nuclear-free world would be U.S. monopoly possession of nuclear weapons. This, however, is a world we have already experienced. Monopoly possession of atomic weapons by the United States in the second half of the 1940s served as an inducement, not a deterrent, to other countries' acquisition of nuclear arsenals. The disarmament scheme premised on the U.S. atomic monopoly—the Baruch Plan—demonstrably failed. Only when other states, most notably the Soviet Union, had built their own nuclear capabilities, were they willing to negotiate restrictions.

It is not difficult to draw the historical parallels to the era of U.S. atomic monopoly and the arms control negotiations of the Cold War. Why would Iran or North Korea forgo the nuclear option given their current security predicaments? A look at the map shows Iran effectively surrounded by nuclear-armed states: Pakistan on its eastern border, India just beyond, Russia to the north, Israel to the west, and the United States with aircraft carriers and nuclear-armed submarines deployed in the Persian Gulf, Mediterranean Sea, and Indian Ocean, as well as the global reach of its land-based intercontinental missiles. The *Korean Times* article about the U.S. nuclear umbrella presents a good approximation of the nuclear threat posed to North Korea, without even taking into account the nuclear arsenals of neighboring Russia and China.

The security environment that confronts Iran and North Korea, and the incentives they face in making judgments about their nuclear options, are obvious to many well-informed international observers. In an interview with the British Broadcasting Corporation, for example, Mohamed El Baradei, then head of the International Atomic Energy Agency, "told the BBC that countries with nuclear weapons were treated differently to those without. He said North Korea, with a bomb, was invited to the conference table, while Saddam Hussein's Iraq, without one, was—as he put it—pulverised." Regarding Iranian motives, he said, "[It] is my gut feeling that Iran would like to have the technology to enable it to have nuclear weapons, if it decides to do so." The Iranians, in his view, "want to send a message to their neighbours, to the rest of the world, don't mess with us." Even recognizing the incentives for Iran to obtain a nuclear weapons capability, El Baradei offered as a solution that the nuclear "haves" take the initiative: "The only safe future, he said, was widespread nuclear disarmament led by the existing nuclear powers."[29] As long as Iran and North Korea perceive those existing nuclear powers—the United States, in particular—as hostile, they are unlikely to disarm first on the promise of future disarmament by their adversaries. But that seems to be the only plan on offer by the Americans.

RELATING NUCLEAR DISARMAMENT TO BROADER SECURITY CONCERNS

Previous efforts at nuclear disarmament suggest that states achieve progress only when they take other states' security concerns into account. During the Cold War that meant U.S. acknowledgment that the Soviet Union would insist on achieving "parity" with the United States before it would pursue mutual reductions. A more significant reduction of the nuclear threat came with the end of the Cold War and the East-West conflict, when the governments on both sides—spurred by nongovernmental organizations and popular movements—recognized the interconnection of security issues with political concerns, including human rights.[30] A key turning point came when the reformist Soviet leadership of Mikhail Gorbachev acknowledged the effect on U.S. and

NATO nuclear policy of the large Soviet conventional armed presence in central Europe and the role that the Soviet Army had played in bolstering the rule of communist parties in the region. Gorbachev's unilateral initiatives—such as deep reductions and restructuring of conventional forces, a halt to Soviet nuclear testing, and an acknowledgment of "freedom of choice" in the domestic political order of the East European states—paved the way to the end of the Cold War and the prospect for further reductions in nuclear weapons. Although Ronald Reagan was sympathetic to the goal of abolishing nuclear weapons, his successors were more skeptical and squandered an opportunity to achieve more dramatic progress. Nevertheless, that the United States and Russia ceased to consider each other mortal enemies in a nuclear stand-off constituted a major achievement.

Picking up where Gorbachev and Reagan left off—an explicit goal of Shultz, Perry, Kissinger, and Nunn, articulated in their first *Wall Street Journal* article—is a sensible first step toward achieving nuclear disarmament. Yet the fact that Russia and the United States are no longer the leaders of rival military alliances does not mean there are no security concerns that could complicate the prospects for nuclear disarmament. Indeed, the Russian government has made clear two of those concerns: the continued expansion of NATO, and U.S. plans, promoted by the administration of George W. Bush, to deploy components of a missile defense system in Eastern Europe, ostensibly to defeat an attack from Iran. Russian officials expressed concern about the system and doubts about the rationale.

Regardless of what one thinks of NATO and of the merits of extending security guarantees to countries along Russia's border with which Moscow has conflictual relations, no one can plausibly argue that NATO expansion enhances the prospects for nuclear disarmament. The Russian armed forces have to plan for the contingency of war, and if they contemplate a war with states allied to a nuclear-armed United States, they must also contemplate the use of nuclear weapons. The continued expansion of NATO—both the eastward expansion and the expansion into a worldwide military force for so-called out of area missions—will hinder nuclear disarmament, much as the deployment of large, offensively oriented conventional forces did during the Cold War. Few countries, Russia included, are going to be willing to give up their nuclear weapons if the United States continues to flaunt its global dominance in conventional military forces.

On missile defense, Moscow still sees the connection between nuclear defense and disarmament in pretty much the traditional way it was understood during the Cold War. One side's deployment of defenses undermines the deterrent effects of the other side's retaliatory nuclear offensive forces. The Russian public interpretation of U.S. plans for missile defense in Eastern Europe held that they were directed against Russia and, in former president Putin's words, would "upset the balance" of nuclear forces. Russian analysts suggested the new deployments were intended to neutralize Russia's capability to launch a retaliatory nuclear attack against Europe if Russia faced a nuclear attack from the West. Secretary of State Condoleezza Rice dismissed these concerns as "ludicrous." In fact, the proposed deployments in the Czech Republic and Poland were not well suited for their stated mission of defending Europe from an Iranian attack; if upgraded, they would have been more effective in hindering a Russian missile attack. In response to the announcement of U.S. deployment plans, Putin proposed to the Bush administration more cooperative means of dealing with a potential Iranian threat, including sharing data from Russian radar systems and even joint operation of early-warning centers in Moscow and Brussels.[31] The Bush administration preferred its own plan. In November 2008, following the election of Barack Obama, Defense Secretary Robert Gates dismissed Putin's offer out of hand rather than let the new administration make its own decision.[32]

The incoming Democratic administration did, in fact, revise the Republican decision—substituting for it one that it described as more plausible from a security standpoint. In the process it opened the possibility for new sites for deployment in Eastern Europe and a redistribution of the contracts to a new set of military industrial firms within the United States.[33]

Although the change in policy on missile defense offered an opportunity to try to address Russian security concerns, Obama's advisers seemed to go out of their way not to do so, even in the interest of negotiating reductions in nuclear arms. As Michael McFaul of the National Security Council staff insisted in July 2009, "[We're] not going to reassure or give or trade anything with the Russians regarding NATO expansion or missile defence."[34] The proposal offered at NATO's Lisbon summit in November 2010 to cooperate with Russia on missile defense suggests a departure from such an obstinate approach. Russia is still, however, likely to find the prospect of missile-defense components in Romania and Poland troubling.

Russia is the easy problem, however, compared to addressing the security concerns of Iran and North Korea. Resolution of the conflict with those two countries may have to await changes in their internal policies, much as the Soviet reforms of the *perestroika* era combined domestic and international change. But as in the Soviet case, the United States must be prepared to recognize genuine initiatives toward reconciliation when they appear. In Prague, President Obama expressed such readiness when he stated that his "administration will seek engagement with Iran based on mutual interests and mutual respect. We believe in dialogue." That line received warm applause compared to his earlier threat to punish violators of the nonproliferation regime. His Czech audience also reacted positively to the prospect that "if the Iranian threat is eliminated, we will have a stronger basis for security, and the driving force for missile defense construction in Europe will be removed." That prospect, however distant, would simultaneously remove one of the barriers to nuclear reductions with Russia. In his June 2009 press conference with the South Korean president, Obama indicated that there "is another path available to North Korea" as well, "a path that leads to peace and economic opportunity for the people of North Korea, including full integration into the community of nations. That destination can only be reached through peaceful negotiations that achieve the full and verifiable denuclearization of the Korean peninsula."[35] The United States is presumably not prepared to put its own nuclear arsenal on the table during such negotiations. Under the circumstances, one may doubt whether the North Korean leadership sees the negotiations as fully "peaceful," when they are conducted under the shadow of the "nuclear umbrella" that the United States extends to its South Korean ally.

The end of the Cold War and the East-West arms race took many observers by surprise. But the proposals that led to the withdrawal of hundreds of thousands of troops from central Europe and substantial reductions in nuclear weapons were many decades in the making. Peace researchers and activists in the United States and Europe worked with their counterparts in the Soviet Union to promote initiatives for restructuring and reduction of military forces and respect for human rights.[36] Sympathetic diplomats and political leaders incorporated many of the ideas into their policies. Today's security challenges seem no less daunting, and the solutions will have to be equally creative and bold.

THE NORMATIVE CONTEXT FOR NUCLEAR DISARMAMENT

Many observers have noted the antipathy toward nuclear weapons that Ronald Reagan shared with Mikhail Gorbachev. These weapons, in order to achieve their deterrent effect, must inspire terror, and they did so by threat of mass destruction of innocent life—even if civilians were not deliberate targets. More than a half-century ago a prominent strategist of the RAND Corporation referred to the U.S.-Soviet nuclear stand-off as a "delicate balance of terror."[37] A quarter-century after that, U.S. and Soviet leaders, fearing that the balance might not be adequate to prevent a nuclear war, thought about the dreadful consequences. In the case of Reagan and Gorbachev that thinking spurred them to action in the cause of nuclear disarmament. They were undoubtedly influenced by the fact that people worldwide shared their fear, and at certain points in history many of them protested against nuclear arms in large numbers. Research has suggested that a prerequisite for meaningful limitations on nuclear weapons has been popular mobilization, and that fear and a sense that political leaders are acting irresponsibly tended to fuel that mobilization.[38] Public reaction to the threat of radioactive fall-out from the massive nuclear tests in the 1950s and the near catastrophe of the Cuban Missile Crisis, for example, contributed toward the first achievements in arms control, such as the Limited Test Ban Treaty. Loose talk by members of the Reagan administration about fighting and winning a nuclear war, combined with a worsening of U.S.-Soviet relations in the 1980s, spurred a worldwide peace movement that inspired Gorbachev's initiatives and gave him some hope that they would be well received.[39] The overall normative context included a stigmatization of nuclear weapons as dangerous and potentially genocidal, no matter who owned them.

A deliberate and forthright condemnation of nuclear weapons by the leaders of the nuclear-armed states could make an important contribution to the prospects for global nuclear disarmament. President Obama made a gesture in that direction by acknowledging U.S. moral responsibility for the atomic bombings of Hiroshima and Nagasaki—implicitly recognizing as morally dubious the disproportionate killing of innocents even in the service of a just cause. Many observers have likened the process of nuclear disarmament, or the more ambitious goal of abolishing war, to the abolition of slavery.[40] Tannenwald has argued that the use of nuclear weapons has already attained the status of a taboo, but that no such stigma attaches to the possession of nuclear weapons, nor to the planning for their use. She argues that the taboo against use could be strengthened by what she calls "virtual abolition schemes" entailing changes in "habit, attitude, norms, law." These might include international pledges of "no first use" of nuclear weapons and criminalization of the use of nuclear weapons, with threats of war-crimes trials of leaders who violate the prohibition.[41] President Obama's commitment of April 2010 not to use U.S.

nuclear weapons against (most) non-nuclear states, however welcome, does not constitute a "virtual abolition scheme" in Tannenwald's sense.

The logic of such proposals assumes that the more a practice is considered morally abhorrent the less likely it is to recur. The process of nuclear disarmament would be bolstered if the leaders of states that possess nuclear weapons not only rejected their use, but apologized for their acquisition and possession. As it stands, their current position—advocating disarmament but retaining the threat of nuclear annihilation—undermines the goal of a nuclear-free world. Imagine if leaders instead emphasized only the negative side of nuclear weapons: the tremendous economic and environmental costs they have imposed over the decades, and even on future generations (if one considers the legacy of genetic damage caused by radioactive fallout); the near misses from accidents and during Cold War crises, and what the consequences might have been had those crises triggered a war; and what the consequences will be if even a small fraction of the world's current nuclear arsenal is used. Consider again the parallel to the abolition of slavery. No one doubts that any country that harbors slave-traders, or individuals found to enslave others, would be subject to unqualified condemnation. No one would argue that one should balance such condemnation against the economic or psychological benefits that accrue to slave-holders. Why should nuclear weapons be treated any differently?

If the possession of nuclear weapons were universally stigmatized, many of the problems that arise in discussions of the merits of nuclear zero would diminish in significance. Consider the problem of verification, and the concern—often associated with Jerome Wiesner, MIT professor and science adviser to President John F. Kennedy—that as fewer nuclear weapons exist the ones that remain become more significant. This formulation applies when countries treat nuclear weapons as valuable additions to their arsenals. But what if they treat them rather as stigmatized instruments of genocide which call forth universal condemnation? On the topic of verifying "nuclear zero," Andrew Mack has pointed to the potential role of whistle-blowers as a way of preventing cheating on a disarmament agreement: "No state that contemplated reneging on its disarmament commitments could be certain that its transgression would not be revealed *from within*. If just one individual refused to go along with the deception, all would be revealed." He points to several familiar cases: "Israel's nuclear-weapons programme had its Mordechai Vanunu, Russia's chemical-weapons plans had their Vil S. Mirzayanov, and Saddam Hussein had his defector son-in-law, Hussein Kamel Hassan."[42] One could imagine that the prospect of whistle-blowing would be even more threatening to potential violators if the weapons in question were publicly condemned by all of the world's leaders and held in revulsion by all of the world's citizens.

The stigmatization of nuclear weapons to the extent that no country would admit to desiring them may seem an unrealistic goal. The history of prior abolition movements, as well as the evidence from moderate successes in arms control during the Cold War, suggest that a prerequisite for such a significant change may be popular mass mobilization contributing to a gradual evolution in the normative context. Unless people experience the right combination of fear and hope, they may not be willing to act. If instead, along with Dr. Strangelove, we stop worrying and learn again to Love the Bomb, our prospects for achieving nuclear disarmament will diminish.

NOTES

1. Fred Kaplan, *The Wizards of Armageddon* (New York: Simon and Schuster, 1983).

2. Henry A. Kissinger, *Nuclear Weapons and Foreign Policy* (New York: Harper, 1957).

3. George P. Shultz, William J. Perry, Henry A. Kissinger, and Sam Nunn, "Toward a Nuclear-Free World," *Wall Street Journal*, 15 January 2008.

4. In August 2007, six cruise missiles armed with nuclear warheads went missing when U.S. Air Force personnel mistakenly loaded them onto a plane and flew them across the country. For an analysis of previous accidents and near-misses, see the masterful study by Scott Sagan, *The Limits of Safety: Organizations, Accidents, and Nuclear Weapons* (Princeton: Princeton University Press, 1993).

5. Shultz, Perry, Kissinger, and Nunn, "Toward a Nuclear-Free World."

6. The White House, Office of the Press Secretary, "Statement by President Barack Obama on the Release of Nuclear Posture Review," 6 April 2010.

7. Yousaf Butt, "Redefining Deterrence: Is RRW Detrimental to U.S. Security Calculus?" *Bulletin of the Atomic Scientists*, 2 December 2008.

8. Tsuyoshi Hasegawa, *Racing the Enemy: Stalin, Truman, and the Surrender of Japan* (Cambridge: Harvard University Press, 2005); Sean L. Malloy, *Atomic Tragedy: Henry L. Stimson and the Decision to Use the Bomb against Japan* (Ithaca, NY: Cornell University Press, 2008).

9. Melvyn P. Leffler, "The American Conception of National Security and the Beginnings of the Cold War, 1945–48," *American Historical Review* 89, no. 3 (June 1984).

10. Matthew Evangelista, "Stalin's Postwar Army Reappraised," *International Security* 7, no. 3 (Winter 1982–83); Philip A. Karber and Jerald A. Combs, "The United States, NATO and the Soviet Threat to Western Europe: Military Estimates and Policy Options, 1945–1963," *Diplomatic History* 22, no. 3 (Summer 1998); and Matthew Evangelista,

"The 'Soviet Threat': Intentions, Capabilities, and Context," *Diplomatic History* 22, no. 3 (Summer 1998).

11. Christopher Paine, "On the Beach: The Rapid Deployment Force and the Nuclear Arms Race," *Middle East Research and Information Project (MERIP) Reports* no. 111 (January 1983), reprinted in Matthew Evangelista, ed., *Peace Studies: Critical Concepts in Political Science* (London: Routledge, 2005), vol. 2.

12. Nina Tannenwald, *The Nuclear Taboo: The United States and the Non-Use of Nuclear Weapons since 1945* (New York: Cambridge University Press, 2007), chs. 4–6.

13. *Nuclear Operations*, Air Force Doctrine Document 2-12 (7 May 2009).

14. "Statement by President Barack Obama on the Release of Nuclear Posture Review," 6 April 2010.

15. *Nuclear Operations*, pp. 4, 8.

16. Tannenwald, *The Nuclear Taboo.*

17. William J. Perry, Brent Scowcroft, and Charles D. Ferguson, "How to Reduce the Nuclear Threat," *Wall Street Journal*, 28 May 2009.

18. Jon Kyl and Richard Perle, "Our Decaying Nuclear Deterrent," *Wall Street Journal*, 30 June 2009.

19. Daniel Dombey and Tobias Buck, "Moment of Truth Looms over Impasse on Enrichment," *Financial Times*, 11 June 2009, p. 4.

20. "President Obama Held a News Conference with South Korean President Lee Myung-bak," 16 June 2009; transcript at http://www.washingtonpost.com/wp-dyn/content/article/2009/06/16/AR2009061601627.html.

21. Jung Sung-ki, "US Nuclear Umbrella: Double-Edged Sword for S. Korea," *Korea Times*, 24 June 2009.

22. Remarks of President Barack Obama, Hradčany Square, Prague, Czech Republic, 5 April 2009, at http://prague.usembassy.gov/obama.html.

23. Carl Bildt and Radek Sikorski, "Next, the Tactical Nukes," *New York Times*, 2 February 2010; Agence France Presse, "Allied Bid for Obama to Remove US European Nuclear Stockpile," 20 February 2010, at http://nz.news.yahoo.com/a/-/world/6830367/allied-bid-for-obama-to-remove-us-european-nuclear-stockpile/; Massimo D'Alema, Gianfranco Fini, Giorgio La Malfa, Arturo Parisi, and Francesco Calogero, "Per un mondo senza armi nucleari," *Corriere della Sera*, 24 July 2008; "New Think and Old Weapons," *New York Times* (editorial), 27 February 2010.

24. David E. Sanger and Peter Baker, "Obama Limits When U.S. Would Use Nuclear Arms," *New York Times*, 5 April 2010.

25. Kyl and Perle, "Our Decaying Nuclear Deterrent."

26. George P. Shultz, William J. Perry, Henry A. Kissinger, and Sam Nunn, "A World Free of Nuclear Weapons," *Wall Street Journal*, 4 January 2007.

27. The term appears frequently in connection with the nuclear ambitions of North Korea and Iran. See, for example, "Blair Condemns 'Completely Irresponsible Act,'" *In-*

dependent (UK), 9 October 2006, on the reaction to a North Korean nuclear test; and Agence France Presse, "US Military Chief Slams Iran's 'Irresponsible Influence,'" *France 24 International News*, 2 May 2008.

28. William J. Broad and David E. Sanger, "Obama's Youth Shaped His Nuclear-Free Vision," *New York Times*, 5 July 2009.

29. BBC, "Iran 'Would Like Nuclear Option,'" 17 June 2009, at http://news.bbc.co.uk/2/hi/middle_east/8104388.stm.

30. This was the explicit program of the European Nuclear Disarmament movement. See, for example, E. P. Thompson, "Protest and Survive," pamphlet put out by the Campaign for Nuclear Disarmament (London, 1980); E. P. Thompson, *Beyond the Cold War* (New York: Pantheon, 1982); E. P. Thompson, *The Heavy Dancers* (New York: Pantheon, 1985); and Jean Stead and Danielle Grünberg, *Moscow Independent Peace Group* (London: Merlin Press, 1982). For a scholarly account of the transnational human-rights efforts, see Daniel C. Thomas, *The Helsinki Effect: International Norms, Human Rights, and the Demise of Communism* (Princeton: Princeton University Press, 2001).

31. George N. Lewis and Theodore A. Postol, "European Missile Defense: The Technological Basis of Russian Concerns," *Arms Control Today* (October 2007).

32. Tom Parfitt and Ian Traynor, "US Rejects Kremlin's Call to Scrap Missile Shield," *The Guardian*, 14 November 2008.

33. On Romania's interest in hosting a system, see Mihaela Iordache, "Après la 'Guerre des étoiles': la Roumanie au centre du nouveau système de défense américain?" *Europolitik*, 15 October 2009, at http://www.newropeans-magazine.org/content/view/10172/1/. On the redistribution of contracts, see Roxanna Tiron, "Missile Defense Shift Redirects Billions in Government Contracts," *The Hill*, 20 September 2009, at http://thehill.com/business-a-lobbying/59449-missile-defense-shift-redirects-billions-in-contracts.

34. Stefan Wagstyl and Edward Luce, "US and Russia Square Up over Missile Shield," *Financial Times*, 3 July 2009.

35. Transcript of press conference, 16 June 2009.

36. The work of Randall Forsberg was particularly important in this regard. See, for example, "The Freeze and Beyond: Confining the Military to Defense as a Route to Disarmament," *World Policy Journal* 1, no. 2 (1984); and "Parallel Cuts in Nuclear and Conventional Forces," *Bulletin of the Atomic Scientists* (August 1985).

37. Albert Wohlstetter, "The Delicate Balance of Terror," *Foreign Affairs* 37, no. 2 (January 1959).

38. Jeffrey W. Knopf, *Domestic Society and International Cooperation: The Impact of Protest on U.S. Arms Control Policy* (New York: Cambridge University Press, 1998); David S. Meyer, *A Winter of Discontent: The Nuclear Freeze and American Politics* (Boulder, CO: Praeger, 1990); and David Cortright, *Peace Works: The Citizen's Role in Ending the Cold War* (Boulder, CO: Westview, 1993).

39. Robert Scheer, *With Enough Shovels: Reagan, Bush and Nuclear War* (New York: Random House, 1982); for a contemporary analysis of Gorbachev's proposal for a nuclear-free world, see Matthew Evangelista, "The New Soviet Approach to Security," *World Policy Journal* 3, no. 4 (Fall 1986).

40. James Lee Ray, "The Abolition of Slavery and the End of International War," *International Organization* 43 (Summer 1989); Randall Forsberg, "Toward a Theory of Peace: The Role of Moral Beliefs" (Ph.D. dissertation, Massachusetts Institute of Technology, June 1997); a summary version is available as "Socially-sanctioned and Non-sanctioned Violence: On the Role of Moral Beliefs in Causing and Preventing War and Other Forms of Large-group Violence," in Evangelista, ed., *Peace Studies*, vol. I, ch. 5.

41. Tannenwald, *The Nuclear Taboo*, ch. 10.

42. Andrew Mack, "America, Russia, and a Nuclear-free World," openDemocracy.net, 7 June 2009, at http://www.opendemocracy.net/article/america-russia-and-a-nuclear-free-world, original emphasis.

17 American Conventional Superiority: The Balancing Act

Dennis M. Gormley

INTRODUCTION

The transformation of the U.S. conventional capabilities has begun to have a substantial and important impact on counterforce strike missions, particularly as they affect counterproliferation requirements. So too have improvements in ballistic missile defense programs, which are also critically central to U.S. counterproliferation objectives. These improved conventional capabilities come at a time when thinking about the prospects of eventually achieving a nuclear disarmed world has never been so promising. Yet, the path toward achieving that goal, or making substantial progress toward it, is fraught with pitfalls, including domestic political, foreign, and military ones. Two of the most important impediments to deep reductions in U.S. and Russian nuclear arsenals—no less a nuclear disarmed world—are perceived U.S. advantages in conventional counterforce strike capabilities working in combination with even imperfect but growing missile defense systems.

The Barack Obama administration has already toned down the George W. Bush administration's rhetoric surrounding many of these new capabilities. Nevertheless, it is likely to affirm that it is a worthy goal to pursue a more conventionally oriented denial strategy as America further weans itself from its reliance on nuclear weapons. The challenge is to do so in the context of a more multilateral or collective security environment in which transparency plays the role it once did during the Cold War as a necessary adjunct to arms control agreements. Considerable thought has already been devoted to assessing many of the challenges along the way to a nuclear-free world, including verifying arsenals when they reach very low levels, more effective management of the civilian nuclear programs that remain, enforcement procedures, and what, if anything, might be needed to deal with latent capacities to produce nuclear weapons.[1] But far less thought has been expended on why Russia—whose cooperation is absolutely essential for abolition to happen—might ever wish to proceed toward such a postnuclear world that would be dominated militarily by American conventional military capabilities and what might be needed to allay legitimate concerns in this regard. At the very least, it will become increasingly important to separate fact from fiction in regard to the state of various conventional offensive and defensive counterproliferation capabilities and begin the challenge of addressing what kind of concrete steps are needed to alleviate Russian concerns. It is precisely that objective to which this chapter is addressed.

The chapter is organized along the following lines. It first examines Russian perceptions of U.S. advances in conventional warfighting, after which it then assesses the extent to which these perceptions are real or exaggerated. Finally, in light of Russia's concerns, the chapter closes with a set of policy options designed to help allay these concerns along the path toward deep reductions in nuclear arsenals.

ALLEVIATING RUSSIAN FEARS

Confronted by both the U.S. lead in conventional capabilities and the erosion of its nuclear forces due to readiness reductions coupled with lapses in its early warning system, Russia has evinced a growing sense of vulnerability. Although this threat perception is only partly justified, it still could impede further steps in achieving deep nuclear reductions. To achieve its ambitious objectives in nuclear arms control, the Obama administration must first understand and then try to alleviate legitimate Russian fears concerning asymmetric American advantages in conventional counterforce capabilities.

RUSSIAN PERCEPTIONS OF U.S. ADVANCED CONVENTIONAL SYSTEMS

American advances in precision global strike capabilities coupled with a seemingly unfettered ability to exploit missile defense technologies in the absence of any treaty constraints provides a challenging backdrop to obtaining deep reductions in Russian and American nuclear arsenals. The cavalier way in which the Bush administration unilaterally opened negotiations with Poland and the Czech Republic on stationing midcourse interceptors and radars, respectively, on these nations' territories catapulted the missile defense issue to center stage. But equally worrisome to Russia are developments in precision conventional strike weapons that are seen as capable of destroying strategic targets. Russia sees the combination of conventional offense and defense as leaving it at a decided and uncomfortable disadvantage vis-à-vis the United States in the aftermath of deep nuclear reductions, no less a world without nuclear weapons.[2]

Controversy surrounding the U.S. decision to negotiate rights to deploy a "third site" for midcourse ground-based interceptors in Poland and the X-band radar in the Czech Republic made missile defense the premier issue standing in the way of progress in deep nuclear reductions. Indeed, Premier Vladimir Putin told Japanese media on May 10, 2009, that U.S. plans for missile defenses in Europe would be linked to strategic arms reductions.[3] Despite the limited technical capacity of U.S. interceptors in Poland to threaten Russian strategic forces, Russia's reaction to U.S. plans was vitriolic for reasons that go beyond technical threat analysis.[4] The Bush administration's discussions with the Poles and Czechs occurred against the backdrop of NATO's inchoate plans for a missile defense system of its own, including one that could conceivably include Russia at some future point. In January 2008, with Germany as the host nation, NATO's Theater Missile Defense Ad Hoc Working Group—operating under the aegis of the NATO-Russia Council—conducted the fourth in a series of theater missile defense exercises, with eleven NATO nations joining Russia in a command and control exercise of missile defense forces. Some might forgive Russians for believing that the U.S. rush to deploy its own missile defense system in Europe represents a way of edging Russia out of any future NATO missile defense system.

Russia might also be excused for worrying about the open-ended U.S. approach toward determining when to deploy new missile defense components as well as the opaque nature of what the U.S. notion of global missile defenses truly means. Missile defense opacity reflects the diametrically opposed acquisition strategies for missile defense practiced before and after the terrorist attacks of September 11, 2001. Before 9/11, particularly in regard to Democratic administrations, support for any complex military system occurred only after the threat had been amply explicated and then the system was subjected to thorough testing—a "fly-before-you-buy" practice in which any particular missile defense system undergoes enough operational tests to determine its reliability and performance effectiveness.[5] The administration of George W. Bush introduced the notion of capabilities-based planning, which overturned the need for a thorough vetting of the threat and instead sought to develop a full range of capabilities needed to cope with likely future contingencies. The logic for capabilities-based planning was laid out in the 2001 Quadrennial Defense Review.[6] It was predicated on the belief that, since one cannot know with enough confidence precisely what threats will emanate from either nations or terrorist groups, defense planners must identify specific capabilities needed to dissuade enemies from pursuing threatening options, deter them by deploying forces for rapid use, and defeat them if deterrence fails. With such a broad writ in hand, the chief lesson of 9/11 for the Bush administration was that a determined adversary would stop at nothing—including even acquiring ballistic missiles—in order to attack the United States.[7] With long-standing metrics for measuring performance no longer applicable, the Bush administration abjured relying on extensive flight tests to determine system reliability and performance. Deployment decisions were based instead on simulations that integrated limited real-world test results with conceptual components reproduced in a model. Moreover, no longer did the Missile Defense Agency specify an overall system architecture. Whatever components passed the muster of this admittedly risky approach were deployed immediately in two-year block intervals, leaving critics aghast at such a something-is-better-than-nothing approach to deployment. But to observers in Russia, such opacity produced confusion and uncertainty with respect to future U.S. missile defense plans and capabilities.[8]

Moscow's more immediate concerns have changed in the face of the Obama administration's revisions to the Bush plans and the 2010 NATO decision to offer Russia inclusion in NATO's plans for territorial missile defenses in Europe. With its decision to scrap the Bush plan to protect Europe and America from Iranian intercontinental-range missiles, the Obama administration quite sensibly has chosen to focus initially on defending against missiles that could threaten American troops in Europe and our European allies: Iranian short- and medium-range ballistic missiles. These missiles are numerous and threatening and to that extent substantially more interceptors than the Bush plan's ten will be needed to deal with this near-term threat. Thus, the Obama plan's missile defense architecture will depend on proven sea-based interceptors—Standard Missile-3 (SM-3)—deployed initially on ships but later also on land. One Aegis cruiser alone carries 100 SM-3 interceptors. The Obama plan banks on the expectation that Iran will not produce a truly intercontinental missile threat until at least 2020, by which time modified versions of SM-3 interceptors are expected to be capable of intercepting potential future intercontinental-range ballistic missiles (ICBMs).[9] Still, absent legal constraints on future American missile defense plans, Russian fears, however relaxed today, could re-emerge in the future.

What animates Russian officials most in light of the absence of formal treaty constraints is that with the U.S. deployment of highly powerful ground- or sea-based X-band radars and space-based infrared sensors (known as the Space-Based Infrared System, or SBIRS-Low), America will have a break-out potential in place for a thick, global system of missile defense.[10] Compared with the poor discrimination performance of earlier warning radars, X-band systems have a resolution of 10 to 15 cm, good enough to discriminate between real warheads and decoys. More ominously, once they are deployed globally, not only will midcourse ground-based interceptors be able to take advantage of their improved resolution, but so too will a growing network of sea-based interceptors on Aegis cruisers/destroyers and land-based upper-tier THAAD (Terminal High Altitude Area Defense) interceptors. Of course, X-band, and especially SBIRS-Low, may not prove to be as effective as promised, but this does not lessen the concern of Russian defense planners who see uncontrolled expansion of American global missile defenses as a potential threat to their diminishing nuclear deterrent.

Prospective missile defense advances represent only the most visible impediment to progress in nuclear arms control. Lurking just behind are concerns about U.S. advanced conventional weapons. In the U.S. debate, much has been made of Russia's fear of U.S. nuclear primacy.[11] But Russian strategic analysts have begun to write in some detail about the prospects that future advanced conventional weapons—together with improved missile defenses—could place Russia in a position of unacceptable vulnerability.[12] This perception is not merely the product of wild speculation by nonspecialists in the Russian press. The well-respected Maj. Gen. Vladimir Dvorkin (Ret.), who formerly directed fundamental research in mathematical modeling in nuclear planning, and then participated in virtually every major U.S.-Soviet strategic arms control negotiation, reflects the broad concern now existing in Moscow that conventional weapons imbalances represent a key roadblock to deep nuclear reductions. As Dvorkin notes:

> [A Russian] concern is the possibility that high-precision conventional weapons could be used to destroy strategic targets. Precision-guided munitions (PGMs) pose a threat to all branches of the strategic nuclear triad, including the silo and

> mobile launchers of the Strategic Rocket Force (SRF), strategic submarines in bases, and strategic bombers. The types of PGMs to be used against each of these components, the vulnerability of these components, the vulnerability of assets, and operation requirements would require . . . study.[13]

U.S. plans to arm Trident D-5 missiles with conventional payloads as part of its plans for prompt global strike have already raised concerns—in the United States and Russia alike—about missile warning ambiguity and inadvertent retaliatory actions. These developments are of sufficient concern to Russian planners that Moscow arms officials have proposed strategic conventional delivery vehicles as candidates for possible limits in future strategic weapons treaties with the United States.[14]

If U.S. strategic conventional denial capabilities are just emerging today, Russian military planners must also worry about where such programs might be in a decade or two. The U.S. Strategic Command's initial complement of forces comprising the Global Strike mission included the U.S. Air Force's F-22 fighter providing penetration corridors for B-52, B-1, and B-2 bombers loaded with conventional precision strike weapons.[15]

The U.S. Navy has converted four of its 18 Trident Ohio-class submarines to each carry 154 Tomahawk land-attack cruise missiles, the latest version of which features a two-way satellite data link that permits the missile to attack one of sixteen preprogrammed targets or take new GPS coordinates to attack a fleeting target of opportunity. Assuming it has reserve fuel, the missile can also loiter in the area for hours awaiting a more important target, as well as pass information from its own TV camera on battle damage. Instead of filling each of the four Trident submarines with its full complement of 154 Tomahawks, a few missiles can be traded for special-operations mini-subs or small reconnaissance UAVs. The Pentagon has also sought, without success thus far, to spend $503 million to outfit a small number of the Trident D-5 nuclear missiles on the remaining fourteen Ohio-class Trident submarines with conventional warheads (either small-diameter bombs or bunker-buster penetrating warheads). Even more robust global strike systems could emerge from current research and development programs, including the Conventional Strike Missile, consisting of pairing converted ICBMs with hypersonic glide vehicles launched from locations on the east and west coasts of the United States not associated with nuclear delivery, and two experimental hypersonic technology programs.[16]

THE U.S. CONVENTIONAL STRATEGIC THREAT TO RUSSIA: SEPARATING FACT FROM FICTION

Any American president—Barack Obama included—wishing to wean the United States from its long-standing reliance on nuclear weapons would find it difficult not to pursue a robust conventionally oriented denial strategy. Yet, the challenge facing the United States is to make more transparent precisely where current advanced conventional and missile defense programs stand today, and what restrictions or operational constraints the United States might be willing to accept, if any, on their development or operation to accelerate the path toward nuclear abolition.

If the U.S. decision to arm a small number of Trident D-5 missiles with conventional warheads is any indication, virtually no thought went into how such plans would be viewed in Moscow or Beijing, or indeed, even in the U.S. Congress. The impervious nature of conventional strategic strike programs is less a matter of intention and more related to the fact that programs are mired in vagueness with differing interpretations of missile requirements and capabilities existing within various bureaucratic stake holders. Programs are diffused across the entire Department of Defense, including the Defense Advanced Research Project Agency and the military services. And rather than being driven by any well-conceived concept of operation dictating how these various programs will transform military operations—the bellwether of truly revolutionary change—these efforts are propelled for the most part by raw technological momentum.[17] The opaque nature of U.S. global missile defense ambitions in the Bush administration largely emanated from the imperative to deploy systems as quickly as possible to meet political, if not threat-driven, needs. Global strike capabilities, on the other hand, have the advantage today and in the future of appearing to transform deterrence-oriented nuclear ballistic missiles that no one ever wishes to be used into denial-oriented counterforce systems possessing an array of future mission possibilities—a factor that surely animates the interest of all three military services. But Global Strike's exclusive affiliation with advanced conventional strike is today more promise than reality. However much the U.S. Air Force may have envisioned the Prompt Global Strike mission as a decidedly conventional one, its initial implementation proved otherwise, not least because of the dearth of truly global conventional capabilities.[18] In fact, Global Strike's June 2004 implementation as an approved operational plan mirrored the Bush administration's 2001 Nuclear Posture Review (NPR) conflation of nuclear and conventional capabilities.

President Bush's elevation of preemption (actually, prevention) from military option to national doctrine in 2002 gave real impetus to making the Global Strike concept operational. Grave concern over the toxic mix of WMD and the presumed nexus between so-called rogue states and a new brand of apocalyptic terrorism led to specific guidance to the U.S. military to integrate selected bombers, ICBMs, ballistic-missile submarines, and cyber-warfare assets into a strike force capable of promptly attacking high-value targets associated with specific regional contingencies. Some advanced conventional capability figured into the original Global Strike operational implementation, probably consisting of joint direct attack munitions launched by B-2 bombers and Tomahawk cruise missiles launched from submarines and surface vessels. But Global Strike as a purely conventional capability was overtaken not only by limited capabilities but also by the Bush administration's desire to make nuclear strike options more credible and tailored to the post–Cold War requirements reflected in its 2001 NPR.[19]

Where does Prompt Global Strike stand today? The Next-Generation Bomber, originally slated for deployment by 2018, has been delayed not only because of budget limitations but also due to uncertainties with respect to what kind of impact current Strategic Arms Reduction Treaty (START) renewal will have on the mix of nuclear delivery systems.[20] According to a congressional staff member on the Senate Armed Services Committee, there is no longer any prospect for either Trident or Minuteman land-based nuclear missiles undergoing conversion to meet the Pentagon's requirement for prompt conventional strikes, while research funding for hypersonic glide vehicles will remain in place, but without prospect for any deployment decisions any time soon.[21] As one senior U.S. Strategic Command officer stated to this writer recently, "Global Strike has been throttled back."[22] Yet the Obama administration's 2010 Quadrennial Defense Review promotes the expansion of long-range conventional strike capabilities, including experimenting with new Prompt Global Strike prototypes, perhaps even ones that would avoid, unlike the Bush administration's plans for Trident conventional conversion, intermingling nuclear and conventional warheads together.[23]

One might argue, of course, and the Russians do, that the requirement for converting Trident might be resurrected in future. They surely observed that an independent study panel of the bipartisan National Research Council (NRC) had endorsed a limited application for the conventionally armed Trident before the 2008 election. The NRC panel only gave its support for the mission of a time-critical strike against a fleeting target of opportunity (for example, counterterrorist target or rogue state activity), which would involve no more than one to four weapons. The U.S. Navy had pressed for funding to convert two Trident missiles on each of twelve deployed Trident submarines for a total of twenty-four conventionally armed Tridents. Importantly, the NRC panel drew a distinction between the more limited mission and conventional Trident's broader application. The limited use would not carry the same stiff operational and political demands as a larger use of conventional Trident would in providing leading edge attacks in support of major combat operations. In the latter regard, Trident would probably join substantial numbers of Tomahawks and other PGMs on bombers as part of a counterforce strike at the outset of a major regional contingency. The NRC panel properly noted that in contrast to using one to four Tridents alone, any large-scale prompt conventional strike would present much stiffer operational demands related to intelligence support and command and control, as well as drastically different political implications with regard to warning ambiguity. Whether the contingency involves using one or many conventional Tridents, as the NRC panel observed, "[T]he ambiguity between nuclear and conventional payloads can never be totally resolved."[24] Yet, the larger the Trident salvo of conventional missiles, the higher the prospects for misinterpretation and inadvertent responses. At the same time, because Russian early-warning systems are incomplete, even smaller numbers may be wrongly interpreted as a larger-than-actual salvo or incoming missiles. Concerns about ambiguity leading to inadvertent nuclear war—rightly or wrongly conceived—largely explain the congressional decision not to support conventional Trident's funding.

Arming Trident with a conventional warhead is not the only way to deal with fleeting terrorist targets. For example, the combination of U.S Special Forces on the ground and armed Predator UAVs in the air represents a potent and now broadly used new capability to deal with fleeting targets. The NRC panel noted the importance of UAVs and special forces as sources of intelligence supporting conventional Trident strikes, which begs the question: why can't less provocative capabilities—if perhaps less effective under some circumstances—obviate the need for conventional Trident in regard to this limited mission?[25] Another option to evaluate would be a new missile altogether, rather than one with a nuclear legacy, like the U.S. Navy's concept of a "Sea-Launched Global Strike Missile," or even the Navy's effort to develop a supersonic version of the Tomahawk cruise missile.[26] For the time being, the Obama administration and Congress have taken an appropriate time out with Prompt Global Strike, which will surely not allay Russian concerns over the long run. But it does provide space to consider future prompt-strike missile options and their effect on military stability in the context of a world that may well become far less dependent on long-range, nuclear-armed ballistic missiles in the future.

Research and development programs attempting to achieve technological breakthroughs in global strike capabilities by 2025 are, frankly speaking, problematic at best. These include the hypersonic cruise vehicle that could take off and land from a U.S runway and be anywhere in the world in one to two hours. The idea for such a space plane has been around since the 1950s.[27] President Ronald Reagan accelerated the push in his 1986 State of the Union Address, yet his director of the Strategic Defense Initiative (Star Wars), Henry Cooper, told a congressional panel in 2001 that after the expenditure of some $4 billion on the development of the space plane concept from the early 1970s to the end of the 1990s (discounting various programs in the 1950s and 1960s, as well as the space shuttle investment), the only thing produced was "one crashed vehicle, a hangar queen, some drop-test articles and static displays."[28] Current Pentagon hypersonic programs face, among many, the difficult challenge of developing lightweight and durable high-temperature materials and thermal management techniques needed to cope with hypersonic speeds. This is because hypersonic glide vehicles require a thermal protection system capable of preventing their payloads from melting at re-entry speeds of up to Mach 25 (or twenty-five times the speed of sound). The quest to master and deploy hypersonic systems will not come easily, not only because of the huge technical challenges associated with these systems but also because the strategic environment is so uncertain. No defense agency would likely be willing to bet on any one solution to the global-strike requirement under such circumstances. However, the U.S. Congress appears to have chosen to continue down the risky and potentially costly path of pursuing hypersonic delivery vehicles. If nothing else, this course removes the nearer-term solutions like conventional Trident from becoming any kind of impediment to progress in strategic arms control negotiations.

If converting Trident to deliver non-nuclear payloads and development of more futuristic advanced conventional programs represent nonexistent threats to Russia today, that is not the case in regard to hundreds of Tomahawk cruise missiles (616 maximum, if UAVs or special forces are not fitted out in launch tubes instead) that comprise the four Ohio-class Trident submarines converted from nuclear ballistic missile submarines (SSBNs) to guided-missile (that is, cruise missile) submarines between 2002 and 2008. In worrying about this threat, Russian analysts take particular note of the precision accuracy and retargeting capability of the latest generation Tomahawk cruise missile. This, it is asserted, means that highly accurate Tomahawks could threaten Russian silo-based intercontinental ballistic missiles, while the fact that they possess their own means of reconnaissance, can loiter in the target area, and can be retargeted after launch, suggests they can find and destroy mobile missiles like the new Topol-Ms. Such a preemptive strike of this sort could, by 2012–15, destroy between 70 and 80 percent of Russian's nuclear forces. The remaining missiles, it is asserted, could then be readily intercepted by the U.S. global missile defense system.[29]

Granting that the current state of Russian strategic missile forces is today substantially below its Cold War form and that they are likely to suffer funding shortfalls over the next decade, the expectation that U.S. conventionally armed Tomahawks, even ones with high accuracy and retargeting capability, could, on their own, accomplish such successful results is—kindly put—the height of excessive imagination. Observing U.S. advances in precision conventional strike linked to advanced reconnaissance systems, Soviet-era military theoreticians did indeed become fascinated with the prospect that "automated search and destroy complexes" could one day come close to approximating the effectiveness of at least tactical nuclear weapons.[30] But a closer look at what Soviet-era planners truly had in mind shows that it had nothing to do with anticipating that missiles alone could dominate a major military campaign. Instead, their role was seen as leveraging the effectiveness of a multiplicity of other strike elements (aircraft, bombers, electronic jamming, airborne assault and heliborne forces, and so forth) in a major combined arms campaign. Tomahawk cruise missiles are surely accurate enough to hit on or very near to a Russian missile silo, but their warhead carries only 450 kg of either blast fragmentation or combined-effects submunitions. The former is a mere pinprick vis-à-vis hardened missile silos; the latter is only relevant against soft targets. Indeed, even a Trident missile armed with a conventional penetrator would require Herculean accuracy and absolutely perfect targeting conditions to have any chance whatsoever of threatening silo-based missiles.[31]

What about advanced Tomahawk's reputed new capabilities against mobile missiles? As discussed earlier, the U.S. Air Force in particular has accomplished major improvements in counterforce targeting of fleeting targets, largely as a by-product of nearly continuous combat operations in Afghanistan and Iraq over the last eight years. Nevertheless, it is critical to distinguish between what piloted aircraft can accomplish against a rogue state's mobile missiles compared with autonomous missiles equipped with a data link and TV camera facing arguably the most skilled nation there even has been when it comes to operating intermediate- and strategic-range mobile missiles.[32] It's one thing to track, detect, and successfully attack fleeting groups of Taliban or al Qaeda fighters in Afghanistan or Iraq, or Iraqi mobile missile units who believed they are impervious to ubiquitous battlefield reconnaissance systems while being otherwise overwhelmingly dominated (in the case of Iraq in 2003) by large numbers of American conventional forces, and quite another to expect 600 or so conventionally armed Tomahawks to do decisive damage to 180 Russian nuclear-armed mobile missiles proficient in the practice of employing camouflage, cover, and concealment methods once they have moved from their peacetime bases. Moreover, there is the stiff challenge of operating impervious to Russia's advanced air and missile defenses. U.S. counterforce targeting against mobile missiles has indeed improved greatly since coming up completely short in the 1991 Persian Gulf War, but even in Iraq in 2003, only anecdotal evidence suggests that more success was achieved against a greatly diminished Iraq missile force compared to its 1991 holdings. Success did not mean halting the admittedly low launch rate over the twenty-one-day war, nor did it mean that Iraq's entire missile stores were eliminated via either counterforce or missile defenses by the war's conclusion. For example, thirty-three Iraqi cruise missiles—a threat that had surprised American missile defenders and contributed to friendly-fire losses—were found intact on the Faw peninsula after the war.[33] Simply put, we fall prey to a fallacy of division to think that because tactical counterforce operations using advanced strike systems (like Tomahawk) have improved remarkably during the last eight years, they can also succeed in strategic counterforce operations where even nuclear strike systems were expected at best to provide only problematic results due to inevitable target location uncertainties.[34] Finally, there is the stark reality that the inevitable failure to locate and destroy all of Russia's strategic nuclear weapons would expose the United States to a devastating nuclear riposte.

The open-ended nature of the U.S. missile defense system raises perhaps the most legitimate area of concern from a Russian perspective, although the Obama administration's decision to cap ground-based midcourse interceptors at thirty ought to allay such concerns. Vladimir Dvorkin has written that Russia has little to worry about from American missile defenses until roughly 2015.

Until then, Russian offensive missiles have adequate "defense suppression systems" to require as many as ten U.S. ground-based interceptors to destroy one warhead. Even the addition of the third site in Poland would not have changed these circumstances. But as time passes, and if the United States were to deploy space-based laser and kinetic-kill weapons "on a massive scale," Russia's nuclear deterrent could conceivably be seen to be at risk.[35] Given the stance of the Obama administration thus far, notably its insistence on demonstrating missile defense performance and system cost effectiveness before deployment decisions are taken, the likelihood of the United States taking the path that worries Russians most is highly doubtful. Yet, without the constraints once associated with the 1972 Anti-Ballistic Missile Treaty, from which the United States unilaterally withdrew in 2002, nothing legally bars a future U.S. administration from pursuing such an open-ended course of action. This stark reality no doubt explains Russian insistence on including, in the text of the "New" START treaty, signed in Prague on April 8, 2010, by presidents Obama and Medvedev, a clause noting the interrelationship between strategic offense and defense, and its growing importance as offensive systems are further reduced.[36]

COOPERATIVE ENGAGEMENT WITH RUSSIA: OPTIONS FOR CONSIDERATION

The daunting challenge of achieving complete abolition of nuclear weapons will surely entail several stages of nuclear reductions along the path to lower, and one hopes, safer arsenals. And dealing with conventional imbalances along this uncertain path not only is a U.S.-Russian dilemma but also includes conventional imbalances in the Middle East, South Asia, and Northeast Asia. Within these three regional settings lately, a contagious outbreak of interest in preemptive strike doctrines linked to advanced conventional strike weapons (most notably cruise missiles) shows worrisome signs of producing even greater instability in the future.[37] For many states on the unequal end of such developments, it will be difficult to imagine why they would wish to eliminate their nuclear weapons. Former Senator Sam Nunn suggests the need to reach a "base camp [or] vantage point from which the summit [a nuclear-free world] is visible and the final ascent to the mountaintop is achievable."[38] The first step along the way to that base camp is for the United States and Russia to restart a critical feature of Cold War arms control negotiations: the elevation of transparency, or making both sides of any competition aware, within the limits of security, of what the other side is doing.

The notion of greatly improved transparency and perhaps even substantial cooperation between the United States and Russia is not a novel concept; it rose to center stage after 9/11. In November 2001, the two presidents signed a "Joint Statement on a New Relationship between the United States and Russia," followed by another in May 2002 specifying a range of possibilities for cooperative engagement, including strengthening confidence and increasing transparency in the area of missile defenses, exchanging information on missile defense programs and tests, reciprocal visits to observe tests, and work on bringing a joint center for exchanging data from early warning systems into effect. Most important, the two sides agreed to study possible areas for missile defense cooperation beyond joint exercises to include joint research and development on missile defense technologies within the limits of security and protecting property rights. The Russia-NATO Council was singled out as the framework to examine cooperative engagement in missile defense.[39]

What greeted Moscow in the aftermath of the 2002 attempt to foster missile defense cooperation with the United States was little in substance and provocative instead of cooperative, namely Washington's unilateral engagement of Poland and the Czech Republic on their involvement in the U.S. missile defense program. U.S. efforts to bring Georgia and Ukraine into NATO didn't help either. U.S. attempts to allay Russia's concerns about these developments failed to impress, and gestures toward transparency and an examination of the potential contribution of Russian radars were less than wholeheartedly dealt with, at least in Russian eyes.

Seek Consensus on Missile Threats to NATO and Russia

The first step in achieving real and lasting cooperation in missile defense is for Russia and the United States, through the NATO-Russia Council, to reach consensus on pace and scope of Iran's ballistic and cruise missile threat to the whole of NATO. Extant threat assessments facing the NATO region focus in the main on ballistic missile systems. The debates focus less on Iran's ballistic missile capacity than on the pace of Tehran's success in weaponizing a suitably compact nuclear reentry vehicle that could survive the rigors of reentry, as well as how quickly their solid-fuel missile developments will mature. Far less attention is given to the growing cruise missile threat on the periphery of Europe. Iran is among a rapidly growing number of countries that have begun pursuing land-attack cruise missile programs. According to a 2004 NATO Parliamentary Committee report, Iran was converting some 300 Chinese anti-ship cruise missiles into land-attack systems by fitting them with turbojet engines and new guidance systems. Such designs have been demonstrated as capable of achieving around 1,000 km range and could be readily launched from merchant ships to target substantial portions of Europe. Even more worrisome over the longer-term was the 2005 disclosure that Russian and Ukrainian arms dealers had collaborated with the head of Ukraine's export control agency in the illegal sale of twelve to twenty Ukrainian/Russian Kh-55 strategic (and nuclear capable) cruise missiles to China and Iran. The Kh-55's range is 3,000 km. Even though the illegal transfer of at least six Kh-55s to Iran also included a ground support system for testing, initializing, and programming the missiles, such a small number of cruise missiles was probably acquired primarily for purposes of examination and reverse engineering, leading eventually to the development of Iran's own long-range cruise missile program.[40] A common view of the threat of both ballistic and cruise missiles offers opportunities for broader cooperation beyond just ballistic missile defense to include warning, detection, and defeat of airborne threats.

U.S. cruise missile defense programs today are not in good shape. Fighters equipped with advanced detection and tracking radars will eventually possess some modest capability to deal with very low volume attacks, assuming advance warning information is available. But existing U.S. programs are underfunded, while interoperability, doctrinal, and organizational issues discourage the military services from producing joint and effective systems for defending U.S. forces and allies in regional military campaigns.[41] NATO's own cruise missile defenses are no better off. The poor state of cruise missile defenses raises the question: can either or both the U.S. and Europe find security by fielding only half a missile defense system, capable of handing but one dimension of the missile threat?

Expand the Cooperative Airspace Initiative (CAI)

Launched within the NATO-Russia Council in 2002, the CAI's goal is to achieve a system of air traffic information exchange along the borders of Russia and NATO member countries. Four sites each currently exist in Russia and NATO countries—from the far north in Russia (Murmansk) and Norway (Bodø) to Turkey (Ankara) and Russia (Rostov-on-Don) in the south. Poland hosts a NATO coordination center in Warsaw, while the companion Russian center is located in Moscow. Besides forming a basis for NATO and Russia to establish greater confidence in working together, the CAI has focused especially on aircraft that might be under the control of terrorists or a rogue state. CAI is complemented as well by a functionally equivalent system of Air Sovereignty Operation Centers (ASOC) that the United States funded in former Warsaw Pact states beginning in 1997. Although the CAI information exchange system had successfully passed joint testing qualifications in July 2008, it along with other bilateral NATO-Russia initiatives were suspended in August 2008 in protest for Russia's intervention in Georgia. CAI only resumed in March 2009.[42]

CAI, working in possible cooperation with the ASOCs, could form the basis for investigating an expansion of air monitoring capabilities to the domain of cruise missile warning and defense. Russia initially balked at the formation of ASOCs, arguing that they together could create a common airspace picture useful for tracking and providing guidance against threats. But to the extent CAI starts taking on the character of ASOCs, the closer it gets to becoming a useful NATO-wide and Russian vehicle for starting collaboration on defending against cruise missiles. About $6.5 million has been invested in CAI thus far, with financial support coming from twelve countries, including Russia and the United States.[43] The virtue of engaging Russia's participation in an expanded CAI concept—including its role in cruise missile defense—goes much beyond trust building and improved air safety and security. Rather, an expanded CAI offers Russia the chance to become a full participant in an inchoate but potentially constructive endeavor to kick-start the lesser-included dimension of missile defense. Russia's long-standing prowess in developing effective air defense systems, including the S-400, which boasts capability to intercept ballistic and cruise missiles as well as aircraft, could fit nicely into a broad-area concept for European cruise missile defense. Directing Moscow's export energies away from S-300 and S-400 transfers to countries like Syria and Iran and toward the prospect of a more effective collaborative working environment within the NATO-Russia Council is worthy of serious evaluation.

Engage Russia on Ballistic Missile Defense

There is already broad support in Washington for engaging Russia in a manner substantially different from the Bush administration's efforts in early 2008 by both secretaries Gates and Rice. Perhaps the easiest way to jump-start missile defense cooperation would be to move toward implementing the Joint Data Exchange Center in Moscow. Russia and the United States first agreed on a joint warning concept involving notifications of ballistic missile flights to each side in 1998, which was formalized in a June 2000 meeting between presidents Clinton and Yeltsin, who agreed to establish the center in Moscow. Legal and tax issues have prevented the center from becoming operational. All of the operational details have been worked out already, so movement toward implementation should be comparatively straightforward. It would also be appropriate to examine more closely Russian president Putin's 2007 proposal to establish a second data exchange center in Brussels.

U.S. officials have already signaled their willingness to examine the use of Russian low-frequency warning radars at Gabala in Azerbaijan and Armavir in Russia's Krasnodar Region as part of the U.S.-led global missile defense system.[44] As nongovernmental radar specialists have noted, there is a chance that combining an X-band radar deployed either in Azerbaijan or Turkey with the Armavir radar could possibly offer three to four more minutes of additional warning than the canceled X-band radar operating on its own from the Czech Republic.[45] At the very least, American radar specialists need to investigate precisely how these two radars might contribute not only to improved missile defense performance but also partnerships with Russia in areas where Russian technological prowess might complement American and European missile defense skills.

If cooperation in missile defense warning isn't difficult enough, it is even more so when it comes to cooperation in interceptors. Security and intellectual property rights issues have always stood in the way of achieving much progress. Assuming, however, that U.S.-Russian relations improve in the aftermath of successful strategic arms control treaties, and particularly in light of NATO's offer to include Russia in its territorial missile defense program, it would make good sense to explore avenues toward cooperation in missile defense interceptors. One competitive advantage that Russia once had is in directed energy technologies. In the early 1990s, U.S. and Russian technical cooperation exchanges disclosed that Russia then led the world in carbon dioxide and high-power solid-state lasers. Again, in the 1990s at least, there was significant cooperation between U.S. and Russian scientific and academic organizations, including in the area of solid-state lasers for nonmilitary applications.[46] The U.S. missile defense program has experienced less than optimal success in the airborne laser program—witness the recent Pentagon decision to cancel the second prototype—an effort seen as critical to achieving some modest capability in defeating ballistic missile threats shortly after they are launched (or during the so-called boost phase). Building on past endeavors in the 1990s, it makes good sense to explore once again opportunities to cooperate in directed energy interceptors.

The purest form of reassurance would resurrect formal arms control constraints designed to allay Russian (and Chinese) concerns about the open-ended nature of the U.S. global missile defense program. Foremost on Russian minds are U.S. intentions to deploy interceptors in space, which could perform double duty as both ballistic missile interceptors, with potentially significant capabilities against Russian offensive forces in the aftermath of deep reductions, and antisatellite weapons to maintain or extend American dominance in space. The American pursuit of such options would be foolhardy, in the first case because no conceivable rogue-state threat would merit such an expansion, and in the latter case, because American dependence on space to sustain its conventional superiority would potentially suffer from such a decision to trigger an arms race in antisatellite weapon capabilities. A preferred alternative would be for the United States to examine what it might be willing to accept in limits on midcourse and upper-tier interceptors, which could be incorporated in a new legally binding treaty with Russia. At the same time, the United States should take the lead with Russia and China to negotiate "rules of the road" for space operations akin to ones that govern air, ground, and naval operations on earth.

Were the Iranian nuclear missile threat to the U.S. homeland to accelerate unexpectedly, which is doubtful, and reasons for deploying the third site in Poland and the Czech Republic determined to be necessary, it is not inconceivable to imagine a significant degree of Russian cooperation nonetheless. This would entail dusting off the assurance proposals of the Bush administration, introduced in 2007, which involved restricting the radar's angle of view so as not to threaten Russian missile launches and agreeing not to activate the site until the Iranian threat was palpable to both sides. Russia had also insisted on a permanent observer presence at both the Czech and Polish bases, but one well-placed Russian observer has suggested that a Polish proposal, allowing for an "almost permanent presence" by Russians, would be satisfactory to Moscow. This would entail aperiodic visits by Russian observers who would be accredited to the Russian embassies in the Czech Republic and Poland and the installation of surveillance cameras for around-the-clock surveillance.[47]

Assuaging Russian Concerns over American Conventional Superiority

This area is perhaps the most intractable, not least because of the Russian tendency to exaggerate U.S. military capabilities. There is little doubt that America possesses greatly superior conventional military forces capable of being projected anywhere around the globe. Russia is today investing in its conventional forces and plans, by 2020, to be in a much better state than it is today. But even the most optimistic estimates suggest that Russia will remain significantly inferior across the board vis-à-vis the United States. From this vantage point Russia is less concerned about the reasons why current U.S. conventional capabilities, such as conventionally armed Trident missiles or hundreds of highly accurate Tomahawk cruise missiles launched from Trident submarines, are incapable of threatening Russia's strategic deterrent. They are concerned about future possibilities, however "fanciful."[48]

If there is a solution to the conventional superiority issue, it lies less in trying to convince Russia that current or prospective U.S. advanced conventional strike systems are incapable of achieving what they fear, and more in conceiving of options that might allay those concerns over the longer run. That said, as much transparency as is possible should nonetheless take place. But so too should the United States evaluate the possibility of constraining the patrol areas where Ohio-class Trident submarines bearing Tomahawks go. Russian analysts are concerned that they will operate sufficiently close to Russian territory to permit them to target their fixed and mobile strategic forces. Indeed, such an operational pattern is not fanciful in light of the speed and quietness of the Ohio-class family of submarines. They could quite conceivably, though not without some risk, operate with impunity not only inside a state's 200 nm exclusive economic zone but also within its 12 nm territorial waters.

To evaluate what the United States would have to do to allay Russian concerns, I examined what constraining Ohio-class submarines to a patrol area just outside the 200 nm economic exclusive zone might accomplish to reduce the perceived threat of striking all Russian strategic nuclear forces (fixed and mobile forces together with submarines bases), comprised of thirteen large-area targets.

Assuming that Tomahawks have a maximum operational range of 2,500 km, Ohio-class submarines would be able to reach nine of the thirteen target areas. Importantly, however, three mobile divisional bases (housing today ninety-nine Topol mobile missiles), and two fixed strategic missile groups (with sixty-eight SS-18 missile silos, each missile armed with ten independently targetable warheads)—together representing 57 percent of Russia's land-based Strategic Rocket Forces—would not be within reach of Tomahawk missiles. Although such an approach seems unnecessary based purely on the highly dubious nature of the Tomahawk threat to such strategic targets, U.S. planners should

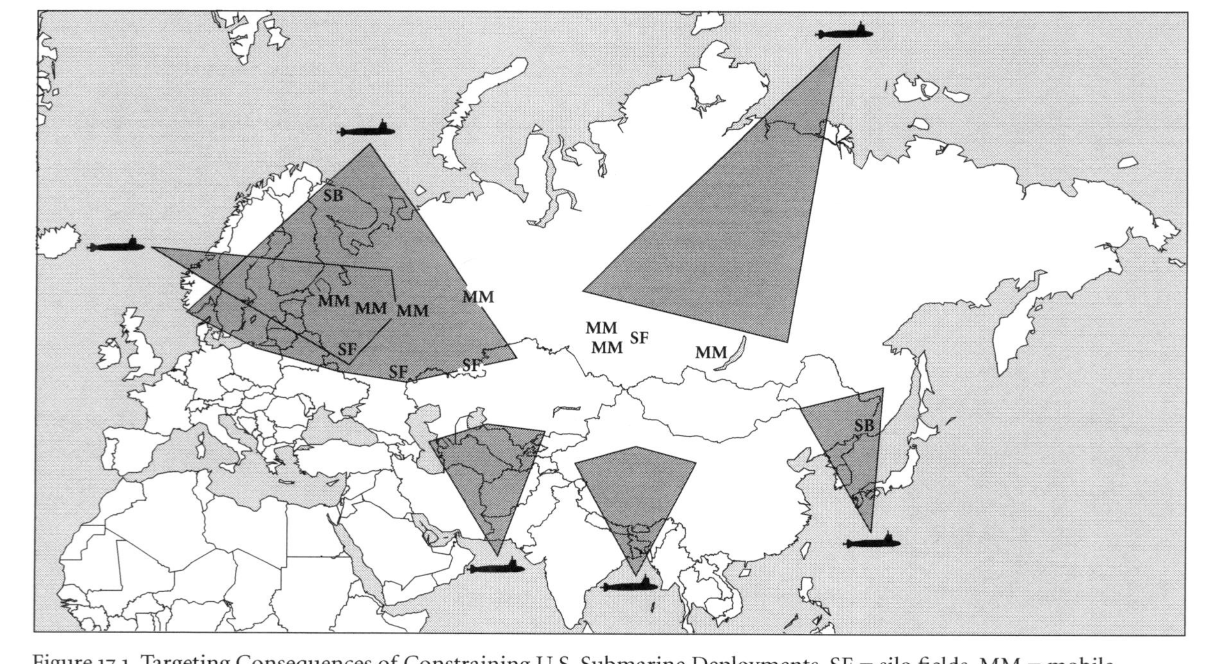

Figure 17.1. Targeting Consequences of Constraining U.S. Submarine Deployments. SF = silo fields, MM = mobile missile garrisons, SB = submarine bases. Shaded areas indicate the reach of Tomahawk cruise missiles launched from Ohio-class submarines positioned 200nm off the coast of any state. Six submarine areas are shown here, but currently the U.S. Navy possesses only four such submarines.

examine in much greater detail the merits and pitfalls of employing such an operational constraint in order to allay Russian fears.[49]

On possible constraints in regard to future U.S. ambitions to restart the conventional arming of Trident for a prompt global strike task, or a broader mission to engage significantly in regional military campaigns, the only solution may lie in counting such strategic conventional delivery vehicles as if they were nuclear armed, which seems to be the case for ICBMs and SLBMs under the "new" START regime signed in April 2010. The same may have to apply as well to future hypersonic cruise vehicles, not least because in fact they would be theoretically capable of delivering nuclear payloads.

CONCLUSION

As U.S. and Russian planners look toward the challenges and pitfalls of achieving deep reductions in nuclear arsenals, they should begin systematically to appraise additional novel ways of achieving stability as arsenals drop to less than 500 warheads and then fall further. The recent turn by many states toward adopting preemptive strike doctrines employing advanced conventional weapons does not augur well for achieving a stable world. However difficult it surely will be for states to shed this predilection toward preemption—or prevention—through prompt action, if history tells us anything, it is that while such practices may succeed in achieving some initial battlefield success, they do so at the grave cost of war and its inevitable political and financial consequences. Witness America's eight-year tragedy in Iraq. Preemptive strike doctrines employing conventional weapons are clearly unacceptably dangerous in a nuclear-armed world. But they will also be dangerous in a world devoid of all nuclear weapons, particularly during regional or international crises. One way is to tone down, if not eliminate, the preemption option, as the Obama administration did in its May 2010 National Security Strategy.[50] It is needlessly reckless to elevate such a military choice—assessed as absolutely critical under dangerously threatening circumstances—to a national doctrine.

Another is to undertake a fresh examination of Ronald Reagan's dream of eliminating offensive ballistic missiles, attempted unsuccessfully at the Reykjavik summit with Mikhail Gorbachev, in 1986.[51] However fanciful such an endeavor may appear today, it may begin to become far more meritorious as the world sheds its nuclear obsession. Land-attack cruise missiles, which today have already become the conventional weapon of choice around which preemptive strike doctrines are being wrapped, also merit much more attention than they have received to date. Besides more effective controls within supply-side mechanisms like the Missile Technology Control Regime, and incorporation of cruise missiles into the Hague Code of Conduct's normative treatment of missile proliferation,[52] all advanced conventional system transfers will merit much closer attention than ever before, perhaps along the lines of global arms trade treaty, a concept that has already been examined closely at the UN. Common international standards, accompanied by greatly improved transparency and verification procedures attending the transfer of all advanced conventional systems, are matters that cannot await the outcome of contemporary efforts to achieve nuclear abolition. They deserve attention on their own merits no matter the outcome of the quest to achieve the abolition of nuclear weapons.

NOTES

This chapter is adapted and updated from a longer treatment of the subject, entitled "The Path to Deep Nuclear Reductions: Dealing with American Conventional Superiority," *Proliferation Papers* No. 29 (Paris, Ifri, Fall 2009). It can be downloaded at www.ifri.org/downloads/pp29gormley1.pdf.

1. These issues are usefully taken up in George Perkovich and James M. Acton, *Abolishing Nuclear Weapons*, Adelphi Paper 396 (New York: Routledge for the International Institute for Strategic Studies, 2008).

2. For a comprehensive treatment of Russian perceptions of growing U.S. military superiority, see Stephen J. Blank, *Russia and Arms Control: Are There Opportunities for the Obama Administration?* (Carlisle, PA: Strategic Studies Institute, U.S. Army War College, 2008).

3. "Russia to Link Missile Defense in Europe with Nuclear Arms Treaty," RIA Novosti, May 10, 2009.

4. For a technical appraisal of how Russian military analysts might plausibly view Polish-based interceptors as a threat, see George N. Lewis and Theodore A. Postol, "European Missile Defense: The Technological Basis of Russian Concerns," *Arms Control Today* (October 2007), at http://www.armscontrol.org/act/2007_10/LewisPostol.

5. For an illustration of this position from a practitioner, see "What Are the Prospects, What Are the Costs? Oversight of Ballistic Missile Defense (Part 2)," testimony of Philip E. Coyle, III, Senior Advisor, World Security Institute, before the House Committee on Oversight and Government Reform, Subcommittee on National Security and Foreign Affairs, April 18, 2008.

6. *Quadrennial Defense Review Report*, September 30, 2001, at http://www.defenselink.mil/pubs/pdfs/qdr2001.pdf.

7. For this author's analysis of 9/11's lessons, see Dennis M. Gormley, "Enriching

Expectations: 11 September's Lessons for Missile Defence," *Survival* 44 (Summer 2002): 19–35.

8. Maj. Gen. Vladimir Dvorkin (retired), observed that "there is no telling how far the United States will go with its missile defense deployment plans." See his "Reducing Russia's Reliance on Nuclear Weapons in Security Policies," in *Engaging China and Russia on Nuclear Disarmament*, ed. Christina Hansell and William C. Potter, Occasional Paper no. 15 (Monterey, CA: James Martin Center for Nonproliferation Studies, April 2009), p. 95.

9. "Fact Sheet on U.S. Missile Defense Policy: A 'Phased, Adaptive' Approach for Missile Defense in Europe," The White House Office of the Press Secretary, September 17, 2009.

10. This was a concern even before the U.S. withdrawal from the ABM treaty in 2002. See Jack Mendelsohn, "The Impact of NMD on the ABM Treaty," in *White Paper on National Missile Defense,* ed. Joseph Cirincione et al. (Washington, DC: Lawyers Alliance for World Security 2000).

11. Most notable was the reaction in both the U.S. and Russia to a 2006 article in *Foreign Affairs* magazine arguing that the U.S is close to obtaining an effective nuclear first-strike capability against Russian and Chinese strategic retaliatory forces. See Keir A. Lieber and Daryl G. Press, "The Rise of U.S. Nuclear Primacy," *Foreign Affairs* (March/April 2006), at http://www.foreignaffairs.com/articles/61508/keir-a-lieber-and-daryl-g-press/the-rise-of-us-nuclear-primacy. For reactions, see "Nuclear Exchange: Does Washington Really Have (or Want) Nuclear Primacy?" *Foreign Affairs* (September/October 2006), at http://www.foreignaffairs.com/articles/61931/peter-c-w-flory-keith-payne-pavel-podvig-alexei-arbatov-keir-a-l/nuclear-exchange-does-washington-really-have-or-.

12. See, for example, "U.S. Can Attack Russia in 2012–2015," *Moscow Agentstvo Voyennykh Novostey* (internet in English), February 26, 2008 [FBIS].

13. Dvorkin, "Reducing Russia's Reliance on Nuclear Weapons in Security Policies," p. 100. For its part, Russia would prefer to proceed along the conventional-oriented path that the United States has pursued since 1991. Russia's National Security Concept, published in 2000, notes that reliance on nuclear weapons is a temporary phenomenon. Once current plans to develop new air- and sea-launched cruise missiles and PGMs come to fruition by 2020, Russia will no longer need to rely predominantly on nuclear weapons for deterrence purposes. See Nikolai N. Sokov, Jing-dong Yuan, William C. Potter, and Cristina Hansell, "Chinese and Russian Perspectives on Achieving Nuclear Zero," in *Engaging China and Russia on Nuclear Disarmament*, ed. Hansell and Potter, p. 4 (see n. 8).

14. The United States reportedly would prefer to keep any conventionally armed delivery systems, like Trident, out of future nuclear arms control treaties. Author interview with a former government official, Washington, DC, April 2009.

15. It should be noted that when the Global Strike mission was first constituted, it counted nuclear weapons among its constituent components.

16. These programs are joint U.S. Air Force/DARPA efforts conducted under the rubric "Force Application and Launch from CONUS [Continental United States]" or FALCON program. See http://www.darpa.mil/tto/programs/Falcon.htm for a brief outline of the FALCON program; and *Alternatives for Long-Range Ground-Attack Systems* (Washington, DC: Congressional Budget Office, March 2006), at http://www.cbo.gov/ftpdocs/71xx/doc7112/03-31-StrikeForce.pdf.

17. The development of the aircraft carrier during the 1930s furnishes perhaps the finest exemplar of concept rather than technology driving revolutionary military innovation. See Williamson Murray and Allan R. Millett, eds., *Military Innovation in the Interwar Period* (Cambridge: Cambridge University Press, 1998), chs. 5, 8.

18. For a pre-9/11 view of U.S. Air Force plans, see Matt Bille and Maj. Rusty Lorenz, "Requirement for a Conventional Prompt Global Strike Capability," briefing presented to the National Defense Industrial Association's Missile and Rockets Symposium and Exhibition, May 2001 (copy available from this chapter's author).

19. For an incisive appraisal of the operational implementation of Global Strike, including the creation of its organizational components to direct planning and execution, see Hans M. Kristensen, "U.S. Strategic War Planning after 9/11," *Nonproliferation Review* 14 (July 2007): 373–90.

20. Bombers are credited with counting rules that apply to capability rather than actual operating load-outs of nuclear weapons. Thus, there is currently a reluctance to firm up a Next-Generation bomber design before START counting rules are made clear. See David Fulghum, "USAF Bomber Grounded by More than Budget," *Aviation Week & Space Technology* (April 22, 2009), at http://www.aviationweek.com/aw/generic/story.jsp?id=news/NGB042209.xml&headline=USAF%20Bomber%20Grounded%20by%20More%20than%20Budget&channel=defense. For details on the new bomber, see Norman Polmar, "A New Strategic Bomber Coming," Military.com (April 14, 2008) at http://www.military.com/forums/0,15240,165805,00.html.

21. Telephone interview, April 2009. My thanks to Monterey Institute colleague Miles Pomper for this information.

22. Interview, March 2009.

23. See Department of Defense Quadrennial Defense Review Report, February 2010, at http://www.defense.gov/QDR/images/QDR_as_of_12Feb10_1000.pdf. On new Prompt Global Strike concepts, including ones offering opportunities for increased transparency with Russia, see David E. Sanger and Thom Shanker, "White House Is Rethinking Nuclear Policy," *New York Times*, February 28, 2010, p. 1.

24. "Conventional Prompt Global Strike Capability," letter report of the National Research Council's Committee on Conventional Prompt Global Strike Capability, dated May 11, 2007, at http://www.nap.edu/catalog/11951.html.

25. A point made by Joshua Pollack in "Evaluating Conventional Prompt Global Strike," *Bulletin of the Atomic Scientists* 65 (January/February 2009): 13–20. The less effective circumstances would entail Predator's problematic survival against sophisticated and thick air defenses, which would be less likely to be the case in the limited counterterrorist scenario and more likely in major combat operations against a regional adversary.

26. The Sea-Launched Global Strike Missile is mentioned in "Conventional Prompt Global Strike Capability," while a related (if not precisely the same) concept for a Submarine-Launched Intermediate-Range Ballistic Missile is discussed in detail at http://www.globalsecurity.org/wmd/systems/slirbm.htm. On the supersonic Tomahawk, see Dennis M. Gormley, *Missile Contagion: Cruise Missile Proliferation and the Threat to International Security* (Westport, CT: Praeger Security International, 2008), p. 54.

27. The first publicly acknowledged program, in 1957, was the U.S. Air X-20 Dyna-Soar, which was supposed to be launched vertically off the ground and then glided back to earth for landing. The current hypersonic cruise vehicle would be expected to operate at between 30 and 50 km altitude.

28. Testimony by Henry F. Cooper to the House Subcommittee on Space and Aeronautics Committee on Science, October 11, 2001, at http://www.tgv-rockets.com/press/cooper_testimony.htm. Cooper largely placed blame on Pentagon management inefficiencies for the program's poor performance.

29. "U.S. Can Attack Russia in 2012–2015," *Moscow Agentstvo Voyennykh Novostey* (Internet in English), February 26, 2008 [FBIS].

30. Most notably, see N. V. Ogarkov, *Krasnaya Zvezda*, May 9, 1984 (BBC Monitoring Service translation [SU/7/639/C/10]).

31. Russian concrete silo covers are dome-shaped and approximately 20 feet in diameter and 5 feet high in the center. This means that they have a radius of curvature of about 12.5 feet. Employing the targeting requirement of approaching the target at less than 2 degrees from the vertical, the penetrator would have to impact less than 5 inches from the absolute center of the silo cover, or within a 10-inch diameter circle whose center is at the apex of the dome. My thanks to Dr. Gregory DeSantis, a former U.S. Department of Defense scientist, for making these calculations based on the penetrator design discussed in Nancy F. Swinford and Dean A. Kudlick, "A Hard and Deeply Buried Target Defeat Concept," Defense Technical Information Center document no. 19961213 060, 1996 (Lockheed Martin Missiles & Space, Sunnyvale, CA) at http://www.stormingmedia.us/86/8678/A867813.html.

32. The Soviet Union first deployed intermediate-range ballistic missiles on mobile launchers in 1976 (the SS-20).

33. Dennis M. Gormley, "Missile Defence Myopia: Lessons from the Iraq War," *Survival* 45 (Winter 2003/04}, p. 71.

34. The Russian supposition that American intelligence, surveillance, and recon-

naissance capabilities are so ubiquitous that anything that moves will be detected and instantly killed flows from the exaggerated expectations of such books as Harlan Ullman and James P. Wade, Jr., *Shock and Awe: Achieving Rapid Dominance* (Washington, DC: National Defense University, 1996). For a more grounded treatment, see Barry Watts, *Clausewitzian Friction and Future War* (Darby, PA: Diane Publishing Co., 2004).

35. Vladimir Dvorkin, "Threats Posed by the U.S. Missile Shield," *Russia in Global Affairs* 2 (April–June 2007), at http://eng.globalaffairs.ru/numbers/19/.

36. Text of the "Treaty between the United States of America and the Russian Federation on Measures for the Further Reduction and Limitation of Strategic Offensive Arms," p. 2. The text also takes note of the impact of conventionally armed ICBMs and submarine-launched ballistic missiles (SLBMs) on strategic stability.

37. This trend is documented in Gormley, *Missile Contagion* (see n. 27).

38. Quoted in Philip Taubman, "The Trouble with Zero," *New York Times*, May 10, 2009, at http://www.nytimes.com/2009/05/10/weekinreview/10taubman.html.

39. Text of "Joint Declaration on the New Strategic Relationship," The White House Office of the Press Secretary, May 24, 2002.

40. Gormley, *Missile Contagion*, chs. 3, 4.

41. Ibid., ch. 9.

42. Brooks Tigner, "NATO and Russia Near Air Traffic Information Exchange," *International Defence Review* (April 29, 2009), at http://idr.janes.com/public/idr/index.shtml. See also press release of the Russian Mission to NATO, at http://natomission.ru/en/societ/article/society/artnews/40/.

43. The other sources of financial support include Canada, France, Greece, Hungary, Italy, Luxembourg, Norway, Poland, Turkey, and the United Kingdom. See ibid.

44. Ellen Barry, "U.S. Negotiator Signals Flexibility toward Moscow over New Round of Arms Talks," *New York Times*, May 5, 2009; and "U.S. Is Ready to Discuss Proposal on Using Gabala Radar as Part of Global Missile Shield—U.S. Ambassador," *Moscow Interfax*, April 27, 2009.

45. See, for example, Theodore Postol, "A Ring around Iran," *New York Times*, July 11, 2007, at http://www.nytimes.com/2007/07/11/opinion/11postol.html. Postol argues that the Gabala radar's lower frequency radar could crudely yet effectively provide earlier warning than a Czech-based X-band radar, whose higher frequencies and resolution are useful to characterize the target initially detected by the Russian radar. Thus, the sum of the two could furnish additional warning time without loss of much-needed target resolution.

46. K. Scott McMahon, *Pursuit of the Shield: The U.S. Quest for Limited Ballistic Missile Defense* (Lanham, MD: University Press of America, 1997), pp. 251–52.

47. Victor Yesin, "Action and Counteraction," *Global Affairs* 1 (January–March 2009), at http://eng.globalaffairs.ru/numbers/26/1262.html. Yesin is a colonel general in the Russian military and a professor at the Russian Academy of Military Sciences.

48. A word used by Ambassador Linton Brooks to describe a practice employed by Soviet-era arms control negotiators, and apparently no less today. Brooks notes that a senior Russian official once noted that Russia was concerned over the possibility of U.S. use of special forces to blow up strategic missile silos. See his comments at an Arms Control Association meeting in Washington, DC, on April 27, 2009, at http://www.armscontrol.org/node/3632.

49. Johan Bergenas of the Monterey Institute's James Martin Center for Nonproliferation Studies designed and constructed Figure 17.1. Even were these submarines to operate from within territorial waters, it is important to note that such cruise missiles would not be programmed to fly a straight-line path to their targets for reasons of survivability. Moreover, were they able to reach mobile missile operating areas, there would be little fuel remaining for advanced Tomahawks to employ their loiter and search capability against mobile missiles.

50. See http://www.whitehouse.gov/sites/default/files/rss_viewer/national_security_strategy.pdf.

51. For a recent appraisal, see Steve Andreasen, "Reagan Was Right: Let's Ban Ballistic Missiles," *Survival* 46 (Spring 2004): 117–30.

52. For reasons why adopting changes in the Hague Code of Conduct make sense, see Dennis M. Gormley, "Making the Hague Code of Conduct Relevant," issue brief, July 20, 2009, at http://nti.org/e_research/e3_hague_conduct_relevant.html.

WHAT NEXT?

18 Steps toward a World Free of Nuclear Weapons

David Holloway

INTRODUCTION

In his speech in Prague on April 5, 2009, President Obama asserted America's commitment "to seek the peace and security of a world without nuclear weapons." "This goal will not be reached quickly," he continued, "perhaps not in my lifetime. It will take patience and persistence."[1] He also listed, under three broad headings, a series of steps his administration would undertake. First, in order to begin movement toward a world free of nuclear weapons, he promised to reduce the role of nuclear weapons in U.S. national security strategy, to negotiate a new Strategic Arms Reduction Treaty (START) with Russia by the end of 2009, to pursue "immediately and aggressively" U.S. ratification of the Comprehensive Test Ban Treaty (CTBT), and to seek a verifiable Fissile Material Cutoff Treaty (FMCT). Second, in order to strengthen the Nuclear Non-proliferation Treaty (NPT), he called for more resources and authority for international inspections, a new framework for civil nuclear cooperation, including an international fuel bank, and a structure that ensures that when any country breaks the rules it will suffer consequences. Third, in order to ensure that terrorists never acquire nuclear weapons, he proposed a new international effort to secure all vulnerable nuclear material around the world and a Global Summit on Nuclear Security in 2010; he also called for turning the Proliferation Security Initiative and the Global Initiative to Combat Nuclear Terrorism into "durable international institutions."

On September 24, 2009, at the initiative of the Obama administration, the UN Security Council held a summit meeting devoted to nuclear disarmament and nuclear nonproliferation. This was intended to "draw attention at the highest levels of government to the nuclear dangers confronting the international community and the urgency of taking concrete steps to address them."[2] Obama presided at the meeting, at which fourteen heads of state and government unanimously adopted Resolution 1887 reiterating the Security Council's support for nuclear disarmament and nuclear nonproliferation.[3] The resolution reaffirms the Security Council's commitment to a world without nuclear weapons and provides a framework for moving toward that goal. It is very largely a reaffirmation of commitments enshrined in treaties and other UN resolutions. It reflects the agenda Obama outlined in Prague, and aims to build on what he called "a consensus that all nations have the right to peaceful nuclear energy; that nations with nuclear weapons have the responsibility to move toward disarmament; and those without them have the responsibility to forsake them."[4]

There is a considerable overlap between the list of steps to be undertaken by the Obama administration and the list of measures proposed by George Shultz and his colleagues in their *Wall Street Journal* articles.[5] This is not coincidental: Obama has acknowledged the work of the four horsemen, whom he invited to be present in the Security Council for the summit. Nor is the overlap surprising. There is a well-established agenda of unfinished items in the area of arms control and disarmament. The Obama administration has already taken some of these in hand. Negotiations with Russia on a successor to START (signed in 1991) began in May 2009, and the New START Treaty was signed by presidents Medvedev and Obama in April 2010. Obama has entrusted Vice President Joseph Biden with the responsibility of steering the CTBT to ratification by the Senate, although that is not likely to happen before 2011. A new Nuclear Posture Review was published by the Department of Defense in April 2010, and this helps to define the role of nuclear weapons in U.S. national security policy. It was hoped that negotiations on a Fissile Material Cutoff Treaty would resume in January 2010 in the Conference on Disarmament in Geneva, but Pakistan has blocked the resumption of those negotiations. In April 2010 an international conference on nuclear materials was held in Washington, DC, and attended by forty-seven heads of state and government. Obama has launched an international effort to secure all vulnerable nuclear material around the world within four years.

The Prague speech set out an ambitious agenda. It is one thing to make proposals; it is another, to translate them into reality. Not even the initial steps could be taken for granted. The New START negotiations raised more issues than anticipated and took longer than expected to negotiate. Republican opposition delayed the ratification of New START, which was only achieved in late December 2010. The Nuclear Posture Review became the focus of sharp debates within the administration, and its completion was postponed more than once. In spite of the difficulties, some of the crucial first steps outlined in the Prague speech have now been taken. Much more needs to be done, of course. Some of the obstacles to progress come from the difficulties of resolving disagreements with other states, but some are embedded in broader debates in the United States about the desirability and feasibility of a world without nuclear weapons. There is no consensus on these issues. The arguments against nuclear disarmament are not new, but they have reemerged with particular force in reaction to Obama's call for a world free of nuclear weapons.

The first question is whether it is in fact desirable to eliminate nuclear weapons. There are those who oppose nuclear disarmament on the grounds that nuclear weapons have helped to keep the peace by making it clear to the great powers that war among them would be so destructive that it could not serve any useful political purpose. In this view, a world without nuclear weapons would merely reopen the way to large-scale wars, unless the international system were so reorganized as to abolish war itself. The present situation, if it could be stabilized, would be better than the search for elimination. There are at least two responses to that argument. The first has already been mentioned in Chapter 1. The current situation is not likely to be stable in the long run, because a discriminatory nuclear order will not last; more states will want to acquire nuclear weapons, leading to recurrent crises as the nuclear weapon states seek to prevent others from going nuclear. The second is that the history of nuclear weapons does not provide reassurance that the world would be safer over the long term with more nuclear weapon states. It is true that nuclear weapons have not been used in war since 1945, but there have been crises in which the possibility that nuclear weapons might be used has appeared to be dangerously close. A world with more nuclear weapon states would offer more scope for nuclear crises.

The second issue is that of feasibility. Many critics of the vision of a world free of nuclear weapons claim that such a world is not feasible, and that it is therefore dishonest to hold out the hope that it can be achieved. Supporters of the vision do not claim to know exactly what a world without nuclear weapons would look like—except for the lack of nuclear weapons of course—and they recognize that many difficult problems will need to be answered before the final goal is reached; they argue nevertheless that it provides an essential compass point in the search for a safer and more secure nuclear order. The dialectic between the vision and the practical steps is central to this approach. "Without the bold vision, the actions will not be perceived as fair or urgent," George Shultz and his colleagues wrote in their first *Wall Street Journal* article. "Without the actions, the vision will not be perceived as realistic or possible."[6]

Disagreement on the feasibility of nuclear disarmament is very sharp. This is clearly shown by the Final Report of the Congressional Commission on the Strategic Posture of the United States.[7] Congress set up the commission in 2008 to help guide the next Nuclear Posture Review. The Democrats appointed six of the commission's twelve members, the Republicans the other six. William Perry (one of the Four Horsemen) served as chairman, and James Schlesinger (a strong critic of the Four Horsemen) as vice-chairman. Among other things, Congress asked the commission to look to the long term in formulating its recommendations about the U.S. strategic posture. The commission found, however, that it had very different visions for the future: "As we have debated our findings and recommendations," the Final Report of the commission states, "it has become clear that we have very different visions of what might be possible in the long term. Fundamentally, this reflects our differences over whether the conditions can ever be created that might enable the elimination of nuclear weapons."[8]

The Congressional commission reached consensus on many near-term issues, with the notable exception of ratification of the CTBT, on which it was split. This consensus shows that disagreement about the possibility of eliminating nuclear weapons need not prevent agreement in many areas of nuclear policy. In spite of their differences over the elimination of nuclear weapons, the members of the commission shared a hopeful vision of the nearer term, "reject[ing] the notion that somehow it is inevitable that international nuclear order will collapse."[9] The commission report portrays the nuclear future as manageable from the point of view of the United States. It thereby rejects what was one of the basic motivations for the Hoover Initiative—namely, that the status quo was tending to a bad outcome. This view of a manageable nuclear future might lessen the pressure for far-reaching policy changes; the tenor of the commission's Final Report is much less urgent than that of Obama's Prague speech.

REDUCTIONS IN NUCLEAR FORCES

The United States and Russia between them have more than 90 percent of all nuclear warheads; their arsenals include thousands of warheads, while according to the best estimates no other country has more than about 300.[10] The

United States and Russia therefore need to take the lead in reducing nuclear forces. This should surely be possible. The Cold War is over, and, notwithstanding the worsening of relations between the two countries in the early years of this century, it is inconceivable that either country would now intentionally attack the other with nuclear weapons. Doctrinal statements by the United States and Russia suggest that it should be possible to make substantial reductions in strategic nuclear weapons. Neither country now regards the other as an imminent nuclear threat or as the main source of nuclear danger, though neither has been willing to dismiss entirely the danger of a nuclear threat arising from the other in the future. There is therefore scope for substantial reductions in strategic nuclear forces with each side retaining an effective nuclear deterrent, the more so since mutual deterrence between them now serves as a hedge against a possible future danger rather than as protection against an immediate and pressing threat.

U.S.-Russian relations reached their nadir after the Georgian war of August 2008, with signs that a new round of nuclear arms competition might be beginning. Barack Obama came into office with the goal of "resetting" relations with Russia in order to secure Russian help in dealing with the nuclear danger, including the threat from Iran. On April 1, 2009, after their meeting in London, presidents Medvedev and Obama issued a Joint Statement setting out a substantive agenda for international security. "We committed our two countries to achieving a nuclear free world," the Joint Statement says, "while recognizing that this long-term goal will require a new emphasis on arms control and conflict resolution measures, and their full implementation by all concerned nations."[11] Obama's September 2009 decision not to go ahead with the planned deployment of the missile defense radar in the Czech Republic and the interceptor missiles in Poland has contributed to an improvement in relations. The New START is a reflection of the improved relationship.

The new treaty could provide the basis for more cuts in nuclear forces. It should be possible to make reductions beyond the 1,550 warhead ceiling enshrined in the new treaty. The next stage could be to aim for 1,000 strategic nuclear warheads apiece, and then proceed by stages with further reductions. It has become clear, however, that further reductions in strategic arms will be contingent on a number of issues, most notably on agreement to regulate ballistic missile defenses. It will be important for the two sides to maintain strategic stability as nuclear forces are reduced to lower levels. In other words, a balance should be maintained that is stable in terms of deterrence theory: lower levels should not create incentives for the use of nuclear weapons in a crisis; nor should they offer incentives to either side to acquire more nuclear weapons.[12]

Strategic stability is often analyzed in purely technical terms, but the political context is crucial. Policy-makers and military planners have to make political judgments as well as technical assessments. The level of destruction that a retaliatory strike needs to threaten, in order to deter a nuclear attack, will vary according to political as well as military circumstances. The forces needed to deter a mortal enemy from attacking will be different from those needed to deter a country with which one has less hostile relations. In the latter case the potential attacker is less likely to give his political goals a value that would outweigh the losses that even the smallest retaliatory nuclear strike would cause. This is an important point, because it means that mutual deterrence can exist at lower levels of forces. Mutual deterrence has its own requirements—the most important being that both sides have an assured retaliatory capability—but those requirements can be satisfied at ever lower levels of forces as long as the political relationship is right.

Ultimately, mutual deterrence need not exist at all in relations between two nuclear states. There is no deterrence if neither side contemplates attacking or being attacked. This means that further reductions in U.S. and Russian nuclear forces should be possible as long as the political relationship develops to the point where fears and suspicions diminish. Indeed, there is an argument to be made that deterrence can operate even when there are no nuclear weapons in the world. That is because we would be entering a post–nuclear weapons world in which the knowledge of how to make nuclear weapons would continue to exist, as well as fissile materials and the industrial technologies for producing them. That knowledge, it has been argued, could serve as a kind of "virtual deterrent" at zero nuclear forces.[13] Nuclear weapons could thus be eliminated, leaving deterrence in place, like the Cheshire cat in *Alice's Adventures in Wonderland*, which disappears apart from its grin; "'A grin without a cat!' said Alice. 'It's the most curious thing I ever saw in all my life.'"

Nuclear disarmament will involve not only the United States and Russia; all the nuclear powers will have to give up their nuclear weapons. None of the other states has anything like the number of nuclear weapons possessed by the United States and Russia. They say, with justification, that it is up to those two countries to make deep reductions first, and then they will join in. Sooner rather than later, however, the other nuclear powers should be brought into the process of disarmament. There are ways in which they could make a contribution, for example, by not increasing their nuclear forces, by agreeing to greater transparency, and by not maintaining their nuclear forces in an operationally deployed status.

Strategic stability in the sense in which it has traditionally been applied in the context of the U.S.-Russian (and Soviet) relationship may become more complex as U.S. and Russian nuclear forces are reduced. More states—and more relationships—will have to be taken into account, and the requirements for verification and monitoring may become more demanding. Is strategic stability in the traditional sense the appropriate way to think about nuclear relationships under those circumstances? Confidence-building measures such as transparency and low states of combat readiness may assume greater importance. The definition of strategic stability may also have to be broadened to include political factors in a more explicit way. These are questions that would merit research and discussion among the nuclear powers.

DISARMAMENT AND NONPROLIFERATION

There has been a shift in American thinking from an emphasis on stopping others from acquiring nuclear weapons to a focus on creating a new nuclear order in which obligations by the nuclear powers to move toward disarmament will play a key role. That of course is what the Nuclear Non-proliferation Treaty mandates: the non–nuclear weapons states that have signed the treaty (that is, almost all states) have made the commitment not to acquire nuclear weapons, while the nuclear weapons states have committed themselves to working toward nuclear disarmament.

The relationship between nuclear disarmament and nuclear nonproliferation is perhaps the central issue in Obama's embrace of the vision of a world free of nuclear weapons. In his Prague speech he described the "basic bargain" of the Nuclear Non-proliferation Treaty as "sound": "[C]ountries with nuclear weapons will move towards disarmament, countries without nuclear weapons will not acquire them, and all countries can access peaceful nuclear energy."[14] In order to realize the vision of a world free of nuclear weapons it is necessary not only to get rid of nuclear weapons through disarmament, but also to prevent new states or nonstate actors from acquiring nuclear weapons.

The view that disarmament will lead to a strengthening of the nonproliferation regime is by no means universally accepted in the United States. There are two main objections. The first is that during the Cold War the U.S. policy of extending deterrence to its allies in NATO and in East Asia dampened the spread of nuclear weapons. The United States was committed to responding, with nuclear weapons if necessary, to attacks on its allies. These commitments were intended not only to deter the enemy but also to reassure allies that they were secure and covered by the U.S. "nuclear umbrella." If the United States were to move to deep reductions in its nuclear forces, and ultimately to the elimination of nuclear weapons, so the argument runs, some of the states that have benefited from the U.S. policy of extended deterrence might seek nuclear weapons of their own. This is, of course, a serious issue that would have to be addressed in moving toward elimination. It obviously would not be desirable if reductions in the existing nuclear arsenals were to encourage states that do not now have nuclear weapons to acquire them. Nevertheless, in the post–Cold War world it should be possible to find ways to deal with this problem. Japan is often pointed to as the most problematic case in this context, relying heavily on the U.S. nuclear guarantee for its security, yet the Japanese prime minister, Yukio Hatoyama, approved Resolution 1887 at the UN Security Council summit in September 2009. "Japan," he said, "would engage in active diplomacy to lead international efforts on nuclear disarmament and non-proliferation."[15]

The second objection is that states that are determined to acquire nuclear weapons have done so in the past, and will do so in the future, without any regard to the moves that the nuclear weapon states are making now, or might make in the future, toward nuclear disarmament. In other words, they acquire nuclear weapons for their own reasons—as Israel, India, Pakistan, and North Korea have done. This is a common argument against the vision of a world free of nuclear weapons, but it is beside the point. The key link between disarmament and non-proliferation, in the minds of those who advance the vision of a world without nuclear weapons, is that if the nuclear weapon states move in the direction of nuclear disarmament it will become easier to construct a nuclear order in which those who break the rules are sanctioned. As Obama said in Prague: "Rules must be binding. Violations must be punished. Words must mean something. The world must stand together to prevent the spread of these weapons."[16] At the UN summit he made the same point: "[We] must demonstrate that international law is not an empty promise, and that treaties will be enforced."[17]

The question is how to do this. Obama seems to have in mind a new approach to international relations in general. The common challenges of the twenty-first century, he said at the UN Security Council summit, "can't be met by any one leader or any one nation. And that's why my administration has worked to establish a new era of engagement in which all nations must take responsibility for the world we seek."[18] Obama is aiming to construct a new nuclear order for which all nations—but especially the great powers—take responsibility. To act responsibly is to abide by commitments already made and to be ready to sanction those who do not live up to their commitments.[19] This new order entails nuclear disarmament on the part of the nuclear powers, in accordance with the Nuclear Non-proliferation Treaty, as well as a willingness to ensure that any country that breaks the rules will suffer consequences. The Obama vision is not that the nuclear powers should get rid of their weapons and in return expect to see a strengthening of the nonproliferation regime, but rather that these two developments should go hand in hand.

IS A WORLD WITHOUT NUCLEAR WEAPONS REALISTIC?

The United States and the other permanent members of the UN Security Council have recommitted themselves to the goal of a world free of nuclear weapons. They have not provided a timetable for attaining that goal, though more than once Obama has said that the goal may not be reached in his lifetime.[20] Nor has it been spelled out what a world free of nuclear weapons would look like. What would it really mean to be "free of nuclear weapons?" Would there be many states with the capacity to produce nuclear weapons in a short time? Would a nuclear weapons–free world require new kinds of intrusive inspection? Are the necessary means of verification available? Would there always be the danger of breakout? What could be done to mitigate that danger? What will the end state look like? These are extremely important questions, which have begun to receive the analysis they deserve.[21]

It would be a mistake, however, to make the initial steps on the journey contingent on agreement about the precise configuration of the end state. The important thing is to start on the journey and with each step to move closer to the goal. There is a great deal that can be done—and should be done—to move in the direction of reductions and elimination before the final destination is clear in all its details. There is a great deal that those who do not share the goal of elimination can agree to: the steps toward such a world would be of value in themselves, even short of the ultimate goal. Nevertheless, elimination should serve as the compass point for nuclear policy: in assessing any given policy one of the questions to ask is whether it moves us in the direction of nuclear disarmament. It is the vision of a world free of nuclear weapons that gives meaning to the specific steps and makes it possible to view them as part of a broader unfolding process.

The key elements of a world without nuclear weapons would be: (a) reduction of nuclear weapons to zero; (b) controlled and guaranteed access to nuclear fuel; and (c) international arrangements to prevent states from breaking out of the non-nuclear regime. These three elements will be central to any system of nuclear disarmament that has the peaceful uses of nuclear energy as one of its goals. All three were present in the Acheson-Lilienthal Report and the Baruch Plan. How does the Obama agenda differ from those early attempts at nuclear disarmament? First, there is now a decades-long experience of negotiations and agreements, which embody shared understandings of the nuclear danger and how to go about dealing with it. There are, of course, differences and disagreements among the nuclear powers in the way in which they see nuclear weapons, but there is also a considerable degree of common understanding, which did not exist in 1946. Second, the proposals put forward by Obama draw on that experience and seek to extend and build on it: by ratifying the CTBT, for example, or extending strategic arms reductions, or negotiating a Fissile Material Cut-Off Treaty. Third, Obama has not presented to the world a blueprint for the end state; rather he is trying to use what has already been agreed upon as the basis for drawing other states into the cooperative project of constructing a new nuclear order. This is, then, an open-ended agenda to be worked on by many different actors—including nonstate actors—although Obama has made it clear that he sees the United States playing a leading role.

CONCLUSION

Obama has laid out an ambitious vision and a full agenda. Many obstacles stand in the way. This chapter has pointed to some of them, especially the divisions inside the United States on the desirability of even the first steps. There are, however, many other obstacles, as the chapters in this book show. First, there is skepticism about American goals and interests: surely the United States wants nuclear disarmament because that would make the world safe for American conventional superiority? Would nuclear disarmament lead to greater U.S. dominance in the world—something that Americans might be happy with but other states could be expected to resist? Are nuclear weapons an essential means for other countries seeking to balance American power?

Second, not all the nuclear powers view nuclear weapons in the same way; nor do they all assign to nuclear weapons the same role in their defense policy.

Russia, to take just one example, places heavy reliance on nuclear weapons in its doctrine and its policy because of the weakness of its conventional forces. It will not be interested in eliminating its nuclear weapons, or even in deep reductions in its nuclear forces, until it feels that there is a balance of conventional forces that guarantees its security.

Third, there are today two international crises caused by the efforts of states that signed the NPT to acquire nuclear weapons. North Korea has tested nuclear weapons and is apparently intent on producing more plutonium. Western governments believe that Iran, which is building the main elements of the nuclear fuel cycle and has conducted many of its nuclear activities in secret, is in the process of developing nuclear weapons of its own. If North Korea continues to add nuclear weapons to its arsenal and Iran proceeds to make the bomb, those will be serious setbacks to the effort to rid the world of nuclear weapons. It does not mean that the effort to rid the world of nuclear weapons should be abandoned, but it will make the task much more difficult and cast doubt on the ability of the international community to act together to carry it out.

It is appropriate therefore to quote the famous concluding paragraph of Max Weber's 1919 lecture on "Politics as a Vocation," in which he stresses how hard politics is and also how important it is to strive for what may seem to be impossible. "Politics," writes Weber,

> is a strong and slow drilling of hard boards. It takes both passion and perspective. Certainly, all historical experience confirms the truth—that man would not have attained the possible unless time and again he had reached out for the impossible.... Even those who are neither leaders nor heroes must arm themselves with that steadfastness of heart that can brave even the crumbling of all hopes. This is necessary right now, or else men will not be able to attain even that which is possible today.[22]

There is a great deal of "drilling of hard boards" to be done by policy-makers, by scholars, and by activists alike, to rid the world of nuclear weapons.

NOTES

1. Remarks by President Barack Obama in Prague, April 5, 2009, at http://www.whitehouse.gov/the_press_office/Remarks-By-President-Barack-Obama-In-Prague-As-Delivered/.

2. "Concept Paper for the Security Council Summit on Nuclear Non-Proliferation and Nuclear Disarmament," annex to the letter dated September 15, 2009, from

the president of the Security Council to the secretary general, at http://www.securitycouncilreport.org/atf/cf/%7B65BFCF9B-6D27-4E9C-8CD3-CF6E4FF96FF9%7D/Disarm%20S2009463.pdf.

3. The text of the resolution can be found at http://www.un.org/News/Press/docs/2009/sc9746.doc.htm.

4. Remarks by the president at the United Nations Security Council Summit, at http://www.whitehouse.gov/the_press_office/Remarks-By-The-President-At-the-UN-Security-Council-Summit-On-Nuclear-Non-Proliferation-And-Nuclear-Disarmament/.

5. See Chapter 1, this volume.

6. George P. Shultz, William J. Perry, Henry A. Kissinger, and Sam Nunn, "A World Free of Nuclear Weapons," *Wall Street Journal*, January 4, 2007.

7. *America's Strategic Posture: The Final Report of the Congressional Committee on the Strategic Posture of the United States*, William J. Perry, chairman, James R. Schlesinger, vice-chairman (Washington, DC: United States Institute of Peace, 2009).

8. Ibid., p. xix.

9. Ibid., pp. xix–xx.

10. The most careful estimates are those provided by Robert S. Norris and Hans M. Kristensen published in the Nuclear Notebook in each issue of *The Bulletin of the Atomic Scientists* (http://www.thebulletin.org).

11. JointStatementbyPresidentObamaandPresidentMedvedev,April1,2009,athttp://www.america.gov/st/texttrans-english/2009/April/20090401125216xjsnommiso.8078381.html&distid=ucs.

12. For further discussion, see David Holloway, "Further Reductions in Nuclear Forces," in *Reykjavik Revisited: Steps toward a World Free of Nuclear Weapons*, ed. George P. Shultz, Steven P. Andreasen, Sidney D. Drell, and James E. Goodby (Stanford: Hoover Institution Press, 2008), pp. 1–45.

13. See especially Jonathan Schell, *The Abolition* (New York: Knopf, 1984).

14. Remarks by President Barack Obama in Prague (cited in n. 1).

15. "Historic Summit of Security Council" (New York: UN Security Council Department of Public Information, September 24, 2009), at http://www.un.org/News/Press/docs/2009/sc9746.doc.htm.

16. Remarks of President Barack Obama in Prague (cited in n. 1).

17. Remarks by the president at the United Nations Security Council Summit (cited in n. 5).

18. Ibid.

19. For a helpful discussion of responsible sovereignty that seems to jibe well with Obama's remarks, see Bruce Jones, Carlos Pascual, and Stephen John Stedman, *Power and Responsibility: Building International Order in an Era of Transnational Threats* (Washington, DC: Brookings Institution Press, 2009), ch. 1.

20. Remarks of President Barack Obama in Prague (cited in n. 1); remarks of the president to the United Nations Security Council Summit (cited in n. 4).

21. See, for example, Sidney D. Drell and James E. Goodby, *A World without Nuclear Weapons: End-State Issues* (Stanford: Hoover Institution Press, 2009).

22. Max Weber, *Politik als Beruf* (München and Leipzig: Verlag von Duncker & Humblot, 1919), at http://de.wikisource.org/wiki/Politik_als_Beruf.

19 Practical Steps toward Nuclear Zero

Peter Dombrowski

During the 2008 presidential campaign, the then-Democratic presidential candidate, Senator Barack Obama (D-Ill), rarely spoke of nuclear weapons or arms control, but when he did he pledged to follow policies similar to those recommended by groups such as the Nuclear Threat Initiative,[1] and various former high-ranking government officials, including former secretaries of state George Shultz and Henry Kissinger, former senator Sam Nunn, and former secretary of defense William J. Perry, among others who had promoted a vision of the world free of nuclear weapons. Senator Obama, along with these distinguished defense and foreign policy experts, came under attack from defense analysts who questioned the wisdom and feasibility of a nuclear-free world. Few of the arguments were new or especially persuasive; indeed, George Perkovich and James Acton have identified them as the "fatuous five."[2] Yet even commentators who generally agreed with the goal of a nuclear-free world questioned whether a new president would or could actually follow through on such a promise, or have the political courage to push the logic of zero in the face of domestic and international opponents.

On the surface, Senator Obama's approach to nuclear weapons was not all that different from that of his Republican rival, Senator John McCain (R-Ariz). In a major speech at the University of Denver, Senator McCain argued, "Today, we deploy thousands of nuclear warheads. It is my hope to move as rapidly as possible to a significantly smaller force."[3] In Denver, as in other campaign speeches, candidate McCain also sought to disassociate himself, cautiously, from the nuclear policies of the Bush administration by offering qualified support for the Non-proliferation Treaty and the Comprehensive Nuclear Test Ban

Treaty, as well as international organizations such as the International Atomic Energy Agency. Moreover, after the election, when President Obama endorsed the logic of zero in Prague and elsewhere, Senator McCain spoke on the Senate floor, arguing, "[L]et us keep in mind the dream of a nuclear free world enunciated so eloquently by our 40th president."[4] Senator McCain, as he had during the presidential campaign, sought to cloak his support for arms control and disarmament by assuming the mantle of President Ronald Reagan, including the spirit of Reykjavik.

As the U.S. presidential candidates were staking out positions on nuclear weapons and their role in maintaining world peace and security, an international movement was growing to abolish nuclear weapons; prominent politicians and policy analysts in the United States, the United Kingdom, Germany, and elsewhere were calling for the United States to lead the way toward a world free of nuclear weapons. One prominent contribution was an article in *Foreign Affairs*, "The Logic of Zero," by Ivo Daalder and Jan Lodal.[5] The public efforts of retired politicians, policy-makers, and academic entrepreneurs helped create a policy window for President Obama and other world leaders to step through and pursue a broad-based agenda for peace based on the simple idea that the very existence of nuclear weapons threatens world peace.

Daalder and Lodal propose that the United States should help create a coalition of countries that accept the logic of zero. They argue that: (1) a world without nuclear weapons is the only way of guaranteeing that such weapons will never be used; (2) in the interim the only valid purpose for nuclear weapons is to prevent their use by others; and (3) all fissile material must be subject to international accounting and control. Their case rests on the strategic logic that the only purpose underlying American nuclear weapons is to prevent use by others, and thus the United States can reduce its own arsenal to roughly 1,000 total weapons. Once this is done the United States should establish a "comprehensive" nonproliferation regime to account for and monitor all fissile materials. Numerous op-ed articles, scholarly assessments, and books echoing Daalder's and Lodal's *Foreign Affairs* piece have followed.[6] Yet as Randy Rydell argues, "[M]any of these zero initiatives suffer from zero follow-up."[7]

This chapter identifies ways to advance and sustain the logic of nuclear disarmament beyond those suggested by Daalder and Lodal and other scholars working in this field. It is aimed, first and foremost, at President Obama and his foreign and security policy teams because, as a practical matter, American leadership is essential to the fate of the movement toward eliminating nuclear weapons. The chapter focuses on the internal actions that the U.S. government could undertake to help ensure that other countries do not discount American efforts as "cheap talk, talk that will not be followed by concrete actions that are not readily reversible."[8] In the language of international relations theory, the chapter urges actions that will demonstrate a "credible commitment" to the logic of zero.[9] As Perkovich and Acton argue, "[E]xploration of the challenges of abolition must take place in parallel with practical near term steps (lest they be nothing more than empty rhetoric)."[10]

First, this chapter supports President Obama's call for a world summit to include the leaders of existing nuclear states, threshold states, and those countries that, presumably, could acquire nuclear weapons relatively quickly given their access to nuclear fuel and the technologies and engineering capacity to produce nuclear weapons. Although progress on bilateral arms control and disarmament between the United States and Russia is important, if for no other reason than that they control roughly 95 percent of the world's nuclear weapons, wider global action will be required to address the risks associated with some of the newer nuclear weapons states.

Second, the chapter argues that the President should put on hold suggestions to introduce new arms control initiatives;[11] further, he should pursue only minimal changes, including extensions, to existing arms control and disarmament agreements. Simplifying the U.S. arms control agenda, and therefore using U.S. leadership to limit the number of arms control initiatives pursued by the international community at any one time, would maximize the attention devoted to the headline goal of eliminating nuclear weapons. This simplification process should commence immediately and continue until world leaders have developed and committed to a comprehensive process for achieving nuclear disarmament.[12]

Third, and most important, the chapter proposes that President Obama should order the U.S. military and national security community to engage seriously with the fact that the nation can no longer rely on nuclear weapons as the ultimate guarantor of American national security. After all, the 2010 Nuclear Posture Review already emphasized "reducing the role of U.S. nuclear weapons" in US defense policy by limiting the circumstance under which the nation reserves the right to employ nuclear weapons and pledging to strengthen conventional capabilities. Specifically, the president must use his executive powers, role as commander-in-chief, and power of persuasion with the American public and Congress to examine how the nation would implement nuclear disarmament. Each of these three steps supports Daalder's and Lodal's idea of developing a "strategic logic that explains how the world can get there from here."[13]

FROM THE BUSH ADMINISTRATION TO THE OBAMA ADMINISTRATION

In eight years in the White House President Bush did not make arms control or disarmament a priority. One of the Bush administration's most prominent foreign policy decisions was to abrogate the Anti-Ballistic Missile (ABM) Treaty unilaterally with little or no consultation with Russia, the other signatory to the agreement. Yet, in the Moscow Treaty and the negotiations to follow-on the achievements of START I, the Bush administration was willing to discuss, within tight limits, further arrangements with Russia. At the same time, the Bush administration, working with the nuclear industrial complex, proponents within the military, and Congress continued to pursue vertical proliferation that greatly troubled arms control proponents. At various points, the president's advisors pushed to develop a new class of so-called bunker buster weapons designed to destroy hardened or buried WMD facilities. They also supported the Reliable Replacement Warhead (RRW) program, reportedly to ensure the viability of existing nuclear weapons far into the future.

Perhaps most troubling was a development that had less to do with nuclear weapons and programs than with U.S. strategic intent. In 2002 the new National Security Strategy focused not only on deterrence but on preemption or even preventive war; administration critics feared that the Bush administration was lowering the threshold for using military force and perhaps even nuclear weapons. Some analysts concluded that the Bush administration's focus on preemption had actually shifted international debates and national strategies in the direction of either preemptive or preventive action.[14] Given loose talk about the need to take preemptive military action against rogue nuclear states or even threshold states, and the well-known difficulties of destroying weapons and facilities buried deep within underground bunkers, some analysts concluded that small-yield, earth-penetrating nuclear weapons were the only viable way to maintain deterrence and threaten the nuclear programs of other states. As the 2001 Nuclear Posture Review briefings suggested, nuclear weapons could "defeat enemies by holding at risk those targets that could not be destroyed by other types of weapons."[15]

In sharp contrast to the previous administration, the Obama administration managed to stake out a strong position on nuclear issues during its first one hundred days in office and to take numerous concrete steps to revive arms control initiatives. On April 5, 2009, President Obama chose Prague as the venue for making his first major speech on nuclear arms and arms control.[16] The president made two notable points: (1) America's commitment to seek the peace and security of a world without nuclear weapons; and (2) a Global Summit on Nuclear Security, to be held within the next year. Four days earlier, in London, Russian president Medvedev and President Obama had essentially, "endorsed a nuclear-free world—zero nuclear weapons—to be achieved on a step-by-step basis,"[17] and laid the groundwork for the START negotiations originally intended to meet a fall 2009 deadline, negotiations that reached fruition with the signing of the New START treaty on April 9, 2010. On September 24, 2009, the United Nations Security Council weighed in by adopting a U.S.-sponsored resolution favoring a "world without nuclear weapons."[18]

With the New START agreement signed and —as of December 2010— ratified, the Obama administration should focus on fine tuning its diplomatic approach and on implementing its public commitment to global zero domestically. For the president's agenda to have a chance to succeed, it must have strong support from all elements of the executive branch, including those agencies and departments that might naturally be skeptical of the zero option, and commitment from key congressional leaders. With the Democratic Party's loss of the majority position within the U.S. House of Representatives and the reduction of its majority in the Senate after the 2010 mid-term elections, the task will not be easy. But President Obama retains powerful rhetorical advantages, executive authorities, and, not insignificantly, the ability to engage in old-fashioned political horse trading with opponents to his arms control and disarmament agendas.

ALTERNATIVE APPROACHES

Summitry and Beyond

As promised in Prague and implicitly supported by the UN Security Council, to earn widespread support for the logic of zero from the nuclear states and the wider international community, the Obama administration should continuously and repeatedly engage the leaders of concerned powers on the issue of global zero. President Obama's team should continue to fan out across the world, engaging all interested parties, not simply the major nuclear powers or threshold states of immediate concern. However, the Obama administration should take a different approach than advised thus far by experts on the question of who should attend nuclear arms control and disarmament meetings, when the meetings should occur, and what agenda the initial meeting should follow.

Attendance. The question of who should attend a global summit is controversial. The past dictates that invitations should be issued to the heads of the five leading nuclear powers—the United States, Russia, China, Great Britain, and France. Yet limiting attendance to the Perm-5 would constrain the overarching ambition of ridding the world of nuclear weapons. It would hold future negotiations hostage to an earlier time, when the individual states either had nuclear weapons or not, and thus were involved in negotiations or not. Today's reality is that two other states—India and Pakistan—admittedly possess nuclear weapons, another—North Korea—has clearly conducted nuclear tests, and a third—Israel—is widely assumed to have nuclear weapons but does not acknowledge possession officially. And this accounting does not include threshold states such as Iran, which could have nuclear weapons within five to ten years or so, depending on who is doing the analysis. Finally, several states have a military-industrial complex capable of building nuclear weapons and may, under present circumstances, soon have the incentives to begin weapons programs themselves.[19]

The bottom line is that all of these states have a stake in getting to zero. All nuclear powers and threshold powers should be included formally as summit attendees. Critics will argue that this would give "rogue" states that have not complied with earlier nuclear agreements the status and respect otherwise denied by the international community. The counterargument is that conferring status and respect is less dangerous than allowing rogue states to pursue their ambitions free from the prying eyes of the international community, and without taking advantage of opportunities to negotiate with states possessing such dangerous weapons.

Schedule. In Prague President Obama pledged to convene the world summit as soon as is practical.[20] Given the numerous items on the administration's international and domestic agendas, the summit should be scheduled for as early in the president's third year in office as is possible, preferably after having won ratification for the New START agreement. This will allow the president several degrees of freedom because the administration's next nuclear diplomatic initiative will take place well past the partisan debates of the 2010 mid-term elections and before the beginnings of the 2012 presidential campaign. With many of the thorny issues of force structure, counting rules, verification, monitoring, and so forth already addressed in the negotiations of the two nuclear superpowers leading to New START, the world summit will allow discussions of these and other issues with the wider range of nuclear states to proceed. The U.S.-Russian agreement, along with the Nuclear Posture Review, provides a baseline against which initial discussion of the most likely problems along the road to general nuclear disarmament can proceed, including the small numbers problem and the technicalities of nonproliferation, and unforeseen issues can receive early attention.

Agenda. The summit agenda must be carefully negotiated. What should be on the summit agenda? First and foremost it aims to focus the world community for the coming decade on the singular purpose of getting to zero. In effect, the nuclear arms control agenda should be reset to prioritize effective disarmament. Second, the summit must establish a process for moving forward. Participants must set a firm timetable for further summits and working groups. Each should have hard deadlines, interim milestones, and hard expectations. One way around the obvious disparities among the size of the nuclear forces involved and the various areas of concern and incentives would be to devise concentric circles of engagement, beginning perhaps with the two largest nuclear powers, and ending perhaps with threshold states or even nuclear-capable states. Third, another not insignificant part of the summit's agenda should be to raise the profile of nuclear issues in world opinion. Public support for nuclear arms control has waned with the end of the Cold War. The nuclear freeze movement that pressured politicians in the United States and Europe during the 1980s has no significant counterpart today. The United States can give the logic of zero momentum by acting unilaterally in ways that publicize its commitment and put pressure on its counterparts. As Freedman observes, "If this undertaking is going to be treated with the seriousness it deserves over an extended period, public opinion will need to be engaged."[21]

Simplification

In many respects, the existing nuclear arms control regime may be part of the problem in getting to zero. Like any regime, arms control consists of "principles, norms, rules, and decision making procedures around which actor expectations converge."[22] Yet the nuclear arms control regime was designed and evolved in another time, during a period of bipolarity, superpower rivalry, and more limited prospects for proliferation. The regime does not necessarily fit the current distribution of power within the international system, or the most immediate challenges to global security. Past nuclear arms control agreements have, of necessity, led to the reification of both international and national bureaucracies devoted to administering a particular agreement or process vice more general solutions to questions of nuclear security. As such, the bureaucracies are not necessarily open to new direction or to political guidance that may dramatically alter their roles, missions, prestige, and, ultimately, usefulness. Of course, this is true, only more so, for the military communities and intelligence agencies whose raison d'être would be most threatened by arms control or disarmament agreements.

Specifically, many if not most of the existing agreements regarding nuclear weapons and materials were decided or had their origins in the rivalry between the Soviet Union and the United States. Everything from decisions on force levels to processes to timetables to verification regimes hinged upon the diplomatic, political, technological, and security needs of the two nuclear superpowers. Daalder and Lodal, for example, explicitly adopt this framing by arguing that Russia and the United States remain at the center of future agreements. Indeed, the Obama administration implicitly endorsed the Russia-first paradigm by agreeing on a bilateral meeting with Russia before the president had even announced its more general commitment in Prague.[23]

While in a numerical sense—Russia and the United States control a disproportionate percentage of the world's nuclear weapons—this is reasonable, it is not a tactic designed to garner the support of the lesser nuclear states, so-called rogue states, and threshold states for a wider push toward zero. Each of these groups will present unique challenges to the push for disarmament, but all would benefit from inclusion rather than exclusion.

Several of the most immediate challenges to nuclear security involve states—Iran, North Korea, and Israel, for example—which have been at the periphery of arms control processes historically and, worse still, at the periphery of most forms of international governance for the entire nuclear age. As such, nuclear and near-nuclear states that are not members of the Non-Proliferation Treaty or other international fora have little stake in the existing state of affairs, and virtually no history of participating in arms control negotiations in a positive way. If anything, they have a vested interest, domestically as well as internationally, in maintaining their outsider status. At home, resistance to pressure from other nuclear powers confers prestige and legitimacy on leaders. In Iran, for example, virtually the entire political spectrum,[24] regardless of their position on other foreign policy issues such as Westernization or an independent approach toward regional security, agree that acquiring nuclear weapons is essential not only for national security, including deterrence, but for the political benefits that would accrue in terms of regional leadership.[25]

CLEAN THE SLATE AND CONSOLIDATE

At the world summit and within all associated negotiations, the United States should encourage other nations, both nuclear and non-nuclear, to table, at least temporarily, existing agreements and ongoing negotiations. Getting to zero will require a clean slate, an international tabula rasa, for building a new nuclear arms control regime from the ground up in a way that recognizes new political realities. The reasons underlying this recommendation extend far beyond beginning with a fresh start.

First, as odd as this may seem, there is a question of efficiency. The number and quality of specialists in nuclear disarmament (and associated disciplines, including monitoring, verification, and nuclear forensics) in both individual countries and the various nongovernmental and supranational organizations that support arms control initiatives are limited. This is especially true with regard to political leaders who have taken the time and effort to gain special expertise in the challenges of nuclear arms control. Participation by the epistemic community of arms control experts, scientists, and engineers and by highly competent national level politicians is essential to moving forward with a broad international effort to implement the zero option. There are five bilateral U.S.-Russia arms control organizations and six multilateral ones on the books. This number does not include the individual bureaucracies within nuclear states charged with the nuclear dimensions of diplomacy and security. Nor does it even hint at the private sector organizations and groups, big and small, which are in the business of studying, promoting, and even defeating arms control measures; such private groups are significant, not only as a source of expertise, talent, and innovative ideas, but because they also provide the personnel and bully pulpits that will be required to capture the public's attention and thus pressure governments to move forward toward zero. For large and wealthy countries, focusing on multiple nuclear arms control and disarmament agendas and processes is difficult enough; for smaller or less well endowed countries, this shortage of expertise might place serious limitations on their ability to engage in new initiatives.

Second, a new set of relatively inexperienced national political leaders will be engaged in negotiations over the next several years in place of the vast experience, knowledge, and long-standing commitment represented by politicians like Mikhail Gorbachev, Helmut Schmitt, George Shultz, and Henry Kissinger. New leaders will operate in an international security environment unlike any other in the post-Hiroshima age. On the positive side, new leaders may be able to jettison old baggage. The mistakes made in the past (such as, perhaps, the U.S. abrogation of the ABM Treaty?), historical disagreements on substance (for example, about counting, verification, monitoring rules), and relatively rare instances of bad faith should be set aside. They happened, they were unfortunate, but current leaders are not bound to repeat earlier errors, settle old scores, or follow in the policy footsteps of previous generations. Further, the current generation of world leaders may be more open to the significance and potential of new techniques and technologies (such as nuclear forensics and the types of audit that James Acton addresses in his chapter in this volume). New leaders can and certainly must learn, but this generation and the next of world political leaders must focus on positive momentum toward zero, rather than short-term jockeying for position or the domestic benefits of resisting international arms control and disarmament negotiations. Providing for long-term, non-nuclear national security, perhaps complete with local and regional confidence-building measures and even security guarantees offered by a strengthened United Nations, could help overcome domestic support for nuclear weapons programs.

Third, the familiar social science concept of path dependence provides insight into why a fresh approach with renewed focus on the specifics of implementing the logic of zero makes political and policy sense. Historians and institutionally minded social scientists of all kinds generally focus on the ways in which past choices shape and constrain existing organizations and outcomes.[26] With sufficient political will, diplomatic savvy, and public support, President Obama and other heads of government have an opportunity to prevent previous decisions, mistakes, and misunderstanding from constraining the future. As later sections of this chapter will suggest, President Obama can take steps as commander-in-chief that will remove obstacles to nuclear disarmament presented by his own national security bureaucracies. And by doing so, he will help other leaders break long-standing patterns of behavior and institutional inertia.

Fourth, public attention like that of domestic bureaucracies and political leaders is limited and fickle. Concentrating on getting to zero, vice incrementally dealing with a wide variety of arms control, disarmament, and nuclear policy issues, will provide the public with greater clarity.

U.S. NUCLEAR POLICIES AND PROCESSES

If the United States is committed to the Zero Option it will need to match its rhetoric and international diplomacy with bold decisions regarding its own nuclear policies, programs, and processes. Reshaping internal policies in ways supportive of zero would demonstrate the nation's commitment without damaging U.S. security. It would provide a road map for the type of actions other nuclear states could adopt as they too walked back from relying on nuclear weapons as the ultimate guarantor of security. It will be difficult politically but, given the stakes at hand, might be the only way to begin the road to zero. It is also in keeping with President Obama's general approach: as Steve Pifer observes, "[T]he Obama administration's view [is] that U.S. nuclear policy and force levels should take account of nuclear non-proliferation, arms control, and broader security objectives."[27]

U.S. Moratorium

President Obama should pledge to defer new programmatic decisions on nuclear weapons and systems until after the world summit, if not beyond; in effect, the United States should impose a moratorium, unilateral if necessary, on the development of nuclear weapons as well as on upgrading or expanding the complex of laboratories and firms involved in weapons production. In practice this would mean working with Congress to defer action on key programs associated with the U.S. nuclear weapons complex. In announcing this decision, the president should encourage allies and others to take similar actions pending the results of the summit. Early accounts of congressional posturing over ratification of the New START agreement suggest that programmatic restraint may not be possible. Senators such as influential Republican arms control expert Jon Kyl (R-AZ) reportedly insisted that the Obama administration's support for large-scale funding increases for nuclear stockpile management and modernization programs was part of their price for voting in favor of ratification.

The president can act decisively to overcome two sticking points for the international community, especially nuclear and near-nuclear states, left over from the Bush administration and, indeed, presidential administrations extending back to the Cold War era itself. The Obama administration could reassure the international community by: (1) ending the RRW once and for all, both metaphorically and in reality, because, despite the formal death of RRW in Congress, proponents continue to lobby for its revival, and (2) declaring plans to build so-called bunker buster weapons,[28] particularly the Robust Nuclear Earth Penetrator (RNEP), to be over and destined to remain just plans.

The RRW program rested on the assumption that "warheads deteriorate with age."[29] Thus, for RRW supporters, to maintain the nation's nuclear deterrent and potential nuclear warfighting required the means to "improve the reliability, longevity, and certifiability of existing weapons and their components."[30] Regardless of the endless policy and technical debates over whether this is a necessity and whether or not RRW is the only way to ameliorate the possibility of deterioration that could lead to warhead unreliability, the symbolism of canceling the program for good would outweigh potential losses in weapons reliability, especially if computer simulations and other measures provide ways to maintain remaining warheads.[31] This would be a bold political statement of the first order. It would also require the Obama administration and its congressional allies to overcome the natural inclination of bureaucracies to survive with existing and preferred missions intact through whatever means necessary; in this case recasting the concerns of RRW proponents as Stockpile Stewardship may help justify continued funding for federal nuclear weapons laboratories without associating the program with efforts to develop new nuclear weapons.[32]

Congress refused to approve funding for the RNEP in 2005 after several reputable groups marshaled technical and operational arguments against the small nuclear weapon. Then-senator Pete Domenici (R-NM) concluded at the time that "[t]he focus will now be with the Defense Department and its research into earth-penetrating technology using conventional weaponry. The NNSA [National Nuclear Security Administration] indicated that this research should evolve around more conventional weapons rather than tactical nuclear devices. With this department change in policy, we have agreed not to provide DOE with funding for RNEP."[33] Even with the seemingly decisive defeat of the RNEP, program scientists and strategists continue to dream of a usable "bunker buster" because many states have buried their nuclear, chemical, and biological weapons research, development, production, and storage facilities deep underground. Preemption or even retaliation against such facilities is difficult with both conventional and nuclear warheads, but the increased yield of nuclear weapons makes their success more feasible according to some analysts. Nevertheless, in the context of efforts to promote the logic of zero, it is in the interest of the United States to renounce the use of nuclear weapons, newly designed or otherwise, for this use because of the signal it would send to the rest of the world.

Assuredly other experts could conceive of other perhaps more acceptable confidence-building measures above and beyond the two discussed here. In his chapter in this volume, for example, Alexei Arbatov argues that the U.S. deployment of cruise missiles on four Ohio class submarines (SSGNs) is destabilizing because it raises serious verification difficulties and could lead to an arms race at sea. SSGNs, while highly touted as transformational by some national security experts, are not essential for striking in-land targets—there are other far more powerful and far more transparent ships available with the vertical launch systems (VLS) necessary to fire ground-attack cruise missiles. The difference is that these ships do not have the SSGN's history of being used as part of the U.S. nuclear deterrent.

The Logic of Zero and Strategic Planning

If the United States wants to demonstrate seriousness in its pursuit of zero it will not only have to shift gears internationally, but it will have to overcome resistance from the military, intelligence, and defense-industrial communities with vested interest in either the status quo or in an alternative future in which nuclear weapons play an even greater part in U.S. defense planning than they do now. This will require tremendous political will, not to mention the expenditure of scarce political capital on the part of key members of the president's national security team. In Prague, the president signaled his resolve by saying, "To put an end to Cold War thinking, we will reduce the role of nuclear weapons in our national security strategy and urge others to do the same."

One way to understand better the implications of zero, and the paths to arriving at zero, is to force the military and defense planning bureaucracies to engage with the logic of zero. As Perkovich and Acton observe, "None of today's nuclear-armed states (and those depending on them for security guarantees) would commit to major proportional reduction in their arsenals without well-vetted studies by their national defense establishments."[34] War-games, planning scenarios, planning guidance, and other midproducts of the entire intelligence and military planning process should be informed by the notion that the United States is preparing for a non-nuclear future. There are a number of planning and analysis processes where the logic of zero and its implications can be examined:

- Defense Planning Scenarios
- Quadrennial Defense Review (QDR)[35]
- Defense Planning Guidance
- National Military Strategy
- Nuclear Posture Review

The Obama administration pushed the 2010 Nuclear Posture Review (NPR) to "continue to reduce the role of nuclear weapons in U.S. national security strategy" and to "continue concrete steps toward a world without nuclear weapons."[36] This step, which ran contrary to the guidance given by President Bush before the last NPR,[37] opened the door for strategists and planners to grapple seriously with the road to zero. Yet the importance of these simple words can be overstated, as the same list of NPR themes focus first on nuclear deterrence and extended deterrence (again a marked contrast to the 2001 NPR guidance from President George W. Bush, which stressed that the "Cold War approach to deterrence is no longer appropriate"—not because he wanted to rid the world of nuclear weapons, but because many of his advisors sought justifications for, and the means to use, conventional and perhaps even nuclear weapons to fight U.S. enemies rather than deter them).[38] Among the specific issues worthy of further study are:

- the low numbers problem, or whether the probability of a catastrophic nuclear event increases as fewer nuclear weapons exist;
- the impact of reducing the numbers and types of nuclear weapons on deterrence and extended deterrence, both in general and in specific regional or dyadic relationships;
- war-fighting without nuclear weapons;
- the effects of reducing nuclear weapons and platforms explicitly designed to deliver nuclear weapons on the conventional force; and
- identification of specific points along the path toward zero which present the greatest challenges or vulnerabilities to U.S. national and international security.

It is highly likely that not all the answers from such explorations will support the logic of zero. In fact, arguing deductively, theorists have already called several of the most important assumptions of proponents of disarmament into question. But understanding the problems and nuances of the process will allow negotiators to find ways around the difficulties and to work with other countries to overcome vulnerabilities.

THE POLITICS OF ZERO

The politics of getting to zero are extremely complex, both internationally and within the domestic arena. Internationally, the United States and like-minded nations will have to overcome the suspicions of other nuclear states that somehow proposals to reduce, if not eliminate, nuclear weapons will leave them vulnerable. Potential risks include but are not limited to:

- the possibility that rival states will maintain their arsenals even as a build-down is negotiated and implemented;
- the opportunity for other, currently non-nuclear capable, states to take advantage of the reductions to develop, accelerate, or regenerate their own nuclear programs;
- the danger that the period, even if it can be measured in decades, preceding the implementation of agreements to eliminate will be destabilizing; and
- the possibility that states without the resources to field large and technologically advanced conventional military capabilities will fear putting themselves at a permanent disadvantage if the world agrees to renounce nuclear weapons (no matter how their immediate security requirements change with time).

Many nations will be wary of American intentions. As the nation with the most powerful conventional military, and both the national will and economic capacity to outspend most if not all rivals or even groups of rivals, the United States might use nuclear disarmament to permanently lock in its own conventional superiority. For potential U.S. adversaries, adopting asymmetric military strategies against the possibility of American military intervention will be made much more difficult without the ready-made solution of acquiring nuclear weapons and delivery systems.[39]

It may be even harder to generate support for the logic of zero within the U.S. national security community than to gain the assent of other governments including both nuclear and non-nuclear powers. Nuclear weapons, even more than the vast economic, political, diplomatic, and conventional military resources available to the U.S. government, remain the foundation of America's superpower status in the first decade of the twenty-first century. Proposing deep cuts in the number of nuclear weapons, and even the elimination of nuclear weapons altogether, challenges the received wisdom of many decades. For the Obama administration and its successors, any steps toward arms control much less toward nuclear zero will also stimulate intense opposition from the most conservative elements of U.S. society, including for example, the so-called Tea Party supporters who tend to vote Republican.

Beyond the concerns of strategists and politicians, resistance is likely to come from the strategic, military, intelligence, and defense industrial/scientific-engineering communities. All have vested interests in maintaining the status quo rather than moving forward into an even more uncertain future.

The military is an interesting case. On the one hand, since the end of the Cold War nuclear weapons have played a reduced role in U.S. strategic thought, at least as evidenced by national strategy documents. In the past two decades defense planning documents have only rarely focused on the role of nuclear weapons. Deterrence, while oft-referenced, has given way first to shaping the international security environment and then, during the presidency of George W. Bush, to more ambitious instruments such as prevention; in fact, even recent references to deterrence have concentrated less on nuclear deterrence than on the role of conventional forces. The Bush administration's Nuclear Posture Review sought both conventional analogs to nuclear deterrence and greater reliance on ballistic missile defense as guarantors of U.S. national security. Military transformation, one of the driving trends in defense planning and budgeting since the Clinton years, is somewhat remarkable for its relative silence on nuclear weapons.[40] Transformation advocates even argue that, properly employed, conventional weapons can achieve the same effects as nuclear weapons without the political and moral baggage.

On the other hand, throughout the administration of George W. Bush the nuclear weapons community waged a campaign to maintain and even expand the roles and mission of nuclear weapons. For example, the nuclear laboratories fought to develop and fund small nuclear weapons, so-called bunker busters capable of destroying hardened facilities. If and when the U.S. armed services are called upon to strike another nation's nuclear arsenal and production facilities, bunker busters and the other parts of the U.S. reconnaissance strike complex will ease the difficult mission of destroying hardened facilities. Thus if the military has not focused on nuclear tactics and strategy in recent years, its focus on strike operations, as embodied, for example, in the establishment and strengthening of U.S. Strategic Command (STRATCOM), indicates the continued importance of nuclear missions to the American military.

Nuclear missions, and the vast infrastructure required to sustain the forces and capabilities required to carry out those missions, constitute a significant portion of U.S. defense spending, especially if the mission is defined broadly to include offensive and defensive weapons, as well as the technical communities and personnel that support them. In 2008 the United States spent roughly $52 billion in aggregate on various programs related to nuclear weapons.[41] Moreover, annual spending figures do not do justice to the capital investment in nuclear programs that remain part of the investment stock supporting U.S. national security. Between 1940, the year the Manhattan Project was initiated, and 1996, Steven I. Schwartz estimates the United States spent a minimum of $5,821 billion (constant 1996 dollars) on nuclear weapons programs.[42] Future spending remains uncertain, given possible changes based on programmatic decisions by the Obama administration, the recommendations of the Nuclear Posture Review, and the Quadrennial Defense Review, not to mention congressional appropriations and other military decisions great and small. Potentially the costs will remain in the $50 billion per year range if policies remain unchanged, or even rise if projects like the NNSA "Complex Transformation" plan to undertake an extensive, multi-billion dollar investment in new nuclear weapons facilities and new nuclear warhead designs costing, according to Department of Energy estimates, more than $200 billion over two or three decades, go forward.[43]

According to the Center for Strategy and Budgetary Assessments,

> Deeper cuts in nuclear forces could also yield significant budgetary savings. . . . Over the longer term, moving toward a force of some 1,000–1,500 nuclear warheads could yield budgetary savings of several billion dollars a year. These savings would be due to both lower operations and support costs and acquisition costs for the Department of Defense, as well as lower costs related to maintaining the U.S. nuclear weapons stockpile for the Department of Energy.[44]

Yet while taxpayers and deficit hawks might view such savings as a reason to support the logic of zero, the reverse logic is that such cuts would result in canceling programs and contracts, weakening the prestige and influence of specific military missions, communities, and their associated organizational support, and putting less public funds in the hands of defense firms. Moreover, the weapons laboratories and associated infrastructure are spread over many states and, more important, congressional districts. As we have learned from many defense programs over the years, from the B-1B bomber to the F-22 to various naval shipbuilding programs, senators and congressmen are more than willing to use their votes to protect programs that support local jobs. There is little reason to assume that when it comes time to make serious cuts in various nuclear-related programs, legislators will remain any less vigilant.

The point is not to emphasize the expense of nuclear weapons, but to indicate the economic, budgetary, and commercial importance of nuclear weapons to the U.S. economy, the military services, and various other government agencies such as the Department of Energy, and to those defense industrial firms contracting with the U.S. government to provide the various products and services required to maintain the nuclear weapons arsenal. With large sums at stake, programmatic cuts, whether dictated by strategic decisions like that to pursue the logic of zero or by efforts to reduce defense spending, will be resisted by both government and private sector organizations.

The intelligence community plays an important if under-recognized role on debates over nuclear weapons and arms control. Recent high-level scenarios and futures work make assumptions about the future of nuclear states, proliferation, and the status of American nuclear forces. Further, much of the intelligence infrastructure to include satellite systems and listening posts was developed during the Cold War. It is optimized for providing strategic warning against nuclear attacks and monitoring other nuclear weapons states. Approaching zero will require new modes of monitoring and verification, as well as dealing with increasingly obsolete systems and processes. Given the new security challenges that have developed since 9/11, there is little doubt the intelligence community can find ways to reallocate resources. But given the long lead times for deploying complex technological systems such as satellite constellations, planning and procurement must occur sooner rather than later to prepare for a world in which nuclear arsenals dwindle below the 1,000-warhead mark for Russia and the United States, and hopefully, to smaller or nonexistent numbers in other existing nuclear or threshold states. Revelations in late 2010 documenting how North Korea and, to some extent, Iran have managed to surprise the U.S. and other international observers with the progress of their nuclear weapons manufacturing capabilities point to the importance of improving intelligence collection and analysis.

CONCLUSION

Implementation of the president's wider agenda for a nuclear-free world depends on the willingness of key nuclear states to press forward, the ability of the president and his senior staff members to push his agenda with the executive branch and the armed forces, and, perhaps most significantly, to shape the attitudes and actions of key congressional national security experts such as Richard Lugar to support the president's policies. Already the groundwork is being laid, but much remains to be accomplished and several important political choices about how to proceed remain open.

Under President G. W. Bush, Secretary of State Rice often spoke of but barely pursued a notion of "Transformative Diplomacy," especially with regard to foreign aid programs. For then-secretary Rice transformation meant, among other things, greater inclusion of the recipients of U.S. assistance into decision-making. Both President Obama and Secretary of State Clinton now have an opportunity to put real transformation into practice by leading international efforts toward nuclear zero. Attaining international "buy in" for the logic of zero will require a major, well-publicized, internationally legitimate forum—the classic bully pulpit. In this case transformative should mean inclusion and transparency. It will also require sustained presidential effort and attention to the domestic dimensions of nuclear disarmament. The U.S. military, the nuclear weapons industrial complex, and their congressional supporters must be convinced that their fears of the consequences of zero are overstated or can be overcome. One way to begin this long process will be to study seriously the specific consequences of nuclear disarmament using the various analytic techniques (war gaming, operations research) and collective decision-making (NPR, QDR, among others) that have guided defense planning since at least the McNamara era.

NOTES

This chapter represents my professional judgments and in no way reflects the policies of the U.S. Naval War College, the U.S. Navy, the Department of Defense or the U.S. government. I would like to thank Judith Reppy and Catherine Kelleher as editors, as well as all participants at the 2009 ISODARCO conference, for useful suggestions. George Quester, Andrew L. Ross, James Acton, Andrew Winner, Thomas Nichols, Jeffrey Arthur Larsen, James M. Smith, James J. Wirtz, Duane Bratt, and Jonathan Pollack graciously read earlier versions of this chapter. As usual, all mistakes are mine and mine alone.

1. Bryan Bender, "Nuclear Agenda Draws Scrutiny: Obama to Seek Largest Cuts in US, Russian Warheads," *Boston Globe*, 22 February 2009, p. 1.

2. George Perkovich and James M. Acton, "Rebutting the Standard Arguments against Disarmament," *Bulletin of Atomic Scientists* (15 July 2009), at http://www.thebulletin.org/web-edition/op-eds/rebutting-the-standard-arguments-against-disarmament.

3. "McCain Calls for Slashing U.S. Nuclear Arsenal," *CNNPolitics.com* (27 May 2008), at http://www.cfr.org/bios/662/john_mccain.html#22.

4. "McCain Supports Goal of a World without Nuclear Weapons," floor statement by Senator John McCain—A World without Nuclear Weapons (3 June 2009), at http://www.ploughshares.org/news-analysis/news/mccain-supports-goal-world-without-nuclear-weapons.

5. Ivo Daalder and Jan Lodal "The Logic of Zero," *Foreign Affairs* (November/December 2008): 80–95.

6. See, for example, George P. Shultz et al., eds., *Reykjavik Revisited: Steps toward a World Free of Nuclear Weapons* (Palo Alto, CA: Hoover Institution Press, 2008).

7. Randy Rydell, "The Future of Nuclear Arms: A World United and Divided by Zero," *Arms Control Today* 39, no. 3 (April 2009): 21–25.

8. Scholars, including Robert Jervis and James Fearon, argue that costly signals reveal more about a state's intentions than does cheap talk; the nature of signaling intentions and how they are interpreted by other actors, however, remains an open research program. Some scholars even support sending cheap signals under specific conditions and within certain issue areas. See Robert Jervis, *The Logic of Images in International Relations* (New York: Columbia University Press, 1970); James Fearon, "Domestic Political Audiences and the Escalation of International Disputes," *American Political Science Review* 88, no. 3 (September 1994): 577–92.

9. One excellent contribution to the vast and growing literature on the problem of credible commitments among nation states is Kurt Taylor Gaubatz, "Democratic States and Commitment in International Relations," *International Organization* 50, no. 1 (Winter, 1996): 109–39.

10. George Perkovich and James M. Acton, "What's Next?" in *Abolishing Nuclear Weapons: A Debate*, ed. George Perkovich and James M. Acton (Washington, DC: Carnegie Endowment Report, February 2009), p. 316.

11. The proposed hold should include, temporarily, important proposals such as efforts to restart work on a comprehensive fissile material treaty. See Arend Meerburg and Frank N. von Hippel, "Complete Cutoff: Designing a Comprehensive Fissile Material Treaty," *Arms Control Today* (March 2009): 16.

12. While ideally the Obama administration could have begun with a clean slate in bilateral negotiations with Russia, the administration chose to pursue a follow-on to START I and START II, and there is no going back. In reality, achieving a modus vivendi with Russia, especially if it somehow includes agreement on pushing for nuclear disarmament, may pressure other states to attend a world summit and, better yet, play a constructive role.

13. Daalder and Lodal, "The Logic of Zero," p. 81.

14. Peter Dombrowski and Rodger Payne, "The Emerging Consensus for Preventive War," *Survival* 48 (Summer 2006): 115–36.

15. Amy F. Woolf, *Nuclear Weapons and US National Security: A Need for New Weapons Programs?* CRS report for Congress (15 September 2003), p. 2.

16. For the full text of President Barack Obama's remarks at Hradčany Square, Prague, Czech Republic, 5 April 2009, see http://prague.usembassy.gov/obama.html.

17. Steven Pifer, *Beyond START: Negotiating the Next Step in U.S. and Russian Strategic Nuclear Arms Reductions*, Brookings Policy Paper no. 15 (May 2009), p. 5.

18. "Nuclear Arms Resolution Passed at UN Summit," *Arms Control Today* (October 2009): 22–23.

19. For a sober discussion of the possibility of additional nuclear programs in view of recent North Korean nuclear and missile tests, see Christopher W. Hughes, "North Korea's Nuclear Weapons: Implications for the Nuclear Ambitions of Japan, South Korea, and Taiwan," *Asia Policy* 3 (January 2007): 75–104, at http://asiapolicy.nbr.org.

20. The "Washington Summit," convened in April 2009, while useful in focusing attention on the need to control access to fissile materials, was far more modest than the world summit discussed here.

21. Lawrence Freedman, "Nuclear Disarmament: From a Popular Movement to an Elite Project, and Back Again?" in *Abolishing Nuclear Weapons*, p. 144, at http://www.carnegieendowment.org/files/abolishing_nuclear_weapons_debate.pdf.

22. Stephen D. Krasner, "Structural Causes and Regime Consequences: Regimes as Intervening Variables," *International Organization* 36, no. 2 (Spring 1982). Reprinted in Stephen D. Krasner, ed., *International Regimes* (Ithaca, NY: Cornell University Press, 1983).

23. On April 1, 2009, President Obama met with President Medvedev and agreed "to begin bilateral intergovernmental negotiations to work out a new, comprehensive, legally binding agreement on reducing and limiting strategic offensive arms to replace the START Treaty." Joint Statement by Dmitriy A. Medvedev, president of the Russian Federation, and Barack Obama, president of the United States of America, Regarding Negotiations on Further Reductions in Strategic Offensive Arms. For more context, see Cole Harvey, "Russia, U.S. Seek START Successor by Year End," *Arms Control Today* (April 2009).

24. John Daniszewski, "Iranians Defend Nuclear Rights," *Los Angeles Times*, 7 March 2006.

25. Abbas William Samii, "The Iranian Nuclear Issue and Informal Networks," *Naval War College Review* (Winter 2006): 74.

26. My thinking here was shaped by, among many others, James Mahoney, "Path Dependence in Historical Sociology," *Theory and Society* 29, no. 4 (August 2000): 507–48.

27. Pifer, *Beyond START*, p. 9.

28. "These new nuclear weapons are sometimes presented as generic 'bunker busters,' including such targets as command centers, for example, but when specifics are included, chemical and biological weapons in particular are likely to be cited." Ivan Oelrich, *Missions for Nuclear Weapons after the Cold War*, Federation of American Scientists Occasional Paper no. 3 (January 2005), p. 36, at http://www.fas.org/programs/ssp/nukes/non-proliferation_and_arms_control/missionsaftercwrptfull.pdf.

29. Jonathan Medalia, "The Reliable Replacement Warhead Program: Background and Current Developments," *CRS Report to Congress* (updated 12 September 2008), p. CRS-1, at http://www.fas.org/sgp/crs/nuke/RL32929.pdf.

30. House Report 108-792, "Making Appropriations for Foreign Operations, Export Financing, and Related Programs for the Fiscal Year Ending September 30, 2005, and

for Other Purposes." Congressional language, at http://thomas.loc.gov/cgi-bin/cpquery/?&db_id=cp108&r_n=hr792.108&sel=TOC_2807988&.

31. The RRW study conducted by the Jason study group outlined the needed measures. It concluded, "The absence of new nuclear explosive testing increases the need for experiments, computational tools, and improved scientific understanding of the connection of the results from such experiments and simulations to the existing nuclear explosive test data. Even when suitably validated simulations can predict device failure, and provide reliable estimates of margins and uncertainties, a continued non-nuclear experimental basis will be required for certification of any new design." See "Reliable Replace Warhead: Executive Summary," JSR-07-336E (7 September 2007), p. 5, at http://fas.org/irp/agency/dod/jason/rrw.pdf.

32. I am grateful for Judith Reppy's insight here. See also George P. Shultz, William J. Perry, Henry A. Kissinger, and Sam Nunn, "How to Protect Our Nuclear Deterrent," *Wall Street Journal*, 19 January 2010, for ideas along these lines that draw on the work of the Strategic Posture Commission led by former defense secretaries Perry and James R. Schlesinger and on a Jason technical study commissioned by the National Nuclear Security Administration in the Department of Energy.

33. Quoted on the Federation of American Scientists (FAS) website, at http://www.globalsecurity.org/wmd/systems/rnep.htm.

34. Perkovich and Acton, "What's Next?" p. 318.

35. William S. Cohen, "Report of the Quadrennial Defense Review," Washington, DC, Department of Defense, May 1997, Section I. Congress directed DOD to perform the 1997 Quadrennial Defense Review as a method to conduct a "fundamental and comprehensive examination of America's defense needs."

36. Nuclear Posture Review 2010 Fact Sheet, "Nuclear Posture Review (NPR) Background," 6 August 2009, p. 1, at http://www.armscontrolwonk.com/file_download/193/NPR_Background.pdf.

37. The out-briefing of the 2001 NPR offered a more ambiguous statement: "Deploy the lowest number of nuclear weapons consistent with the security requirements of the US, its allies and friends." Department of Defense, "Findings of the 2001 Nuclear Posture Review," 9 January 2002, slide 6, at http://www.defenselink.mil/dodcmsshare/briefingslide/120/020109-D-6570C-001.pdf.

38. Ibid.

39. At the most simple level, asymmetric strategies "attack vulnerabilities not appreciated by the United States and capitalize on limited U.S. preparations against such threats." Often they involved nuclear, biological, or chemical threats or, in more recent usage, terrorism. See, for example, Bruce W. Bennett, Christopher Twomey, and Gregory F. Treverton, *What Are Asymmetric Strategies?* DB-246-OSD (Santa Monica, CA: RAND Corp., 1999).

40. For one example, a Congressional Research Service review of U.S. Department

of Defense transformation efforts barely mentions the U.S. nuclear arsenal. When it refers to nuclear weapons at all it is to point out the reasons why advocates argue that transformation is necessary; for example, the acquisition of nuclear weapons by potential U.S. adversaries. Ronald O'Rourke, "Defense Transformation: Background and Oversight Issues for Congress," *CRS Report to Congress* (updated 4 April 2005), at http://www.globalsecurity.org/military/library/report/crs/crs_rl32238_apr05.pdf.

41. Stephen I. Schwartz with Deepti Choubey, *Nuclear Security Spending: Assessing Costs, Examining Priorities* (Washington, DC: Carnegie Endowment for International Peace, 2009), at http://carnegieendowment.org/files/nuclear_security_spending_complete_high.pdf.

42. Steven I. Schwartz, *Atomic Audit: The Costs and Consequences of U.S. Nuclear Weapons since 1940* (Washington, DC: Brookings Institution, 1998). The table estimating the details of historical spending on nuclear weapons programs can be found at http://www.brookings.edu/projects/archive/nucweapons/figure1.aspx.

43. William D. Hartung, "Nuclear Bailout: A Critique of the Department of Energy's Plans for a New Nuclear Weapons Complex," New America Foundation, Submitted in Conjunction with the Public Comment Period on the Supplemental Programmatic Environmental Impact Statement (SPEIS) for the Department of Energy's "Complex Transformation" Plan (25 March 2008), at http://www.newamerica.net/files/Nuclear_Bailout.pdf.

44. The Center for Strategic and Budgetary Assessments, "Cost of Defense Plans and Forces: Nuclear Forces and Proliferation," at http://www.csbaonline.org/2006-1/2.DefenseBudget/Nuclear_Forces.shtml.

CONTRIBUTOR BIOGRAPHIES AND INDEX

CONTRIBUTOR BIOGRAPHIES

James M. Acton

Carnegie Endowment for International Peace, USA

James Acton is an Associate in the Nuclear Policy Program at the Carnegie Endowment for International Peace. A physicist by training, Acton is co-author of the Adelphi Paper, *Abolishing Nuclear Weapons*, and co-editor of the follow-up book, *Abolishing Nuclear Weapons: A Debate*. He is currently a member of the International Panel on Fissile Materials.

Ian Anthony

Stockholm International Peace Research Institute (SIPRI), Sweden

Ian Anthony is currently Director of Research and Head of the Arms Control and Nonproliferation Programme at the Stockholm International Peace Research Institute. Dr. Anthony received his PhD from the University of London. He is the editor of four volumes and the author of five monographs, the most recent of which are *Reforming Nuclear Export Controls: The Future of the Nuclear Suppliers Group* (Oxford: Oxford University Press, 2007), and *Reducing Threats at the Source: A European Perspective on Cooperative Threat Reduction* (Oxford: Oxford University Press, 2004).

Alexei G. Arbatov

Carnegie Moscow Center, Russia

Alexei G. Arbatov was the Deputy Chairman of the Defense Committee of the State Duma in the Federal Assembly of the Russian Federation from 1993 to 2003, where he was responsible for Russia's defense budget, arms control treaties, and defense industries. At present he is the Head of the Center on International Security in IMEMO (Russian Academy of Sciences) and the head of the project on nuclear nonproliferation in the Carnegie Moscow Center. He has published five individual books and numerous chapters, papers, and articles on international security and strategic issues, including *Lethal Frontiers: A Soviet View on Nuclear Weapons* (Praeger, 1988), *Security: Russia's Choice* (Epicenter, 1999), *Beyond Deterrence* with Vladimir Dworkin (Carnegie, 2008), and *The Security Equation* (Yabloko, 2010).

Nadia Alexandrova-Arbatova

Institute of World Economy and International Relations, Moscow

Nadia Alexandrova-Arbatova is Head of the Department on European Political Studies at the Institute for World Economy and International Relations (IMEMO), Russian Academy of Sciences. Her recent publications include *Russia and Europe, the Foreign Policy of Yeltsin Russia* (Stockholm: Forsvarshogskolan, 2001), "The Russia-EU Common Space of External Security: Imperatives and Obstacles," *Security Index* 3, no. 86 (2009) (in Russian and English), "The Impact of the Caucasus Crisis on Regional and European Security," *Southeast European and Black Sea Studies* 9, no. 3 (September 2009): 287–300.

Avner Cohen

James Martin Center for Nonproliferation Studies

Avner Cohen is a Senior Fellow at the Washington office of the James Martin Center for Nonproliferation Studies, Monterey Institute of International Studies. He wrote this paper while he was a Public Policy Scholar at the Woodrow Wilson Center for International Scholars in Washington, DC. He is the author and co-editor of *Nuclear Weapons and the Future of Humanity* (1986), *The Institution of Philosophy* (1989), and the author of *The Nuclear Age as Moral History* (in Hebrew, 1989), *Israel and the Bomb* (1998), and *The Worst Kept Secret: Israel's Bargain with the Bomb* (2010).

Marco De Andreis

Fondazione Ugo La Malfa, Italy

Marco De Andreis has published extensively on international security and international political economy, and has worked on energy projects in association with the Fondazione Ugo La Malfa, Rome. He is now Director of Economic Studies at Italy's Customs Agency. He has also served as political advisor to Italy's Minister of European Affairs, in Rome, and to a European Commissioner, in Brussels.

Peter Dombrowski

Naval War College, USA

Peter J. Dombrowski is Professor and Chair of the Naval War College's Strategic Research Department and an Adjunct Professor at the Watson Institute, Brown University. He holds a BA in political science from Williams College, and an MA and PhD in political science from the University of Maryland. He is the co-author with Eugene Gholz of *Buying Military Transformation: Technological Innovation and the Defense Industry*, among other publications.

Lynn Eden

Stanford University, USA

Lynn Eden is Associate Director for Research and a Senior Research Scholar at the Center for International Security and Cooperation, Freeman Spogli Institute for International Studies, Stanford University. She is also Co-chair of U.S. Pugwash. Eden's most recent book, *Whole World on Fire: Organizations, Knowledge, and Nuclear Weapons Devastation,* won the American Sociological Association's 2004 Robert K. Merton Award for best book in science, knowledge, and technology.

Matthew Evangelista

Cornell University, USA

Matthew Evangelista is President White Professor of History and Political Science and Chair of the Department of Government at Cornell University, Ithaca, New York, where he teaches courses in international and comparative politics. He is the author of four books: *Innovation and the Arms Race* (1988), *Unarmed Forces: The Transnational Movement to End the Cold War* (1999), *The Chechen Wars: Will Russia Go the Way of the Soviet Union?* (2002), and *Law, Ethics, and the War on Terror* (2008), and the editor of several others.

Dennis M. Gormley

University of Pittsburgh, USA

Dennis M. Gormley is on the faculty of the Graduate School of Public and International Affairs at the University of Pittsburgh. He is also a Senior Research Fellow at the university's Matthew B. Ridgway Center for International Studies. His most recent book is *Missile Contagion: Cruise Missile Proliferation and the Threat to International Security* (Praeger, 2008), while his journal articles have appeared in *Survival*, the *Washington Quarterly*, the *Bulletin of the Atomic Scientists, Nonproliferation Review, Orbis*, and others.

David Holloway

Stanford University, USA

David Holloway is the Raymond A. Spruance Professor in International History, Professor of Political Science and of History, and Senior Fellow at the Freeman-Spogli Institute for International Studies at Stanford University. He is the author of *The Soviet Union and the Arms Race* (1983) and *Stalin and the Bomb: The Soviet Union and Atomic Energy, 1939–1956* (1994). With Sidney Drell and Philip Farley he wrote *The Reagan Strategic Defense Initiative: A Technical, Political, and Arms Control Assessment* (1985).

Venance Journé

International Center on Environment and Development, France

Venance Journé is a researcher at the International Center on Environment and Development (CIRED-CNRS) in France. Her recent publications include: *From*

Chernobyl to Chernobyl with Georges Charpak and Richard L. Garwin (2005), and "The Real Story behind the Making of the French Hydrogen Bomb: Chaotic, Unsupported, but Successful" with Pierre Billaud, *Non-Proliferation Review* (July 2008). She has long been active in Pugwash, including serving on the Executive Council, and recently prepared the publication in French of the text, history, and context of the Weapons of Mass Destruction Commission Report (the Blix Commission).

Catherine McArdle Kelleher

Brown University and University of Maryland, USA

Catherine McArdle Kelleher is a Senior Fellow at the Watson Institute, Brown University, a College Park Professor at the University of Maryland, and Professor Emerita at the U.S. Naval War College. For nearly a decade she led the Dialogue of Americans, Russians, and Europeans (DARE), based first at Aspen Berlin and then at the Watson Institute, Brown University. In the Clinton administration she was the Personal Representative of the Secretary of Defense in Europe and Deputy Assistant Secretary of Defense for Russia, Ukraine, and Eurasia. She is the author of more than seventy books and articles and founder of Women in International Security (WIIS).

Jeffrey Lewis

Monterey Institute for International Studies, USA

Jeffrey G. Lewis is Director of the East Asia Nonproliferation Program at the James Martin Center for Nonproliferation Studies at the Monterey Institute for International Studies. Dr. Lewis founded and maintains the leading blog on nuclear arms control and nonproliferation, ArmsControlWonk.com. He is the author of *Minimum Means of Reprisal: China's Search for Security in the Nuclear Age* (MIT Press, 2007).

Jill Marie Lewis

Physicians for Social Responsibility, USA

Jill Marie Lewis is now a Foreign Affairs Specialist for the National Nuclear Security Administration at the U.S. Department of Energy. She wrote her chapter for this volume while serving as Deputy Director for Security Programs at Physicians for Social Responsibility, where her work focused on domestic and international nuclear weapon and energy policy, and promoting scientific engagement opportunities with Iran.

Simon Moore

University of Maryland, USA

Simon Moore is a Research Associate, Center for International and Security Studies at Maryland (CISSM), where he specializes in energy security policy, focusing at present on cooperative policies in energy resourcing in Eastern Europe. Previously he was lead researcher in London for the Stockholm Network's energy and environment program, and edited *Beyond the Borders*, on reform movements in non-EU Europe.

Götz Neuneck

University of Hamburg, Germany

Götz Neuneck is Deputy Director at the Institute for Peace Research and Security Policy, and head of the Interdisciplinary Group for Arms Control and Disarmament. He is a member of the Council of the Deutsche Physikalische Gesellschaft (DPG)/German Physical Society; Chairman of the working group "Physik und Abrustung"/Physics and Disarmament of the DPG, and Pugwash representative of the Verband Deutscher Wissenschaftler (VDW)/Association of German Scientists, as well as a member of the Council of Pugwash Conferences on Science and World Affairs. His most recent publication is *South Asia at a Crossroads: Conflict or Cooperation in the Age of Nuclear Weapons, Missile Defense, and Space Rivalries* (Baden-Baden, 2010), for which he is co-editor (with Subrata Ghoshroy).

Laicie Olson

Center for Arms Control and Non-Proliferation, USA

Laicie Olson is a Senior Policy Analyst at the Center for Arms Control and Non-Proliferation, where her work focuses on global weapons proliferation and military spending. Olson has published research on the annual defense budget, Comprehensive Test Ban Treaty, U.S.-India nuclear deal, and Iran, and she is a regular contributor to the blog Nukes of Hazard.

Judith Reppy

Cornell University, USA

Judith Reppy is Professor Emerita in the Department of Science and Technology Studies and Associate Director of the Judith Reppy Institute for Peace and Conflict Studies at Cornell University. From 1995 to 2000, she served as Co-chair of the U.S. Pugwash Conferences on Science and International Affairs. Reppy is the co-editor and contributing author of *The Genesis of New Weapons: Decision Making for Military R and D*, and *The Relations between Defense and Civil Technologies*, among other publications.

Randy Rydell

United Nations, USA

Randy Rydell is Senior Political Affairs Officer in the Office of Mr. Sergio Duarte, the High Representative for Disarmament Affairs at the United Nations. He served from January 2005 to June 2006 as Senior Counsellor and Report Director of the Weapons of Mass Destruction Commission (Blix Commission) and Senior Fellow at the Arms Control Association in Washington, DC.

Waheguru Pal Singh Sidhu

East-West Institute, New York

Waheguru Pal Singh Sidhu is Vice President of Program at the East West Institute in New York. Prior to this he was the Director of the New Issues in Security Course at the Geneva Centre for Security Policy. Dr. Sidhu has researched, written, and taught extensively on the United Nations, disarmament, arms control, and nonproliferation issues. His recent publications include: *Arms Control after Iraq: Normative and Operational Challenges,* and *Kashmir: New Voices, New Approaches.* He has published extensively in leading international journals, including *Arms Control Today, Asian Survey, Disarmament Diplomacy, Disarmament Forum, International Peacekeeping, Jane's Intelligence Review, Politique Etrangère,* and the *Bulletin of Atomic Scientists.*

INDEX

Made in the USA
Columbia, SC
23 January 2019